EMILY DICKINSON IN CONTEXT

Long believed to be untouched by contemporary events, ideas, and environments, Emily Dickinson's writings have been the subject of intense historical research in recent years. This volume of thirty-three essays by leading scholars offers a comprehensive introduction to the contexts most important for the study of Dickinson's writings. While providing an overview of their topic, the essays also present groundbreaking research and original arguments, treating the poet's local environments; literary influences; social, cultural, political, and intellectual contexts; and reception. A resource for scholars and students of American literature and poetry in English, the collection is an indispensable contribution to the study not only of Dickinson's writings but also of the contexts for poetic production and circulation more generally in the nineteenth-century United States.

ELIZA RICHARDS is an associate professor of English and Comparative Literature at the University of North Carolina at Chapel Hill. Author of *Gender and the Poetics of Reception in Poe's Circle* (Cambridge, 2004), she has published essays on American literature and culture in journals such as *Arizona Quarterly*, *ESQ*, *Amerikastudien/American Studies*, *Poe Studies*, *Yale Journal of Criticism*, and *Victorian Poetry*.

EMILY DICKINSON IN CONTEXT

EDITED BY

ELIZA RICHARDS

University of North Carolina, Chapel Hill

CAMBRIDGE
UNIVERSITY PRESS

32 Avenue of the Americas, New York NY 10013-2473, USA

Cambridge University Press is part of the University of Cambridge.

It furthers the University's mission by disseminating knowledge in the pursuit of education, learning, and research at the highest international levels of excellence.

www.cambridge.org
Information on this title: www.cambridge.org/9781107022744

© Cambridge University Press 2013

This publication is in copyright. Subject to statutory exception and to the provisions of relevant collective licensing agreements, no reproduction of any part may take place without the written permission of Cambridge University Press.

First published 2013
Reprinted 2013

A catalog record for this publication is available from the British Library.

Library of Congress Cataloging in Publication data
Emily Dickinson in context / [edited by] Eliza Richards, University of North Carolina, Chapel Hill.
  pages cm
Includes bibliographical references and index.
ISBN 978-1-107-02274-4 (hardback)
1. Dickinson, Emily, 1830–1886 – Criticism and interpretation.
I. Richards, Eliza, editor of compilation.
PS1541.Z5E3966 2013
811'.4–DC23   2013009542

ISBN 978-1-107-02274-4 Hardback

Cambridge University Press has no responsibility for the persistence or accuracy of URLs for external or third-party Internet Web sites referred to in this publication, and does not guarantee that any content on such Web sites is, or will remain, accurate or appropriate.

Contents

List of Illustrations	*page* viii
Contributors	ix
Acknowledgments	xv
List of Abbreviations and Textual Note	xvii
Chronology	xix

    Introduction   1
    Eliza Richards

PART I. LOCAL ENVIRONMENTS

1 Amherst   13
   Domhnall Mitchell

2 Reading in the Dickinson Libraries   25
   Eleanor Elson Heginbotham

3 Education   36
   Angela Sorby

4 New England Puritan Heritage   46
   Jane Donahue Eberwein

5 Nature's Influence   56
   Margaret H. Freeman

PART II. LITERARY CONTEXTS: SOURCES, INFLUENCES, INTERTEXTUAL ENGAGEMENTS

6 The Bible   69
   Emily Seelbinder

Contents

7   Shakespeare   78
    Páraic Finnerty

8   Renaissance and Eighteenth-Century Literature   89
    David Cody

9   British Romantic and Victorian Influences   98
    Elizabeth A. Petrino

10 Transatlantic Women Writers   109
    Páraic Finnerty

11 Immediate U.S. Literary Predecessors   119
    Cristanne Miller

12 U.S. Literary Contemporaries: Dickinson's Moderns   129
    Mary Loeffelholz

13 Periodical Reading   139
    Joan Kirkby

PART III. SOCIAL, CULTURAL, POLITICAL,
AND INTELLECTUAL CONTEXTS

14 Religion   151
    James McIntosh

15 Death and Immortality   160
    Joan Kirkby

16 Gendered Poetics   169
    Shira Wolosky

17 Democratic Politics   179
    Paul Crumbley

18 Economics   188
    Elizabeth Hewitt

19 Law and Legal Discourse   198
    James Guthrie

20 Slavery and the Civil War   206
    Faith Barrett

21 Popular Culture   216
    Sandra Runzo

22 Visual Arts: The Pentimento   226
    Alexander Nemerov

23 Natural Sciences   236
    Sabine Sielke

24 Nineteenth-Century Language Theory and the
    Manuscript Variants   246
    Melanie Hubbard

25 "Say Some Philosopher!"   257
    Jed Deppman

PART IV. RECEPTION

26 Editorial History I: Beginnings to 1955   271
    Martha Nell Smith

27 Editorial History II: 1955 to the Present   282
    Alexandra Socarides

28 On Materiality (and Virtuality)   292
    Gabrielle Dean

29 The Letters Archive   302
    Cindy MacKenzie

30 Critical History I: 1890–1955   311
    Theo Davis

31 Critical History II: 1955 to the Present   321
    Magdalena Zapedowska

32 Dickinson's Influence   332
    Thomas Gardner

33 Translation and International Reception   343
    Domhnall Mitchell

Further Reading   353
Index   369
Index of Emily Dickinson's Poems   384

Illustrations

1. *Wild Flowers Drawn and Colored from Nature*, ed. Mrs. Badger (New York: Scribner, 1859; EDR 467) and *Morrison's Stranger's Guide to the City of Washington* (Washington: Morrison, 1852; EDR 222) page 27
2. Emily Dickinson's cardinal points symbolism (based on Rebecca Patterson, *Imagery*, 183–200) 61
3. Winslow Homer, *The Veteran in a New Field*, 1865. Oil on canvas, 24 1/8 × 38 1/8 in. Bequest of Miss Adelaide Milton de Groot (1876–1967), 1967 (67.187.131). The Metropolitan Museum of Art, New York, New York. Image copyright The Metropolitan Museum of Art 227
4. *The Veteran in a New Field* (detail) 228
5. Winslow Homer, *Prisoners from the Front*, 1866. Oil on canvas, 24 × 38 in. Gift of Mrs. Frank B. Porter, 1922 (22.207). The Metropolitan Museum of Art 230
6. Winslow Homer, *The Brush Harrow*, 1865. Oil on canvas, 24 × 37 13/16 in. Harvard Art Museums/Fogg Museum, Anonymous Gift, 1939.229 231

Contributors

FAITH BARRETT is Associate Professor of English at Lawrence University. She is the author of *To Fight Aloud Is Very Brave: American Poetry and the Civil War* (2012) and coeditor with Cristanne Miller of *Words for the Hour: A New Anthology of American Civil War Poetry* (2005).

DAVID CODY is Professor of English at Hartwick College. His articles on Dickinson, Hawthorne, Melville, Poe, Cooper, Whitman, Henry Adams, Faulkner, and other American and British authors have appeared in numerous scholarly journals, books, and annual volumes.

PAUL CRUMBLEY is Professor of English at Utah State University. He is the author of *Inflections of the Pen: Dash and Voice in Emily Dickinson* (1997) and *Winds of Will: Emily Dickinson and the Sovereignty of Democratic Thought* (2010).

THEO DAVIS is Associate Professor of English at Northeastern University. She is the author of *Formalism, Experience, and the Making of American Literature in the Nineteenth Century* (2007).

GABRIELLE DEAN is the Curator of Modern Literary Rare Books and Manuscripts at Johns Hopkins University. She is working on a book titled *Picturing the Grid: Emily Dickinson, Gertrude Stein and the Photographic Turn.*

JED DEPPMAN is Irvin E. Houck Associate Professor in the Humanities and Director of Comparative Literature at Oberlin College. A former vice president of the Emily Dickinson International Society, he is author of *Trying to Think with Emily Dickinson* (2008) and coeditor of *Emily Dickinson and Philosophy* (2013).

JANE DONAHUE EBERWEIN is Distinguished Professor of English (Emerita) at Oakland University. She is the author of *Dickinson: Strategies of Limitation* (1985), editor of *An Emily Dickinson Encyclopedia*

(1998), and coeditor with Cindy MacKenzie of *Reading Emily Dickinson's Letters: Critical Essays* (2009).

PÁRAIC FINNERTY is a Senior Lecturer in English and American Literature at the University of Portsmouth. He is the author of *Emily Dickinson's Shakespeare* (2006); he is currently working on his second monograph, *Dickinson and Her British Contemporaries,* and a co-authored book, *Victorian Celebrity Culture and Tennyson's Circle.*

MARGARET H. FREEMAN is Emeritus Professor of Los Angeles Valley College and Co-Director of Myrifield Institute for Cognition and the Arts. She has published widely on cognitive poetics and the poetry of Emily Dickinson.

THOMAS GARDNER is Alumni Distinguished Professor of English at Virginia Tech. His most recent books are *John in the Company of Poets: The Gospel in Literary Imagination* (2011) and *A Door Ajar: Contemporary Writers and Emily Dickinson* (2006).

JAMES GUTHRIE is Professor of English at Wright State University. He received his doctorate from University at Buffalo / SUNY. He is the author of *Emily Dickinson's Vision* (1998) and *Above Time: Emerson's and Thoreau's Temporal Revolutions* (2001), as well as several articles concerning Dickinson's poetry.

ELEANOR ELSON HEGINBOTHAM, Professor of English (Emerita) at Concordia University St. Paul, is the author of *Reading the Fascicles of Emily Dickinson* (2003) and coeditor of a forthcoming collection of essays on the fascicles, along with some dozen essays in other collections and journals, including *EDJ* and the *ED Bulletin*. In "retirement" she teaches in the Washington, DC, area.

ELIZABETH HEWITT is an Associate Professor in the Department of English at The Ohio State University, Columbus. She is author of *Correspondence and American Literature, 1770–1865* (2004).

MELANIE HUBBARD is an independent scholar writing a book on Emily Dickinson's rhetoric and poetics, for which she won a National Endowment for the Humanities (NEH) grant; she has published articles in the *Emily Dickinson Journal* and *MOSAIC*. Essays are forthcoming in *Dickinson and Philosophy* (2013) and *Spectrum of Possibility*, a collection of essays on Dickinson's fascicles. She has also published a book of poems, *We Have With Us Your Sky* (2012).

JOAN KIRKBY is the author of *Emily Dickinson* (1991). Recent publications include "[W]e thought Darwin had thrown 'the Redeemer' away: Darwinizing with Emily Dickinson" (*EDJ*, 2010) and "'A crescent still abides': Emily Dickinson and the Work of Mourning" (in *Wider Than the Sky: Essays and Meditations on the Healing Power of Emily Dickinson* [2007]).

MARY LOEFFELHOLZ is Professor of English and Vice Provost for Academic Affairs at Northeastern University. She is the author of *From School to Salon: Reading Nineteenth-Century American Women's Poetry* (2004).

CINDY MACKENZIE teaches nineteenth-century American literature at the University of Regina in Saskatchewan, Canada. She is the author of *A Concordance to the Letters of Emily Dickinson* (2000), coeditor of *Reading Dickinson's Letters: Critical Essays* (2010), and coeditor of *Wider Than the Sky: Essays and Meditations on the Healing Power of Emily Dickinson* (2007).

JAMES MCINTOSH is Professor of English and American Culture (Emeritus) at the University of Michigan. His most recent book is *Nimble Believing: Dickinson and the Unknown* (2000).

CRISTANNE MILLER is SUNY Distinguished Professor and Edward H. Butler Professor of Literature at the University at Buffalo SUNY. Author of *Emily Dickinson: A Poet's Grammar* (1987) and coeditor of *The Emily Dickinson Handbook* (1998), her most recent book is *Reading in Time: Emily Dickinson in the Nineteenth Century* (2012). She is currently preparing a new reading edition of Dickinson poems for Harvard University Press.

DOMHNALL MITCHELL teaches nineteenth-century American literature at the Norwegian University of Science and Technology. He is the author of *Emily Dickinson: Monarch of Perception* (2000) and *Measures of Possibility: Emily Dickinson's Manuscripts* (2005). With Maria Stuart, he edited *The International Reception of Emily Dickinson* (2009). His essays have appeared in *American Literature*, *EDJ*, *Legacy*, and *Nineteenth-Century Literature*.

ALEXANDER NEMEROV is the Carl and Marilynn Thoma Provostial Professor in the Arts and Humanities at Stanford University. His most recent book is *Wartime Kiss: Visions of the Moment in the 1940s* (2012).

ELIZABETH A. PETRINO is Associate Professor and Chair of English at Fairfield University. She is the author of *Emily Dickinson and Her Contemporaries: Women's Verse in America, 1820–1885* (1998). She has published articles on Dickinson and her female literary peers in several journals and anthologies. Her research interests include Dickinson's transatlantic influences and literary allusion, especially relating to British and Continental writers.

ELIZA RICHARDS is Associate Professor in the Department of English and Comparative Literature at the University of North Carolina at Chapel Hill. She is the author of *Gender and the Poetics of Reception in Poe's Circle* (2004) and is completing a book entitled *Correspondent Lines: Poetry and Journalism in the US Civil War*.

SANDRA RUNZO is Associate Professor of English at Denison University. She has published several essays on Emily Dickinson and is currently at work on a book-length study of Dickinson and popular culture.

EMILY SEELBINDER is a Professor of English at Queens University of Charlotte, where she joined the faculty in 1989. She is also the editor of "My Criterion for Tune," an occasional series in the *Emily Dickinson International Society Bulletin* that explores musical settings of Dickinson's work.

SABINE SIELKE is Chair of North American Literature and Culture and Director of the North American Studies Program and the German-Canadian Centre at the University of Bonn. She is the author of *Reading Rape: The Rhetoric of Sexual Violence in American Literature and Culture, 1790–1990* (2002) and *Fashioning the Female Subject: The Intertextual Networking of Dickinson, Moore, and Rich* (1997). She also coedited *Orient and Orientalisms in US-American Poetry and Poetics* (2009).

MARTHA NELL SMITH is Professor of English and Distinguished Scholar-Teacher at the University of Maryland. She is the author or editor of five books on Emily Dickinson, as well as a digital scholarly edition, *Emily Dickinson's Correspondences* (2008) and the *Dickinson Electronic Archives*. She is on the Advisory Board of Harvard University Press's *Emily Dickinson Archive* (2013).

ALEXANDRA SOCARIDES is Assistant Professor of English at the University of Missouri. She is the author of *Dickinson Unbound: Paper, Process, Poetics* (2012).

ANGELA SORBY is the author of the critical study *Schoolroom Poets* (2005); two poetry collections, *Distance Learning* (1998) and *Bird Skin Coat* (2009); and a forthcoming anthology of nineteenth-century children's poetry, *Over the River and Through the Woods,* coedited with Karen Kilcup. She teaches literature and creative writing at Marquette University.

SHIRA WOLOSKY is Professor of English and American Literature at the Hebrew University of Jerusalem. She is author of *Emily Dickinson: A Voice of War* (1984), *Language Mysticism* (1995), *The Art of Poetry* (2001), *Poetry and Public Discourse* (2010), and other books and articles on literature and literary theory.

MAGDALENA ZAPEDOWSKA is a former faculty member at Adam Mickiewicz University in Poznan, Poland; she now works at the Writing Center at Amherst College. Her articles on Dickinson and other nineteenth-century authors have appeared in U.S. and Polish journals and essay collections.

Acknowledgments

I thank Ray Ryan for commissioning this book; the anonymous reviewers of the proposal, who offered strengthening suggestions; and the staff at Cambridge University Press and Newgen Knowledge Works for seeing the manuscript through the publication process: Bindu has been particularly helpful. Elisa Faison helped build the index with care, and I greatly appreciate the time and effort she devoted to this challenge. It has been inspiring to work with the passionate and knowledgeable community of Dickinson scholars. I would like to express particular gratitude for the generous help of those with whom I consulted most closely during the editing process: Jed Deppman, Jane Eberwein, Cristanne Miller, Domhnall Mitchell, Marianne Noble, and Martha Nell Smith. Cristanne Miller and Domhnall Mitchell reviewed my chronology and offered useful suggestions and corrections (any remaining errors are my own). Thanks also go to the staff at the National Humanities Center, where I was a Fellow in 2010–2011 and a Resident Associate during the fall semester of 2011 while working on this project. Karen Dandurand, a distinguished Dickinson scholar, died before she completed her contribution for this volume. Her influence and memory inform the work in countless ways.

Abbreviations and Textual Note

Capps   Capps, Jack, *Emily Dickinson's Reading, 1836–1886* (Cambridge, MA: Harvard University Press, 1966).
EDJ   *The Emily Dickinson Journal* (Johns Hopkins University Press).
F   Franklin, R.W., ed., *The Poems of Emily Dickinson: Variorum Edition*. (Cambridge, MA: The Belknap Press of Harvard University Press, 1998).
Habegger   Habegger, Alfred, *My Wars Are Laid Away in Books: The Life of Emily Dickinson* (New York: Random House, 2001).
Handbook   Grabher, Gudrun, Roland Hagenbüchle, and Cristanne Miller, eds., *The Emily Dickinson Handbook* (Amherst: University of Massachusetts Press, 1998).
J   Johnson, Thomas H., ed., *The Poems of Emily Dickinson, Including Variant Readings Critically Compared with All Known Manuscripts* (Cambridge, MA: The Belknap Press of Harvard University Press, 1955).
L   Johnson, Thomas H. and Theodora Ward, eds., *The Letters of Emily Dickinson*. (Cambridge, MA: The Belknap Press of Harvard University Press, 1958).
Leyda   Leyda, Jay, *The Years and Hours of Emily Dickinson*, 2 vols. (New Haven: Yale University Press, 1960).
Reception   Buckingham, Willis J., *Emily Dickinson's Reception in the 1890s: A Documentary History* (Pittsburgh: University of Pittsburgh Press, 1989).
Sewall   Sewall, Richard, *The Life of Emily Dickinson* (Cambridge, MA: Harvard University Press, 1980 [1974]).
Whicher   Whicher, George Frisbee, *This Was a Poet: A Critical Biography of Emily Dickinson* (New York and London: Charles Scribner's Sons, 1939).

Unless otherwise indicated, quotations from Dickinson's poems follow the text of Franklin's variorum edition; both Franklin and Johnson numbers are cited parenthetically within the text for the convenience of readers. When the particular version of a poem is important to the essay's argument, the letter has been added in addition to the number. Dickinson's letters are cited by Johnson's letter numbers. Dickinson's idiosyncratic spelling, capitalization, and punctuation have been retained throughout, and her dashes are represented by spaced hyphens, as in Franklin's edition. Some contributors have chosen to represent line breaks as they appear in Dickinson's manuscripts, though neither Johnson nor Franklin editions represent them in this way.

Chronology

1828	Dickinson's parents, attorney Edward Dickinson of Amherst and Emily Norcross of Monson, marry.
1829	(William) Austin, Dickinson's brother, is born in Amherst.
1830	Edward buys one half of the brick Homestead on Main Street that belongs to his father. Emily Elizabeth Dickinson is born here on December 10.
1833	Lavinia Norcross (Vinnie), Dickinson's sister, is born.
1835	Dickinson begins four years at Amherst Female Seminary. Edward Dickinson is appointed treasurer of Amherst College.
1838	Edward Dickinson begins first term in the Massachusetts legislature. Samuel Fowler Dickinson, his father and a founder of Amherst College, dies in Ohio.
1840	Dickinson enters Amherst Academy, with Lavinia: "I have four studies. They are Mental Philosophy, Geology, Latin, and Botany. How large they sound, don't they?" (L6). The Dickinsons move to West Street (now North Pleasant Street).
1846–7	The only known daguerreotype of Dickinson was made by William C. North in Amherst.
1847	Dickinson graduates from Amherst Academy and enters Mount Holyoke Female Seminary, where she completes a single year of studies: "I am now studying 'Silliman's Chemistry' & Cutler's Physiology, in both of which I am much interested" (L20). There she refuses to confess faith publicly during a period of evangelical Protestant religious revivalism.
1850	The Amherst College *Indicator* publishes a valentine by Dickinson, "Magnum bonum." Dickinson continues to resist religious conversion, even though many of her loved ones convert: "I am standing alone in rebellion" (L35). During

Dickinson's lifetime a handful of poems were published, always anonymously, and some perhaps without her permission.

1852 The *Springfield Republican* publishes Dickinson's "Sic transit gloria mundi" (F2 J3) as "A Valentine." Edward Dickinson is elected to the US House of Representatives. Emily writes to Susan Gilbert: "Why cant *I* be a Delegate to the great Whig Convention?" (L94).

1853 Austin enters Harvard Law School.

1855 With Lavinia, Dickinson travels to Washington, DC, and spends several weeks there in February and March. On the way home they visit Philadelphia, where Dickinson meets the Reverend Charles Wadsworth. In November, the Dickinsons move back to the Homestead on Main Street. Emily and Lavinia never marry; they live their adult lives with their parents in this house.

1856 Austin marries Susan Huntington Gilbert. They move into a house built for them next door to the Dickinson Homestead, which they call The Evergreens, where they raise a family and have an active social life. The relationship between Dickinson and Susan is important: "Dear Sue - With the exception of Shakespeare, you have told me of more knowledge than anyone living - To say that sincerely is strange praise" (L757).

1857 Ralph Waldo Emerson lectures in Amherst and is entertained at The Evergreens: "It must have been as if he had come from where dreams are born!" (Prose Fragment 10, in *Letters*).

1858 Dickinson begins recording poems in hand-sewn booklets later known as fascicles. The practice continues until 1864. After this, she gathers some poems in loose anthologies called sets (in 1865, and from 1871 until 1875, when she stops). "Nobody knows this little Rose" (F11 J35) appears in the *Springfield Republican* as "To Mrs. - - , with a Rose. [Surreptitiously communicated to The Republican]." Circa 1858–1865: Dickinson's poetic production increases dramatically, reaching an estimated peak of 295 in 1863, and more than 200 in 1862 and 1865. She becomes increasingly reclusive, but maintains an extensive and engaged correspondence with family and friends, many of whom are also prominent public figures (Thomas Wentworth Higginson, Samuel Bowles, Josiah Gilbert Holland, Helen Hunt Jackson, Judge Otis P. Lord). The "Master Letters," drafts of love letters with an unknown recipient, are probably composed during this time (it is unknown if the letters were sent).

1861	US Civil War begins. "I taste a liquor never brewed - " (F207 J214) is published in the *Republican* under the title "The May-Wine." Elizabeth Barrett Browning dies: "Silver - perished - with her Tongue - " (F600 J312).
1862	"Safe in their Alabaster Chambers - " (F124 J216) is published in the *Republican* as "The Sleeping." Dickinson begins correspondence with Thomas Wentworth Higginson, responding to his essay in the *Atlantic Monthly* that offers advice to young writers: "Are you too deeply occupied to say if my Verse is alive?" (L260). Higginson departs for South Carolina as the Colonel of the first black Union army regiment. Amherst native Frazar Stearns is killed in action, "his big heart shot away by a 'minie ball'" (L255).
1864	Dickinson suffers from eye problems and moves to Cambridge, MA, for treatment, April–November: "yet I work in my Prison, and make Guests for myself - " (L290). Austin is drafted to fight in the Civil War and pays for a substitute. "Flowers - Well - if anybody" (F95 J137) published by *Drum Beat*, *Springfield Republican*, and *Boston Post* under the title "Flowers"; "These are the days when Birds come back - " (F122 J130) published by *Drum Beat*, a Brooklyn paper raising funds for the Union cause, under the title "October." "Some keep the Sabbath Going to Church - " (F236 J324) published in the *Round Table* under the title "My Sabbath." "Blazing in Gold and quenching in Purple" (F321 J228) published by *Drum Beat* and the *Springfield Republican* under the title "Sunset." "Success is counted sweetest" (F112 J67) published in the *Brooklyn Daily Union*.
1865	Dickinson returns to Cambridge for eye treatment in April, and stays another seven months. Vision improves.
1866	"A narrow fellow in the grass" (F1096 J986) is published by the *Republican* as "The Snake"; Dickinson tells Higginson: "it was robbed of me - defeated too of the third line by the punctuation" (L316).
1869	Dickinson refuses Higginson's invitation to come to Boston: "I do not cross my Father's ground to any House or town" (L330).
1870	Higginson visits Dickinson in Amherst.
1871–2	George Eliot's *Middlemarch* published: "'What do I think of *Middlemarch*? What do I think of glory - " (L389).

1873	Higginson visits Dickinson again.
1874	Edward Dickinson dies in Boston: "His Heart was pure and terrible and I think no other like it exists" (L418).
1875	Emily Norcross Dickinson has a stroke and is paralyzed.
1876	In a letter, well-known writer Helen Hunt Jackson rebukes Dickinson for refusing to publish: "You are a great poet – and it is a wrong to the day you live in, that you will not sing aloud" (L444a).
1877	Samuel Bowles visits Dickinson in Amherst: "You have the most triumphant Face out of Paradise" (L489).
1878	Helen Hunt Jackson visits Dickinson in Amherst. At her insistence, Dickinson allows "Success is counted sweetest" to be published anonymously in *A Masque of Poets*. It is attributed to Emerson. Around this time Dickinson begins writing to Judge Otis P. Lord, a relationship that lasts to his death: "It is strange that I miss you at night so much when I was never with you" (L645). Most letters, like this one, survive only in draft form, or as fair copies. It is unknown if they were sent.
1880	Reverend Charles Wadsworth visits Dickinson in Amherst. Judge Lord and nieces visit Amherst. Lord gives Dickinson *Complete Concordance to Shakespeare* at Christmastime: "While Shakespeare remains Literature is firm" (L368).
1882	Dickinson's mother dies after a long illness: "The dear Mother that could not walk, has *flown*" (L779). Reverend Wadsworth dies. Judge Lord visits Dickinson in Amherst.
1883	Dickinson's beloved nephew Thomas Gilbert (Gib) dies at age eight; she writes to Susan, "I see him in the Star, and meet his sweet velocity in everything that flies" (L868).
1884	Judge Lord dies: "I work to drive the awe away, yet awe impels the work" (L891).
1886	Dickinson dies on May 15; her final letter to Louise and Frances Norcross reads simply: "Little Cousins, Called back. Emily" (L1046). Funeral takes place on May 19 in the Homestead library. Higginson attends and reads Emily Brontë's "No coward soul is mine." Susan Dickinson writes an obituary that appears in the *Republican*. Soon afterward Lavinia discovers a trove of Dickinson manuscripts in a wooden trunk – no one seems to have been aware during her lifetime of how many poems she was writing (more than 1,700 are extant, many in multiple versions) – and decides to enlist help in publishing them.

Introduction
Eliza Richards

Unlike Charles Dickens, "a man so imbricated in his age as to be synonymous with it," Emily Dickinson does not obviously demand to be read within historical contexts.[1] Indeed, when asked to imagine Dickinson, readers may picture a woman dressed in white, sitting at a small desk in her bedroom, receiving "Bulletins all Day / From Immortality," and writing them down in the form of her "letter to the World / That never wrote" to her (F820 J827, F519 J441). A famously retiring poet, dubbed "Queen Recluse" by her close friend Samuel Bowles, Dickinson witnessed just a handful of her poems published in newspapers and magazines during her lifetime, often without her permission (quoted in Sewall, 474). More of her poems circulated in letters to a diverse array of friends. But not even her sister Lavinia, with whom she lived, knew of the extent of her opus until after her death, when hundreds of poems were discovered, many of them neatly sewn into little booklets later known as fascicles. This scenario of consummately private poetic production framed the early publication of her "portfolio" poems, as one of her correspondents and earliest editors, Thomas Wentworth Higginson, called them.[2] From 1890 to 1945, competing factions of Dickinson's family and friends offered this treasure trove to the public bit by bit, in volume after volume, underscoring the poet's eccentric, isolated genius all the while, setting terms of reception that endure to the present day. (Martha Nell Smith discusses this history and argues for its continued relevance in Chapter 26.)

This image served Dickinson's reputation well in the early periods of recognition. Turn-of-the-century readers were fascinated with her strange writings, which seemed "like poetry torn up by the roots, with rain and dew and earth still clinging to them" and presented to the public.[3] Speculative biographies followed the earlier family memoirs, as readers entranced by the riddling poems and letters sought to piece together a narrative of Dickinson's outwardly uneventful, inwardly spectacular life. Who or what motivated the great crisis of the early 1860s that spurred such a powerful outpouring of poems? Who was the "Master" addressed in three of her letter drafts; was he or she the motivating force? Until the present day – three book-length biographical studies and a historical novel entitled *The Secret Life of Emily Dickinson* (2011) have been published in recent years – people have enthusiastically inquired into the mysteries of Emily Dickinson, arriving at a range of more or less plausible, more or less intriguing answers.[4]

If the first decades of criticism cast Dickinson as an eccentric, idiosyncratic genius, criticism of the mid-twentieth century confirmed and extended that picture by casting her as a protomodernist, a writer who had more to do with the twentieth century than with the one in which she lived. In the 1930s and 1940s the New Critics sharply countered psychological and biographical studies, insisting that Dickinson's work should be judged by "the poetic relation of the words" alone.[5] (Theo Davis offers a fascinating analysis of New Critical engagements with Dickinson in Chapter 30.) Dickinson's compact, compressed "fusion of sensibility and thought" made Dickinson an ideal poet for these formalists, who devoted their energies to intensive explications of individual poems, modeling an influential strategy of close reading that remains one of the most rewarding and commonly practiced approaches to reading Dickinson, especially in the classroom.[6] As much as close reading strategies have enriched the study of her complex poems, however, they have also tended to reinforce the tendency to think of her as work as context-less, as if her world of words swung free, its "Boundaries - forgot - ," like the spider in one of her poems whose web was swept away by a housewife's broom (F513 J605). These context-less readings themselves constitute a somewhat paradoxical historical context, for the formalist strain in Dickinson criticism continues to flourish in transformed ways, allying itself with linguistic, psychological, philosophical, and even some historicist approaches.[7]

Starting in the 1960s, New England religious life offered one of the earliest historical and intellectual contexts for analyzing Dickinson's poetry – particularly Puritanism and Calvinism, the Second Great Awakening, and Transcendentalism.[8] Although the range of theological frames for reading her work has multiplied over the years, there is no abatement of interest in the topic. It is clear that Dickinson's poetry is an exercise in "nimble believing," but it is not as clear how to define that process or the goals of her rigorous but open-ended spiritual inquiry.[9] It is therefore not surprising, and certainly not redundant, that dozens of articles and at least four monographs published recently have concentrated on spiritual issues: on religion's role in Dickinson's writing process, on the "problem of human suffering," and on Dickinson and "hymn culture."[10] Several of the essays in this volume take up the question of Dickinson's engagements with religious traditions and writings: Jane Donahue Eberwein writes on Dickinson's New England heritage; Emily Seelbinder examines the particular copy of the King James Bible that Dickinson owned; Joan Kirkby discusses ideas about death and immortality in the poet's time; and James McIntosh evaluates her conflicted thinking about Christian traditions.

Feminist criticism initiated a comprehensive revolution in Dickinson studies in the 1970s and 1980s, as scholars became increasingly interested in finding ways of locating Dickinson's complex verbal artifacts within their gendered cultural surroundings. From Susan Gilbert and Sandra Gubar's landmark study *Madwoman in the Attic* (1979), to Margaret Homans and Cristanne Miller's deconstructionist-inspired readings of Dickinson's language and poetic practice, to Cheryl Walker and Joanne Dobson's historicist studies of Dickinson's relation to her female contemporaries, feminist criticism opened Dickinson studies to new forms of historically, politically, and psychologically inflected approaches.[11] Mary Loeffelholz offered a Lacanian reading not only of Dickinson, but also of her feminist critics in 1991; Martha Nell Smith's 1992 study *Rowing in Eden* powerfully raised the possibility of Dickinson's same-sex attraction to and love for Susan Dickinson as a motivating force in her poetic production; and Elizabeth A. Petrino explored the relationships between Dickinson and her popular female poetic peers in 1998.[12] Though studies of gender and sexuality have become increasingly alloyed with other approaches in recent years (as Shira Wolosky in Chapter 16 argues they should be), the conceptual frameworks established by the feminist legacy in Dickinson criticism are a powerful force that continues to shape work on a range of topics today.

Because Dickinson's poetry was so long approached through meditative, presentless, dislocated modes of reading, the energies drawn from historicist and cultural approaches have taken time to infuse that intensely private and individualized atmosphere. If Dickinson was long figured as "the exception," and if she continues to impress readers as startlingly original, critics have nevertheless been increasingly fascinated with the ways in which she comments on contemporary events and surroundings.[13] Barton St. Armand's landmark study *Emily Dickinson and Her Culture* (1984) helped inaugurate the historical trend, with chapters on Victorian death rituals, the popular hobby of scrapbooking, and the aesthetics of John Ruskin.[14] Shira Wolosky's study of Dickinson and the U.S. Civil War appeared the same year and set the terms for an ongoing inquiry into the poet's oblique commentary on the war that continues unabated today (Faith Barrett has contributed an excellent essay on the topic for this volume).[15] During the late 1980s and 1990s, substantial work on Dickinson's relation to popular literary culture, abolitionist and feminist rhetoric, and visual culture emerged.[16] These pioneering studies persuasively demonstrated that although her work may be private, it nevertheless registers important intellectual, social, and political currents of her time.

In the twenty-first century, contexts for the study of Dickinson have multiplied as never before. Domhnall Mitchell's *Monarch of Perception* (2000) considers Dickinson's work in relation to contemporary contexts such as railroads, domestic space, and autograph anthologies. Alfred Habegger's biography, *My Wars Are Laid Away in Books* (2001), takes a decidedly cultural turn. In *Dickinson's Misery: A Theory of Lyric Reading* (2005), Virginia Jackson deconstructs the iconography of Dickinson as the isolated lyric poet and powerfully raises the question of precisely what contexts are appropriate for reading her work; Páraic Finnerty examines cultures of reading and performance surrounding Dickinson in *Emily Dickinson's Shakespeare* (2006); Aife Murray undertakes a full-scale excavation of the lives of the family's servants and their influence on Dickinson's work in *Maid as Muse* (2009). In *Winds of Will* (2010), Paul Crumbley explores the ways democracy informs the poet's work. In the same year, Robin Peel published the first book-length study of the impact of nineteenth-century sciences – paleontology, natural theology, geology, astronomy, and so forth – on Dickinson's thinking. Most recently, Cristanne Miller's *Reading in Time: Emily Dickinson in the Nineteenth Century* (2012) situates the poet within nineteenth-century literary culture, examining the ways she engages contemporary forms, conventions, and writing practices.[17] Other recent book-length studies address Dickinson's international reception, her engagements with textiles and clothing, and her critical reception history since 1960.[18] A special issue of *The Emily Dickinson Journal* (19.1) in 2010, edited by Daniel M. Mannheim and Marianne Noble, focused on her reading of a broad range of writings that circulated in her time. Articles and book chapters have treated Dickinson's legacy in the American schoolroom, her sense of interior space, her engagements with new technologies such as photography and telegraphy, her interest in news and current events, Darwin's influence, her portrayal and understanding of animals, and her global sensibility.[19] This is just a sampling of the recent outpouring of work on Emily Dickinson in historical contexts that shows no sign of dwindling, and Magdalena Zapedowska offers an admirably concise and comprehensive overview of the multiplying trends in Dickinson studies from 1955 to the present in Chapter 31. Studies of the philosophical, linguistic, and scientific contexts for Dickinson's writing are all in the works, and there are certainly others of which I am not yet aware. As Mary Loeffelholz astutely notes in her essay for this volume, "a Dickinson who can remain our contemporary must increasingly be pried away from modernism and affixed to practices more *au courant*," and historicism is certainly an *au courant* current in Dickinson studies today. In part because her work for so long seemed impervious to cultural contexts, critics are now fascinated with what seems like a great reservoir of unexplored engagements with the events, ideas, social movements, politics, arts, education, religion, everyday practices, environments, entertainments, and writings of her time.

Ongoing innovations and insights in editorial studies have informed many of these contextualizations and serve as an important context themselves (both Gabrielle Dean and Alexandra Socarides take up this important topic in their essays for this volume). Dickinson's manuscripts – her fascicles, unbound poems, scraps, and letters – have undergone intense scrutiny in the past few decades. Insights and hypotheses abound regarding the organization and chronology of the writings, the lineation of the poems, her tendency to include multiple word choices even in final drafts, and Dickinson's material practices more generally. Since Thomas Johnson's revolutionary scholarly edition, which treated seriously Dickinson's own idiosyncratic punctuation, capitalization, syntax, and word variants, a number of editorial projects have opened possibilities for scholarly inquiry and raised new questions about the best ways to represent Dickinson's manuscripts. R. W. Franklin first made many of the manuscripts available to the broader public in 1981, when he published facsimiles in *The Manuscript Books of Emily Dickinson*; critics were newly able to analyze lineation, word location, and other nuances of the manuscript page, which is especially important for a poet who declined to publish (or at least, to "print" – critics have suggested she made a distinction) during her lifetime. In 1995, Marta Werner drew attention to the scraps and fragments of Dickinson's writing, reproducing them within her editorial study and encouraging readers to speculate about the choices that resulted in the forms in which they appear. Innovative digital projects such as *Emily Dickinson's Correspondences: A Born-Digital Textual Inquiry* and *Radical Scatters: Emily Dickinson's Late Fragments and Related Texts, 1870–1886* continue to make new presentations of Dickinson available, which constitute, as well as enable, new interpretations of her texts.[20] In the fall of 2013, Harvard University Press will launch the *Emily Dickinson Archive*; available to the public around the world, the site will pair manuscripts with transcriptions and other resources, enabling new scholarship and fresh directions in teaching. Readers are making new sense of Dickinson in the digital age.

This proliferation of cultural, political, social, intellectual, and editorial frames has generated a need for a volume that orients readers to the shifting, unsettling, expanding world of Emily Dickinson. Though complete coverage is of course impossible, I have aimed at comprehensiveness and balance in the book's design, while asking contributors to draw on their extensive expertise to offer fresh insights into their topics. The outstanding essays that make up this volume offer lasting contributions to Dickinson scholarship. Several of the essays break new ground in crucial yet understudied areas: see especially Elizabeth Hewitt on economics, James Guthrie on the law, Sandra Runzo on popular culture, Paul Crumbley on Dickinson's democratic poetics, Jed Deppman on her philosophical engagements, Sabine Sielke on the natural sciences, and Melanie Hubbard on nineteenth-century theories of language. Essays that cover more familiar topics bring fresh insight grounded in impressive levels of original research: Domhnall Mitchell on Amherst; Eleanor Elson Heginbotham on the Dickinson library; Angela Sorby on Dickinson's education; David Cody on eighteenth-century influences, particularly Dickinson's interest in Sir Thomas Browne's writings; Elizabeth A. Petrino on Romantic influences; Joan Kirkby on periodical reading; and Páraic Finnerty on Shakespeare as well as transatlantic women writers.

Some essays are particularly striking for their innovative methodological approaches: Margaret Freeman's emphasis on Dickinson's transformations of nature into metaphor, Cristanne Miller's comparative approach to metrical innovation, Alexander Nemerov's striking comparison of the use of "pentimento" in Winslow Homer's paintings and Dickinson's poems. Other contributions stand out for offering a provocative argument even while presenting a responsible overview of a topic: Emily Seelbinder stresses the importance of the aberrant spelling of a single word for understanding Dickinson's engagements with the King James Bible; Mary Loeffelholz emphasizes Dickinson's competition with her female contemporaries over writing a "modern" form of literature; Sabine Sielke argues that Dickinson critiques the limitations of scientific inquiry, championing poetry's alternative forms of knowledge; Cindy MacKenzie thinks about the ways Dickinson's letters are haunted by the writer as well as by her readers; Theo Davis challenges the longstanding assumption that Dickinson's poems were strange and incomprehensible to her earlier readers while estranging common understandings of new critical modes of inquiry; and Thomas Gardner traces the ways that writers since Dickinson have engaged in conversations with her poetry in their own work.

Several of the scholars contributing to this volume live and work outside the United States, one indication of Dickinson's growing reputation around the world. In Chapter 33, Domhnall Mitchell discusses this global expansion of interest, offering an overview of the trends in international reception and the challenges posed by translating Dickinson into very different languages and cultures. It is my hope that this volume abets the expanding circulation of Dickinson's work by offering accessible and well-informed critical insights to students, teachers, and scholars everywhere.

If the book itself could continue expanding, many more essays might have been written: on Dickinson's fascination with foreign places, for example, or on her deep engagement with the flora and fauna that populated her immediate surroundings. Her family relationships and close friendships, many of them mediated through her extraordinary letters, merit more extensive treatment than they could receive here. Luckily, readers can look to studies that lie outside the scope of this volume, and I begin to offer suggestions for additional reading in the notes to this introduction. Other recommendations are available in the list of further readings, arranged by chapter, at the end of this book. There is much to offer here as well, however, and I hope readers linger over the information and ideas in this volume, offered by a thoughtful, innovative, and deeply knowledgeable group of scholars.

NOTES

1 Preface, *Charles Dickens in Context*, ed. Sally Ledger and Holly Furneaux (Cambridge: Cambridge University Press, 2011).
2 Thomas Wentworth Higginson, "An Open Portfolio" (1890), *The Recognition of Emily Dickinson*, ed. Caesar R. Blake and Carlton F. Wells (Ann Arbor: University of Michigan Press, 1964), 3.
3 Thomas Wentworth Higginson, "Preface to Poems by Emily Dickinson" (1890), Blake and Wells, eds., *The Recognition of Emily Dickinson*, 11.
4 Jerome Charyn, *The Secret Life of Emily Dickinson* (New York: Norton, 2011); Lyndall Gordon, *Lives Like Loaded Guns: Emily Dickinson and Her Family's Feuds* (London: Virago, 2010); Christopher Benfey, *A Summer of Hummingbirds: Love, Art, and Scandal in the Intersecting Worlds of Emily Dickinson, Mark Twain, Harriet Beecher Stowe, and Martin Johnson Heade* (New York: Penguin Press, 2008). Brenda Wineapple, *White Heat: The Friendship of Emily Dickinson and Thomas Wentworth Higginson* (New York: Alfred A. Knopf, 2008).

5 R. P. Blackmur, "Emily Dickinson: Notes on Prejudice and Fact" (1937), Blake and Wells, eds., *The Recognition of Emily Dickinson*, 209.
6 Allen Tate, "New England Literary Culture and Emily Dickinson," *Symposium* (April, 1932). Blake and Wells, eds. *The Recognition of Emily Dickinson*, 161.
7 See, e.g., Sharon Cameron, *Lyric Time: Dickinson and the Limits of Genre* (Baltimore: Johns Hopkins University Press, 1979); Helen Vendler, *Poets Thinking: Pope, Whitman, Dickinson, and Yeats* (Cambridge MA: Harvard University Press, 2004).
8 See, e.g., Charles Anderson, *Emily Dickinson's Poetry: Stairway of Surprise* (New York: Holt, Rinehart and Winston, 1960); Albert Gelpi, *Emily Dickinson: The Mind of the Poet* (Cambridge, MA: Harvard University Press, 1965).
9 James McIntosh's book title, a paraphrase of something Dickinson wrote in L750 to Judge Lord. *Nimble Believing: Dickinson and the Unknown* (Ann Arbor: University of Michigan Press, 2000).
10 Aliki Barnstone, *Changing Rapture: Emily Dickinson's Poetic Development*. Hanover: University Press of New England, 2006); Linda Freedman, *Emily Dickinson and the Religious Imagination* (Cambridge: Cambridge University Press, 2011); Patrick Keane, *Emily Dickinson's Approving God: Divine Design and the Problem of Suffering* (Columbia: University of Missouri Press, 2008); Victoria Morgan, *Emily Dickinson and Hymn Culture: Tradition and Experience*. (Burlington, VT: Ashgate, 2010).
11 Sandra M. Gilbert and Susan Gubar, *The Madwoman in the Attic: The Woman Writer and the Nineteenth-Century Literary Imagination* (New Haven, CT: Yale University Press, 2000 [1979]). Margaret Homans, *Women Writers and Poetic Identity: Dorothy Wordsworth, Emily Brontë, and Emily Dickinson* (Princeton, NJ: Princeton University Press, 1980); Cristanne Miller, *Emily Dickinson, a Poet's Grammar* (Cambridge, MA: Harvard University Press, 1987); Cheryl Walker, *The Nightingale's Burden: Women Poets and American Culture before 1900*. (Bloomington: Indiana University Press, 1982); Joanne Dobson, *Dickinson and the Strategies of Reticence: The Woman Writer in Nineteenth-Century America* (Bloomington: Indiana University Press, 1989).
12 Mary Loeffelholz, *Dickinson and the Boundaries of Feminist Theory* (Urbana: University of Illinois Press, 1991). Martha Nell Smith, *Rowing in Eden: Rereading Emily Dickinson* (Austin: University of Texas Press, 1992); Elizabeth A. Petrino, *Emily Dickinson and Her Contemporaries: Women's Verse in America, 1820–1885* (Hanover, NH: University Press of New England, 1998).
13 Max Cavitch, "Dickinson and the Exception," *A Companion to Emily Dickinson*, ed. Martha Nell Smith and Mary Loeffelholz (Malden, MA: Blackwell, 2008).
14 Barton Levi St. Armand, *Emily Dickinson and Her Culture: The Soul's Society* (Cambridge: Cambridge University Press, 1984).
15 Shira Wolosky, *Emily Dickinson: A Voice of War* (New Haven, CT: Yale University Press, 1984).
16 David Reynolds, *Beneath the American Renaissance: The Subversive Imagination in the Age of Emerson and Melville* (Cambridge, MA: Harvard University Press,

1988); Karen Sánchez-Eppler, *Touching Liberty: Abolition, Feminism, and the Politics of the Body* (Berkeley: University of California Press, 1993). Judith Farr, *The Passion of Emily Dickinson* (Cambridge, MA: Harvard University Press, 1992).
17 Domhnall Mitchell, *Emily Dickinson: Monarch of Perception* (Amherst: University of Massachusetts Press, 2000). Páraic Finnerty, *Emily Dickinson's Shakespeare* (Amherst: University of Massachusetts Press, 2006); Aife Murray, *Maid as Muse: How Servants Changed Emily Dickinson's Life and Language* (Hanover, NH: University Press of New England, 2009); Paul Crumbley, *Winds of Will: Emily Dickinson and the Sovereignty of Democratic Thought* (Tuscaloosa: University of Alabama Press, 2010), Robin Peel, *Emily Dickinson and the Hill of Science* (Madison, NJ: Fairleigh Dickinson University Press, 2010). Cristanne Miller, *Reading in Time: Emily Dickinson in the Nineteenth Century* (Amherst: University of Massachusetts Press, 2012).
18 *The International Reception of Emily Dickinson*, ed. Domhnall Mitchell and Maria Stuart (London: Continuum, 2009); Fred White, *Approaching Emily Dickinson: Critical Currents and Crosscurrents Since 1960* (Rochester, NY: Camden House, 2008).
19 Angela Sorby, *Schoolroom Poets: Childhood, Performance, and the Place of American Poetry, 1865–1917* (Durham, NH: University of New Hampshire Press, 2005). Diana Fuss, *The Sense of an Interior: Four Writers and the Rooms that Shaped Them* (New York: Routledge, 2004). Eliza Richards, "'Death's Surprise, Stamped Visible': Emily Dickinson, Oliver Wendell Holmes, and Civil War Photography," *Amerikastudien/American Studies* 54.1 (2009), 13–33. Jerusha Hull McCormack, "Domesticating Delphi: Emily Dickinson and the Electro-Magnetic Telegraph," *American Quarterly* 55 (2003): 569–601. Eliza Richards, "'How News Must Feel When Traveling': Dickinson and Civil War Media," *A Companion to Emily Dickinson*, ed. Martha Nell Smith and Mary Loeffelholz (Malden, MA: Blackwell, 2008); Joan Kirkby, "Dickinson Reading," *EDJ* 5.2 (1996); Colleen Boggs, "Emily Dickinson's Animal Pedagogies," *PMLA* 124.2 (2009), 533–41; Aaron Shackelford, "Dickinson's Animals and Anthropomorphism," *EDJ* 19.2 (2010), 47–66; Paul Giles, "'The Earth Reversed Her Hemispheres': Dickinson's Global Antipodality," *EDJ* 20.1 (2011), 1–21.
20 *Poems; Including Variant Readings Critically Compared with All Known Manuscripts*, ed. Thomas H. Johnson. 3 vols. (Cambridge: Belknap Press of Harvard University Press, 1955); *The Manuscript Books of Emily Dickinson*. Ed. R. W. Franklin. Cambridge, MA: Belknap Press, 1981; *Emily Dickinson's Open Folios : Scenes of Reading, Surfaces of Writing*, ed. Marta L. Werner (Ann Arbor: University of Michigan Press, 1995); *Emily Dickinson's Correspondences: A Born-DigitalTextual Inquiry*, ed. Martha Nell Smith and Lara Vetter (available at: http://rotunda.upress.virginia.edu/edc/default.xqy); *Radical Scatters: Emily Dickinson's Fragments and Related Texts, 1870–1886*, ed. Marta Werner (available at: http://libxml1a.unl.edu:8080/cocoon/radicalscatters/default-login.html).

PART I

Local Environments

CHAPTER I

Amherst

Domhnall Mitchell

The town and inhabitants of Amherst, Massachusetts, where Emily Dickinson lived all her life, are at their most visible in the poet's correspondence. Family, friends, servants, neighbors, and places are given their proper names (or versions of them), and even cats, horses, and hens make appearances. There are multiple references to church meetings and sermons, to economic and political ambitions, rivalries and anxieties, to the seasons and weather, to concerts, a reading club, the stagecoach and a circus, and to the immediate and everyday in general. Founded in 1759, Amherst was a small town with a population of 2,613 when Dickinson was born there in 1830, but it boasted an elite private school – the Amherst Academy, founded by her paternal grandfather and Noah Webster, among others, in 1814 – and a college, which the same grandfather had helped to found in 1821. The college in particular dominated the cultural, religious, and social life of the community; it provided an intellectual environment that fostered lifelong interests in the poet. Emily Dickinson's was an important family in Amherst, but that status waxed, waned, and waxed again: they built the town's first brick house in 1813, effectively lost it by 1833, and triumphantly repurchased and refurbished it in 1855 – then added another next door in 1856. By the 1860s, a hemlock hedge and fence surrounded the perimeter of both houses fronting Main Street, giving a strong dynastic impression that began to fade only after the poet's death in 1886. But although Amherst sustained the poet enough for her to have left it for extended periods only three times as an adult (in February and March of 1855 she traveled to Washington and Philadelphia, and from April to late November 1864 and April to October 1865 she stayed in Cambridge for eye treatment), it is mentioned only twice in 1,789 poems, as opposed to 88 times in 1,048 letters. For many different reasons, the most decisive of which were aesthetic, she was careful to hide the traces of her local referents.

After five years at the Amherst Female Seminary, Dickinson began attending the Amherst Academy in 1840, where the subjects taught included arithmetic and algebra, botany, chemistry, composition, foreign languages, geography, geology, history, Latin, mathematics, "mental philosophy," religion (including the hymns of Isaac Watts), rhetoric, and science.[1] Biographer Alfred Habegger has argued that the school "stimulated Emily's ambition by turning essay writing into a public contest," with the best examples included in *Forest Leaves*, a class anthology made up of handwritten contributions (Habegger, 164). But it stimulated in other ways too: pupils of the Academy were occasionally allowed to attend lectures given by Professor Edward Hitchcock (1793–1864) of Amherst College, a leading geologist of the day and the author of several textbooks used in the Academy – but also someone for whom science was a powerful explanatory tool in the cause of religion, enriching rather than undermining belief. His textbooks were also set reading at the Academy: "When Flowers annually died and I was a child," Dickinson wrote in 1877, "I used to read Dr Hitchcock's Book on the Flowers of North America. This comforted their Absence - assuring me they lived" (L488).

Dickinson's education was supplemented further by the family library, which amounted to five hundred volumes and included four sets of Shakespeare, the writer she referred to most often, as well as a "Lexicon," her "only companion" (L261).[2] Though there were several small libraries serving the (six) school districts of the town by 1840, the Dickinsons typically had no need of them: books were either purchased privately (in L261 she describes her father buying her "many Books - but [begging her] not to read them"), or received as gifts; private loans; or in exchange with friends, especially Dickinson's sister-in-law Susan Huntington Gilbert Dickinson. The Dickinsons subscribed to fifteen magazines and newspapers, more than the family average in Amherst; the multiple references in her poems to foreign places, history, and geological phenomena, including volcanic activity and mountain formation, is profoundly mediated both by an education that was fairly comprehensive by the standards of her day and by the stories Dickinson read in *The Atlantic Monthly*, *Harper's Monthly Magazine*, and *Scribner's*. Amherst's books and print culture, in short, provided her with a set of references that extended well beyond the local – Cristanne Miller counts "around seventy poems referring to the 'Orient' or mentioning people, animals, or products from Asia" between 1858 and 1881; she argues convincingly that periodicals helped Dickinson understand and question "her New England identity in direct relation to multiple aspects of global exchange."[3]

Amherst was a religious town – the impact of the Second Awakening manifested itself in the foundation of the college, designed to educate and train young ministers, and, slightly further afield, Mount Holyoke Female Seminary, which Dickinson attended as a boarder from 1847 to 1848: at the funeral of its founder, Mary Lyon, in 1849, it was revealed that there had been "eleven revivals in twelve years" there (quoted in Habegger, 198). Dickinson's family did not remain untouched by successive waves of revivalism: her mother, Emily Norcross Dickinson, joined the First Church in 1831; her father and younger sister Lavinia (Vinnie) converted in 1850; and her brother Austin followed them in making a profession of belief in 1856, in part under the influence of his bride-to-be Susan, who was to become one of Dickinson's most important familiars. Dickinson, then, was surrounded on both sides of her family by men and women who were religiously active and prominent. Her maternal grandfather, Joel Norcross, was a "bright-minded, vigorous man who participated in civic and religious activities, promoted quality education, and succeeded in a multiplicity of entrepreneurial enterprises," while her paternal grandfather Samuel Fowler Dickinson "stood at the heart of the village's religious life; clerk and treasurer of the town and frequent delegate to the state legislature, he was at its political center; his legal practice kept him engaged in local commerce, especially the buying and selling of local land."[4] Emily Dickinson herself, though, remained unwilling to express any experience of grace during her year at Mount Holyoke, and never formally belonged to a church. It is perhaps telling that her brother had been deeply skeptical before meeting his future wife, and that her father had run the business affairs of the First Church for around twenty years before his own conversion. There is a (possibly apocryphal) story about Edward being reprimanded for wanting "to come to Christ as a lawyer" when he had to do so "as a poor sinner"; something of that proud reserve finds its way into the occasionally skeptical and aloof voices of Dickinson's religious poems, as when a speaker asks of God in F1675/J1601 "that we may be forgiven - / For what, he is presumed to know" (quoted in Sewall, 66). Nevertheless, her poetry shows the impact of Amherst's religious culture in both its subject matter and form. A concern with the meaning of death and the possibility of an afterlife is often dramatized in poems that are spoken posthumously, as well as the struggle between a yearning to believe and a refusal to do so on unequal terms. Her basic unit, the quatrain, was taken from hymns, and she adopted and adapted various structures of rhythm and rhyme from Watts's hymns.

Sermons were another influence, from which Dickinson learned a great deal about poetic effects. Responding to one given by Edwards Amasa Park (1808–1900) at the First Church on November 20, 1853, she wrote:

> I never heard anything like it, and don't expect to again, till we stand at the great white throne . . . . And when it was all over, and that wonderful man sat down, people stared at each other, and looked as wan and wild, as if they had seen a spirit, and wondered they had not died. (L142)

Park was associated with a "theology of the feelings" that emphasized a creative and imaginative use of language rather than careful rational exposition, and Dickinson's own writing often creates a cumulative emotional impression on the reader that begins with a strong opening line and intense, sometimes violent, imagery: "He fumbles at your Soul" (F477 J315) is a famous example. Dickinson's poetic method can therefore be related more broadly with currents of nineteenth-century theology that originated in Germany and found their way to Amherst. Park had been Professor of Moral Philosophy and Metaphysics at Amherst College from 1835 to 1836; he was influenced by the Higher Criticism associated with Friedrich Schleiermacher (1768–1834), who stressed the importance of intuition, mystery, and personal feelings in religious experience. Henry Boynton Smith (1815–77), whose preaching Dickinson noted in a letter to Austin (L22), was Professor of Moral Philosophy and Metaphysics at Amherst College from 1847 to 1850, and "had studied in the universities of Halle and Berlin" (where Schleiermacher had taught) (Sewall, 359). Lyman Coleman (1796–1882) was married to Dickinson's maternal first cousin, Maria Flynt; a minister of the Congregational Church in neighboring Belchertown, he too had studied in Berlin before becoming principal of Amherst Academy (from 1844 to 1846), where Dickinson took German with him (her habit of capitalizing certain nouns is believed to have been influenced by German convention). The Rev. George Henry Gould (1827–99), an early family and personal friend, was another minister who "had an ear for music – the 'music of words'," which finds its corollary in Dickinson's F1577/J1545 "The Bible is an antique Volume," where the speaker aligns herself with Orpheus, who captivates and charms through music, rather than the Scripture that condemns.[5]

Emily Dickinson is not obviously like Walt Whitman ("I'm Nobody!" from F260/J288 seems at first glance to be very far removed from the "I sing myself" of *Leaves of Grass*), but in fact her inner gaze ("I" is the most often-used word in her poetic vocabulary) is made at least partly possible by a self-confidence generated by her family's prominence in a regionally vital town. Many of her references to Amherst are in the context of invitations to visit that reveal pride as much as attachment, the earliest in 1842 (L3, "I do wish you would come to Amherst…"). There are even times when Dickinson becomes a self-appointed spokesperson or ambassador for the place, as in August 1878 when she represents her own concern as that of "Amherst's Face" in responding to news of an accident involving Mrs. Sarah Jenkins, wife of the former pastor of the First Church, who had only recently relocated to Pittsfield after eleven years (L564). At one level, this identification of town and self was derived from her family's long and distinguished association with Amherst's most significant institutions. In reaction to the perceived encroachment of liberalism from elsewhere, her grandfather, Samuel Fowler Dickinson, had helped finance and found Amherst College in 1821, and her father and brother served as its treasurers – Edward from 1835 to 1872, and Austin from 1873 to 1895. The three generations of Dickinson men were all lawyers, with the poet sometimes serving as a witness to legal documents, and to a greater or lesser extent politically active: Samuel and Edward both served on the state legislature, and Austin was a driving force behind new buildings in the town and college, as well as the landscaping of the town Common (in consultation with Fredrik Law Olmsted, designer of New York's Central Park) and Wildwood cemetery. The poet's mother, Emily Norcross Dickinson, was also very well educated and a supremely gifted gardener who in 1858 was mentioned in the local paper for her ability to grow figs, a "great rarity… in this latitude." In the same note, "Mr. D" was praised for "the extreme beauty of the house and grounds" and for "the great variety and beauty of the fruits and plants" that Mrs. Dickinson, in truth, was responsible for (Leyda I, 359). Commencement Week activities in the autumn included events and visits hosted by the Dickinson family, with Emily's sister-in-law Susan assuming the role of social leader from 1857 onwards. An early and shared sense of familial distinction is clearly articulated in an 1853 letter to Austin, in which Emily observes that their cousins "The Newmans seem very pleasant, but they are not *like us*. What makes a few of us so different from others? It's a question I often ask myself" (L118).

Edward Dickinson's own leading role in Amherst as a lawyer and politician carried over into the personal sphere; in July 1851 he took an active part in helping to extinguish a fire in town, but also rang the church bells (often a fire alarm) in October of the same year to draw attention to a rare instance of the Aurora Borealis (L53). And of Austin it was said that "nobody in the town could be born or married or buried, or make an investment, or buy a house-lot, or a cemetery-lot, or sell a newspaper, or build a house, or choose a profession, without [him] close at hand."[6] The same remarks could be applied equally well to Emily Dickinson herself – except that where her male relatives had roles that were public and institutional, hers were epistolary, literary, and informal: for example, in 1853, her brother became the first secretary of the Amherst Ornamental Tree Association, but Dickinson kept an extensive herbarium, cultivated plants (as did her sister Lavinia), and wrote about flowers extensively and knowledgeably in both letters and poems.[7] In an 1866 letter to her close friend Elizabeth Holland, Dickinson remarked that "My flowers are near and foreign, and I have but to cross the floor to stand in the Spice Isles" (L315). In 1862, she repeated this sense of the exotic in describing "Carnations" that "tip their spice" along with daisies, fuchsias, geraniums, hyacinths, and "Globe Roses" (F367 J339).[8] In a letter (L53) to her brother, she celebrated exactly the same Northern lights as had her father: "The sky was a beautiful red, bordering on a crimson, and rays of a gold pink color were constantly shooting off from a kind of sun in the centre." She later turned to them again in two poems, F319/J209, "Of Bronze - and Blaze" and F321/J228, "Blazing in Gold - and / Quenching - in Purple!," both dating from 1862.

The extent to which the Dickinson family interests and attitudes overlap in relation to Amherst can be seen in F383/J585 "I like to see it lap the Miles - ," another 1862 poem that may take some of its impetus from the description of a train in Charles Dickens's *American Notes for General Circulation* (1842) but much more from the successful part played by Edward Dickinson in securing the extension of the railroad network to Amherst in 1852. On the day that the first train arrived, Edward led a parade that is memorably described by the poet in a letter of June 1853:

> Father was as usual, Grand Marshal of the day, and went marching around the town with New London at his heels like some old Roman General, upon a Triumph Day. Mrs Howe got a capital dinner, and was very much praised. Carriages flew like sparks, hither, and thither and yon, and they all said t'was fine. I spose it was - I sat in Prof Tyler's woods and saw the train move off, and then ran home again for fear somebody would see me, or ask me how I did. (L127)

It is not always easy to recognize how active a commentator on public or social events in Amherst Dickinson was – in letters, the connections are more obvious, but in poems she works hard to erase specific origins. "I like to see it lap the Miles - " makes no mention of a train, a historically identifiable person or place, but something of the ambivalence about the arrival of the railroad in the letter carries over into the poem, especially in the apparently uncontrollable nature of its movement ("hither, and thither and yon" in L127: seventeen lines with eight conjunctions but no full-stop in F383/J585). There is a kind of triumph in the ending, however, where the "omnipotent" beast is made "docile" at "it's own stable door - ," a not-insignificant detail for a family with a reputation for owning fine horses and its own stable: that the engine was named "Amherst" and the station positioned adjacent to the Dickinson meadow added to that sense of private eminence.

The Dickinson standing in Amherst was never negligible, but its base was not always entirely secure either. The impressive house that the poet lived in from 1830 to 1840, and again from November 1855 to her death in 1886, was associated with both achievement and distress. Built in 1813 and described as probably the first brick dwelling in town, it was originally painted red and designed in the Federal style. Within twenty years it had to be sold to pay off crippling debts. However, though Samuel Fowler Dickinson and his wife Lucretia Gunn Dickinson relocated to Cincinnati, Ohio in a move that the family and town read as an enforced exile, Edward continued to occupy the western half of the building with his wife Emily Norcross Dickinson and three young children, sharing the property with the new owner, David Mack (a storeowner and manufacturer of ladies' hats) until April 1840, when the Dickinsons moved to West (now Pleasant) Street. By April 1855, after Mack's death the year before, Edward was ready to reverse both the journey and his family's fortunes, repurchasing the building and embarking on an ambitious and costly makeover: he added a cupola in the Italian style, a conservatory on the southern side, a veranda facing west, and a kitchen and laundry to the rear, and he repainted the house in a light ochre color with off-white trim and dark green shutters.[9] To the west of the house he commissioned an Italianate villa, the Evergreens, designed by Northampton architect William Fenno Pratt in consultation with Austin and Susan Huntington Gilbert as an incentive to keep them in town. In 1856 the house was completed, Austin and Susan married, and the dynasty seemed to have been secured. Edward came close to overreaching himself, however, in trying to regain the family honor, for the redevelopment and expansion were so much beyond his means that there is still some speculation as to how he managed to finance them. There were other costs as well: Dickinson herself was reluctant to relocate, and her mother suffered an apparent breakdown from which she began to recover only several years later. The poet's physical withdrawal started then, as a side effect of domestic necessity, for Dickinson and her younger sister were left in charge of their mother's convalescence and of the day-to-day management of the household.

Dickinson's anxieties about the family standing in Amherst emerge even earlier in an 1847 letter, again to Austin (and written while she was a pupil at the Mount Holyoke Female Seminary), in which she described a nightmare in which:

> Father had failed & mother said that "our rye field which she & I planted, was mortgaged to Seth Nims." I hope it is not true but do write soon & tell me for you know "I should expire with mortification" to have our rye field mortgaged, to say nothing of it's falling into the merciless hands of a loco!!! (L16)[10]

As Thomas H. Johnson points out in his notes to the letter, a "loco-foco" had, in the 1840s and 1850s, become a collective term used by the conservative Whigs about Democrats – one of whom was Seth Nims, the village postmaster during terms of office served by a Democratic president. By the 1860s, however, the Whig party, which Edward Dickinson represented, had effectively ceased to exist. The economic and political status of the Dickinsons was subject to change, then, and its fluctuations were reflected in both the history of the family home and the poet's concern with transience – in both her letters and her poems. Edward's repurchase and refurbishment of the homestead, and his commission of a second one for Austin and Susan in the Evergreens next door, was a powerful and public statement that the family fortunes had been restored, but the long-term effects of his risk-taking and that of his father made themselves felt in Dickinson's poetry, where evanescence and loss can be linked to the specter of social and financial failure – for example, in F1144/J1119, "Paradise is that old mansion," where an Edenic state is made "Bankrupt once through [Adam's] excesses." By contrast, she identified poetry (in a memorable image that invokes John 14:2 "In my Father's house are many mansions") as a "fairer House than Prose - / More numerous of Windows - / Superior - for Doors - " (F466 J657) – a space associated with status, but removed from its anxieties. One of Dickinson's most famous lyric utterances, "Publication - is the Auction / Of the Mind of Man - " (F788 J709), makes a very clear pronouncement of abhorrence at the prospect of subjecting the pure products of the "Human Spirit" to the "Disgrace of Price"; the poem's aesthetic and class-related distance from a potentially compromising encounter with the literary marketplace has some of its background in her family's mixed economic and civic history.[11]

The Dickinsons had fourteen acres of meadowland, with a barn behind the house where they kept a cow, horses, and chickens. The family "wintered their stock on hay from their own field, visible from the poet's south window," and took part in different cattle shows during the 1850s and 1860s (as the town gained a reputation for agricultural innovation that would eventually result in the formation of the Massachusetts Agricultural College in 1879) (Habegger, 376). Although rural life was never far away, Amherst evolved over the course of the nineteenth century from a predominantly agrarian economy to a mixed one that included manufacturing on a small but notable scale. Two streams that ran through the town provided natural power for mills, particularly in North Amherst, and the industries included paper (from 1814 onwards, and especially from the 1830s to the end of the century), wood-working and wire goods, textiles (cotton from 1809 and wool from 1830), and hoop-skirts (in 1863). When Dickinson writes "I tie my Hat - I crease my Shawl" in 1863 (F522 J443), it is useful to know that ladies' bonnets had been produced in Amherst from the 1840s, and that hat making was an important town industry, especially from 1829, when her neighbor Leonard M. Hills arrived. By 1871, a year before his death, his workforce numbered more than one hundred, and his first factory was established in East Amherst, on Main Street – not far from where the poet lived. When another of Dickinson's speakers reports that the "Carriage held but just Ourselves - / And Immortality," the tension between the everyday and supernatural is given added weight when one considers that fine-quality carriage-making was an established industry in Amherst at the time of the poem's composition (in 1862), having begun as early as 1827. Even the reference (in F475 J488) to the act of writing as "the Art of Boards," with "Tools" and a "Plane" for its instruments of labor, can be seen in this context – for specialist tool making, and particularly the manufacture of highly sought after planes, started in Amherst in 1835.[12] Amherst's greatest period of productivity overlapped to some extent with her own (in the 1860s) – but small businesses came and went, so that by drawing on images of crafts and implements that had a locally specific as well as a personal resonance, Dickinson was able to promote a sense of her own skills and excellence in relation to a larger community of artisans and workers, within the nexus of a wider awareness of competition, limitation, and transience.

By the 1870s, as her poetic output dwindled (from more than two hundred poems in 1865 to fewer than fifty every year after) and she withdrew from the possibility of any broader public attention or encounter, Dickinson's epistolary version of her brother's centrality in Amherst expanded: "two-thirds of [her] surviving notes and letters date from her last sixteen years," and many of these went to neighbors in and from the town on the occasion of births, deaths, and marriages, or as acknowledgement for acts of kindness (Habegger, 541). "Expulsion from Eden grows indistinct in the presence of flowers so blissful," she wrote to Mrs. Thomas P. Field in 1878 (L552). To her neighbor Mrs. Lucius Boltwood, whose son died at the age of 34 in July of 1871, she offered the thought that "flowers might please him, though he made like Birds, the exchange of Latitudes" (L363). Again in 1873, she consoled Mrs. Hanson L. Read on the drowning of her two teenage sons by reporting her sister Lavinia saying that "your martyrs were fond of flowers" and hoping that a bouquet would not "profane their vase" (L404). These short and beautifully written notes, gnomic and too original to be understood as routine, comprise some of her most tender and moving pieces; they also reveal Dickinson contributing to and benefitting from a culture of informal exchange with Amherst at its core. Although she published only ten poems in her lifetime (and all of those anonymously), Dickinson did have a contemporaneous audience, a group of people in or from her local community who were to a greater or lesser extent aware that she wrote: though the record is necessarily incomplete, more than 500 poems that we know about were circulated separately to friends, 252 of them to Susan, and this is a not insignificant aspect of the history of her reception. Even the physical materials on which she wrote, as a number of commentators have pointed out, are visibly related to Amherst life: compositions survive on the backs of envelopes, advertising flyers, and pharmacy wrappers from businesses in the neighborhood and farther afield.

But we need to be careful here: a tender, apparently intimate, elegy such as F1641/J1599 "Though the great waters sleep" was sent in condolence to separate recipients who would have thought that they referred only to newspaper editor Samuel Bowles, nephew Gilbert, Judge Otis Lord, or (possibly) Edward Tuckerman, the Amherst College botanist. Amherst was vitally important to Dickinson's identity and that of her family, but she related to it (as Adrienne Rich so memorably puts it) "on [her] own premises."[13] There were occasions when she connected poems directly to public events in town: she sent F1514/J1474 "A Counterfeit - A Plated Person" to her brother and sister-in-law's house, The Evergreens, and signed it "Lothrop," thus linking it to a sensational case of physical abuse involving the daughter of an Amherst minister, Charles D. Lothrop.[14] But, intriguingly, she retained no copy for herself: in the 1870s and 1880s Dickinson sent many poems without keeping any personal or archival record, suggesting either that she did not value them herself (which is not the same as saying that they are without value) or trusted that recipients would conserve them. Perhaps the provenance of this particular composition made it unappealing or limited in her eyes, but whatever the cause of the indifference, we need to remind ourselves again of the distinction mentioned at the beginning of this essay: Amherst is mentioned almost a hundred times in that portion of the correspondence that is extant, but only twice in the poems. Thus, when Jerome McGann writes of "Because I could not stop for Death" (F479 J712) that "the journey being presented is not some unspecified drive in the country, but a funeral ride which is located quite specifically in relation to Emily Dickinson and her Amherst world" and goes on to name the streets and the cemetery that he presumes are being described in that poem, one stops short: the fact is that Dickinson did *not* name those streets, and recovering them runs counter to the practice of this and most of her other poems.[15] Reading F260/ J288 "I'm Nobody! Who are you?" with its imperious dismissal of being "public - like a Frog," it is interesting to know that Amherst Common before her brother's intervention had a frog pool and was sometimes used as the venue for rallies and agricultural festivals, but the significance of the poem relies on the tension it independently seeks to generate between a "Somebody" or somebodies associated with (commercial, political, and sexual) self-aggrandizement and a withdrawn and selective minority whose work and value are more refined and exclusive. Emily Dickinson did not date or place her poems precisely because she wanted them to be as timeless and free of local context as possible – in order to survive her. The paradox of Dickinson is that she was very much of her time and town in believing that poetry was a form of immortality – a belief that depended in its turn on the assumption that culture would remain permanent and stable, with verse the sun at its center – and she worked very hard, and successfully, to cover the tracks of her poems' provenance. For example, the events of the Civil War (1861–5), including the loss of Amherst natives such as Frazer Stearns, son of the Amherst College president, are not mentioned directly, but can be detected more obliquely in some of her themes, tropes, and images. In the end, Amherst's greatest gift to her, in addition to a local field of study for her favourite topics of "Love and Death" (L873), was its own significance – and the additional success of her family within that municipal success: her father and grandfathers, her brother and sister-in-law, in Richard B. Sewall's words, were "River Gods" of the Connecticut valley (Sewall, 120). And as the Irish poet Patrick Kavanagh puts it, river gods – and literary ones especially – "make their own importance."[16]

NOTES

1. Carlton Lowenberg, *Emily Dickinson's Textbooks* (Lafayette, CA: Carlton Lowenberg, 1986); Habegger, 139–66, 191–212.
2. Edward Carpenter and Charles Morehouse, *The History of the Town of Amherst, Massachusetts* (Amherst, MA: Press of Carpenter & Morehouse, 1896), 347–9; Daniel Lombardo, *A Hedge Away: The Other Side of Emily Dickinson's Amherst* (Northampton, MA: Daily Hampshire Gazette, 1997), 75–6; Daniel Lombardo, "What the Dickinsons Read," *Tales of Amherst: A Look Back* (Amherst, MA: The Jones Library, 1986), 100–2.
3. Cristanne Miller, *Reading in Time: Emily Dickinson in the Nineteenth Century* (Amherst, MA: The University of Massachusetts Press, 2012), 119, 145–6.
4. Mary Elizabeth Kromer Bernhard, "Portrait of a Family: Emily Dickinson's Norcross Connection," *The New England Quarterly* 60.3 (September 1987), 364. Polly Longsworth, "The 'Latitude of Home': Life in the Homestead and the Evergreens," *The Dickinsons of Amherst* (Hanover, NH: The University Press of New England, 2001), 23.
5. Nellie Gould-Smith, "Introduction," *What Life Consists, and Other Sermons*, by Rev. George H. Gould (Boston: The Pilgrim Press, 1903), 3.
6. Polly Longsworth, *Austin and Mabel: The Amherst Affair and Love Letters of Austin Dickinson and Mabel Loomis Todd* (New York: Farrar, Straus & Giroux, 1984), 356.
7. *Emily Dickinson's Herbarium: A Facsimile Edition* (Cambridge, MA: Harvard University Press, 2006).
8. Judith Farr, *The Gardens of Emily Dickinson* (Cambridge, MA: Harvard University Press, 2005).
9. "'You're Painting the Homestead?!? Why?!' at Emily Dickinson Museum July 22." News Release of the Emily Dickinson Museum, June 21, 2004.
10. Christopher Clark, *The Roots of Rural Capitalism: Western Massachusetts, 1780–1860* (Ithaca, NY: Cornell University Press, 1990), 203.
11. Betsy Erkkila, "Emily Dickinson and Class," *American Literary History* 4 (1992), 1–27.
12. Carpenter and Morehouse, *The History of the Town*, 276–301.
13. Adrienne Rich, "I Am in Danger - Sir - ," *Necessities of Life* (New York: Norton, 1966), 33.
14. Lombardo, "Amherst and the Dickinsons' Fight against 'Gross Brutality'," *A Hedge Away*, 256–8.
15. Jerome McGann, "The Text, the Poem, and the Problem of Historical Method," *The Beauty of Inflections: Literary Investigations in Historical Method and Theory* (Oxford: Clarendon Press, 1988), 128.
16. "Epic," *Patrick Kavanagh: Collected Poems* (London: Martin Brian & O'Keefe, 1972), 136.

CHAPTER 2

Reading in the Dickinson Libraries

Eleanor Elson Heginbotham

Emily Dickinson eased her famine at her lexicon (F754 J728); she equated books to transporting frigates and coursing prancers (F1286 J1263), poetry to Lamps (F930 J883), and one novel, *Middlemarch*, to "Glory" (L389). Today those "kinsmen of the shelf" (F512 J604), her books and those of her family, are at Harvard's Houghton Library, Brown's John Hay Library, Amherst College's Frost Library, and the Jones Library, the latter two within walking distance of the Dickinson homes, the Homestead and the Evergreens. To judge from the contents of these collections, the homes must have had little space for anything other than books. The thousands of volumes in these libraries are, says Houghton's Leslie Morris, "the last great lode for Dickinson scholars to mine."[1] Mining them thoroughly will be a major project; this essay is, as Jack Capps said of his in *Dickinson's Reading*, "a task only suggested and begun here" (Capps, 9).

Capps and many others have reflected on Dickinson's reading as it inspired her verse. This essay is less about potential influence than about the cultural context for that influence: the books with their leather and paper and gold embossing; the care and conveying of these materials to their present homes; and the possibilities the collections hold for mining. Mining them, as Gary Stonum reminds us, gives insight into "Dickinson's primary access to a world beyond Amherst," but he and others caution against hasty conclusions when we cannot usually know *which* thin marks in *which* existing editions were made by *which* book-devouring member of the Dickinson reading circle.[2] Astounding volume aside, moreover, the collection is incomplete: books were loaned and lost; a fire, for example, destroyed Austin's office in 1888, perhaps consuming books. Nevertheless, looking at what is left, we, too, have the "mouldering pleasure" of meeting "an Antique Book - / In just the Dress his Century wore - " (F569 J371).

25

READING SPACES FOR A READING FAMILY

Gathering such a collection was the natural enterprise of a family of educators on both the Dickinson and Norcross sides. The seeds of such a passion show up in the courtship letters between Emily's future parents. The sober law student besieged young Emily Norcross with borrowed books and sermons. He urges her to read, for example, "a new novel," *Hope Leslie,* "which I presume you will find interesting," following up three weeks later with new reading material, noting that he needs to return the book to its owner.[3] When they married, the home became "a fortress," with its independent "monarchs" constantly reading.[4] Letters from daughter Emily created what I have called her "Epistolary Book Club" and speak of a literal "Reading Club" (L43, L44);[5] a less-remarked list of literary activities made by Vinnie records her, and possibly also Emily's, attendance at book groups at least once a month (Sewall, 249).

Books in the "fortress" came from many sources. Although there were the beginnings of libraries in the town (notes in the *Hampshire and Franklin Express* for November 25, 1853 and May 18, 1855 announce plans for reading cooperatives), although at least once Emily attempted to use the college library (L191), and although books were shared among friends, the family generally purchased books. In Amherst, as Jane Wald reports, the family could buy from JB and C Adams; from Boston, the Norcross sisters could send books purchased from Burnham Antique Bookstore.[6] The newspapers advertised booksellers, and the family could also order by mail in response to "subscription" notices (such notes appear in the back of many of the extant books). Some of the most valued books were gifts; for example, the poet daughter's "seriousness of purpose was fostered ... by friends such as Benjamin Franklin Newton [who] sent her Ralph Waldo Emerson's poems, 'a beautiful copy' (L30)."[7]

Given the vastness of the current collection, one struggles to picture where the books were located in the Dickinson homes. From 1840 to 1855, the family moved from the Homestead to a large house on North Pleasant Street. Although it was "a grand old house,"[8] there is no mention of a library other than Emily's teasing note to Austin that "Father says your letters are altogether before Shakespeare, and he will have them published to put in our library" (L46). Writing to Austin in 1851, Dickinson describes the family scene: "Father and mother sit in state in the sitting room perusing such papers only, as they are well assured have nothing carnal in them" (L63). In another scenario the family gathers in the kitchen, "Mr. Dickinson reading a 'lonely and rigorous' book ... Austin

Figure 1. *Wild Flowers Drawn and Colored from Nature*, ed. Mrs. Badger (New York: Scribner, 1859; EDR 467) and *Morrison's Stranger's Guide to the City of Washington* (Washington: Morrison, 1852; EDR 222). Reproduced by permission of Houghton Library, Harvard University.

studying …Vinnie scanning the columns of the newspaper for items of local gossip," while, according to family lore, "Emily sits, trying with all her might to keep up with the thoughts rushing past."[9]

When the Dickinsons moved back to the Homestead in 1855, their books had a room of their own. The "library" in the front of the house on the Main Street side was opposite to and as large as the front parlor (Leyda II, 2). A table "behind the door" held wine and an "unclaimed flower" that Dickinson told Samuel Bowles she would leave him (L205). There must also have been a soft chaise or reading chair: "Mother is asleep in the Library - Vinnie - in the Dining Room," Emily reports to Mrs. Holland (L432). Open to the hallway and the conservatory, the room's three doors, two windows, and fireplace afforded little wall space for the numbers of volumes currently counted as Dickinson family books. Books must have been everywhere: in the four bedrooms and in the two parlors, in one of which "Higginson noticed among other books, copies of his *Out-Door Papers* and *Malbone: An Oldport Romance.*"[10]

After Austin's 1856 marriage to Sue and their move to the Evergreens a hedge away from the Homestead, space doubled for books that passed between the households. Symbolically, the French doors of the library at the Evergreens were kept open, so that Austin's sister could enter the house through this sacred room.[11] The Jerome Liebling photographs of the library and the parlor in the Evergreens reveal shelves mounting to about chest height and topped with objets d'art.[12] Books were probably stacked on tables as well, especially the beautiful oversized flower book given to Emily by her father on New Year's Day, 1859 (Figure 1).[13] This flowery treasure is one sample of the pleasures of mining the Dickinson library now scattered to the four new repositories.[14] In an age when "literature and trade books advanced at a rate ten times faster than that of population growth," it was not surprising that the Dickinson library grew almost boundlessly.[15]

THE COLLECTIONS

I began at the Jones Library. In addition to a taped conversation with the longest inhabitant of the Evergreens and a poetic book on astronomy that was used as a textbook at the college, the library offers riches within newspaper microfilms.[16] Dickinsonians know the influence of editors on the Dickinson family: *Scribners'* Josiah Holland; the *Springfield Republican*'s Samuel Bowles, who "brought the sense of this 'yeasty time' into their very living rooms" (Sewall 466); and Thomas Wentworth Higginson, whose *Atlantic* editorial, "Letter to a Young Contributor" "saved" Dickinson's life (L330). Aife Murray has noted the shifting class awareness brought to the Dickinson home through the family's newspapers, and Alfred Habegger, the shifting gender awareness brought particularly by the *Springfield Republican*.[17] In the Jones Library one realizes that journals not only brought news *to* the Dickinsons; they also provided news *of* the Dickinsons. In the *Hampshire and Franklin Express*, one reads, for example, of Edward's generosity to the church: a donation of $100 for each $1,000 expended (June 29, 1860); of his speeches to students and soldiers' families; and of his legal work on behalf of a defendant in a rape case (July 20, 1860). Emily could not escape the fame that belonged to her father, news of which entered the family library, where newspapers were well read.

If "Bulletins all Day" came from newspapers, they also came, as Dickinson said, "From Immortality" in scores of religious volumes (F820 J827). That the Dickinson household owned so many bibles, hymnals, and diverse devotional material does not make them oddly zealous. To most at that time and place "the Bible was ... at hand throughout the day, beside the bed at night," said Millicent Todd Bingham, adding that Edward Dickinson led his family in worship "each morning, like other householders."[18] His daughter's mind was "saturated" with the Bible.[19] Her poetic beat was that of the meters in Isaac Watts's hymnals, such as the Houghton's green morocco edition that belonged to Dickinson's mother.[20] The 1810 Watts volume at Harvard is pocket-sized. In contrast, one of the dozens of religious texts – this one at Brown – intrigues for its largeness: Henry Ward Beecher's 1871 *Life of Jesus the Christ*, with its rich paintings by William E. Marshall. Although this book is unmarked, it is tempting to think of Dickinson's maturing theology encountering Beecher's emphasis on Jesus as a socially aware teacher with a "sudden addiction ... to parables."[21]

Five secular works, selected from the four libraries, illustrate the breadth of the family interests and the nourishing of Emily's grasp of the material world. The jewel of the Jones collection – an 1838 book that, if Dickinson read it (it was a text at the Academy) – must have opened her eyes to the heavens. The first page of Elijah H. Burritt's *Geography of the Heavens and Class Book of Astronomy* linked the science to Dickinson's art: "Astronomy is a science which has, in all ages, engaged the attention of the poet, the philosopher, and the divine." The astronomy book is unmarred, but across town at the Frost Library is a battered, much marked copy of another 1838 textbook, *Publii Virgilii Maronis Opera; or*

The Works of Virgil. With copious Notes. In pencil, next to this subtitle, is an exclamation point from the saucy student, Emily. On the free flyleaf page of the Latin text are algebraic formulations, as though the student took the book to more than one class and used it for scratch reckoning. Something like chocolate fell on pages 236–7, and a flower was inserted between pages 342 and 343.

From the heavy boxes brought from a satellite warehouse at Brown's John Hay Library, one pulls out a crumbling *Amherst Record* for August 21, 1895: the obituary for Austin, who "hated sham and hypocrisy ... and despised the cheap wit and shallow 'smartness' which some employ to curry favor." Emily Dickinson would not have read that, but she may well have read the other contents, a pamphlet transcript of the 1865 "Trial of the Conspirators for the Assassination of President Lincoln," and a splotched pamphlet containing "Mr. Dickinson's / Agricultural Address" (October 1831).

In contrast to the boxed surprises at Brown, the Houghton's meticulously organized collection offers such pleasures as the two books pictured (see Figure 1): the small brown leather 1858 guidebook, *Morrison's Stranger's Guide to the City of Washington,* and a heavy, ornately decorated coffee-table-sized book on tiny flowers. The first, with its catalogue of rooming houses, schools, burial sites, and parks, is fascinating as a history of the capital city during the brief term in Congress of Edward Dickinson, who inscribed the book in two places. He inscribed the bigger book on flowers as well – "To my daughter Emily / from her father Edw. Dickinson January 1 1859." Each page contains the scientific Latin name and the familiar name of the flower, painted beautifully enough to be framed, and a poem. Although the poems do not reach the level of Dickinson's, the lovely book is almost a match to the herbarium Dickinson herself made as a schoolgirl.[22] Amherst's remarkable President Edward Hitchcock, renowned for scientific studies read by Dickinson, was also the author of a nonscientific study in Houghton's collection: that of Mt. Holyoke's founder, Mary Lyon.[23] Dickinson, who knew both subject and author well, may have made the marks therein.

Although scholars have not yet mined such books as Hitchcock's and Badger's, many *have* written about the rich literary holdings with their suggestive marginal marks. The house was full of them. There were at least seven editions of Shakespeare, so it is surprising to read Vinnie's 1850 letter to her brother: "Why did'nt you come home, Friday? We expected to see you .... Can you spare your Shakespeare to us for a day or so? We want to read Hamlet before the lecture."[24] Emily, too, asked Austin and others for specific books, and she talked about or paraphrased a wide range of classic and contemporary authors. Much could be – and has been – made of the set of poetry books, including *Aurora Leigh* in the Frost Library and *Paradise Lost* in the Houghton. As Benjamin Lease says, she read these books "voraciously" as "Sacred Texts Transformed." Listing some dozen of the usual suspects, Lease concludes that they were "catalysts to release Dickinson's distinctive voice and vision."[25] It is beyond pleasure to hold, as she may have, the compilations of poems in their neat, uniform, gilded bindings: Longfellow and Elizabeth Barrett Browning, for example, at the Frost and Wordsworth and Donne at the John Hay.

As a sample of the less expected pleasures of holding these "mouldering books," I pause on one she noted in a teasing letter about her father's strictness – his "trimming about 'Uncle Tom' and 'Charles Dickens' and these 'modern Literati'" (L113). The mutilated Stowe novel (at the John Hay) is missing part of its cover, and has dramatic droppings of something – wax? tears? tea? – on pages that apparently interested the reader (Dickinson?): one such page is the illustration of "Little Eva Reading the Bible to Uncle Tom in the Arbor," in which the little girl famously points to the lake and says, "Don't you see, – there?" and tells Tom, "I'm going there" (64). Most marred with splotches is "The Victory" chapter, where Stowe muses, "But to live, – to wear on, day after day, of mean, bitter, low, harassing servitude ... this is the true searching test of what there may be in man or woman" (240). Of course, we cannot know whether the marks are Emily's, Sue's, Martha's, or even Mary Hampson's, which brings us to the most dramatic element of the Dickinson Library: its salvation and movement to the two major holding sites: the Houghton and the John Hay.

TRACING "THE SPOILS"

Most are familiar with the members of the Dickinson family: Edward (1803–74); Emily Norcross (1804–82); Austin (1829–95); Emily (1830–86); Lavinia (1833–99); Susan Gilbert Dickinson (Austin's wife, 1830–1913); and the children, particularly Martha Dickinson Bianchi (1866–1943), who owned, borrowed, read, and discussed the books and journals now held in the three university libraries, marking them in many ways. How the Dickinson family library entered the current collections involves others; they, too, are characters in plotlines worthy of a Henry James novel. Before briefly tracing that gothic tale of "the spoils of the Dickinson legacy" as Elizabeth Horan calls it, it is worth applauding Charles Green, a far-seeing director at Amherst's Jones Library, who was the first – as early as 1921 – to anticipate the urgency of maintaining artifacts from the family of the increasingly famous first daughter of Amherst.²⁶ That collection now contains some 7,000 items.

The rest of the story is "notoriously contentious," proving that "when it came to the market, Emily Dickinson, [who called publication 'the Auction / Of the Mind of Man' (F788 J709)] was right."²⁷ The competitive intrigues of saving and re-collecting the Dickinson holdings has been well told by Leslie Morris, Curator of Modern Manuscripts and Rare Books at Harvard's Houghton, and by Barton Levi St. Armand, Elizabeth Horan, Lyndall Gordon, and others.²⁸ The drama begins with the well-documented contest between "sister" Sue and Mabel Loomis Todd (1856–1932), family friend and Austin's mistress. Both women – especially Sue – had stashes of Emily Dickinson's writings, and both had daughters who joined them in publishing competing versions of the poems: Millicent Todd Bingham (1880–1968), who earned a Radcliffe doctorate in geography, and Martha Dickinson Bianchi, poet and musician. Both daughters dedicated their lives to Emily Dickinson and to the memories and rights of their respective mothers. Their rivalry influenced the destination of the treasures in their keeping.

Although her ownership rights were challenged by Dickinson heirs and, later, by Harvard University, Mrs. Todd's collection – the manuscripts and letters entrusted to her by Lavinia and Austin – went to Amherst's Frost Library. Although most of the Bingham collection comprises manuscripts, The Frost Library has since purchased such valuable Dickinson family books as that thoroughly marked-up Latin textbook and a number of sets of collected literary works: Longfellow in two volumes, Mrs. Browning's *Essays on Greek Christian Poets*, Barrett Browning's *Aurora Leigh*, and more, all bound handsomely in matching blue covers with gilded lettering.

Most Dickinson materials – those from the house of Sue and Martha Dickinson Bianchi – had already ended up at Harvard's Houghton and Brown's John Hay. The story of how they did so involves a third cast of characters. The last surviving member of her household, Martha, who "was well on my way to becoming an author, when I was forced to become a niece!" asked a literary friend, Alfred Leete Hampson (1890–1952), for assistance with the legacy in 1923.²⁹ His help in editing Bianchi's Dickinson collections in the 1930s merged into cataloguing the works. At a New York arts event Martha met Mary Landis (1894–1988), who joined her and Hampson in caring for the documents. In 1943, when Martha Dickinson Bianchi died, "Hampson inherited her [Bianchi's] copyrights and her parents' house in Amherst, the Evergreens and all its contents, including the Dickinson papers."[30] In 1947, Landis married Hampson.

The next year, 1948, the Hampsons considered selling the Dickinson collection, thus adding a fourth cast of characters to the story of the disposition of manuscripts – and books: William H. McCarthy, who had helped Madame Bianchi with the 1930 centennial celebration of Dickinson, was a friend of the Hampsons and worked at the Rosenbach Company, rare book dealers in New York, who became agents for the Hampsons; William A. Jackson, Librarian of the Houghton, suggested purchasing the Hampson Dickinson collection to Gilbert Holland Montague (1889–1961), who, with a gift of $50,000 (honoring his alma mater and his wife), became the donor of the collection at Harvard that would make possible most subsequent scholarship on Emily Dickinson, including that unmined lode of books. Beginning in 1950, during negotiations for storing and copyrighting, treasures from Amherst began arriving. Along with the manuscripts and the letters, which would become the basis for the volumes edited by Thomas H. Johnson, were many books from the Dickinson family library. Today Harvard's 591 volumes await more scholars to decide which books made Dickinson "a great reader and a dainty reader" (quoted in Sewall, 270).

Mary Hampson, who scoured the Evergreens for material and sent it to Harvard in small increments, lived alone in the Evergreens for some thirty years after Alfred died in 1952. Her determination to exorcise the influence of the Todd/Bingham family and to protect the reputation and possessions of the Dickinsons leads to a sad coda. The Hampsons and Montague appended a condition to the use of the material they gave the Houghton: in return for giving up all rights to the materials themselves, they stipulated that Millicent Todd Bingham, who had once spoken in hope of conjoining the materials, and one or two scholars who used the Todd material, could not have access to them. Mrs. Hampson, "keeper of the keys," as St. Armand called her, had also become responsible for the enormous collection of books, pamphlets, and other material that is now at Brown University's John Hay Library. Hampson, who threw away nothing but rather added her own books, left the jumble that eventually found a home at Brown, thanks largely to the work of Barton St. Armand and George Monteiro; in the boxes they rescued are three generations of Dickinson books and a plethora of books belonging to Hampson. In a building adjunct to the John Hay Library, some 232 closely packed cartons of items – hundreds of them political and legal documents mysteriously marked from the "buttery" – remain to be examined. Future doctoral work surely lies in doing what the caretakers at Harvard have done with their share of the Dickinson materials: organizing and annotating the contents. Indeed, the mining of the Dickinson Library has just begun. As Little Eva told Tom, "Don't you see, – there?"

NOTES

1. Interview with Leslie A. Morris at Houghton Library, August 2, 2011.
2. Gary Lee Stonum, "Dickinson's Literary Background," *Handbook*, 45.
3. Quoted in Vivian Pollak, *A Poet's Parents: The Courtship Letters of Emily Norcross and Edward Dickinson* (Chapel Hill: University of North Carolina Press, 1988), 121, 131.
4. Millicent Todd Bingham, *Emily Dickinson's Home: The Early Years as Revealed in Family Correspondence and Reminiscences* (New York: Dover Publications, 1955), 5.
5. Eleanor Elson Heginbotham, "'What are you reading now?': Emily Dickinson's Epistolary Book Club," *Reading Emily Dickinson's Letters: Critical Essays*, ed. Jane Donahue Eberwein and Cindy MacKenzie (Amherst: University of Massachusetts Press, 2009), 126–60.
6. Jane Wald, "'Pretty Much Real Life': The Material World of the Dickinson Family," *Handbook*, 44–60; Sewall, 628, n. 3.
7. Vivian R. Pollak, "Emily Dickinson, 1830–1886: A Brief Biography," *A Historical Guide to Emily Dickinson*, ed. Vivian R. Pollak and Marianne Noble (New York: Oxford University Press, 2004), 37.
8. Bingham, *Emily Dickinson's Home*, 63.
9. Ibid., 255.
10. Benjamin Lease, *Emily Dickinson's Readings of Men and Books, Sacred Soundings* (New York: St. Martin's Press, 1990), 89.
11. Barton Levi St. Armand, "Keeper of the Keys: Mary Hampson, the Evergreens, and the Arts Within," *The Dickinsons of Amherst*, ed. Jerome Liebling, Christopher Benfey, and Barton Levi St. Armand (Hanover: University Press of New England, 2001), 132.
12. Ibid., 117.
13. Mrs. C. M. Badger, *Wild Flowers Drawn and Colored from Nature* (New York: Scribner, 1859). The copy consulted is from the Houghton Collection, EDR 467.
14. For use of rare materials in this essay thanks to the following: at Harvard's Houghton, Leslie Morris, Rachel Howarth, Mary Haegert, and others; at Brown's John Hay, Rosemary Cullen and Timothy Engels; at Amherst's Robert Frost, Peter Nelson, Michael Kelly, Mimi Dakin, and others; and at the Jones Library, Tevis Kimball and Kate Boyle.
15. David S. Reynolds, "Emily Dickinson and Popular Culture," *The Cambridge Companion to Emily Dickinson*, ed. Wendy Martin (Cambridge: Cambridge University Press, 2002), 209.

16 Taped interview with Mary Landis Hampson conducted by Sheila Rainford (December 17, 1978); Elijah H. Burritt, *Geography of the Heavens and Class Book of Astronomy* (New York: FJ Huntington & Co, 1838).
17 Aife Murray, *Maid as Muse: How Servants Changed Emily Dickinson's Life and Language* (Durham, NH: University of New Hampshire Press, 2009), 142–8; Habegger, 382–92.
18 Bingham, *Emily Dickinson's Home*, 31.
19 Fordyce R. Bennett, *A Reference Guide to the Bible in Emily Dickinson's Poetry* (Lanham, MD: The Scarecrow Press, 1997), Preface.
20 Isaac Watts, *Watts Psalms carefully suited to the Christian Worship* (New York: Williams and Whiting, 1810).
21 Henry Ward Beecher, *Life of Jesus the Christ* (New York: J. B. Ford, 1871), 300.
22 Badger, *Wild Flowers*. Dickinson's "Herbarium," also in the Houghton, has been re-created in facsimile: *Emily Dickinson's Herbarium* (Cambridge, MA: The Belknap Press of Harvard University Press, 2006).
23 *The Power of Christian Benevolence Illustrated…in Mary Lyon* (Northampton & Philadelphia, 1851).
24 Bingham, *Emily Dickinson's Home*, 109.
25 Lease, *Emily Dickinson's Readings*, 35.
26 Elizabeth Horan, "Mabel Loomis Todd, Martha Dickinson Bianchi, and the spoils of the Dickinson legacy" in *A Living of Words: American Women in Print Culture*, ed. Susan Albertine (Knoxville: The University of Tennessee Press, 1995), 65–93.
27 Ibid., 65, 68.
28 Leslie A. Morris, "Foreword," *Emily Dickinson's Herbarium*, 7–14; St. Armand, "Keeper of the Keys," 107–67; Lyndall Gordon, *Lives Like Loaded Guns: Emily Dickinson and her Family's Feuds* (New York: Viking, 2010), 345–405.
29 Quoted in St. Armand, "Keeper of the Keys," 138.
30 Morris, Foreword, 9.

CHAPTER 3

Education

Angela Sorby

Emily Dickinson's own words complicate the story of her education. In 1862, she wrote to Thomas Wentworth Higginson: "I went to school - but in your manner of the phrase - had no education" (L261). Although Dickinson did not attend Harvard like Higginson, she was actually superbly educated at home, at Amherst Academy, and at Mt. Holyoke Female Seminary. So why disavow this background? Why draw a distinction between "school" and "education"? Jed Deppman has argued that "for those who seek to join their thought with Dickinson's, the issue of word definitions represents a key mediation between her private poetic concerns and the larger, volatile cultural climate of metaphysical instability that included but far transcended the making of dictionaries."[1] Any account of Dickinson's education, then, must consider what education meant in the worlds that she inhabited, and how she negotiated it to meet her evolving needs as a poet. In her poems and letters, Dickinson displays a strong autodidactic streak; she uses educational texts and mentors to study what she wants to learn, not necessarily what they want to teach. However, even as she asserts her individuality, she continually cultivates pedagogical relationships that are affective as well as intellectual. Dickinson draws on the spiritual, romantic, and scientific dimensions of her schooling, but she defines education, above all, as a labor of love – with all the risks and intimacies that love entails.

Dickinson's earliest educational experiences were steeped in what Deppman calls metaphysical instability, for competing strains of Calvinism, romanticism, and affective sentimentalism contributed to her emerging worldview. Dickinson's formal schooling reflected the religious orthodoxy of her community. From the Calvinist perspective, literacy matters because it is a crucial path to salvation. In *Corderius Americanus*, Cotton Mather cautions parents not to let their children "die without instruction," because through careful study children can steer their inherently evil natures toward redemption.[2] Dickinson's community was still steeped in Calvinist doctrine and treated education (including girls' education) as a serious enterprise with clear aims.

At the same time, as Jane Donahue Eberwein has argued, Connecticut Valley Calvinism was under tremendous pressure from early nineteenth-century advances in Biblical scholarship, the arts, and the sciences. Geographically isolated Amherst was hardly a hotbed of romantic revolution, but outside influences trickled in: students arrived at Amherst College from elsewhere (and many taught at Amherst Academy after graduation); *Parley's Magazine*, and later *Harper's Monthly* and *The Atlantic Monthly*, came through the mail; and of course Dickinson cultivated far-flung friends and mentors, especially in her youth. Her Calvinist education was thus supplemented with fragments of transatlantic romantic thought, scientific rationalism, and secular liberalism. Romantics believed that education should draw out the natural genius of the individual. In his essay "Education," Emerson amplifies:

> I believe that our own experience instructs us that the secret of Education lies in respecting the pupil. It is not for you to choose what he shall know, what he shall do. It is chosen and foreordained, and he only holds the key to his own secret.[3]

Puritans want to teach children through direct instruction, so they can apprehend the word of God. Romantics, by contrast, want to teach children indirectly, through experience, so they can discover the voice within themselves. Dickinson acknowledged her debt to Emerson when she wrote to Otis Lord, "Ralph Waldo Emerson, whose name my Father's Law Student taught me, has touched the secret spring" (L750). Here, Dickinson succinctly describes Romantic pedagogy: Emerson, like all good teachers, simply led her to the wellspring of her own genius.

The third discourse in Dickinson's education is perhaps the most strongly influential, trumping both Calvinist orthodoxy and Romantic individualism. It is, however, also the hardest to define, because it is neither an intellectual movement nor a moral stance. In 1887, a year after Dickinson's death, Higginson tried to put his finger on the *zeitgeist* of antebellum New England, lamenting the decline of "the sentimental," which he defines as

> ... a certain rather melodramatic self-consciousness, a tender introspection in the region of the heart, a kind of studious cosseting of one's finer feelings. Perhaps it is not generally recognized how much more abundant was this sort of thing forty years ago than now, and how it moulded the very temperaments of those who were born into it, and grew up under it.[4]

During her education, Dickinson wrestled with Calvinism and experimented with Romanticism, but she also cultivated a vast archive of emotional responses that made everything she learned personal almost to the point of pain. This sentimental education served as an overarching frame for all of her other lessons, and ultimately infused her poetry with a life-or-death urgency that went beyond teleological questions of spiritual salvation or transcendence.

Dickinson's education began at home. The Dickinson family owned two editions of the *New England Primer*, from 1830 and 1843. The *Primer* was frequently updated during its long reign, but Webster's 1843 *Primer* is "certified" as an exact reprint of the 1691 Benjamin Harris version, indexing the Dickinson family's allegiance to "true and fundamental doctrines" that were otherwise on the wane. To learn from the *Primer* was to read against the expansively liberal grain of Jacksonian America. However, as Pat Crain has argued, even the conservative *Primer* is an internally inconsistent document that reveals tensions within Calvinism, and here Dickinson found provocative raw materials for her imagination.[5] For instance, in February of 1850 Dickinson sent a valentine to William Cowper Dickinson, containing an original verse that begins: "Life is but a strife / 'Tis a bubble / 'Tis a dream" (L33). To illustrate, she pasted in a woodcut of a sleeping king, clipped from the *Primer*. Such repurposing, from textbook to valentine, registers Puritan individualism, while also marking the human connections that were so crucial to Dickinson's art.

The *Primer* also contains hymns and verses by Isaac Watts, whose meters echo through Dickinson's quatrains. As late as 1882, Dickinson was reworking Watts's famous lines, "Now I lay me down to sleep," from the *Primer*:

> Now I lay thee down to Sleep -
> I pray the Lord thy Dust to keep -
> And if thou live before thou wake -
> I pray the Lord thy Soul to make -
> (F1575 J1539)

Dickinson's prayer is disconcerting because the body – dust – takes precedence over the soul; indeed, the speaker hopes that the dead person will remain at peace as a physical corpse, inverting the Christian dream of resurrection. To use Watts prayer – and his familiar meter – is to mark the distance between her early training and her later heterodoxies.

Ironically, Dickinson's confidence in her creative powers probably stemmed in part from her Calvinist upbringing, which stressed the profundity of every soul. As another Watts poem from the *Primer* begins:

> Though I am young a little one,
> If I can speak and go alone,
> Then I must learn to know the Lord
> And learn to read his holy word.[6]

If anyone learned well how to "speak and go alone," it was Emily Dickinson. Dickinson was sent to a District common-school at the age of seven, but her serious institutional education began at the age of nine, in September of 1840, when she and her sister Lavinia enrolled in Amherst Academy. Amherst Academy was a rigorous school that had been co-founded by her grandfather, Samuel Fowler Dickinson, in 1814. Its published aims were Calvinist, but its pedagogical approach was progressive, reflecting the influences of Romantic educators who tried to engage children's natural passions and interests. As early as 1827, a school flier announced that "Languages will be taught in such a manner, that the study of text books may be a study of interesting *facts* and *sentiments* as well as of words and their grammatical relations."[7] Dickinson attended the school on and off for seven years, between 1840 and 1847. Her letters reflect an ardent enthusiasm for her classes; as she wrote to Abiah Root in 1845, "We have a very fine school.... I have four studies. They are mental Philosophy, Geology, Latin, and Botany. How large they sound, don't they?" (L6).

In the 1840s it was unusual for girls to be classically trained, but Dickinson took the Academy's Latin course for three years, and Alfred Habegger suggests that she "would have been a very different poet if she hadn't studied the language." Citing Lois Cuddy, he argues that her background in Latin explains Dickinson's "extreme dislocations of standard English word order and her use of such grammatical terms as 'ablative'" (Habegger, 141–2). However, Dickinson's stylistic quirks cannot be solely rooted in her classical training. After all, the classically educated Higginson was confounded by these very dislocations. Rather, as with the *New England Primer,* Dickinson wrestled with her school textbooks, intellectually and emotionally, breaking the barrier between "*facts* and *sentiments.*" On the flyleaf of her copy of Virgil's *Aeneid,* Dickinson wrote:

> Forsan et haec olim memnisse juvabit.
>   Aeneid 1–203
> Afterwards you may rejoice at the remembrance of these (our school days)
> When I am far away then think of me
>   – E. Dickinson (quoted in Habegger, 141)

This inscription reveals several nascent habits of mind. First, Dickinson is fusing a "feminine" genre, the autograph album, with a "masculine" genre, the Latin textbook. Second, she is not just translating Virgil *verbatim*, but also adding her own addendum of *our school days*. And third, she is imagining reading and writing as intimate, affective strategies: "When I am far away then think of me." Virgil may have influenced Dickinson, but she in turn inflected Virgil, applying both the literal pressure of her pencil and the interpretive pressure of her highly personalized gloss on the *Aeneid* as a token of girlhood friendship.

Ironically, Dickinson's gender, which restricted her on so many fronts, may have helped her cultivate idiosyncratic habits of mind precisely because her educational goals were less fixed than those of most boys. For instance, her brother Austin (and, for that matter, T. W. Higginson) had to master Latin to succeed at college. But because Dickinson was not Harvard-bound, she could pick and choose among "college prep" subjects. Indeed, in her final year at the Academy, she switched from the Classical course back into English, a zigzag she also performs in one of her earliest poems:

> "Sic transit gloria mundi,"
> "How doth the busy bee,"
> "Dum vivimus vivamus,"
> I stay mine enemy!
>
> Oh "veni, vidi, vici!"
> Oh caput cap-a-pie!
> And oh "memento mori"
> When I am far from thee!
> (F2 J3)

Dickinson's parodic recitation mixes Latin phrases with Isaac Watts, whose didactic "busy bee" diligently "improves each shining hour."[8] But she also inserts a plea that she be personally remembered, just as she did in her copy of the *Aeneid*.

This poem is animated by an ironic voice that overwrites even stock phrases with its cheeky individuality. Textbook passages lose their original meaning when breathlessly juxtaposed, working to express the speaker's own idiosyncratic vision. For instance, "Dum vivimus vivamus" technically means "while we live, let us live," but in Dickinson's poem the v-v-v alliteration links it to the noise a bee makes. Isaac Watts's insect is no longer a Calvinist worker-bee; rather, he buzzes aimlessly in a pagan tongue. Likewise the speaker is not a child of Amherst, where evangelical Christianity pervaded every school textbook. Rather, she is a discursive product of the nineteenth-century marketplace of ideas, in which everything is possible but nothing is certain. Random phrases, thrown together, create an amusing pastiche that lampoons authorities from Isaac Watts to Isaac Newton but never settles on any fixed truth.

Amherst Academy did not rely solely on the kind of mindless recitation that Dickinson parodies in "Sic transit gloria mundi." Teachers also required students to write and perform original compositions. In an 1842 letter to Jane Humphrey, Dickinson described one such performance:

> ...this Afternoon is Wednesday and so of course there was Speaking and Composition - there was one young man who read a Composition the Subject was think twice before you speak - he was describing the reasons why any one should do so - one was - if a young gentleman - offered a young lady his arm and he had a dog who had no tail and he boarded at the tavern think twice before you speak .... I told him I thought he had better think twice before he spoke - . (L3)

Two critical aesthetic tendencies are evident in this early letter. First, Dickinson is delighting in the split between the cliché "think twice before you speak" and its potential undoing by an incompetent speaker. Also, she is observing that ordinary language can quickly devolve into nonsense, and that nonsense can destabilize consensus reality. Later she would use these insights to unpack social bromides; for example, "They say that 'Time assuages,' / Time never did assuage" (F861 J686). Conventional phrases – think twice before you speak, time heals all wounds – are a source of inspiration precisely because they contain (but do not assuage) troubling ambiguities.

Erika Scheurer makes a case that these Wednesday composition sessions contributed to Dickinson's original voice. She points out that Amherst Academy's approach was Pestalozzian, reflecting "the beginnings of a larger nationwide transition in the area of writing pedagogy from a focus on rote learning and correctness to more of an emphasis on the actual practice of original composition, with the goal of students gaining fluency and agency as writers."[9] However, although Dickinson was surely capable of fluent prose, her poems and letters frequently disrupt their own flow. Indeed, her leaps of logic, twisted syntax, and dislocated imagery echo the roughness of the passage about the dog with no tail, although of course her textured style is deliberate.

Science pedagogy was especially strong at Amherst Academy, and also at Amherst College, where Academy students could attend lectures. One important figure in Dickinson's early scientific education was Edward Hitchcock, a geologist who became president of Amherst College and a close friend of the Dickinson family. Hitchcock had discovered the world's largest collection of dinosaur tracks, but he was a lifelong anti-Darwinist and offered science courses predicated on the "argument from design," that the natural world proves the existence and majesty of God. At the same time, Hitchcock's *Elementary Geology* (used at both Amherst Academy and Holyoke) proceeds carefully from physical evidence, distinguishing between science and religion: "Revelation does not attempt to give instruction in the principles of science: nor does it use the precise and accurate language of science; but the more indefinite language of common life. Nor does science attempt to teach the peculiar truths contained in revelation."[10] Dickinson would take the split between science and religion only a half-step further when she declared,

> 'Faith' is a fine invention
> When Gentlemen can *see* -
> But *Microscopes* are prudent
> In an emergency.
> (F202 J185)

Hitchcock might have recoiled in horror at the notion of faith as an invention, but his *Elementary Geology* establishes – in spite of its evangelical slant – that scientific truths can be accessed only through microscopes, not through the Bible. In terms of Dickinson's education, what matters is the unsettled quality of so much scientific knowledge and evidence in the 1840s: it was possible to shoehorn dinosaur tracks into a Biblical understanding of the universe, but it was not easy.

Dickinson's formal education was predicated on the assumption that students were progressing toward a full acceptance of Christianity. After Amherst Academy, Dickinson proceeded to Mt. Holyoke Female Seminary, and had she confirmed her faith there, her career as a student would have reached its expected culmination. The school's founder, Mary Lyon, was an Amherst Academy alumna and a Hitchcock protégée, but she exerted greater spiritual pressure on her students than Dickinson had previously encountered. Amanda Porterfield has observed that conversion offered nineteenth-century Christians reassurance about death, a release from social constraints, and the easing of an "emotional despair to which women especially were prey."[11] However, Dickinson remained what Lyon called a "no-hoper," a student who would never accept Christ. She could not attend Harvard, left Holyoke within a year, and was barred from most professions; without the end-point of conversion, her formal schooling lost its raison d'être.

Because she could not (and/or would not) convert, Dickinson was forced to construct her own aims as she continued her education beyond school. Her personal accounts always put greater emphasis on teachers than on institutional trajectories. In the letter that dismisses her formal education as "no education," she gives a glowing account of mentoring:

> When a little girl, I had a friend who taught me Immortality; but venturing too near, himself, he never returned. Soon after my tutor died, and for several years my lexicon was my only companion. Then I found one more, but he was not contented I be his scholar, so he left the land. (L261)

This passage outlines an ideal vision of an education based on relationships and processes, rather than outcomes. For Dickinson, the best teachers teach through indirection and example. She is seeking, not direct instruction, but intuitive, mutual, Emersonian pedagogy, replete with the emotional highs and lows of a close friendship.

Thomas H. Johnson notes that the "Immortal" friend was almost certainly Benjamin Franklin Newton, a Unitarian who shared his transcendental enthusiasms with her and – after he left Amherst in 1850 – sent her Ralph Waldo Emerson's *Collected Poems*. Other critical mentors included Joseph B. Lyman, the Reverend Charles Wadsworth, Samuel Bowles, and, of course, Thomas Wentworth Higginson. Higginson was baffled by Dickinson's insistence on her role as his student; as he recalled in *The Atlantic Monthly*: "From this time and up to her death (May 15, 1886) we corresponded at varying intervals, she always persistently keeping up this attitude of 'Scholar,' and assuming on my part a preceptorship which it is almost needless to say did not exist. Always glad to hear her 'recite,' as she called it, I soon abandoned all attempt to guide in the slightest degree this extraordinary nature, and simply accepted her confidences, giving as much as I could of what might interest her in return."[12] Perhaps, however, Dickinson's sense of Higginson as a "preceptor" was not rooted in a need for guidance, but in a desire for emotional exchange. Naoko Saito points out that for Emerson, friendship is critical to education, because as we learn "we are not engaged in isolated or secluded meditation, or in a kind of aesthetic self-indulgence. It is in the patient process of the conjoint metamorphosis of the self and the culture that the human soul is reborn."[13] To flourish as a poet, Dickinson did not require (or accept) Higginson's literary advice, but surely she cultivated his friendship as part of an affective pedagogy, or "conjoint metamorphosis," that linked her to her culture.

In many of Dickinson's poems, intersubjective emotions do not merely facilitate learning. Rather, in keeping with her sentimental outlook, the full articulation of emotional experiences is one key purpose of education. Here she works out the possibilities:

> We learned the Whole of Love -
> The Alphabet - the Words -
> A Chapter - then the mighty Book -
> Then Revelation closed -
>
> (F531 J568)

At first, the learners seem fixed on a path toward conversion, but Revelation closes and they veer off course. By the final two stanzas they are gazing on each other rather than at their book:

> But in Each Other's eyes
> An Ignorance beheld -
> Diviner than the Childhood's
> And each to each, a Child -

In the first line, "Each Other" is capitalized and the focus is on the students as they try to talk about "What Neither - understood - / Alas! that Wisdom is so large - / And Truth - so manifold!" Have the students in this poem wasted their education? No: the first stanza asserts that they have learned something – love – even if they remain suspended in partial ignorance. The very act of studying together results in a "conjoint metamorphosis," whereby the divine self – the Child – is revealed. Dickinson is often celebrated as an isolated autodidact. Her poetry and her letters, however, show that she also saw education as an ateleological emotional process: a way to encounter, but not necessarily to understand fully, the self and the world through others.

NOTES

1 Jed Deppman, *Trying to Think with Emily* Dickinson (Amherst: University of Massachusetts Press, 2008), 110.
2 Cotton Mather, *Corderius Americanus: A discourse on the good education of children, &c. &c. delivered at the funeral of Ezekiel Cheever, principal of the Latin school in Boston; who died, August, 1708, in the ninety-fourth year of his age. With an elegy and an epitaph* (1708, reprint 1827), 13.
3 Ralph Waldo Emerson, "Education," *Emerson's Complete Works*, ed. JE Cabot (New York: Riverside Edition, 1883), 142.
4 Thomas Wentworth Higginson, "The Decline of the Sentimental," *The New World and the New Book* (New York: Lee & Shepherd, 1891), 178.
5 Patricia Crain, *The Story of A: The Alphabetization of America from the New England Primer to the Scarlet Letter* (Palo Alto, CA: Stanford University Press, 2000), 15–38.

6 *The New-England Primer: improved for the more easy attaining the true reading of English: to which is added The Assembly of Divines, and Mr. Cotton's Catechism* (Ira Webster, 1843), 44.
7 Quoted in John Luke Parkhurst, *The Teacher's Guide and Parent's Assistant* (1827), 332.
8 Isaac Watts, "Against Idleness and Mischief," *Divine and Moral Songs for Children* (1715), n.p.
9 Erika Scheurer, "'[S]o of course there was speaking and Composition - ': Dickinson's Early Schooling as a Writer," *EDJ*, *18.1* (2009), 1–2.
10 Edward Hitchcock, *Elementary Geology* (New York: Dayton and Saxton, 1840), 281.
11 Amanda Porterfield, *Mary Lyon and the Mt. Holyoke Missionaries* (New York: Oxford University Press, 1997).
12 Thomas Wentworth Higginson, "Emily Dickinson's Letters," *Atlantic Monthly*, (October 1891), 450.
13 Naoko Saito, *The Gleam of Light: Moral Perfectionism and Education in Dewey and Emerson.* (New York: Fordham University Press, 2006), 16.

CHAPTER 4

New England Puritan Heritage

Jane Donahue Eberwein

When Edward Dickinson escorted his wife and daughters to the Edwards Church in Northampton, in July 1851, it was to hear not a sermon but a concert by Jennie Lind. Emily's letter to her brother, Austin, specifically mentioned "the old Edwards Church," so it seems likely that the contrast between Jonathan Edwards's reputation as a formidable Puritan preacher and this musical experience heightened her amusement (L46). Passing quickly over Lind's performance, she focused on their father's reaction, which struck her "as if old Abraham had come to see the show, and thought it was all very well, but a little excess of *Monkey*." Dickinson's comments indicate attraction to Lind herself despite resistance to unfamiliar musicianship, but she concluded with the judgment, "I'd rather have a Yankee."

Three decades later, the poet referred again to Jonathan Edwards in a humorous assemblage composed for her little nephew. After copying the poem she titled "The Bumble Bee's Religion," Dickinson attached a dead bee to the paper and then added a brief dialogue, with "All Liars shall have their part" ascribed to Edwards and "And let him that is athirst come" credited to Jesus (L712; F1547 J1522). As Karl Keller points out, this comment facetiously misattributes to the Puritan writer a threatening biblical passage actually drawn from Revelation 21.8.[1] She used Edwards to represent the cruelly judgmental side of Christianity in contrast to Jesus' magnanimity and the bee's instinctive tribute to "the divine Perdition / of Idleness and spring."

This message exemplifies Dickinson's habit of embellishing writings to close friends with flowers or cut-out pictures that amplified verbal imagery. Martha Nell Smith calls attention to two situations in which Dickinson clipped woodcut illustrations from *The New England Primer* to amuse her sister-in-law Susan, a reader sure to recognize visual allusions to the region's most traditional alphabet book.[2] In the first example, a clipping of a printed robin accompanied what seems to have been a real flower to draw out implications of "Whose cheek is this?" (F48 J82). Intertextual wit also shows up in a note Emily sent her sister-in-law about her father's outrage when she visited too late one evening with Austin, Susan, and their friends. The cut-out from the *Primer* illustrated how "Young Timothy / Learnt sin to fly," and Emily elaborated on that picture to identify "the unfortunate insect upon the left" as "Myself" and "the Reptile upon the *right*" as "my more immediate friends, and connections" (L214). On another occasion, Dickinson cast herself in the role of moral authority figure when chastising her brother good-naturedly on the hotel tryst he arranged with Susan in Boston. "Am glad our Pilgrim Fathers got safely out of the way, before such shocking times," she wrote in a comical letter that included references to Puritan classics *Pilgrim's Progress* and *Baxter upon the Will* (L110).

One point these examples illustrate is Emily Dickinson's awareness of her Puritan roots. Even if not herself a professed Calvinist Christian, she shared in the religious tradition that permeated Connecticut Valley culture in her formative years. They also illustrate the droll humor with which the poet appropriated this Puritan heritage for her own purposes. Humor helped her distance herself from Puritanism's most threatening features while letting her share amusement with like-minded friends. Yet to be a Dickinson, a daughter of Amherst, or a Yankee was to share in a daunting intellectual and moral heritage, and the poet turned to that background for more than humor. It also gave her a vocabulary and an approach to writing as spiritual self-examination.

Even though Dickinson took a comical tone in her direct references to the Puritans and often played with diction drawn from church language, she took their fundamental concerns seriously. This poet was in earnest when she claimed "Immortality" as her "Flood subject" in a letter to T. W. Higginson (L319). She did not need conventional emblems of deaths' heads inscribed on moldering New England gravestones to remind her of mortality. The appeal of Christianity was that it offered hope of eternal life, and Emily Dickinson's poems reflect a seriousness in exploring grounds for hope even though they employ a variety of modes (prayer, question, definition, meditation) and tones (angry, helpless, loving, joyous, ironic). This combination of spiritual honesty and tenacity prompted Richard Sewall to parallel her writing to that of Puritan diarists (Sewall, 23), inspired Wendy Martin to term her a "heart's remembrancer," and led Diane Gabrielsen Scholl to read Dickinson's fascicles as following "the pattern of Calvinist conversion narratives which testify to the speaker's anguished and inconsistent struggle to obtain an elusive faith."[3] To record doubts, glimmering hopes, seasons of despair, and anger with God was to be honest in scrutinizing one's soul, as Anne Bradstreet or Edward Taylor could have shown her, and as Edwards himself demonstrated.

John Calvin's theology underlay New England's Puritan heritage. Puritans worshiped an absolute, inscrutable God and stressed the cavernous divide between His perfection and the worthlessness of sinful human nature. As Trinitarians, they believed in the Father, Son, and Holy Spirit and looked to Christ's sacrificial death as atonement to the Father for original sin and its consequences. Accepting the five precepts of the Synod of Dort, they understood atonement to be limited in its effect to those predestined for salvation. What distinguished New England Puritans from their Calvinist brethren elsewhere was their attempt to restrict church membership to "visible saints" whose testimonials to spiritual renewal convinced others of their regenerate condition. As the one member of her household never to make such a public claim, Emily Dickinson was no doubt regarded by neighbors – as she has often been by scholars – as a rebel and unbeliever; although it is just as credible that her spiritual journey simply bypassed communal judgment as a factor in the soul's relationship with God. If a saint, she remained invisible.

In any case, it is anachronistic to refer to Dickinson as rejecting Puritan culture, as she knew of it only indirectly as an admirable yet harsh formative element in New England life. Although Edwards may have been the greatest of the American Puritans, he was also in a sense the last, as church unity gave way to Old Light/New Light divisions and proliferation of sects. The Edwards Church, where her family heard Jennie Lind, was not the meeting house in which Edwards had preached. It had been built in her own lifetime to house an offshoot of Northampton's First Church. Back in 1750, in the troubled aftermath of what came to be known as the Great Awakening, Edwards's congregation had dismissed him ignominiously as their pastor. Joseph Conforti argues that Edwards's masterful image was a product of the Second Awakening in the decades just before and during Dickinson's youth. New Divinity churchmen at Yale and Andover divinity schools "'classicized' Edwards and his writings and in turn used his religious authority to 'traditionalize' nineteenth-century piety, revivalism, and theology."[4] It is surprising, actually, that Dickinson's misattribution of that frightening scriptural passage to Edwards linked his memory to terror because "Sinners in the Hands of an Angry God" (now often the only example of Edwards's writing known to most readers) was much less read in her time than his personal writings, especially the *Faithful Narrative*. *The Life of the Late Reverend Mr. David Brainerd* was his most frequently published book in Dickinson's century because it accorded so well with her evangelical culture's missionary zeal. At Mount Holyoke Female Seminary, Dickinson may also have read his *History of the Work of Redemption*, a series of sermons tracing God's work in history from the creation to the expected second coming with particular attention to revivals.

Edwards's biography reflected the same religious tendencies that factored in Dickinson's family history, although the Calvinist religious culture of his day had been much modified before her religious formation. Her earliest paternal ancestors in America, Nathaniel Dickinson and his wife, had joined Thomas Hooker's migration to Hartford shortly after reaching Massachusetts Bay from Lincolnshire, settled for a while in Wethersfield, and then responded to dissensions in the church by establishing a new settlement in Hadley, Massachusetts. In 1745, their great-grandson Nathan Dickinson joined other Hadley neighbors in settling Amherst, where they founded the First Church – with Nathan Dickinson its first deacon. Congregational churches in all these places (as in Windsor, Connecticut and Northampton, Massachusetts, where Edwards lived) reflected the impact of Hooker's preparationist theology, which held that persons predestined to salvation could – and generally would – take steps to open their hearts to converting grace and that the church was the usual agent of spiritual awakening. Although this concept of gradual conversion ran counter to Calvinist orthodoxy, which upheld God's absolute sovereignty in contrast to the worthlessness of all human effort, it became strongly embedded in Connecticut Valley Congregationalism and fostered its culture of revivalism. Yet the theology professed by the churches and schools influencing Dickinson's religious formation had been substantially reshaped by neo-Edwardsian teachings and then by the New Divinity. Edwards had dedicated his ministry to fighting Arminianism, but his successors trusted in a person's ability to contribute to her or his own salvation. While holding firm against the rationalist-moralist strain of New England religion that resulted in Unitarian dominance at Harvard and in many churches close to the seaboard, Connecticut Valley Congregationalists gradually adopted views Edwards himself condemned.

Born in 1830, Emily Dickinson grew up in an intensely revivalist environment. Amherst's First Church recorded notable seasons of awakening in 1831, 1834, 1841, 1845, 1850, 1857, 1858, 1869, and 1870. Revivals also occurred with great regularity at local colleges – almost annually at Mount Holyoke, although Dickinson apparently resisted pressures for conversion. Revivalism in her area was a genteel religious force that served largely to reinforce social order. As Roger Lundin notes of the 1850 Amherst revival (spurred, in part, by the closing of alehouses in the college town), it "was a frenzy for the ordered life, a drunken quest for spiritual sobriety."[5] In the course of Dickinson's lifetime, however, her church's governing documents softened repeatedly. According to the Rev. Edward Dwight, one effect of the 1858 revival over which he presided in Amherst was that "among the new candidates for church-membership were many, to whom the phraseology of our confession of faith – theological, antiquated, clumsily expressed – was hardly intelligible" so that prudence dictated an attempt "to *recast* both creed and confession."[6]

Educational practices complemented religious teaching, but textbooks reflected a similar trend away from doctrinal rigor. The *New England Primer* had been widely used to teach the first elements of reading in the eighteenth century and probably earlier, but the Dickinson children would not have used it as a text. They did have a copy at home that the poet eventually raided to make the comical assemblages I noted earlier. Dickinson's exclamation "Hurrah for Peter Parley" in her 1852 valentine identifies the dominant series of nineteenth-century elementary readers (F2 J3): Samuel Griswold Goodrich's series of books on geography, history, and other subjects that relied on storytelling to convey moral and patriotic lessons. Nonetheless, Rowena Revis Jones and Carlton Lowenberg have documented how texts from Noah Webster's *Speller* to science and philosophy books read in college reinforced church teachings.[7] The *New England Primer*, customarily bound along with the *Westminster Assembly Shorter Catechism* that had been adopted by New England churches in 1648, was valued for its antiquarian interest and its impact on earlier generations who had learned their alphabet by following its verses and woodcuts all the way from "In Adam's Fall / We sinned all" to "Zaccheus he / Did climb the Tree / His Lord to see." Although it had been dismissed in favor of books more likely to entertain nineteenth-century children, the catechism, especially, still had defenders. Heman Humphrey, president of Amherst College 1823–45, associated it with members of a yet older generation when he reminisced "how delightful it is to hear, as we sometimes do, the aged disciple, repeating with thrilling interest, and feasting his soul upon the definitions of *justification, sanctification, glorification*, and the like, which, three quarters of a century before, were imprinted upon his memory in the nursery."[8] Emily Dickinson could have learned something about rhyme, religion, and visual art from leafing through the *Primer*, but it became more a quaint resource for her to play with than an educational force.

New England Puritan heritage

This pattern of gradual detachment from Puritan New England roots shows up also in Emily's whimsical comment to Austin about the Pilgrim Fathers being safely out of the way before his amorous adventure. Strictly speaking, the Pilgrims were those separatist colonists who reached Plymouth on the *Mayflower*, not Puritans like Nathaniel Dickinson who arrived in Massachusetts Bay a decade later with John Winthrop's Great Migration. In her youth, the idea of "Puritan" seems to have applied to early generations and to the ancestors whose stern rectitude built New England. Dickinson's paternal and maternal ancestors had fought and died in King Philip's War and exerted their energies for God's honor as they founded towns, churches, and schools. In his address on "Representative Men of the Parish" for the 150th anniversary of Amherst's First Church, her brother would pay homage to Ebenezer Dickinson as "a man of serious nature, confident, direct, without doubts, with a natural aptitude for affairs, active, and always present in everything pertaining to the welfare of the church or community."[9] The traits Austin emphasized were those he knew himself and his father to share, and his tribute reflects a growing sense of identification with Puritan ancestors. As young people, however, he and his witty sister regarded their elderly neighbor, Deacon David Mack, a militia general who bought the Homestead after Samuel Fowler Dickinson's bankruptcy and who shared space there with Edward Dickinson's young family from 1834 to 1840, as a throwback to the region's past. Emily remarked to Austin in 1851 that "when I hear the query concerning the pilgrim fathers … it becomes a satisfaction to know that they are there, sitting stark and stiff in Deacon Mack's mouldering arm chairs" (L52). Later, Austin commended Mack as "strong as a lion, pure as a saint, simple as a child, a Puritan of the Puritans."[10] Their father once echoed William Stoughton's 1668 election sermon to declare that "we should render devout thanks to Almighty God … that the kingdoms of the Old World were sifted to procure the seed to plant this continent; that the purest of that seed was sown in this beautiful valley; that the blood of the Puritans flows in our veins," and the *Springfield Republican* characterized Edward Dickinson himself as "a Puritan out of time for kinship and appreciation" in its obituary.[11] Even the poet herself began to identify somewhat with that heritage in later years, perhaps reflecting a tendency among descendants of New England's colonial settlers to distinguish themselves from new immigrant populations.

Dickinson's 1883 reference to "my Puritan Spirit" that "'gangs' sometimes 'aglay'" (L866) alludes to Robert Burns's famous lines about how the "best laid plans of mice and men" often fail, but it also reminds us of a massive gap in her knowledge of the Puritans. Aside from rhymes in the *Primer*, she apparently knew nothing of their poetry. John Harvard Ellis's 1867 edition of *The Works of Anne Bradstreet* could have introduced her to the Puritan "mother of American poetry," but there is no evidence that she knew of this book, nor of the spiritually revealing yet often witty prose and verse meditations that Ellis published for the first time. Even more regrettable was the impossibility of Dickinson's reading Edward Taylor's poetry, which was first introduced to American readers in 1937 by Thomas H. Johnson, Dickinson's own first scholar-editor. Taylor's creative energy, startling range of imagery, rough-hewn versification, and combination of playfulness with intense spiritual introspection would have revealed him as a kindred spirit.

She lived in the nineteenth century, however, and the writers who most influenced her views of the Puritans were Nathaniel Hawthorne and Henry Wadsworth Longfellow, both of whom felt free to employ romantic imagination to embellish stories of New England's grim past while using colonial subject matter to comment on American life in their own time. In a November 1851 letter to her brother, Emily Dickinson likened the two of them to characters from Hawthorne's *The House of the Seven Gables* (published earlier that year), representing herself as the weary yet loyal Hepzibah and Austin as Clifford (L62). One could easily expand that reflection on melancholy to consider how the nineteenth-century Pyncheons suffered for the sins of their Puritan ancestor, but it is also worth considering that it was Clifford's pitiful condition as a blighted artist that inspired Hepzibah's protectiveness. An 1863 poem, "God is a distant - stately Lover" (F615 J357), shows Dickinson's witty adaptation of Longfellow's "The Courtship of Miles Standish" to comment on the mysteries of the Trinity by which the Father delegates the Son to woo the soul: "Verily, a Vicarious Courtship - / 'Miles,' and 'Priscilla,' were such an One." When this poem first appeared in the April 2, 1891 issue of the *Christian Register*, its irreverence drew such angry reactions from readers that Mabel Loomis Todd dropped it from the 1891 *Poems*. Dickinson's poem was accused of Unitarianism, but it also suggests a more artistically interesting possibility for interpreting Longfellow's message: that Priscilla, in spurning the militant would-be groom and choosing the clerk who acted as his envoy, opted for writing as key to New England's future.

It was as a writer that Dickinson assimilated and transformed her Puritan heritage, both her community's historical legacy and the lore doubly refracted for her in the fictions of her literary contemporaries, and her chief debt to that tradition turned out to be language. One cannot imagine her reciting catechism terminology with the rapture Heman Humphrey reported among elderly New Englanders, but she certainly derived a rich vocabulary from the Bible and from sermons, hymns, her lexicon, and schoolbooks, and she made active use of theologically freighted words and phrases. Even the letter to Austin about Jennie Lind featured an account of Sunday's events in their parish with the conclusion "Our church grows interesting, Zion lifts her head - I overhear remarks signifying Jerusalem" (L46). Concordances to her poems and letters document frequent reliance on religious terminology (words like heaven, hell, immortality, savior, sacrament), some of it strongly associated with New England Puritanism and its Calvinist origins (election, ordinance, covenant). A striking trait of Dickinson's usage, however, is her preference for the hopeful language of grace, glory, and election over negative terminology such as damnation, reprobation, and hell. Her 1844 edition of Noah Webster's *American Dictionary of the English Language* furnished solidly orthodox definitions of theological terms while also showing alternative meanings for key words. Often Dickinson's usage exploited layerings of sacred and secular diction. In "My Reward for Being, was This - " (F375 J343), for example, the second stanza reads:

> When Thrones accost my Hands -
> With "Me, Miss, Me" -
> I'll unroll Thee -
> Dominions dowerless - beside this Grace -
> Election - Vote -
> The Ballots of Eternity, will show just that.

As often happens with Dickinson's poems, this one is ambiguous in its address. If "Thee" is a human lover (as seems more likely in the version found in fascicle 24 than this from fascicle 18), this is a celebration of the empowerment that comes of being chosen. If "Thee" is Jesus, it expresses a claim to heaven based on the wholly unmerited gift of saving grace. But what are we to make of the democratic diction of "Vote" and "Ballots"? Apparently more than one elector exercises power in this choice. Similar ambiguity may be found in the sacramental language of "I'm ceded - I've stopped being Their's" (F353 J508), where the new identity claimed by the speaker may be that of an elected soul but may also refer to poetic self-recognition. Even "Mine - by the Right of the White Election!" (F411 J528) can be read as an exultant proclamation of artistic status or a lover's choice instead of the election by Jesus that its combination of legal and sacramental diction suggests with its apparent reference to the "seal" of baptism and God's covenant with his saints.

There was another side to her New England heritage from which Dickinson derived strength: her Yankee identity. When she brushed off Jennie Lind's "trills" with "I'd rather have a Yankee" (L46), she distinguished between European and American musical tastes. "Yankee," however, had regional implications; it referred to rustic New Englanders and habits they developed in leading a hardscrabble existence. Dickinson suggested a natural harmony between Yankee character and New England's ecology when she declared "The Robin's my Criterion for Tune" (F256 J285) – preferring the commonplace bird in her garden and in the *Primer* to English cuckoos or the Swedish nightingale. When she wrote "I think the Hemlock likes to stand / Opon a Marge of Snow - / It suits his own Austerity - / And satisfies an awe" (F400 J525), she suggested how her region's bleak winter landscape emblematized Puritan grimness and integrity. Yankee habits of linguistic economy show themselves in her explosively condensed language as well as in her zeal to make use of every possible space on the manuscript page. Yankee canniness applied to the spiritual life as well as to business affairs in a region where people were said to be on the alert at all times for wooden nickels, and Dickinson applied that watchfulness even to her relationship with God when she remarked that "God was penurious with me, which makes me shrewd with Him" (L207). Perhaps most important with regard to spiritual searching was an insistence on personally convincing evidence. It was doubt of that evidence that had long kept honest New Englanders, like her, from seeking admission to churches. Emily Dickinson's comment shortly after her father's death that "I am glad there is Immortality - but would have tested it myself - before entrusting him" (L418) bespeaks that guarded Yankee temperament even as it suggests how this descendant of Puritans regarded her own prospects of immortality as no less promising than Edward Dickinson's. She both mocked and pitied her formidable ancestors, identified with them increasingly, but never let them daunt her.

NOTES

1 Karl Keller, *The Only Kangaroo among the Beauty: Emily Dickinson and America* (Baltimore: Johns Hopkins University Press, 1979), 68–9.
2 Martha Nell Smith, "The Poet as Cartoonist," *Comic Power in Emily Dickinson*, ed. Suzanne Juhasz, Cristanne Miller, and Martha Nell Smith (Austin: University of Texas Press, 1993), 72, 82–4.
3 Wendy Martin, "Emily Dickinson," *Columbia Literary History of the United States*, ed. Emory Elliott (New York: Columbia University Press, 1988), 623; Diane Gabrielsen Scholl, "Emily Dickinson's Conversion Narratives: A Study of the Fascicles," *Studies in Puritan American Spirituality 1* (1990), 202.

4 Joseph Conforti, *Jonathan Edwards, Religious Tradition, and American Culture* (Chapel Hill: University of North Carolina Press, 1995), 38.
5 Roger Lundin, *Emily Dickinson and the Art of Belief* (Grand Rapids, MI: Eerdmans, 1998), 51.
6 First Church in Amherst, *An Historical Review: One Hundred and Fiftieth Anniversary of the First Church of Christ in Amherst* (Amherst Record, 1889), 82.
7 Rowena Revis Jones, "The Preparation of a Poet: Puritan Directions in Emily Dickinson's Education," *Studies in the American Renaissance* (1982), 285–324; Carlton Lowenberg, *Emily Dickinson's Textbooks*, ed. Territa A. Lowenberg and Carla L. Brown (Lafayette, CA, n.p., 1986).
8 Jones, "The Preparation of a Poet," 296–7.
9 First Church, *An Historical Review*, 60.
10 Ibid., 65.
11 Keller, *The Only Kangaroo*, 99; Habegger, 562.

CHAPTER 5

Nature's Influence

Margaret H. Freeman

Every Landscape is, as it Were, a State of the Soul[1]

"Travel why to Nature," Dickinson wrote to Elizabeth Holland, "when she dwells with us?" (L321). Emily Dickinson avoided travel, preferring to remain within the environs of her own home. As a result, her natural surroundings were especially influential in shaping her poetic imagination. Dickinson transformed her experience of nature into metaphors that formed her poetic art, structured her philosophy of life, and created her emotional self-identification with nature. The landscapes of her natural surroundings became the basis of a philosophical worldview that fused nature and self within the scope of poetic expression.

After 1866, Dickinson never ventured far from the grounds of her home in Amherst, a small Connecticut River Valley town in western Massachusetts. The valley's configuration provided a natural setting for her life's work. Over millennia, its geological formations created a rich, fertile plain, which, with occasional river flooding, boasts the richest alluvial soil on the East Coast.[2] A circumference of hills encloses the valley and its river. Mabel Loomis Todd describes the natural scenery she observed one "warm August afternoon" just a few years after Dickinson's death in 1886:

> Toward the west flowed a noble river, not less than eight hundred feet wide, reflecting the sky on its placid surface. Still further west, ranges of misty blue hills filled the distance, while nearer rose Mount Warner, the pioneer of all that ancient mountain brotherhood.
>
> In the south lay the rugged and picturesque Holyoke range, and the steep sides of Mount Tom beyond the opening where the river has scooped its passage. Northward, Mount Toby showed itself in a luminous, purple atmosphere, a rich tone modified in Sugarloaf, across the river, by its more scarred sides of red sandstone. The gentle slope of the Pelham hills eastward was densely green, and but little colored by distance.[3]

Todd's vivid description of the valley's flora and fauna, with its profusion of flowers, ferns, and mosses, and the "the songs of numberless wild birds" echoing in the mountains, provides a contemporary picture of Dickinson's natural world.[4] To appreciate its effects on the poet, we must imagine her world as one with many more creatures than we see today; a lush growth of native plants unchallenged by later invasive species; a more luxuriant display of vibrant fall color from trees unstressed by modern technology; a colder climate with greater snow accumulation; and the brilliance of starry skies unaffected by light pollution: "Should you ask me my comprehension of a starlight Night," Dickinson wrote, "Awe were my only reply" (L965).

Todd's lyrical tone masks nature's harsher elements. Although Dickinson herself describes nature as "the Gentlest Mother" (F741 J790), she was also well aware of the fury nature can wreak. Daniel Lombardo documents the damage caused in Amherst by floods, tornadoes, and hurricanes in Dickinson's lifetime.[5] Dickinson's letters and her sister's journal entries refer often to inclement weather, especially heavy snowstorms, rain, and wind.[6] Harsh winters threw into exceptional relief the coming of spring, the sunny skies of June, and the colorful splendor of fall.

The idyllic view of Connecticut Valley nature in its pre-lapsarian splendor was tempered by the development of agriculture and the coming of the Industrial Revolution. Originally an eastern section of the town of Hadley, Amherst became a township in 1759 and quickly thrived as an agricultural, light-manufacturing, and college community. In the early part of the nineteenth century, Amherst was surrounded by swamps, which were slowly dredged and drained to create agricultural pastureland.[7] Dickinson saw the first train come to Amherst and witnessed the rise of new industries that replaced hand-crafted goods with machine-made products, as workplaces moved from cottage to factory.

It is no accident that these technological advances, asserting man's control over nature, had their genesis in the Western Hemisphere. Western science sprang from the philosophical traditions of the Greeks and of Cartesian thought, which separated mind from body, reason from feeling, man from nature. By positioning ourselves "outside" nature, we act, James P. Carse tells us, as finite players who "take nature on as an opponent to be subdued for the sake of civilization."[8] Western religion sprang from a Judeo-Christian tradition that reflected this alienation in its account of man's expulsion from the Garden of Eden. Steeped as Dickinson was in the biblical tradition of her Puritan heritage, she nevertheless could not accept the idea that God had banished us from Eden. Home, for Dickinson, was "a bit of Eden which not the sin of *any* can utterly destroy" (L59), and she invariably describes her surroundings as "a real Eden" (L131). "Eden," she tells us, "is that old-fashioned House / We dwell in every day" (F1734 J1657).

Dickinson rejects Western alienation from nature: "When much in the Woods as a little Girl, I was told that the Snake would bite me, that I might pick a poisonous flower, or Goblins kidnap me, but I went along and met no one but Angels" (L271). Dickinson does not approach nature like a scientist, who looks at a leaf to explore its characteristics, but as an artist, who asks: "What does this leaf mean to me?" Experiencing what nature in all its manifestations means to the self, the artist transcends conscious rationalization to access the emotional, subconscious self that is part of nature. This nature is the unseen reality of the world, hidden from us by our conceptualizing minds. As Carse notes, because nature is ultimately unknowable, it makes metaphor and language possible.[9] John Burnside describes it as "that nonfactual truth of being: the missed world, and by extension, the missed self who sees and imagines and is fully alive outside the bounds of socially-engineered expectations – not by some rational process ... but by a kind of radical illumination, a re-attunement to the continuum of objects and weather and other lives that we inhabit."[10] The very process of making art or poetry, Peter London notes, summons up through the medium of brush or pen the preconscious, subliminal activities of the experiencing, embodied mind: "For as we draw closer to Nature, we simultaneously draw closer to our Selves."[11] Dickinson expresses this self-identification with nature through the flowers of her conservatory and garden, the New England seasons, and the imaginative expansion of her landscape into horizons of infinite possibility.

For Dickinson, nature, self, and poetry are unified. Her intimate connection with surrounding woods and fields, with insects, birds, and animals that visited her garden, with the changes of the seasons, and with the nightly spectacle of the moon and stars, created in her an identification with the natural world which, together with her reading, inspired the imagery and structures of her poetic imagination.

Both Judith Farr and Marta McDowell describe in particular the contexts surrounding Dickinson's relationship with flowers.[12] McDowell details the physical characteristics of Dickinson's nineteenth-century surroundings, from the still-unpaved roads, where telephone poles and automobile traffic had not yet appeared, to the meadows and woodlands in which the poet wandered with her dog, Carlo; she describes the herbarium of four hundred specimens that Dickinson created from the wildflowers she collected on her walks. Richard Sewall comments that "the spirit of the herbarium – that device which gives flowers themselves a kind of immortality – spanned her life, a constant joy and inspiration."[13] Farr explores more deeply this connection of flowers to Dickinson's own life, noting how Dickinson drew on the Victorian "language of flowers," so that gifts of flowers conveyed particular messages.[14] Farr notes that for Dickinson, "flowers were metaphors, of both her own self and others."[15] Drawing attention to the pun between "posies" and "poesie," she notes that Dickinson often "spoke of the written word as a flower."[16]

The flora and fauna of Dickinson's natural surroundings shaped her emotional and imaginative life, as well as her words. To Dickinson, nature signified life itself as we experience it. This ability to link inner feelings with outer sensations is explained by the theory of conceptual integration or "blending."[17] Blending occurs when we perceive identity between elements in different domains to create new meaning. It provides a model that shows how Dickinson fuses self, flower, and poem in her creative imagination. In the following poem, Dickinson sets up a series of mental spaces to deliver a flirtatious message with the gift of a flower to her friend Samuel Bowles (F60A J44):

> If *she* had been the Mistletoe
> And I had been the Rose -
> How gay opon your table
> My velvet life to Close -
> Since I am of the Druid -
> And she is of the dew -
> I'll deck Tradition's buttonhole
> And send the Rose to you.

The speaker identifies herself as a sprig of mistletoe and fantasizes exchanging identities with the rose she is sending to her friend. By flirtatiously withholding herself while sending a symbol of love, Dickinson suggestively alludes to the fact that both participants have to be physically present to kiss under the mistletoe. The ability to create multiple mappings of mental spaces enables us to construct new conceptualizations of the world. Both poems and flowers become the "material anchors" of Dickinson's own self, as expressions of her love for others and her own spirit.[18] "By a flower - By a letter / By a nimble love - " she wrote in an early poem (F163 J109).

Gardening is an activity that is open to unknown horizons, as the seasons change in a ceaseless cycle of death and rebirth. Dickinson's close observations of nature led her to two important insights: nature's boundlessness and its indifference to human affairs. The cycle of the seasons and the horizons surrounding Amherst – Dickinson's beloved Pelham hills and the broad expanse of sky above the Connecticut Valley – produced in Dickinson a vision that encompassed appreciation of the unknown, that which lies beyond the limits of our experience. Because we can never fully comprehend the natural world, we can only speak of it through metaphor, the mapping between two totally unlike domains.

Throughout her poetry, Dickinson employs metaphors of her natural surroundings to reflect an identification with the unknown, whether it is the daily cycle in "I'll tell you how the Sun rose ... / But how he *set* I know not" (F204A J318); the passing of the seasons, as in "As imperceptibly as Grief / The Summer lapsed away" (F935D J1540); or the weather, describing the wind as "the fairer - for the farness - / And for the foreignhood - " (F883 J719). Nature infuses her poetics in expressions of ecstatic freedom, whether it is the bee who touches "Liberty - then know no more - / But Noon, and Paradise - " or the soul itself that has "moments of escape - " (F360 J512).

Metaphor has traditionally been understood as a figure of speech, used "for adornment, liveliness, elucidation, or agreeable mystification," as opposed to a means by which we structure our understanding of the world.[19] Rebecca Patterson was perhaps the first to articulate Dickinson's use of metaphor as structural.[20] She identifies in Dickinson's poems a symbolism that aligns the four points of the compass with the seasons and the time of day, assigning them colors and elements and giving them emotional significance (Figure 2).

Whereas Patterson focuses mainly on the cultural context of Dickinson's reading to explain Dickinson's poetic symbolism, George Lakoff and Mark Johnson probe the very nature of metaphoric reasoning itself.[21] In showing how conceptual metaphors express abstract ideas such as love, beauty, or justice through concrete images that reflect the material world, they developed the idea, not new to Western thought, that our conceptual reasoning is based on our physical experience of the world, that our minds are "embodied." Dickinson's linking of the west with evening sunsets and autumn has a physical basis in the way she oriented herself in the world (F468 J658, F1681 J1642). This orientation gives rise to the evening of day metaphorically marking the end of life and death as departure.

Cognitive research provides new tools to determine how Dickinson's natural surroundings influenced her poetic imagination. Even though Patterson's cardinal points symbolism associates the west with water, it does not explain the extraordinary frequency of sea imagery in Dickinson's poetry. Given Amherst's inland location, and the claim of Dickinson's lyric persona that she "never saw the Sea" (F800 J1052), how does the sea

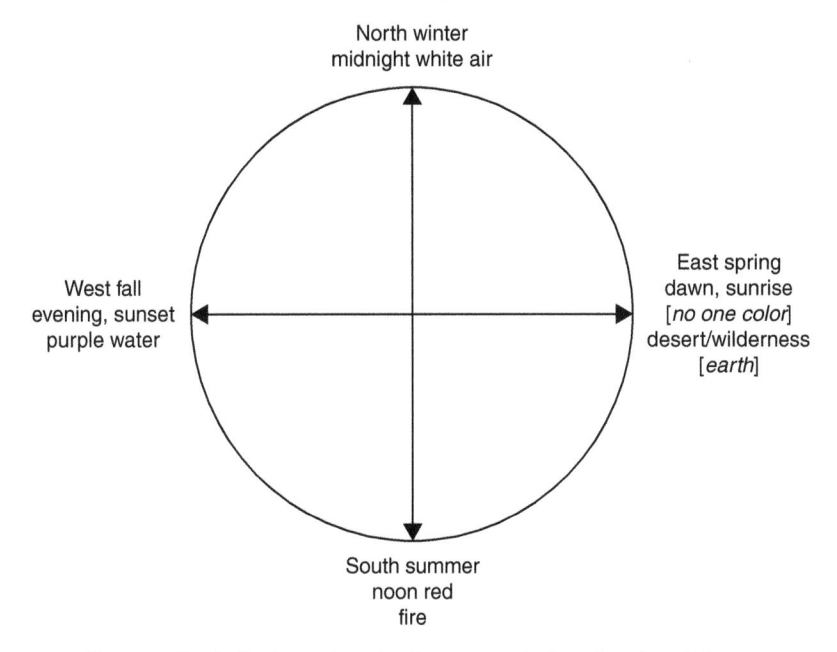

```
              North winter
              midnight white air
                    ↑
                    |
West fall           |           East spring
evening, sunset  ←——+——→        dawn, sunrise
purple water        |           [no one color]
                    |           desert/wilderness
                    |           [earth]
                    ↓
              South summer
              noon red
              fire
```

Figure 2. Emily Dickinson's cardinal points symbolism (based on Rebecca Patterson, *Imagery*, 183–200).

enter her natural surroundings as a source for her poetic imagination? Conceptual metaphor theory provides an answer.

Throughout Dickinson's poetry, an AIR IS SEA metaphor produces many poetic images to simulate her natural surroundings: "A soft Sea / washed around / the House / A Sea of Summer / Air" (F1199 J1198).[22] This metaphor entails many other correspondences that map elements from SEA to AIR. Thus, everything that flies is associated with the sea: "For Captain was / the Butterfly / For Helmsman / was the Bee" (F1199 J1198); "As Bird's far Navigation / … / A plash of Oars, a Gaiety - " (F257 J243). With air as part of sky, and sky as part of space, the sea becomes a metaphor for space and the sun for a ship: "A Sloop of / Amber slips away / Upon an Ether / Sea" (F1599B J1622). Human beings also participate in the metaphor: "Myself endued Balloon / By but a lip of Metal - / The pier to my Pontoon - " (F348 J505). AIR IS SEA thus becomes a structuring metaphor for the way Dickinson experiences and perceives her world.

This brief account does not explain *why* Dickinson adopted the AIR IS SEA metaphor. The answer lies in a further understanding of how Dickinson's natural surroundings inspired her philosophy of life.

Dickinson draws upon two long-standing conventional metaphors: the SEA OF LIFE and LIFE IS A JOURNEY. However, she treats these metaphors very differently. Her images of roads and journeys are almost always negative. They are "lonely" (F43 J9), a "Scarlet way" associated with pain, renunciation, and crucifixion (F404 J527); the speaker on such a journey "felt ill - and odd - " (F439 J579); the paths do not so much achieve, or lead to, or even end at, as come to a "stop" at their destination (F376B J344):

> 'Twas the old - road - through pain -
> That unfrequented - one -
> With many a turn - and thorn -
> That stops - at Heaven -

Dickinson transforms her aversion to travel into a rejection of the LIFE IS A JOURNEY metaphor that underlies Calvinist theology. Structuring the metaphor is a linear path schema that has a beginning, an ending, and points along the way. In the LIFE IS A JOURNEY metaphor, birth maps on to the beginning of the journey; death on to the end. However, in Dickinson's Puritan heritage, death is perceived as a point along the path, serving as a gateway to the soul's final destination of heaven or hell. To hold a linear, Calvinist viewpoint is to value immortality over life. This view conflicts with Dickinson's experiences of the natural world, with its seasonal cycles: the annual return of birds, bees, and butterflies to her garden; the regrowth of flowers and the re-leafing of trees each spring; the fullness of summer; the colors of fall; and then the snows of winter heralding death until new life begins again. Seasonal cycles suggested to Dickinson an alternate, nonlinear view, better represented by the SEA OF LIFE metaphor.

Dickinson's sea metaphors transform LIFE IS A JOURNEY "THROUGH" TIME into LIFE IS A VOYAGE "IN" SPACE. Voyages are associated predominately with the sea, and often end where they began, creating a circular movement. From the details of nature in its annual cycles and the circumference of hills that enclose the Amherst valley, Dickinson created metaphors based not on linear time, but on circular, cyclical space. These metaphors involve three schemata, which Mark Johnson defines as "*structures for organizing* our experience and comprehension": CYCLE, CONTAINER, and CHANGE.[23] These schemata are linked by the notion of movement through space and time within the circle of life.

The circular schema of CYCLE evokes images of arcs, discs, circumference itself, so that Dickinson conceives of motion as circular: "Butterflies from St Domingo / Cruising round the purple line - " (F95B J137); "Within my Garden, rides / a Bird / Opon a single Wheel - " (F370 J500). Together with the sun and moon, Dickinson describes in similar terms the seasons, weather, and life itself: autumn "eddies like a Rose - away - / Opon Vermillion Wheels - " (F465 J656); "As Floods - on Whites of / Wheels - " (F739 J788); "Of Life's penurious Round - " (F283C J313). A direct consequence of this metaphorical association of life with the cycles of nature is that death is no longer a point along a path, a gate to a final destination; it has no location.

Along with the CYCLE, the CONTAINER and CHANGE schemata structure Dickinson's poetry, whether expressed in the man-made images of houses, rooms, and graves, or in the flora and fauna of the natural world. Dickinson's CONTAINER schema has two forms: closed and open. Only death can ensure a closed CONTAINER, one that is unchanging, static, safe, as in "Doom is the House without / the Door - " (F710 J475), or "Safe in their Alabaster Chambers - " (F124B J216). In life, the CONTAINER is an open one that provides the environment for change to occur, whether it is in the "building of the soul" in "The Props assist the House - " (F729A J1142) or the emergence of the butterfly from its cocoon in "My Cocoon tightens - / Colors teaze - " (F1107 J1099). The schema of CHANGE, associated with the CONTAINER schema of life, is dynamic. Nature, Dickinson saw, was continually changing, as time and the seasons moved around Patterson's symbolic compass. Just as day gives way to night and the seasons proceed in order, so life follows the same cycle, from birth to maturity to old age to death.

Although Dickinson is adopting these metaphors from centuries of literary expression, she nevertheless puts her own Amherst-oriented slant on them. Perhaps the most trenchant in this regard is a poem that expresses Dickinson's identification with her natural world, its flora and fauna and seasons (F256 J285):

> The Robin's my Criterion
> for Tune -
> Because I grow - where
> Robins do -
> But, were I Cuckoo born -
> I'd swear by him -
> The ode familiar - rules the
> Noon -
> The Buttercup's my whim
> for Bloom -
> Because, we're Orchard sprung -

> But, were I Britain born,
> I'd Daisies⁺ spurn⁺ -   [⁺Clovers - ⁺scorn -]
> None but the Nut - October
> fit -
> Because - through dropping it,
> The Seasons flit - I'm taught -
> Without the Snow's Tableau
> Winter, were lie - to me -
> Because I see - New Englandly -
> The Queen discerns like me -
> Provincially -

Dickinson sets up self-identification with her natural surroundings by comparing her experience of "growing" in New England with being "born" in Great Britain. Her standards are shaped by her environment: as the seasons pass, she documents the differences. Spring is marked in New England by the arrival of robins, not the cuckoo of Shakespeare in his "Spring" poem at the end of *Love's Labour's Lost*: the poet's "tunes" rise from the familiar "ode" of the robin's song. The Connecticut Valley's fields and orchards, with their summer wildflowers, stand in stark contrast to England's well-tended gardens. In New England, the month of October marks the height of the fall, before the season lapses into the snows of winter. The poet learns and sees through her immediate, intimate, surroundings.

Dickinson's relation to her world is expressed in one of her most famous poems, "This is my letter to the World" (F519 J441). Dickinson's reference to nature sending her message to an unseen recipient suggests that this also is a flower letter-poem. The opening word "This" points to the actual poem Dickinson is writing; Nature's "simple News" and "Message" are her flowers. In the final stanza, the speaker identifies herself with both nature and poetry:

> Her Message is committed
> To Hands I cannot see -
> For love of Her - Sweet - country-
> men -
> Judge tenderly - of Me

The phrase "Sweet - country - men" is syntactically ambiguous. It might describe the flowers, the poem's recipients, or it might request that "men," "For love of Her - Sweet - country - ," judge the poet tenderly, thus drawing us all into self-identification with nature.

By fusing the world of nature, consciousness of the self, and the writing of poetry in such metaphoric blends, Dickinson transforms her natural surroundings into poetry expressing Nature infused with our own life experiences.

NOTES

1. Henri Frédéric Amiel, *Amiel's Journal: The Journal Intime of Henri-Frédéric Amiel*. Trans. Mrs. Humphrey Ward (London: Macmillan, 1921 [1885]), 30.
2. Richard D. Little, *Dinosaurs, Dunes, and Drifting Continents: The Geohistory of the Connecticut Valley* (Greenfield, MA: Valley Geology Publications, 1986).
3. Mabel Loomis Todd, "The Connecticut Valley," Frederick H. Hitchcock, ed. *The Handbook of Amherst* (Amherst, MA: Appleton Press, 1894), 16–17.
4. Ibid., 21.
5. Daniel Lombardo, *A Hedge Away: The Other Side of Emily Dickinson's Amherst* (Northampton, MA: The Daily Hampshire Gazette, 1997), 201–21.
6. Leyda, references scattered throughout.
7. "Wetlands Protection and Permitting." Available at: http://www.amherstma.gov/index.aspx?NID=1268.
8. James P. Carse, *Finite and Infinite Games: A Vision of Life as Play and Possibility* (New York: Random House, 1986), 119.
9. Ibid., 123.
10. John Burnside, "Travelling into the Quotidian: Some Notes on Allison Funk's 'Heartland' Poems," *Poetry Review* 95.2 (2005), 60.
11. Peter London, *Drawing Closer to Nature: Making Art in Dialogue with the Natural World* (Boston and London: Shambala, 2003), 2.
12. Judith Farr, with Louise Carter, *The Gardens of Emily Dickinson* (Cambridge, MA: Harvard University Press, 2004); Marta McDowell, *Emily Dickinson's Gardens: A Celebration of a Poet and Gardener* (New York: McGraw-Hill, 2005).
13. Richard Sewall, "Science and the Poet: Emily Dickinson's Herbarium and 'the clue divine'," *Emily Dickinson's Herbarium: A Facsimile Edition* (Cambridge, MA: The Belknap Press of Harvard University Press, 2006), 20.
14. Farr, *Gardens*, 42.
15. Ibid., 23.
16. Ibid., 4, 11.
17. Gilles Fauconnier and Mark Turner, *The Way We Think: Conceptual Blending and the Mind's Hidden Complexities* (New York: Basic Books, 2002).
18. Edwin Hutchins, "Material Anchors for Conceptual Blends," *Journal of Pragmatics* 37.10 (2005), 1555–77.
19. George Whalley, "Metaphor," *Princeton Encyclopedia of Poetry and Poetics*, ed. Alex Preminger (Princeton, NJ: Princeton University Press, 1965), 490.
20. Rebecca Patterson, *Emily Dickinson's Imagery*, ed. Margaret H. Freeman (Amherst: University of Massachusetts Press, 1979), 180–1.

21 George Lakoff and Mark Johnson, *Metaphors We Live By* (Chicago: The University of Chicago Press, 1980).
22 Margaret H. Freeman, "Metaphor Making Meaning: Emily Dickinson's Conceptual Universe," *Journal of Pragmatics 24* (1995), 643–66. Capitalization indicates that the metaphor in question is conceptual, not linguistic.
23 Mark Johnson, *The Body in the Mind: The Bodily Basis of Meaning, Imagination, and Reason* (Chicago: The University of Chicago Press, 1987), 29.

PART II

Literary Contexts: Sources, Influences, Intertextual Engagements

CHAPTER 6

The Bible

Emily Seelbinder

Since 1950, Emily Dickinson's personal Bible has resided in an acid-free box in the Houghton Library at Harvard University. This King James Bible, about two inches thick and measuring approximately four inches by six inches, is small enough to hold comfortably in one's hand. Bound in straight-grained, green Moroccan leather, decorated in gilt filigree, with the poet's name stamped in the center of the front cover, it is inscribed on the third fly leaf "Emily E. Dickinson / A present from her / Father / 1844." On the pages that follow are a variety of additions and alterations, glimpses of Dickinson in the act of reading the text from which she selected for her poetry and letters more direct references than from any other single source. Among these are a torn scrap of paper serving as a bookmark, stains from dried plant specimens, several pages from which passages have been excised with scissors, a few dog-ears, and, in some margins, light marks, mostly in pencil and occasionally in pen, of the sort Dickinson is known to have used in marking her books.

Until recently, only a few scholars have been privileged to examine this volume, which has become too delicate to allow frequent handling. In the summer of 2011, however, Harvard opened Dickinson's Bible to a worldwide audience through a digitized copy made available online. Now, anyone seeking insight into the ways Dickinson used – and abused – her Bible can examine her personal copy from cover to cover.[1] Turning these virtual pages, one might soon abandon any attempt to decipher the little dots and dashes that are the Morse Code of Dickinson's reading habits. Though the photographs are remarkably clear and the site allows magnification, the marks are only faintly visible, and they are often so far removed from the printed text that it is difficult to determine exactly which passages have been marked. The bolder marks, however, offer many possibilities for enriching our understanding of Dickinson's complex relationship with her Bible.

One of these marks is a bracket – the only one in the entire volume – penciled beside Psalm 121 ("I will lift up mine eyes unto the hills …").

Next to the bracket is a notation in the margin: "E. M. C. 14th Augt. 1854." Jay Leyda identifies this as the work of Eliza Coleman, daughter of Lyman Colman, who "brought his family to Amherst when he took charge of Amherst Academy in Nov. 1844, and taught Greek and German at the College." Frequently suffering from ill health, the "frail Eliza became an intimate of Emily" and continued to maintain contact with the Dickinsons after she left Amherst, including a stay with the family in August 1854 (Leyda I, xxxiv–xxxv). Alfred Habegger suggests that Eliza may have been aware of a quarrel at that time between Emily and Sue and offered this "counsel to look unto the hills for strength" (Habegger, 324). Whatever its purpose, the notation reveals that Dickinson was not always a solitary reader of her Bible and may have sought guidance there in a time of crisis. Further evidence of the significance of this shared experience are stains on the page just above where the psalm begins and on the page opposite, indicating that a flower was pressed between those pages at one time. Readers of the digitized text will find between the two pages a photograph of that flower – a bright, surreal blue one – now removed to a separate folder.

Three other dried plant specimens from Dickinson's Bible have been removed to separate folders and photographed for inclusion in the digitized text. According to the list of Dickinson family books compiled by a Harvard librarian in 1950, one of these is a clover blossom with stem and leaves that came from Edward Dickinson's grave. How this origin was ascertained is not clear, but there is evidence of Dickinson's having attached special significance to clover brought to her from her father's grave by Elizabeth Holland, whom she thanked for that gift in at least two letters written more than a year apart (L432, L475). The placement of the flower also suggests an association with a loved one: at the top of the first page against which it was pressed are these words of Jonathan to David in 1 Samuel 20:18: "thou shalt be missed, because thy seat will be empty."

Although the provenance of the clover cannot be firmly established, two other items preserved in Dickinson's Bible can be confirmed as mementos of a deceased friend. Pasted along the interior edge of one of the last fly leaves in the volume is a two-line obituary notice for Amherst dentist Jacob Holt, which Leyda identifies as having been clipped "from a Boston newspaper" (Leyda I, 147). Next to this notice, in Dickinson's handwriting, is a poem entitled "The Bible," with her notation beneath that it was "Composed by Dr. J. Holt / during his last sickness." Dickinson seems to have followed that illness closely, twice asking Austin in letters from Mount Holyoke how he was doing, sending him her "love" and promising to write to him soon (L17, L19). She herself was recovering from illness in Amherst while Holt was on his deathbed. Only two days after she returned to Mount Holyoke to complete her studies there, he died of consumption at the age of twenty-six. The text for the sermon preached at Holyoke that day was Genesis 49:33, the verse announcing the death of Jacob. Leyda has suggested that Holt was the "friend" Dickinson later mentioned to Higginson as one "who taught [her] Immortality" (Leyda I, 144; L261).

At the time of Holt's death, Dickinson probably already knew he had written some poetry. Johnson and Ward report that "he [twice] published some verses in the *Northampton Courier*" while he and Dickinson were both students at Amherst Academy.[2] "The Bible" was published in the *Hampshire and Franklin Express*, an Amherst weekly, on June 8, 1848. Dickinson transcribed it as follows:

> The Bible.
> "It is a pure & holy word,
> It is the wisdom of a God,
> It is a fountain, full & free,
> It is *the* book for you & me,
> It will the soul's best anchor be,
> Over life's tempestuous sea,
> A guardian angel to the tomb,
> A meteor in the world's dark gloom,
> It is the shining sun at even
> It is a diamond dropped from heaven"[3]

Holt was probably not the first to tell Dickinson the Bible was "*the* book" for her. Even as she copied these words, she was resisting efforts by Mary Lyon (the founder of Mount Holyoke Seminary, where Dickinson was studying) and others to persuade her to cast aside her doubts about the Bible and matters of faith. Her preservation of the poem, therefore, should not be taken as an endorsement of its sentiments. The conventional tropes Holt and others employed, however, do appear in Dickinson's own poems about the Bible and the transformative power of reading. Holt's "fountain, full & free" could be the one from which a Dickinson subject "ate and drank the precious Words" until "His spirit grew robust - " (F1593 J1587). "The soul's best anchor ... / Over life's tempestuous sea" becomes in Dickinson's work a "Frigate ... / To take us Lands away" and "the Chariot - / That bears the Human Soul - " (F1286 J553). Holt's images – a meteor, a diamond dropped, an angel guarding one to the tomb – descend; Dickinson's soar: "What Liberty / A loosened Spirit brings - " (F1593 J1587).

More than three decades after transcribing the poem, Dickinson sent verses to another young man that are the antithesis of Holt's, declaring "The Bible is an antique Volume / Written by faded Men / At the suggestion of Holy Spectres - " (F1577A J1545). This "Diagnosis of the Bible, by a Boy" has long been a divining rod for readers seeking to characterize Dickinson's approach to scripture. Placed side by side with other poems that interrogate scripture and find it wanting – the several poems questioning God's treatment of Moses, for example (F180 J168; F521 J597; F1273 J1201) – the poem can be read as a critique of the conservative Calvinist tradition in which she had been educated and of preachers who breathed no life into the Word. It can also be understood as a comic distillation of "higher critical" readings of the Bible as literature she would have encountered in the work of Romantics and Transcendentalists, as well as that of favorite author George Eliot.

Considered radical in Dickinson's youth, but much more mainstream at the time of her death, higher criticism employed rhetorical, historical, and scientific analysis of scripture and placed less emphasis on the textual analysis of "lower criticism." This approach led some of its adherents to reject the idea of the Bible as having been received directly from God and to treat scripture instead as myth or history. For these critics, including American Transcendentalists such as Emerson, the text was not sacrosanct. As such, the Bible was one of many texts from which a reader might obtain truths and spiritual guidance and to which he or she might bring new and fresh readings by recasting, rearranging, and reimagining what others had written. Dickinson appears to have embraced wholeheartedly this approach to reading. Nowhere is her sense of not being bound by the literal text more evident than in her having excised portions of several pages in her Bible, including lines from the final two chapters of The Revelation of St. John the Divine that were printed only inches away from this dire warning: "if any man shall take away from the words of the book of this prophecy, God shall take away his part out of the book of life" (Rev 22:19). For Dickinson, "A word made Flesh" might be "tremblingly partook," but it could be adjusted to "our specific strength - " (F1715 J681).

In adjusting her Bible to specific strengths, Dickinson generally employed a combination of higher and lower criticism. The former equipped her with skepticism, contexts, and possibilities for playing with texts, the latter with a variety of ways to effect close readings of those texts. An examination of some of the aids to the study of scripture found in the Dickinson family library shows that Dickinson's training in close reading was much more sophisticated than twentieth and twenty-first century readers might have supposed. Among these volumes is a biblical concordance apparently consulted so frequently that it arrived at Harvard "precariously held together with a shoestring" – evidence of the importance the poet attached to words and textual analysis.[4] At least two works simplified the process of comparing verses found throughout the King James Bible, one reorganizing "the whole of the Old and New Testaments" into books on such subjects as "External Nature," "Sacred Seasons," and "Eschatology (or, The Last Things),"[5] and the other offering a selection of verses "designed to facilitate the finding of proof texts" for discussion of such matters as "Female piety, sympathy, and kindness" and "Personality of the Holy Spirit."[6]

Particularly interesting, because it was a common reference text in many nineteenth-century American homes and is comprehensive in its scope, is a collection of books and pamphlets assembled by William Jenks as *A Companion to the Bible*.[7] This massive volume included a concordance, biographies of biblical commentators, a Bible index, a symbol dictionary, a geographical dictionary, maps, and "A Guide to the Reading and Study of the Bible." The study guide, nearly two hundred pages of densely packed text, covers the history of biblical literature and criticism; the principles of biblical interpretation; background on the biblical books; biblical theology; and biblical history, geography, science, arts, and domestic usages. Though its contents might suggest it is prescriptive, the guide's purpose, asserted on its title page and reiterated throughout its discussion, is not to mandate, but to assist, to provide the reader with tools for reading intelligently. Of utmost importance, regardless of the methods a reader might choose to employ, is individual interpretation of scripture, unmediated by others – a bedrock principle of Calvinism and a hallmark of Dickinson's reading of her own Bible.

Unmediated does not, however, imply that the process was solitary. In the many poems and letters in which she employs scripture, Dickinson often poses questions about interpretation and appears eager to engage her readers in a dynamic interpretive process. One especially intriguing example of this occurs in her early correspondence with T. W. Higginson. In her first letter she equates poetry with the living Word (L260). In the second, she identifies "the Revelations" as a favorite book and encloses "There came a day - at Summer's full - ," which makes intriguing use of imagery from Chapter 7 of the Book of Revelation in remembering a secret meeting between lovers who anticipate a "New Marriage" after their deaths (L261, F325C J250). With her fourth letter she encloses "Of Tribulation - these are They" (F328 J325), another poem replete with imagery from Revelation 7. At the end of that poem, she appends a note calling attention to a misspelling in her text. Examining her reason for including this note suggests that her reading of her Bible was especially acute.

Revelation 7 apparently held strong interest for Dickinson. In her Bible, the chapter is framed by dog-eared pages, a means of marking employed rarely elsewhere and never so emphatically. References to this chapter appear at least a half dozen times in her letters and poems, including the two poems mentioned earlier. The chapter describes the triumphant celebration of the "hundred and forty and four thousand of all the tribes of the children of Israel" who have been "sealed the servants of our God in their foreheads" (Rev. 7:3–4) and express their gratitude "to our God which sitteth upon the throne, and unto the Lamb" (Rev. 7:10). The celebration occurs just after the opening of the sixth seal and before the opening of the seventh and last seal of the book of God, at which time the destruction of the earth begins. Of special significance in this vision is "a great multitude, which no man could number, of all nations, and kindreds, and people, and tongues ... clothed with white robes, and palms in their hands" (Rev. 7:9), about which the narrator of Revelation has this discussion with an elder:

> And one of the elders answered, saying unto me, What are these which are arrayed in white robes? and whence came they? And I said unto him, Sir, thou knowest. And he said to me, These are they which came out of great tribulation, and have washed their robes, and made them white in the blood of the Lamb. (Rev. 7:13–14)

Commentaries on this passage point to the palms as signs of victory and the white robes as emblems of righteousness. They also emphasize how "the last [have become] first" (Matt. 19:16): those most scorned on earth have been made "kings and priests" in heaven (Rev. 1:6). As explained in one of the reference texts Dickinson might have consulted, "the kingdom, which is the subject of this prophetic book, is ...'not a kingdom of this world,' not established by the means and apparatus of worldly pomp, not bearing the external ensigns of royalty."[8]

This other-worldliness is evident in "There came a Day," but it is even more pronounced in "Of Tribulation," which reimagines the scene described in the biblical passage. Dickinson's speaker notes the differences between worldly pomp and heavenly victory by remarking on the garments worn by those in the procession. "Spangled Gowns" might denote persons of higher rank on earth, but in heaven these "a / lesser Rank /

The Bible

Of Victors, designate - ." Their wearers are "Victors" in having arrived in heaven. The martyrs, who have a special place among redeemed souls, are "Denoted by the White" robes: "the Ones who / overcame most times - / Wear nothing commoner / than Snow - / No Ornament - but Palms - ."

Further evidence of the inversion of worldly signs is introduced in the third stanza: the "Surrender" and "Defeat" the martyrs experienced as mortals have been transformed, the former now "unknown / On this Superior Soil - " and the latter "an Outgrown / Anguish" apparently experienced in the final hours of life on earth, for it is now "Remembered - as the Mile // Our panting Ancle [sic] / barely passed / When Night devoured / the Road - ." The transformation of earthly grief into heavenly triumph appears almost too much for the speaker and her companions to comprehend. At the end of the poem, they hover at the edge of the procession, interlopers "whispering - / in the House - / And all we said - / was / Saved!"

In a version of the poem she sent to Higginson (F328B),[9] Dickinson placed special emphasis on four words that are not stressed in the fascicle copy (F328A). The first two – "Surrender" and "Defeat" – are set off by quotation marks. This device stresses the paradox of the poem: in surrendering to death and suffering, the martyrs have actually defeated their conquerors. This is true not only for the martyrs, but also for the speaker and her companions. Their wonder at this is evident not only in their whispering, but also in the final word – "Saved!" – writ large and centered on a line by itself at the end of the poem, a breath-taking declaration of triumph. Each of these emphases provides a visual cue underscoring the experiences of the speaker and her companions and signaling for the reader ways of comprehending those experiences and the scripture on which they are based. Each guides the reader in the first and all subsequent readings of the poem. Dickinson's fourth point of emphasis, the misspelling of the noun in the striking image "panting Ancle," might be overlooked in a first reading of the poem. It becomes an intriguing part of rereading, however, when one encounters the note Dickinson added for Higginson at the end of the poem she sent him: "I spelled - Ankle - Wrong - ."

Why call attention to the "error"? Brita Lindberg-Seyersted treats this note as one of several "apologetic references" Dickinson made in her letters "to her occasional mistakes in spelling," which were "often unorthodox," but likely "a weakness, rather than an intended 'privateness.'"[10] The intentionality with which this poem was presented to Higginson, however, suggests that Dickinson's misspelling is neither weak nor private. Rather, it appears the poet has challenged her reader to connect the scene in Revelation 7 to a similar scene somewhere else in the Bible and to do so through the distinctive spelling of *ancle*. Though the more modern spelling had already been incorporated into her lexicon, the archaic spelling remained in the King James Bible. Dickinson's own concordance, an edition of the one originally compiled by Alexander Cruden and still in use in seminaries today, has no listings for the spelling *ankle*, but it does have one for *ancles* in Ezekiel 47:3 and one for *ancle-bones* in Acts 3:7. A glance at Dickinson's Bible reveals the latter as her choice for a parallel to the story in Revelation: there the key word is spelled two different ways, in Ezekiel as *ankles* and in Acts as *ancle*. Higginson might have found the same differences in his own Bible, for the older spelling continued to appear in the King James New Testament well into the 1890s. He might also have found further ways of understanding Dickinson's "panting Ancle" image.

Acts 3 reports an encounter Peter and John had with a lame man at the gate of the temple. Peter spoke to the man: "In the name of Jesus Christ of Nazareth rise up and walk. And he took him by the right hand, and lifted him up: and immediately his feet and ancle-bones received strength" (Acts 3:6–7). Before he was healed, this man's ancles might have been described as "panting," particularly in light of one of the definitions in Dickinson's lexicon for the verb "pant": "To play with intermission or declining strength." This and another definition, "to beat with preternatural violence or rapidity, as the heart in terror, or after hard labor, or in anxious desire or suspense," could apply to the final moments on earth of those in "Of Tribulation" who suddenly found themselves transported to heaven.[11] With her deliberate misspelling and this vivid image, Dickinson invites a comparison of two stories of sudden, unexpected transformation, of healing and salvation, one occurring shortly after the death of Christ, the other at the end of time. By including the formerly lame man among those newly transported to heaven, she emphasizes that the Chosen are not just the martyrs, but also common sufferers, who respond to their newfound strength with muted wonder ("whispering" the single word "Saved!") or shouts of praise.

Dickinson's note to Higginson on his copy of "Of Tribulation" might be taken as declaration of her own strength both as biblical scholar and as poet. Around the same time that she began her correspondence with Higginson, Dickinson reported to Joseph Lyman that the Bible had once seemed to her "an arid book," but now she "saw how infinitely wise [and] how merry it is," offering "fathomless gulfs of meaning ..., hints about some celestial reunion - yearning for a oneness - has any one fathomed that sea?"[12] As her Bible demonstrates, Dickinson plumbed that sea for the rest of her life. The result was a body of work offering incisive, imaginative, and insightful readings of scripture and life that are as endlessly fascinating for us as her Bible was for her.

NOTES

1. *The Holy Bible, containing the Old and New Testaments: translated out of the original tongues* (Philadelphia: J. B. Lippincott, 1843). Dickinson Family Library copy. EDR 8. Houghton Library, Harvard University, Cambridge, MA. Available at: http://nrs.harvard.edu/urn-3:FHCL.Hough:4906292.
2. Thomas H. Johnson and Theodora Ward, "Biographical sketches of recipients of letters and persons mentioned in them." *The Letters of Emily Dickinson*, Vol. *III*, 946.
3. A comparison of Dickinson's copy with the printed version in Leyda reveals several differences: "'Tis" and "'Twill" become "It is" and "It will"; "and" is replaced by an ampersand; emphasis on "you" and "me" in line four is shifted to "the"; semicolons at the ends of lines four and eight become commas; a comma is added at the end of line five; "dropt" becomes "dropped"; the final four words of the poem are not underlined (they are italicized in the original); and periods have been added after each word in the title and after "dropped" in the last line. The added periods are particularly interesting: in the two letters in which she asks about Holt, Dickinson adds periods to his name. The periods in the first letter are particularly emphatic: "How is Jacob. Holt. now?" (L17).
4. Dorothy Huff Oberhaus, "Emily Dickinson's Books," *EDJ*, 2.2 (1993), 63.
5. Roswell D. Hitchcock, *New and Complete Analysis of the Holy Bible* (New York: A. J. Johnson & Son, 1873).
6. Charles Simmons, *A Scripture Manual* (New York: M. W. Dodd, 1845).
7. William Jenks, ed., *A Companion to the Bible* (Brattleboro, VT: Brattleboro Typographic Company, 1838).
8. Jenks, *Companion*, "Guide," 112.
9. The manuscript of the poem, written on two sides of a single sheet and identified as "Ms. Am. 1093(14)," may be viewed online in the photostream made available by the Boston Public Library of its collection of Emily Dickinson Papers. Available at: http://www.flickr.com/photos/boston_public_library/2403508512/in/set-72157604466722178/lightbox/ and http://www.flickr.com/photos/boston_public_library/2403508688/in/set-72157604466722178/lightbox/.
10. Brita Lindberg-Seyersted, *The Voice of the Poet: Aspects of Style in the Poetry of Emily Dickinson* (Uppsala, Sweden: Alquist & Wiksells, 1968), 180–1.
11. Noah Webster, *An American Dictionary of the English Language*, 2 vols. (Amherst, MA: J. S. & C. Adams Brothers, 1844). Available at: http://edl.byu.edu/webster.
12. Richard B. Sewall, *The Lyman Letters: New Light on Emily Dickinson and Her Family* (Amherst: University of Massachusetts Press, 1965), 73.

CHAPTER 7

Shakespeare

Páraic Finnerty

Dickinson's engagements with Shakespeare are culturally representative; the complexity of her response to him reflects his multifaceted reception in nineteenth-century America. By the 1840s, Shakespeare's "artistic supremacy had ceased to be debated; it was simply assumed" and in Anglo-American culture all things associated with him took on new economic and artistic value; the greatest of poets was worshipped as a quasi-divine figure.[1] Dickinson generally agreed with this cultural consensus; in one 1877 letter, she readily associated Shakespeare's birthplace with heaven, declaring "'Stratford on Avon'- accept us all!" (L487). In one of the period's most influential essays on Shakespeare, published in *Representative Men* (1850), a book Dickinson described as "a little Granite Book you can lean upon" (L481), Ralph Waldo Emerson explained why literature, philosophy, and thought had become "Shakespearized":

> [Shakespeare] wrote the text of modern life; the text of manners: he drew the man of England and Europe; the father of the man in America: he drew the man, and described the day, and what is done in it: he read the hearts of men and women, their probity, and their second thought and wiles; the wiles of innocence, and the transitions by which virtues and vices slide into their contraries.[2]

Emerson correctly delineates the constitutive role Shakespeare's works had in nineteenth-century American life and the way they informed and anticipated the nation's most pertinent and personal emotional, intellectual, and ethical concerns.

Other prominent American critics, such as Richard Henry Dana and Henry Norman Hudson, emphasized the plays' didactic and moral function, suggesting that they offered insight into the timeless truths of human nature and universal moral principles. Dickinson's references to Shakespeare as well as the markings in her edition of his works suggest that she did not view him as Dana and Hudson did, but instead regarded him as a "Beloved" guide (L478), whose powers of identification and sympathetic understanding were all encompassing, and who fearlessly represented all sides of human life, even darker ones. Whereas critics such as Dana and Hudson advocated Shakespeare's docile and modest heroines as paragons of virtue and models of proper femininity, Dickinson identified with his transgressive and disruptive female characters – Lady Macbeth, Cleopatra, and Queen Margaret – and with his tragic heroes Othello, Antony, and Macbeth.

The apotheosis of Shakespeare coexisted and overlapped with dissonant voices that challenged and questioned his status in and appropriateness for America. The imperative that Shakespeare should be universally read as a means of moral enlightenment, self-improvement, and cultivation was accompanied by anxieties about his bawdy language and a latent Puritan prejudice against the theater. For these reasons Heman Humphrey and Edward Hitchcock, who were presidents of Amherst College during Dickinson's formative years, condemned the "Immortal Bard of Avon"; Humphrey argued that "Shakspeare as he *is*, is not a fit book for the *family* reading. What Christian father, or virtuous mother, would allow him, if he were now alive, to come into a blooming circle of sons and daughters and recite his plays, just as they stand in the best editions?"[3] Edward Dickinson does not appear to have worried about his children reading Shakespeare; he purchased the unexpurgated Charles Knight eight-volume edition of Shakespeare's works for his family in 1857, despite the production and proliferation of censored or bowdlerized versions specifically for women and children (Leyda I, 352). One incident in Dickinson's early life offers an excellent example of the felt need to supervise and monitor women's reading of Shakespeare, and also provides an indication of the way Shakespeare was being incorporated into social and educational activities. Dickinson's friend Emily Fowler Ford recalls:

> We had a Shakespeare Club ... and one of the tutors proposed to take all the copies of all the members and mark out the questionable passages. This plan was negatived at the first meeting, as far as "the girls" spoke, who said they did not want the strange things emphasized, nor their books spoiled with marks. Finally we told the men to do as they liked – "we shall read everything." I remember the lofty air with which Emily took her departure, saying, "There's nothing wicked in Shakespeare, and if there is I don't want to know it." The men read for perhaps three meetings from their expurgated editions, and then gave up their plan, and the whole text was read out boldly.[4]

Although on this occasion female readers, including the forthright Dickinson, refused male censorship and Shakespeare was read out boldly, the event highlights the subversive nature of Shakespeare's texts. Of course, Dickinson may have been most attracted to the "wicked" side of Shakespeare: his illicit and socially disruptive texts allowed her to imagine new possibilities in constructions of gender and sexuality and historically located alternatives to her culture's standards and dictates, giving Dickinson "access to a dissonant and oppositional 'order of things.'"[5]

For other Americans, it was not Shakespeare's immorality that was the problem, but the way he was deployed in debates about America's national identity, and about whether, despite its political separation from Britain, the United States was still culturally dependent on its former ruler. Richard Grant White, the most respected nineteenth-century American critic and editor of Shakespeare, argued that reading Shakespeare was beneficial because it reconnected Americans with their "Englishhood."[6] Moreover, Dana and Hudson, who were also Anglophiles, embroiled Shakespeare in their attacks on democratic ideals of freedom and equality and their disparaging views about American writers. These critics drew attention to Shakespeare's nationality and politics at a time when anti-English sentiment was still "a feature of American nationalism" – inspiring patriotic zeal and creating a sense of communality – and "many things English were often considered symbols of 'the enemy' of freedom, liberty and democracy."[7] In an 1850 essay championing Nathaniel Hawthorne's literary genius, Herman Melville accused such critics of suffering from "Anglo-Saxon superstitions" that pronounced "Shakespeare absolutely unapproachable."[8] Going even further, Walt Whitman argued that Shakespeare was not suitable reading for Americans because his works celebrated and sympathized with aristocratic and upper-class characters and were "poisonous to the idea of the pride and dignity of the common people, the life-blood of democracy."[9] Like Emerson, Melville and Whitman greatly admired Shakespeare, but abhorred Shakespeare idolatry and worship, which they believed hampered the pursuit of American cultural nationalism. Dickinson heard Dana expound his views in his Amherst lectures in 1850 (Leyda I, 179–80) and would have been familiar with these topical literary debates. In this context, her statements about Shakespeare might be regarded as unpatriotic and elitist: "While Shakespeare remains Literature is firm" (L368); "He has had his Future who has found Shakespeare" (L402); "Pity me, however, I have finished Ramona. Would that like Shakespeare, it were just published!" (L976). Her Shakespeare is literature's foundation, its beginning and end; his timeless works are ever relevant and always current, as contrasted with time-bound texts, such as her friend and contemporary Helen Hunt Jackson's *Ramona* (1884).

Although divisive in some circles, Dickinson's comments reflect the dominant views of an era in which America was "Shakespearized" and Shakespeare Americanized, and American critics, editors, actors, collectors, and individual readers claimed him as their own, exemplifying a "massive transfer of authority and of cultural capital [from Britain] to American society."[10] Shakespeare was not merely an author; he was a brand name that symbolized quality and could be used to advertise or sell anything, from peanuts to patented medicines. This increased his works' circulation and ensured that his language entered common parlance and was as readily found in political speeches, daily newspapers, and almanacs as in private letters, diaries, and journals. Critics and editors established their cultural credentials by involving themselves in the explication and interpretation of his texts and took great pleasure in pointing out the errors of their British precursors and in underlining Shakespeare's American associations. The periodicals Dickinson read most avidly – *Harper's New Monthly Magazine*, *The Atlantic Monthly*, *Scribner's Monthly*, and *The Century* – frequently published such criticism, as the discussion of Shakespeare confirmed these publications' cultural kudos and potentially increased sales. Dickinson was familiar with this intellectual investment in Shakespeare, and even referred to one controversial critic, Delia Bacon, who set out to prove that Shakespeare did not write the plays attributed to him (L721). Less contentiously Bacon argued that the plays were coded critiques of European hierarchy that heralded the coming of American ideals of democracy, freedom, social mobility, and individualism. In a manner analogous to Bacon's, Herman Melville, Louisa May Alcott, and Harriett Beecher Stowe transformed Shakespeare's lines, plots, and imagery to suit American tastes, aiming to advance the reputation of their works through association with his.

Shakespeare's absorption into so many aspects of nineteenth-century American culture is related to his plays' incorporation into contemporary elocution lessons. Like her contemporaries, Dickinson probably first encountered Shakespeare in school textbooks that used his lines to instruct students about rhetoric and reading aloud. In such lessons, a student was advised "to strive to adopt as his *own*, and as his *own at the moment* of utterance, every sentiment he delivers; – and to *say* it to the audience, in the manner which the occasion and subject spontaneously suggest to him who has abstracted his mind both from all consideration of *himself*, and from the consideration that he is reading."[11] Following such instruction, when reading Shakespeare Dickinson would have aimed to offer a self-effacing representation of the emotions of his characters. Not only did Dickinson hear her friends and tutors read Shakespeare aloud during club meetings, but she also may have attended the public readings of Shakespeare that were fashionable at the time (Leyda I, 250). In an 1859 letter to her cousin Louise Norcross, Dickinson refers to the most famous Shakespeare reader of the day: "Do you still attend Fanny Kemble?," adding, "I have heard many notedly *bad* readers, and a fine one would be almost a fairy surprise" (L199). Readings such as Kemble's were popular because they afforded those squeamish about attending the theater the opportunity to hear Shakespeare's words spoken by a professional actor or actress. In another letter, dated March 1865, to Louise and Frances Norcross, Dickinson gives an account of reading scenes from *Henry VI* Part 1 and Part 2 in the attic, after a period of eye trouble when she was forbidden from reading: "I read a few words since I came home – John Talbot's parting with his son, and Margaret's with Suffolk. I read them in the garret, and the rafters wept" (L304). In a culture that esteemed declamation and oration, Dickinson believed herself to be a good reader, who could bring Shakespeare's characters to life – the rafters were certainly moved.

Shakespeare's cultural omnipresence in America was also a direct result of his popularity and prominence on the stage, where his plays were enjoyed by heterogeneous audiences and performed alongside afterpieces and divertissements, which "*integrated* [Shakespeare] into American culture."[12] On September 9, 1851, when Dickinson's sister, Lavinia, most likely accompanied by Austin – and perhaps Dickinson – saw *Othello* at the Boston Museum, the play was performed alongside other forms of entertainment, including singing, dancing, and a farce (Leyda I, 211). Dickinson lived through a good proportion of the century when attitudes toward Shakespeare were shifting. Whereas the popular Shakespeare of the stage had existed alongside the erudite Shakespeare of the schoolroom and periodical, by the end of the century Shakespeare came to be predominantly associated with scholarship, sophistication, education, and cultural standards, and opposed to lowbrow entertainment. Even before this time, the highbrow Shakespeare was deployed by Americans who cherished their Anglo-Saxon origins as a defense against multiculturalism. For them, Shakespeare was a vital component in the nation's educational, cultural, and political system; they used Shakespeare's authority and supremacy to ensure that English language and literature were fundamental to American national identity.

Dickinson draws on features of the public side of Shakespeare's reception in her appropriation of his works in her letters and poems. She first referred to Shakespeare in two letters from 1845, both addressed to her friend Abiah Root. In the first, dated May 7, Dickinson commented that the "bustling" and "whizzing about" of a fellow student at Amherst Academy reminded her of "Shakespeare's description of a tempest in a teapot" (L6); this allusion could be to any number of speeches from Shakespeare's plays, for example, Puck's account of the foolishness of the lovers in the forest scenes from *A Midsummer Night's Dream*.[13] In the second, written on September 25, Dickinson's expression of sadness, "Since I wrote you last, the summer is past and gone, and autumn with the sere and yellow leaf is already upon us" (L8), quotes directly from Macbeth's words: "my way of life / Is fallen into the sear, the yellow leaf" (5.3.22–3). In these early letters and in many later ones, Dickinson participated in her culture's love of quoting from and alluding to Shakespeare, and assimilating his works into daily life; after the Bible, his works were the texts to which she most frequently referred.[14] In other letters, she acknowledged his central role in her intellectual and literary development, comparing his influence to that of her beloved sister-in-law, Susan Gilbert Dickinson (L757), and her friend and mentor Thomas Wentworth Higginson (L593).

In letters, Dickinson usually placed his words or her paraphrased version of them in quotation marks, using Shakespeare to display her cultivation and education, and also to entertain and amuse her correspondents by wittily and provocatively connecting her circumstances and theirs to Shakespeare's plays. Shakespeare was part of forging intimacies through epistolary communication, especially with female correspondents. She assumed her correspondents shared her love and knowledge of Shakespeare, and expected them to understand each allusion and how it related to her letter as a whole. But sometimes her references are so coded that only her most intimate correspondents could have possibly understood. For example, critics debate the meaning of her references to *Antony and Cleopatra* in letters to Susan Dickinson: do they have biographical import, in which the poet saw herself as a self-divided Antony and Sue as a seductive Cleopatra? Or do they merely indicate Dickinson's philosophical and aesthetic appreciation of "Cleopatra as a sign of the infinite attraction of that which is unknowable and unknown"?[15]

Regardless, like her contemporaries, Dickinson domesticated and localized Shakespeare's works, and claimed ownership of them. To take an example, on April 17, 1886, Dickinson, in one of her last letters, told her aunt Elizabeth Currier:

> "I do remember an Apothecary" said that sweeter Robin than Shakespeare, was a loved paragraph which has lain on my Pillow all Winter, but perhaps Shakespeare has been "up street" oftener than I have, this Winter. Would Father's youngest Sister believe that in the "Shire Town," where he and Blackstone went to school, a man was hung in Northampton yesterday for the murder of a man by the name of Dickinson, and that Miss Harriet Merrill was poisoned by a strolling Juggler, and to be tried in the Supreme Court next week? Don't you think Fumigation ceased when Father died? Poor, romantic Miss Merrill! But perhaps a Police Gazette was better for you than an Essay - (L1041).

Here her aunt is transported to this most intimate scene in which Dickinson lies with an edition of *Romeo and Juliet* on her pillow. The reference to Romeo's quest for a dram of poison (5.1.37) may suggest that Dickinson, like Romeo, has been contemplating death. But she used this line in an earlier letter – Dickinson had a fondness for reusing her favorite Shakespearean references – to thank her cousin Fanny Norcross for her recipe for graham bread by light-heartedly comparing it to Romeo's desired-for apothecary (L737). As is often the case, Shakespeare is integrated into Dickinson's hyperbolic style and wry sense of humor. In the later letter, Dickinson comically contrasts the life-weary and soon-to-be-dead Romeo and her convalescing, bed-bound self with an energetic Shakespeare. Shakespeare is literally "up street" because the events of *Romeo and Juliet* have been "unconsciously" reenacted by Amherst locals: the murdered Moses Billings Dickinson and executed murderer Allen J. Adams are equivalent to the victims of the Capulet and Montague feud, and the poisoned spinster Miss Merrill and the "Juggler," her much younger husband Dr. De Vore, are distorted versions of Juliet and Romeo (Leyda II, 468–9). Here and in other letters, Dickinson utilizes his works in a manner comparable to their appropriation by the period's Shakespeare burlesques, two of which were performed in Amherst College in the early 1880s. Like these popular burlesques, Dickinson "elevat[es] a daily occurrence, by a strained hyperbole of language, into a situation of classic dignity" or "[invests] subjects or events of 'great pith and moment' in the costume and dialect of vulgar life."[16] This burlesquing of Shakespeare demonstrates that his power and authority in America were inextricably connected with the way his works seemed to facilitate, invite, and encourage appropriation.

Although Shakespearean allusions and echoes are less frequent in Dickinson's poetry, some poems do explicitly feature his characters, phrases, or tropes.[17] In one such poem, Dickinson mentions Shakespeare by name, but instead of praising him she points to the limitations of his art:

> Drama's Vitallest Expression is the Common Day
> That arise and set about Us -
> Other Tragedy
>
> Perish in the Recitation -
> This - the best enact
> When the Audience is scattered
> And the Boxes shut -
>
> "Hamlet" to Himself were Hamlet -
> Had not Shakespeare wrote -
> Though the "Romeo" left no Record
> Of his Juliet,
>
> It were infinite enacted
> In the Human Heart -
> Only Theatre recorded
> Owner cannot shut -
>
> (F776 J741)

Whereas in letters Dickinson seems to aggrandize her friends, family, and acquaintances through Shakespearean association, here she reverses this, suggesting that the infinitely and internally enacted dramas of their "Common" lives are more "Vital" than his staged tragedies: it is Shakespeare's plots, lines, or characters that are revitalized through such contemporary application. Dickinson's undermining of Shakespeare's literary authority evokes the skepticism in her culture about his value; by making him the playwright of finite public dramas, she produces a space for herself as the poet of the secret theater of the human heart. The poem confirms that Shakespeare's plays and, in particular, Dickinson's experience of reading them aloud, had a profound influence on her creation of dramatic lyrics and presentation of an array of voices that dramatize a range of different emotional, existential, and cerebral states. Referring to this, Susan Howe comments, "Anonymous shape-changer, she carried the concealing farther. Her poems are monologues without a named narrator, their supreme source is Shakespeare."[18] Whereas Shakespeare's carefully delineated characters die at the end of the play, Dickinson's mysterious speakers experience the highs and lows of Shakespearean drama condensed and truncated into lyric form; they communicate without theatrical props, scene-setting devices, or character introductions until their voices fade into silence rather than move toward a denouement or resolution. So whereas Shakespeare's plays perish in recitation and end when theaters shut, Dickinson's poems do not.

That Dickinson wanted her poems, unlike Shakespeare's plays, to remain unfinished and open-ended is made very apparent when we examine poems in which she alludes to his works. For when Dickinson includes Shakespearean phrases, characters, or imagery, the context they provide fails to stabilize and instead expands the poem's interpretative possibilities. For example, the poem "What if I say I shall not wait!" (F305 J277) seems to evoke *Hamlet:*

> What if I say I shall not wait!
> What if I burst the fleshly Gate -
> And pass Escaped - to thee!
>
> What if I file this mortal - off -
> See where it hurt me - That's enough -
> And step in Liberty!
>
> They cannot take me - any more!
> Dungeons can call - and Guns implore -
> Unmeaning - now - to me -
>
> As laughter - was - an hour ago -
> Or Laces - or a Travelling Show -
> Or who died - yesterday!

The allusion to Hamlet's famous line about shuffling off "this mortal coil" might suggest that this poem is Dickinson's version of Hamlet's "To be or not to be" speech (3.1.55–89); like Hamlet, her speaker contemplates suicide and sees it as a means of achieving personal liberty and ending the uncertainty and misfortunes that accompany life. Or perhaps this is Dickinson's shortened account of the entire play, as the final stanza's "laughter," "Laces," "Travelling Show," and one "who died yesterday" might refer respectively to the court jester Yorick; the fine clothing of the Danish court; the visiting troupe of players; and the death of Ophelia. Yet Dickinson's speaker does not experience Hamlet's trademark hesitancy or his fears about death, and, in fact, sounds more like a dagger-wielding Juliet or Othello. Like these characters, Dickinson's speaker believes he or she will be reunited with a beloved figure, free of the oppressive forces that prevented their love. But what happens next? Instead of offering interpretative closure, Dickinson's Shakespearean reference draws attention to the generic difference between his character-driven, climax-reaching dramas and her lyrics spoken by unnamed figures who simply stop speaking.

Nineteenth-century Americans were given mixed cultural signals about Shakespeare, warned against him and encouraged to read him: he was immoral, elitist, and anti-American; or he was a moral guide, a popular entertainer, and so thoroughly American that he united the country's diverse population. Women, in particular, found it easy to relate to this multifarious Shakespeare: like them he was both a cultural insider and outsider; his powers of sympathy and identification were abilities culturally associated with femininity. For women writers, Shakespeare was not an oppressive or stifling male force, but an enabling, inspiring, and almost nurturing one, and his achievement of literary immortality while circumventing personal revelation was a feat they sought to replicate. Similarly, Shakespeare was Dickinson's supreme literary model, and she absorbed his works into her life and writings, yet she also carefully differentiated her words from his to assert her identity as a fellow writer.

NOTES

1 Gary Taylor, *Reinventing Shakespeare: A Cultural History from the Restoration to the Present* (London: Vintage, 1991), 168.
2 Ralph Waldo Emerson, *The Collected Works of Ralph Waldo Emerson*, ed. Alfred R. Ferguson et al., 5 vols. (Cambridge, MA: Harvard University Press, 1971–94), Vol. IV, 121.
3 Heman Humphrey, *Domestic Education* (Amherst: JS & C Adams, 1840), 94–5.
4 Mabel Loomis Todd, ed., *Letters of Emily Dickinson*, 2 vols. (Boston: Roberts Brothers, 1894), Vol. I, 129–30.
5 Páraic Finnerty, "Queer Appropriations: Shakespeare's Sonnets and Dickinson's Love Poems," *Borrowers and Lenders: The Journal of Shakespeare and Appropriation*, *3* (2008). Available at: http://www.borrowers.uga.edu/781869/display.
6 Richard Grant White, *Memoirs of the Life of William Shakespeare* (Boston: Little Brown, 1865), x.
7 Kim C. Sturgess, *Shakespeare and the American Nation* (Cambridge: Cambridge University Press, 2004), 46, 47.
8 Herman Melville, "Hawthorne and His Mosses," *The Literary World* (August 17, 1850), 126.
9 Walt Whitman, *Prose Works 1892*, ed. Floyd Stovall, 2 vols. (New York University Press, 1863), Vol. II, 388.
10 Michael Bristol, *Shakespeare's America, America's Shakespeare* (London: Routledge, 1990), 10.
11 Richard Whately, *Elements of Rhetoric, Comprising the Substance of the Article in the Encyclopaedia Metropolitana*, 3rd ed. (Oxford: John Murray, 1830), 364.

12 Lawrence W. Levine, *Highbrow / Lowbrow: The Emergence of Cultural Hierarchy in America* (Cambridge, MA: Harvard University Press, 1988), 23.
13 William Shakespeare, *The Comedies, Histories, Tragedies and Poems of William Shakespeare; The Pictorial and National Edition*, ed. Charles Knight, 8 vols. (Brown: Little Brown and Company, 1853), 3.2.110–15. All subsequent references are to Knight's edition.
14 See Capps, 61–2, 67, 168–9.
15 Páraic Finnerty, *Emily Dickinson's Shakespeare* (Amherst, MA: University of Massachusetts Press, 2006), 157.
16 Charles Cowden-Clarke, "On the Comic Writers of England. VII. – Burlesque Writers," *Gentleman's Magazine*, 5 (1871), 557.
17 See F266 J247; F1489 J1463; F869 J939; F1247 J1175; F1348 J1279.
18 Susan Howe, *My Emily Dickinson* (Berkeley, CA: North Atlantic Books, 1985), 71.

CHAPTER 8

Renaissance and Eighteenth-Century Literature
David Cody

The nature and extent of Emily Dickinson's engagements with literary works produced in England between the late sixteenth and the late eighteenth centuries have long been a subject of considerable interest to students of her work. We might note at the outset that in any enterprise of this sort the writings of Shakespeare and the King James Bible loom so large that they require – and, in the present work, duly receive – chapters of their own. The present essay, therefore, is concerned with Dickinson's encounters with other significant works, both in poetry and in prose, which appeared during this period of more than two hundred years.

Where some of this literary territory is concerned, there is very little to say. Dickinson's early letters in particular, however, are crowded with pregnant quotations and references, many of which have yet to be traced to their original sources.[1] Some invoke texts to which she had been exposed, more or less forcibly, at school, but others, generally of later date, are records of her own voluntary reading. Passages that she had encountered in anthologies, or in articles or essays in some contemporary periodical, may serve, of course, as hints revealing some aspects of her larger intellectual, spiritual, and poetic endeavors. Both a prodigious reader and an enthusiastic borrower, she was also quite capable of closing the "Valves of her attention," and in fact left a remarkable number of important authors and works not only unmentioned but, for all we know, unperused (F409 J303). In his edition of her letters Thomas H. Johnson identified sources for many of her overt allusions and quotations, and since then scholars have not only managed to identify sources for many others, but also detected (or supposed that they have detected) a number of additional quotations sans quotation marks, paraphrases, and "echoes" – real or imagined – in both the letters and the poems. Most of these quotations are from the Bible, Shakespeare, hymns, contemporary prose by authors ranging from Dickens to "Ik Marvell," and contemporary poetry, but we also encounter material borrowed from collections of proverbs, German grammars, old drinking songs, and many other unexpected sources. She quotes, for example, from Edward Young (1681–1785) in L14; from Thomas Gibbons, the biographer of Watts (1720–85) in L29; from Robert Burns (1759–96) in L31, L42, and L77; from Queen Elizabeth (1533–1603, from a letter to Lord Burghley) in L37; from Joshua Marsden, the English Wesleyan missionary and hymn-writer (1777–1837) in L43; from James Grahame, the Scottish poet (1765–1811) in L85; from Thomas Moore (1779–1852) in L542; and from the elder Samuel Butler (1612–80) in L560.

In many instances the charm, poignance, or gleeful humor that a letter might have held for its original reader will be lost on others unfamiliar with references and allusions that range from the commonplace to the deeply personal, private, and enigmatic. Attempts to document borrowings of this sort have been complicated by the fact that as she created her poems (reworking, rephrasing, distilling, transforming), her sources, however rich and strange in themselves, were often so thoroughly transmuted that they left barely a wrack behind, as though she had internalized Thomas Wentworth Higginson's suggestion (in his "Letter to a Young Contributor") that literature was an "attar of roses, one distilled drop from a million blossoms."[2] In some cases – when she mentions a particular author or work by name, or when the quotation is a commonplace – it is clear that she expected her reader to take up the reference, but where less obvious "echoes" are concerned the case for indebtedness, as we have already noted, becomes much more problematic. In her recent article on "Allusion, Echo, and Literary Influence in Emily Dickinson," Elizabeth A. Petrino points both to the benefits and the dangers inherent in such scholarship when she reminds us that Dickinson's poems and letters can evoke other literary works in ways that are "subtle and barely discernible," and that her poems in particular often "cast literary allusions subtly and anonymously."[3]

Those listening for such echoes must proceed, therefore, with great caution, if only because in finished poems they may be so faint, evanescent, and tenuous that belief in their ghostly existence may be a matter more of taste or faith than of actual evidence. We are often on firmer ground in her letters, but even in her most intimate correspondence Dickinson, so far from making a show of her knowledge, generally maintained a certain discreet reticence: she tended, as Nathaniel Hawthorne puts it in "The Custom House," to "keep the inmost Me behind its veil."[4] In the many hundreds of poems and letters still available for our perusal she fails to mention even the names of many then-canonical authors whose works must have been familiar to her. In an age when epistolary allusion was all the rage the number of canonical authors whom Dickinson fails to mention, invoke, or echo, however faintly, is surprisingly large. There is nothing to suggest, for example, that her interest in early Renaissance literature extended far beyond the aforementioned Shakespeare and the Bible. She mentions Francis Bacon only once, in L721 (1881), and then only to point out that to assume that he might have written Shakespeare's works was to pay him an undeserved compliment. On the other hand, internal evidence suggests at least the possibility that she may have been aware of and interested in authors whom she seems never to have mentioned by name. Ruth Miller's 1968 analysis of structural similarities between Dickinson's fascicles and Francis Quarles' *Emblems, Divine and Moral*, for example, helped to inspire an ongoing inquiry into Dickinson's relationship with the larger emblem tradition.[5] The list of worthies of this period (most of them dramatists) whom she appears to have ignored altogether, however, includes Beaumont, Dekker, Donne, Fletcher, Ford, Jonson, Kyd, Marlowe, Massinger, Middleton, Sidney, Spenser, Webster, and Tourneur.

Even Milton seems to have received little of her attention, though the landscape has altered somewhat since 1938, when George Frisbie Whicher could still suggest that "There is no positive indication that Emily knew Chaucer or Spenser or Milton" (Whicher, 210). In 1966 Jack Capps suggested that a reference in L181 (1855) to "the maiden and married life of Mary Powell" was an indication that Dickinson's interest in Milton had led her to Ann Manning's biography of Milton's first wife; that in the Dickinson family copy of Charles A. Dana's *Household Book of Poetry* the last twenty lines of "Il Penseroso" and two ten-line passages from "L'Allegro" have been marked, perhaps by the poet herself; that Emily quoted from Milton's sonnet "To the Lord General Cromwell" in an 1884 letter to Mrs. Sweetser (L892); and that although she may have encountered it in George Eliot's *Daniel Deronda* L802's "Nothing is here but tears" (1883) is originally from *Samson Agonistes* (Capps, 71–2). That she was more familiar with *Paradise Lost* than these slim pickings might lead us to assume is suggested by quotations in two early letters in which Dickinson offers a cheerful and cheeky blend of literary and popular-cultural allusions. In L17, written to her brother Austin in 1847, she informs him that "I am anticipating much in seeing you on this week Saturday & you had better not disappoint me! I will harness the 'furies' & pursue you with a 'whip of scorpions,' which is worse, you will find, than the 'long oat' which you may remember." A quotation in a subsequent letter to Austin (L57, dating from October 10, 1851) makes it clear that Dickinson had been recalling *Paradise Lost* all along, for when she writes "How soon you will be here! Days, flee away - 'lest with a whip of *scorpions* I overtake your lingering!'" she is recalling the scene in which Death, the son of Satan and Sin and "Fierce as ten Furies," threatens his father before the gates of Hell: "Back to thy punishment / False fugitive! and to thy speed add wings, / Lest with a whip of scorpions I pursue / Thy lingering" (2.699–702). The reference in L17 to "the long oat" robs the Miltonic reference of a bit of its sting, for in the colloquial a horse (or a child) given "long oats" was being thrashed or whipped – an ordeal to which, apparently, Austin had at some point been subjected.

The nature and extent of Dickinson's purportedly more extensive relationship with the seventeenth-century English "metaphysical" poets is a subject that has engendered a great deal of scholarly interest – and debate. In this context "metaphysical" has long been employed to characterize a rather vague poetic tradition delighting in self-consciously learned, sophisticated, and often obscure language; ingenious, witty, and unexpected conceits; intense, extravagant, and fanciful verbal subtleties; and a certain passionate intensity where both the carnal and the spiritual are concerned. Where Dickinson's relationships with these seventeenth-century poets are concerned we have a bit more to go on, for occasional brief and fleeting references to and quotations from their works do in fact appear in her letters. A brief quotation appearing in L653 (1880), for example – a letter written by Dickinson to Thomas Wentworth Higginson, then mourning the recent death of his infant daughter Louisa – embodies both the promise and the difficulty of scholarship that seeks to understand the nature of her engagement with the metaphysicals: "'Twas noting some such Scene," Dickinson writes, "made Vaughn humbly say 'My Days that are at best but dim and hoary.' - I think it was Vaughn."

A general resemblance, a host of more specific similarities, Dickinson's own determinedly gnomic reticence where her own creative process was concerned, and the fact that she could indeed quote from a poem by Henry Vaughan are the sorts of things on which the suggestion that there was a substantial engagement between our poet and her spiritual ancestors among the Metaphysical poets has been based. For skeptics, on the other hand, that tentative "I think," that same gnomic reticence, and a few ancillary facts point toward a different conclusion. Her quotation is inaccurate, she misspells Vaughan's name, she does not appear to have mentioned him again, and so far as we know the Dickinson family libraries did not contain an edition of *Silex Scintillans* – all of which has suggested to some that Dickinson's engagement with Vaughan (and with the larger English "metaphysical" tradition of poetry as it manifested itself in the works of fellow poets such as John Donne, George Herbert, and Edmund Waller) may not, in fact, have been a particularly deep or significant one. We might begin by acknowledging that although several generations of scholars have labored in this particular vineyard, the work has been difficult and the harvest of proof a relatively scanty one, leaving plenty of room for supposition on both sides of the argument. As things stand at present, cases rest on relatively limited evidence, most of it in the form of Dickinson's brief and often apparently casual references to relevant authors, or equally brief and, as we have already seen, often inaccurate (as though recalled from memory) quotations from works with which she may have had only a passing acquaintance.

The most detailed summaries of the evidence for Dickinson's familiarity with works by Herbert, Crashaw, Marvell, and Vaughan have been made by Capps, Benjamin Lease, and a few other scholars, all of them obliged to make the best of limited material. Where Herbert is concerned, for example, we know that the family library held a copy of his *Poetical Works*; that lines from "The Church-Porch" were marked in pencil (perhaps by Dickinson herself) in Susan Dickinson's copy of *The Temple*; that two stanzas from Herbert's "Matin Hymn" were transcribed by Dickinson (who had encountered them, it appears, in *The Springfield Republican* for October 28, 1876); and that Millicent Todd Bingham, laboring under the impression that they were the poet's own work, later published this transcription in *Bolts of Melody* (1945) (Capps, 68–9). Lease believes that Dickinson was also familiar with Herbert's "Virtue," which she could have seen in the Dickinson family copy of Griswold's *Sacred Poets of England and America*.[6] Various works by Donne, Marvell, Crashaw, and others were also available to her in anthologies; while there is no reason to think that she would not have encountered them there, there is also very little evidence to prove that she did.

Few battles are so intense as those waged over the interpretation of Dickinson's poems, and over the decades many scholars have taken positions on one or the other side in this matter of possible influence. In *This Was a Poet* Whicher admitted a "close parallel between her work and that of Donne, Herbert, and Vaughan," but concluded that after all "she was not well acquainted with her distant predecessors," and subsequent critics including Ruth Miller, Gary Lee Stonum, and Sarah Emsley have doubted that any perceived indebtedness was substantial.[7] On the other hand, Judith Farr argued in 1961 that parallels between Dickinson's verse and that of Donne and Herbert were "not accidental," and thereafter Capps, Cristanne Miller, Lease, and Scholl went even further: Capps, for example, saw Dickinson as "highly susceptible to the imagery of the metaphysical poets," Miller identified Herbert as one of Dickinson's "favorite writers," and Lease included "the devotional poetry of ... Herbert and ...Vaughan" in his list of the "sacred texts" that elicited Dickinson's "most passionate involvement."[8] Richard Sewall occupied a middle ground when, in 1974, he acknowledged that Dickinson was "undoubtedly indebted" to the "seventeenth-century Metaphysicals," but concluded that her "more precarious stance, her more self-conscious, detailed, and poignant exploration of the dark interior, her distant and often paradoxical God, set her apart from these poets and made for a different rhythm and language" (Sewall II, 708).

Beyond the works of Shakespeare and the Bible, the only seventeenth-century author for whom Dickinson seems to have nursed a real passion was Sir Thomas Browne, who had been a favorite as well with Hawthorne, Melville, Poe, Emerson, Thoreau, and Higginson. Browne and "the Revelations" occupy two thirds of her prose universe in the now-famous list of favorite authors that Dickinson provided for Higginson in 1862: "You inquire my Books - for Poets - I have Keats - and Mr and Mrs Browning. For Prose - Mr Ruskin - Sir Thomas Browne - and the Revelations" (L261). At this point Shakespeare's may have been a name too sacred to invoke, but because all of the names that she does include had also been mentioned in Higginson's "Letter to a Young Contributor," and because she seems never to have mentioned Keats or Ruskin again, it has sometimes been assumed that she was being less than candid with the man who was becoming her "Preceptor," perhaps because she wanted to keep her true interests judiciously in the shade. Although Higginson had also mentioned Pope and Addison, whom he saw as epitomizing "the smoothness of the eighteenth century," no eighteenth-century author appears on Dickinson's list – like her preceptor, for whom Browne and Marvell embodied the "vital vigor" of the seventeenth century, Dickinson seems to have preferred vigor to smoothness.[9] Although a number of scholars have contributed to our understanding of the Browne–Dickinson relationship, there appears to be a good deal left to say. *Religio Medici* (1643) may well have been one of those works that Dickinson, in a letter to Joseph Lyman, referred to as her "dearest ones of time, the strongest friends of the soul,"[10] although after her initial mention of Browne she seems to have mentioned him only once more, in a draft fragment of a letter/poem probably intended for Judge Otis P. Lord: "My little devices to live till Monday would darken all your glee - for you have a good deal of glee (many a glee) in your nature's corners the most lurking - and never to be trusted as Brown said of sleep - without ones prayers - " (L695). Her reference is to the passage in *Religio Medici* in which Browne refers to sleep as "that death by which we may be literally said to die daily; a death which Adam died before his mortality; a death whereby we live a middle and moderating point between life and death. In fine, so like death, I dare not trust it without my prayers, and an half adieu unto the world, and take my farewell in a colloquy with God."[11]

Dickinson would have responded strongly to many such passages in *Religio Medici*, including Browne's passionate declarations of love for his friend, which seem to anticipate her own responses to Susan Dickinson and "Master." Browne's antiquarian musings, too, may have helped to shape some of her own poetic ventures into the same realm: "In Ebon Box, when years have flown" (F180 J169), for example, with its delicate, nostalgic references to "shriveled cheek" and "mouldering hand," artfully recalls both the macabre exhumations of the celebrated dead carried out with such grim delight by seventeenth-century enthusiasts and the general theme of Browne's *Hydriotaphia*. The rapturous appreciation of mid-nineteenth-century antiquarians for the "quaint" works of Browne, Robert Burton, Jeremy Taylor, and others of their ilk very probably influenced Dickinson's poetic efforts in the same vein, including "A precious - mouldering pleasure - 'tis - " (F595 J371) and "A Word dropped careless on a Page" (F1268 J1261). In her nature poetry, too, Dickinson shared Browne's perception that the natural world was a divinely written text equal with the Bible, a "universal and publick manuscript, that lies expansed unto the eyes of all," full of "mystical letters," "hieroglyphics," and "flowers of nature" from which it was possible to "suck divinity"; in the same way, when she describes Judgment Day in poems such as F653/J515 – "Circumference be full - / The long restricted Grave / Assert her Vital Privilege - / The Dust - connect - and live - / On Atoms - features place - " – she may be recalling his description (in *Religio Medici*) of physical palingenesis, which reads in part: "I beleeve that our estranged and divided ashes shall unite again: that our separated dust, after so many pilgrimages and transformations into the parts of minerals, plants, animals, elements, shall, at the voice of God, return into their primitive shapes, and join again to make up their primary and predestinate forms."[12]

Where the Augustans are concerned, things still remain as they were when Whicher suggested that "No eighteenth-century author, so far as we can judge, came very close to her."[13] Dickinson does not mention Dryden, or Sterne. A passing reference (in L685, written in 1881) to a "Little Boy" who had run away from home as "My pathetic Crusoe" seems to be her only mention of a work by Defoe. Swift is mentioned only once, in L393, and then not as a satirist but as a lover, in the company of Dante and Mirabeau. In L18, written while she was at school in 1847, she notes without enthusiasm that she is about to "recite a lesson in Pope's 'Essay on Man' which is merely transposition." Pope is alluded to again in L85, but never mentioned again. A playful and fairly detailed reference in L212 suggests familiarity with and perhaps fondness for Johnson's *Rasselas*. Exposed to some of Goldsmith's works at school, she refers to *The Vicar of Wakefield* in L285. Her only reference to a work by Cowper is to "John Gilpin's Ride," mentioned (and, in the first instance, misquoted) in two letters (L213 and L888). In letters both early and late (see, for example, L1, 13, 31, and 979) she quotes (more often and more extensively than we have tended to think) from Young's lugubrious *Night Thoughts* and from hymns by Watts and others. From the more congenial Robert Burns she quotes, as we have noted, with some frequency and a good deal of enthusiasm. Despite this paucity of references, it would probably be a mistake to conclude that Dickinson did not comprehend or internalize the neoclassical sensibility, for an occasional flash of wit suggests otherwise. In L141, for example, she invokes Joseph Addison in the course of a diatribe against George Allen, an "Amherst youth" whose rudeness at John Leland's tea-table (with Sue Dickinson in attendance, Allen had dared to praise the election of one of her father's bitter political rivals to the Massachusetts House of Representatives) she labels "the apex of human impudence." "If Addison were alive," she writes, "I would present him to him, as the highest degree of absurdity, which I had yet discerned." This allusion, loyally indignant, apparently casual but self-consciously "learned," will serve to remind us of the challenges still awaiting scholars who seek to shed light on the extent of Dickinson's familiarity with seventeenth- and eighteenth-century British literature. On the one hand, of course, it is possible that Addison was being introduced only in a general (and comedic) way, as an antiquated arbiter of taste. On the other, she may well have had a specific reference in mind – as, for example, the assertion in the *Spectator* No. 350 that a "[Bold] Spirit exerts it self in an impudent Aspect, an over-bearing Confidence, and a certain Negligence of giving Offence. This is visible in all the cocking Youths you see about this Town, who are noisy in Assemblies, unawed by the Presence of wise and virtuous Men; in a word, insensible of all the Honours and Decencies of human Life."[14] This, in turn, might suggest a greater degree of familiarity with Addison's works in particular (and, perhaps, with eighteenth-century literature in general) than event, occasion, or inclination gave her any reason to admit. In this as in so many other matters Dickinsonian, there is still much to discover.

Notes

1 As a rule Dickinson was careful to use quotation marks to avoid even the appearance of plagiarism, but this was not always the case where early letters are concerned. Two lengthy and apparently quintessentially Dickinsonian passages in L34, for example (the now-famous "Valentine" letter that became her first published work when it appeared in the Amherst *Indicator* in February 1850), were "borrowed" nearly verbatim (and without acknowledgment) from an unlikely source – two articles in the *Boston Medical and Surgical Journal* for 1846 and 1847.
2 Thomas Wentworth Higginson, "Letter to a Young Contributor," *Atlantic Monthly* (April, 1862), 410.
3 Elizabeth Petrino, "Allusion, Echo, and Literary Influence in Emily Dickinson," *EDJ*, *19*.1 (2010), 80.
4 Nathaniel Hawthorne, "The Custom House," *The Scarlet Letter* (Boston: Ticknor, Reed, and Fields, 1850), 6.
5 Ruth Miller, *The Poetry of Emily Dickinson* (Middletown, CT: Wesleyan University Press, 1968).
6 Benjamin Lease, *Emily Dickinson's Readings of Men and Books* (London: Macmillan, 1990), 64.
7 Whicher, 210. See also Miller, *The Poetry of Emily Dickinson*; Gary Lee Stonum, "Dickinson's Literary Background," *Handbook*, 44–60; Sarah Emsley, "Is Emily Dickinson a Metaphysical Poet?" *Canadian Review of American Studies/Revue Canadienne d'Etudes Américaines 33*.3 (2003), 249–65.
8 Judith Farr (as Judith Banzer), "'Compound Manner': Emily Dickinson and the Metaphysical Poets." *American Literature 32* (1961), 418; Capps, 66; Cristanne Miller, *Emily Dickinson, A Poet's Grammar* (Cambridge, MA: Harvard University Press, 1987), 138; Lease, *Emily Dickinson's Reading*, 35.
9 Higginson, "Letter," 405.
10 Richard Sewall, ed. *The Lyman Letters: New Light on Emily Dickinson and Her Family*. (Amherst: University of Massachusetts Press, 1965), 76.
11 Sir Thomas Browne, *Religio Medici*, in *Sir Thomas Browne's Works*, ed. Simon Wilkin. 4 vols. (London: William Pickering, 1835) II, 113.
12 Browne II, 21–2; 69.
13 Whicher, *This Was a Poet*, 211.
14 Joseph Addison, *The Works of Joseph Addison*. 3 vols. (New York, 1842), III, 57–8.

CHAPTER 9

British Romantic and Victorian Influences
Elizabeth A. Petrino

Writing in 1864 during the U.S. Civil War to her cousins, Louise and Frances Norcross, Dickinson comments on the importance of her transatlantic literary peers: "I noticed that Robert Browning had made another poem, and was astonished - till I remembered that I, myself, in my smaller way, sang off charnel steps" (L298). Even a brief survey of Romantic and Victorian writers suggests that her poetry grew in power and confidence as she carefully read and distinguished herself from them. Based on the markings in several volumes from the family library, now housed at Harvard, and the periodicals read by her family, we might infer the importance of the Romantics and Victorians to Emily Dickinson and other readers of her generation. Typical pencil markings include vertical lines or double parallel lines drawn in margins, brackets, dots or "x's" placed against titles, turned corners of pages, wavy lines, and the occasional question mark or, rarely, word. Because these volumes were owned and read by others, the methodological difficulty of deciding which markings were Emily Dickinson's presents a challenge. Beyond these markings, one might also consider how newspapers and magazines solidified the reputations of British authors and spread their works abroad. Present not only in the volumes in her family's library, British writers were also familiar figures in genteel literary journals, such as *The Atlantic Monthly* and *Harper's Magazine*. Essays and reviews often quoted large swaths of their poems and frequently recounted their life histories and personal views. Focusing on John Keats, George Gordon Byron, Percy Bysshe Shelley, William Wordsworth, and Alfred Tennyson, I argue that Dickinson distinguished herself from her Romantic precursors and Victorian peers in several ways. She shared the Romantics' affection for nature and Keats's tendency to subsume his voice as the "camelion Poet" into the landscape.[1] But she rejected Keats's quest for literary fame, as well as Wordsworth's and Shelley's desire to employ a prophetic voice and to draw analogies between nature and human beings. Instead, like Tennyson, who wrote during the Crimean War (1853–56),

Dickinson's exposure to scientific and medical advancements during the Civil War led to a heightened concern about distinguishing between mental and physical states. Whereas many Victorian writers questioned the limits of knowledge even while firmly held in the grip of religious orthodoxy, Dickinson explored bodily states outside of religious doctrine and found in nature an antidote to metaphysical anxiety.

John Hollander explores intertextual resonance not only through direct quotation or allusion but echo – the fragmentary, subtle, often barely heard phrases, sounds, and cadences of precursor texts. Rebecca Harding Davis's "Life in the Iron Mills; or, the Korl Woman," for instance, appeared in 1861 in *The Atlantic Monthly*, an issue that Dickinson sought to borrow from her sister-in-law, Susan Gilbert. Davis's epigraph directly alludes to these lines from Tennyson's *In Memoriam*: "O life as futile, then, as frail! / O for thy voice to soothe and bless! / What hope of answer, or redress? / Behind the veil, behind the veil."[2] Published in 1850, though written as a series of elegies over a twelve-year period, Tennyson's *In Memoriam* concerns the death of Arthur Hallam, his friend, fellow poet, and the fiancé of his sister. Davis's allusion to Tennyson emphasizes the degree to which Americans revered his poetry and shared his view about the inadequacy of language to express human tragedy. In contrast to quotation or allusion, Hollander contends that literary echoes may appear through a chain of references because "we may observe that even some well-known and often-heard resonances are frequently reechoes, and that allusive fragments occur in chains of rebound."[3] Turning to several Romantic and Victorian writers, we can explore how Dickinson's poems and letters rework key themes through echoes in creative and generative ways rather than through direct quotation or allusion.

BYRON AND KEATS

Byron figured prominently in the popular mind of the generation immediately preceding Dickinson's as a soldier of fortune, lover, and poet, a figure both to be admired and avoided. She pored over Byron's travel poem "Childe Harold's Pilgrimage" and the melancholy "The Corsair," which explore the struggles of the solitary hero against society and the limits of illicit erotic desire. But she also delighted in the satirical mock-epic *Don Juan*, which stages a critique of Romantic high seriousness, attacking Wordsworth for being "unintelligible" and reducing Coleridge from poet to mere "metaphysician."[4] Dickinson also admired "The Prisoner of Chillon" for its elevation of the inner wealth that resulted from solitude.

Written in 1816, Byron's "The Prisoner of Chillon" concerns the fate of Francois Bonnivard, a political prisoner, whose forced exile prompts him to recognize his inner liberty. As Christopher Benfey explains, "What Byron's poetry promised – for Stowe, Dickinson, and Henry James – was escape from the wintry prison-house of custom and Calvinism, and access instead to nature and to feeling."[5] Captured in her frequent shorthand references to "Chillon," Dickinson's affection for Byron underscores the degree to which he represented liberation from Calvinistic conceptions of self-hood and puritanical attitudes toward sexuality. "'Chillon' is not funny," she writes in a letter to her unnamed "Master," alluding to Bonnivard's forced exile as a trope for her own separation (L233). Her familiarity with Byron's reputation as a scandalous charismatic hero and playboy was furthered by Edward John Trelawney's 1859 *Recollections of the Last Days of Byron and Shelley* and an 1869 article by Stowe, "The True Story of Lady Byron's Life," in which she defended Lady Byron against charges of being a "narrow-minded, cold-hearted precisian, without sufficient intellect to comprehend [Byron's] genius or heart to feel for his temptations," lodged by his Italian mistress, Countess Guiccioli.[6] During her medical treatment in Boston, Dickinson wrote to her sister, Lavinia, about her self-chosen and productive isolation: "You remember the Prisoner of Chillon did not know Liberty when it came, and asked to go back to Jail" (L293).

Besides her immersion in Byron, Dickinson was familiar with Keats's major poems through Charles Anderson Dana's *The Household Book of Poetry* (1860), containing fourteen of Keats's poems, and Robert Chambers's *Cyclopedia of English Literature* (1844), which includes a biographical essay and several poems.[7] Similarly, two essays, "Recollections of Keats," written by "An Old School-Fellow" (1861), and Joseph Severn's "The Vicissitudes of Keats's Fame" (1863), both published in *The Atlantic Monthly*, testify to the poet's desire for posthumous fame, which might have sparked Dickinson's meditations on the same theme. Thomas Wentworth Higginson's "The Life of Birds," published in *The Atlantic Monthly* in 1862, further stresses Keats's descriptive fidelity to nature and enshrines his fame. In contrast, Dickinson writes that "Fame is a fickle food," since "Men eat of it and die" (F1702 J1659). Besides reflecting on the delusiveness of literary fame, a view strengthened by reading about critical attacks on his poetry and his self-perceived failure as a poet, she shared Keats's desire to subsume the individual's perspective and expressed a skeptical view of nature's constancy. In an 1818 letter to Richard Wodehouse, Keats distinguished his poetical character from "the wordsworthian or egotistical sublime" in favor of a morally neutral negative capability that "has no self – it is every thing and nothing ... [w]hat shocks the virtuous philosop[h]er, delights the camelion Poet."[8] As Joanne Feit Diehl explains, "For both, negative capability combines an inclusive receptivity, a refusal to take sides, and the willingness to lose one's individuality in unmediated experience."[9] Dickinson shares Keats's "negative capability" that effaces the poet's perspective and offers a radical openness toward multiple points of view. In "Midsummer, was it, when They died - " (F822 J962), she recasts the imagery of Keats's "To Autumn" to suggest that seasonal change reveals mortality and undercuts the celebration of ripeness. Keats's images, such as "a wailful choir" of gnats that follow the "river sallows, borne aloft / Or sinking as the light wind lives or dies," meditate on death by contrasting the fall's plenitude with the coming winter.[10] Dickinson similarly conveys the mortality underpinning human life: rather than fall's harvest, midsummer offers a "Consummated Bloom" that implies the season comes to its close at its zenith, rather than its waning.

Dickinson also registers Keats's awareness that the perception of natural constancy, while appealing to our human needs, is delusive. Keats's "On the Grasshopper and the Cricket" might reflect his belief in the continuity of nature, as the grasshopper delves into "summer luxury," singing until "tired out with fun."[11] Despite the winter's arrival, however, the cricket's call tricks the listener "in drowsiness half lost" into thinking "the Grasshopper's among some grassy hills."[12] Dickinson tersely portrays the theme of unfulfilled promises held out by nature's signs:

> September's Baccalaureate
> A combination is
> Of Crickets - Crows - and Retrospects
> And a dissembling Breeze
>
> That hints without assuming -
> An Innuendo sear
> That makes the Heart put up it's Fun -
> And turn Philosopher.
>   (F1313 J1271)

"Crickets - Crows - and Retrospects" echoes Keats's autumnal imagery but transforms the mellifluous nightingale popular among the Romantics into the harsh, grating sound of the crow. "Retrospects" summarizes the speaker's delusive winter reflection on the fullness of mid-summer, when birdsong and chirping grasshoppers promise the continuation of life, aptly suggested in the line "The poetry of the earth is ceasing never."[13] Whereas

Keats's poem invokes the theme of sleep and dreaming to explore our tendency toward self-delusion, Dickinson never allows us to transform nature into our own reality. In her stoicism, she translates the voice of nature into "a dissembling Breeze / That hints without assuming." With its pun on "seer"/"sear," an "Innuendo sear" implies that the higher vision afforded by the autumn asks the reader to turn away from a complacent belief in nature's continuity and "turn Philosopher."

WORDSWORTH AND SHELLEY

In contrast to her affinity for Keats, Dickinson drew more selectively from Shelley and Wordsworth, who tend to animate nature through a prophetic voice. In *The Prelude,* Wordsworth contends that nature contains for the impassioned soul the "characters of the great Apocalypse, / The types of symbols of Eternity."[14] For him, nature responds organically to human life – what Paul de Man calls the "intimate and sympathetic contact between human and natural elements."[15] Whereas other American Romantic writers, such as Walt Whitman and Ralph Waldo Emerson, embraced the reading of "types" and "symbols" in nature, Dickinson rejected the philosophical moments of the British Romantic poets in favor of their salient images. In the volume of Shelley's poems she shared with Susan Gilbert, his most striking intellectual poems, such as "The Sunset," "Hymn to Intellectual Beauty," and "Mont Blanc," are unnoted. Rather, maritime imagery, such as the lines "Many a green isle needs must be / In the deep wide sea of misery, / Or the mariner, worn and wan, / Never thus could voyage on," is bracketed from "Lines Written Among the Eugenean Hills."[16]

Similarly, in reading Wordsworth's "Elegiac Stanzas, suggested by a Picture of Peele Castle," Dickinson found an image of integrity and the survival of grief amidst a solitary life. Wordsworth wrote the poem to commemorate his brother's death by drowning, which occurred while he summered there, as well as the effect suffering had on his perceptions of the landscape. Recalled through his memory, stimulated by the painting, Wordsworth's grief over his brother's death transforms his impressions of the landscape, as he laments his inability to represent the still, serene atmosphere:

> Ah! Then, if mine had been the Painter's hand,
> To express what then I saw; and add the gleam,
> The light that never was, on sea or land,
> The consecration, and the Poet's dream .... [17]

Referring twice to *Elegiac Stanzas* in her letters, Dickinson might have been reminded of the sea imagery and fortress-like castle, symbols of the individual's triumph over loss, like Shelley's mariner at sea. In an 1866 letter to Mrs. Holland, she writes about spring's arrival: "Here is the 'light' the Stranger said 'was not on land or sea.' Myself could arrest it but we'll not chagrin Him" (L315). Although we might understand her confidence to "arrest" the light, why does Dickinson call Wordsworth a "Stranger," if his lines resonated with her? The answer might lie in his conviction that natural and human worlds were relatable. In 1873, writing to Louise and Frances Norcross, Dickinson questions the ability to ascertain the reality of other beings except imaginatively: "I wish you were with me, not precisely here, but in those sweet mansions the mind likes to suppose.... 'The light that never was on sea or land' might just as soon be had for the knocking" (L394).

While she selectively refers to Wordsworth, Dickinson rejects Shelley's prophetic voice and tendency to etherealize nature. Shelley's "To a Skylark," marked with an "x" next to its title, emphasizes the bird's elusive and disembodied presence, as he portrays birdsong as natural and unpremeditated poetry:

> Hail to thee, blithe Spirit!
> Bird thou never wert,
> That from Heaven, or near it,
> Pourest thy full heart
> In profuse strains of unpremeditated art.[18]

Shelley uses direct address ("Hail to thee, blithe Spirit!") to signal an "I/Thou" relationship with the bird as a representation of poetic inspiration. The abstract skylark originates ambiguously either "from Heaven, or near it," suggesting that nature serves as a substitute for its divine origins. Unseen, but heard through calls of "shrill delight," the bird can be grasped only through emotion.[19] Using a series of analogies to define its presence – a poet, captive, glowworm, and rose – Shelley cannot ascertain the bird's essence except through comparisons to actual natural phenomena. Drawing an analogy between the bird's call of "unpremeditated art" and the poet, who sings "hymns unbidden," Shelley seeks to embody in his own voice the "harmonious madness" of its song.[20]

Although the European skylark, cuckoo, and nightingale represent spiritual transcendence for British Romantics, the North American hummingbird, bobolink, robin, blue jay, sparrow, and other birds in Dickinson's lyrics do not promise a resurgence of confidence. Rather,

Dickinson's lyric beginning "'Hope' is the Thing with Feathers" (F314 J254) explores precisely the inner state of being – hope – that the bird symbolizes. Most notably, the apostrophe is absent: whereas Shelley addresses the skylark, Dickinson internalizes the bird, stressing its concrete though undefined form and removing the sacred connotation. Like Robert Frost's oven bird that "knows in singing not to sing,"[21] her bird "perches in the soul - / And sings the tune without the words - " (F314 J254). Whereas Shelley imagines that he will become "the trumpet of a prophecy" (as he notes in "Ode to the West Wind") through which nature speaks, Dickinson does not take a vatic stance: the bird communicates directly and outside of language to the soul.[22] This inner voice sustains us in adversity and is accentuated by difficulties, as the speaker notes that hope is heard "sweetest" in the "Gale." The geographical locations where it appears – the "chillest land" and "strangest Sea" – suggest that hope survives despite dire circumstances. Although Shelley listens to the skylark and wishes to be taught to sing, Dickinson reverses the equation between poet and nature: rather than expect a "crumb," her bird or poet relies on its inner resources, a lesson we need to learn to survive trials "in Extremity." Dickinson's anti-prophetic voice does not attempt to speak for others, nor does she assert any truth outside of her own experience of nature.

TENNYSON AND THE VICTORIANS

In contrast to Romantic views that nature responded sympathetically to human desires, Dickinson embraced Victorian writers who explored scientifically and stylistically the relation between physical and spiritual realms. Even before Charles Darwin penned *The Origin of Species* (1859), geological study had begun to dislodge the notion of a divine world order. Dickinson's textbooks at Mount Holyoke Female Seminary included Edward Hitchcock's *Elementary Geology* (1842), which sought to reconcile evolutionary science and religion. The rise of archaeology and travel to Old World sites further supported the view that the creation followed a vaster period of time than identified in Genesis. As Robert Ross claims, scientific determinism held "that the cosmos is a purposeless agglomeration of matter; that Nature, contrary to the Romantic view, is neither sentient nor benign ...; and that life is controlled by mechanical laws of necessity which preclude both free will in man and cosmic control by God."[23] Challenging the predominant Christian narrative, Elizabeth

Barrett Browning in her 1844 "A Drama of Exile" recounts the expulsion of Adam and Eve from paradise to allow Eve a greater, more rational voice. Dickinson was deeply influenced by her verse-novel *Aurora Leigh* (1857), framed with evocations of Genesis and Revelations at beginning and end, which explores a female artist's creativity. Robert Browning's *Dramatis Personae* (1864) and *The Ring and the Book* (1869) also employ dramatic monologues that might have been the model for Dickinson's staged conversations of a "supposed person" (L268). Through their use of literary personae and dialogue, Robert and Elizabeth Barrett Browning imply that various individual perspectives might be equally valid within a seemingly coherent worldview.

Tennyson's *In Memoriam* also captivated Dickinson, perhaps for its exploration of metaphysical and physical realms. Among the poem's central themes are distrust of nature to respond sympathetically to human suffering and the belief that language may be inadequate to conveying human experience. But whereas Tennyson often vacillates between Christian piety and nihilism, Dickinson explores these limits through bodily states outside of religious orthodoxy. Marked with light pencil in Dickinson's copy, the following lines of Tennyson meditate on nature's obscurity and convey the difficulty of language to express human grief:

> I sometimes hold it half a sin
> To put in words the grief I feel;
> For words, like Nature, half reveal
> And half conceal the Soul within.
>
> But, for the unquiet heart and brain,
> A use in measured language lies;
> The sad mechanic exercise,
> Like dull narcotics, numbing pain.
>
> In words, like weeds, I'll wrap me o'er,
> Like coarsest clothes against the cold:
> But that large grief which these enfold
> Is given in outline and no more.[24]

As "narcotics" suggests, advances in medical technology – in anesthesia, antisepsis, and x-rays – allowed the Victorians to explore the suspension of sensation. Despite these achievements, they could not be sure that ether completely anesthetized patients because they often moved or moaned during surgery. For Tennyson, "measured language" might evoke a steady rhythm and decorous speech that, like narcotics, were thought to still the "unquiet" mind.

Dickinson transforms the "measured language" that allays grief into the actual bodily experience of grieving and the treading of the mourner:

> After great pain, a formal feeling comes -
> The Nerves sit ceremonious, like Tombs -
> The stiff Heart questions 'was it He, that bore,'
> And 'Yesterday, or Centuries before'?
>
> The Feet, mechanical, go round -
> A Wooden way
> Of Ground, or Air, or Ought -
> Regardless grown,
> A Quartz Contentment, like a stone -
>
> This is the Hour of Lead -
> Remembered, if outlived,
> As Freezing persons, recollect the Snow -
> First - Chill - then Stupor - then the letting go -
> (F372 J341)

Dickinson creatively reworks Tennyson's stanzas to transform grief into a bodily, rather than intellectual, experience. The mourner's inner monologue reflects the insular stages of grieving: the "stiff Heart" asks herself first in disbelief whether the trauma has been real, and, second, how much time has passed. Dickinson's "This World is not Conclusion" (F373 J501) similarly describes the inability for religion to redress spiritual doubt: "Narcotics cannot still the Tooth / That nibbles at the soul - ." Much as *In Memoriam* refutes the ability of traditional rituals to offer consolation, Dickinson implies that sacred rites, as suggested by a "formal feeling" and "ceremonious," cannot redress spiritual doubt or, perhaps, that these rituals afford comfort in the absence of larger consolatory myths. Either way, the experience of grief is intensely physical and registered through a near-death experience. Dickinson's poem describes the emptiness and sense of purposelessness in performing daily routines. "Ought" might imply those responsibilities that drive individuals forward or, alternatively, the sense of indifference and annihilation brought on by grief. In contrast to the Romantics, who sought to meld the self with nature, Dickinson underscores the impossibility of transcending the physical body. For Tennyson, language operates as a defense – "coarsest clothes against the cold" – even while he acknowledges its inability to express his inner pain. For Dickinson, each metaphor allows the speaker to inhabit more closely the feelings of the mourner, whose grieving resembles the stages of insensibility in freezing to death: "First - Chill - then Stupor - then the letting go - ." Like Tennyson's elegy, Dickinson's lyric attempts to move beyond individual, personal loss. But Dickinson finds the experience of grief more profoundly realized in imagining the bodily state of the mourner.

CONCLUSION

Although Dickinson admired the Romantic poets, she distanced herself from the prophetic voice that animated nature and asserted a sympathetic connection between the natural and human. Even more deeply than the British Victorians, she embraced the body and nature as her ultimate laboratory of the senses. Nevertheless, her affection for both Romantic and Victorian writers suggests that she was fully immersed in the transatlantic conversations of her age. Beyond these writers, other poets and novelists, including Robert Burns, Thomas De Quincey, Christina Rossetti, Charlotte and Emily Brontë, George Eliot, and Charles Dickens, among others, bear further scrutiny. In the cases of Keats and Tennyson, her lyrics evoke their lines through echoes, words, or images that deliberately recast many of their themes. As critics, we might consider, following Hollander, how Dickinson absorbed their influence without becoming overwhelmed. Reading her works against theirs provides an opportunity to engage in a stimulating and rich debate, across at least one continent and several national literary traditions, which underscores how her extraordinarily creative lyrics were formed in dialogue with other poets of the age.

NOTES

1 *Letters of John Keats*, ed. Robert Gittings (Oxford: Oxford University Press, 1970), 157.
2 Alfred, Lord Tennyson, *In Memoriam*, ed. Robert H. Ross (New York and London: Norton, 1973), 36, lines 25–8.
3 John Hollander, *The Figure of Echo: A Mode of Allusion in Milton and After* (Berkeley: University of California Press, 1984), 79–80.
4 *Byron: Poetical Works*, ed. Frederick Page (New York: Oxford University Press, 1970), 647, Canto XC, line 8; Canto XCI, line 8.
5 Christopher Benfey, *A Summer of Hummingbirds: Love, Art, and Scandal in the Intersecting Worlds of Emily Dickinson, Mark Twain, Harriet Beecher Stowe, and Martin Johnson Heade* (New York: Penguin, 2008), 131.
6 Quoted in ibid, 116.
7 I thank Tricia Kannen for mentioning these sources to me.
8 *Letters of John Keats*, 157.
9 Joanne Feit Diehl, *Dickinson and the Romantic Imagination* (Princeton, NJ: Princeton University Press, 1981), 99.
10 *Keats: Poetical Works*, ed. H. W. Garrod (Oxford: Oxford University Press, 1978), 219, lines 27–9.

11 Ibid., 40, lines 6–7.
12 Ibid., 40, lines 13–14.
13 Ibid., 40, line 9.
14 Quoted in Diehl, *Dickinson and the Romantic Imagination*, 35.
15 Paul de Man, *The Rhetoric of Romanticism* (New York: Columbia University Press, 1984), 77.
16 Percy Bysshe Shelley, *The Poetical Works* (Philadelphia, 1853), 242.
17 *Wordsworth: Poetical Works*, ed. Thomas Hutchinson, revised by Ernest De Selincourt, (London: Oxford University Press, 1969), 373, lines 13–16.
18 *Shelley: Collected Poetry*, ed. Neville Rogers (Oxford: Oxford University Press, 1968), 369, lines 1–5.
19 Ibid., 369, line 20.
20 Ibid, 320, line 38; 371, line 103.
21 *The Poetry of Robert Frost*, ed. Edward Connery Lathem (New York: Henry Holt and Company, 1969), 120.
22 *Shelley: Collected Poetry,* 357, line 69.
23 Tennyson, *In Memoriam*, 6 n. 3.
24 Ibid., 6, section 5, lines 1–12.

CHAPTER 10

Transatlantic Women Writers

Páraic Finnerty

Although Dickinson became increasingly committed to one location, her Amherst home, her poems use tropes and images of foreignness and exoticism, drawn from her extensive reading, to describe worldly and otherworldly journeys. Her fantasies of going "abroad" (F886 J784) reflect her nation's inescapable transatlantic and transnational connections, despite its declarations of cultural nationalism and emerging discourses of American exceptionalism. America's most reclusive poet was also a "virtual tourist" who imaginatively experienced environments both diverse and comparable.[1] Consequently, when Dickinson depicts intransigent confinement to one location, she asserts the power of the human mind to escape and transcend an oppressive locality. The most famous version of this motif appears in her poem, "They shut me up in Prose - " (F445 J613), in which an imprisoned "little Girl" describes the ability of her "Brain" to "go round," symbolized by a "Bird" who can escape the "Pound" he is lodged in and as "easy as a Star / Look down opon Captivity - / And laugh." In other poems, reading fuels the imagination's flight toward this roaming bird's eye view that invests human vision with personal freedom and a familiarity with foreignness. One poem declares there "is no Frigate like a Book / To take us Lands away" (F1286 J1263); in another, books grant a "Bequest of Wings," loosening the spirit with "Liberty" (F1593 J1587). Some of the literature that most nourished Dickinson's soul was written by her British female contemporaries, Emily and Charlotte Brontë, Elizabeth Barrett Browning, and George Eliot; and although her response to these writers registers a "complex of attitudes," their powerful influence on her writings and her artistic vocation is unquestionable.[2] Whereas other contemporary women writers wrote solely for social or ethical purposes, celebrating the domestic realm, innate female morality, and ideals of femininity associated with virtuousness, piousness, and wholesomeness, Dickinson's favorites, in their lives and in their fictional creations, aimed to challenge the valorization of the sentimental domestic sphere and of female submissiveness, passivity, and docility. These writers' often controversial works explicitly engaged from a female perspective with themes of freedom, travel, and captivity; they featured heroines that suffered as a result of, fought against, and sometimes triumphed over the limitations imposed on them. Dickinson transported these themes into her own poetry. In her admiration for and engagement with these writers, Dickinson participated in a larger cultural movement in which American women writers looked across the Atlantic to their European peers for models of female creativity and artistic professionalism.

That Dickinson's "little Girl" trapped in prose summons up a defiant, captivity-defying male bird to represent her powerful imagination evokes the frequent use of male pseudonyms by women writers. The most famous literary cross-dressers of her day were the Brontë sisters, Emily, Charlotte, and Anne, who published their 1846 poems and their subsequent novels as Ellis, Currer, and Acton Bell. Charlotte's explanation for this was recorded in Elizabeth Gaskell's *The Life of Charlotte Brontë* (1857), a book Dickinson owned: "we did not like to declare ourselves women, because without at the time suspecting that our mode of writing and thinking was not what is called 'feminine,' – we had a vague impression that authoresses are liable to be looked on with prejudice."[3] What Brontë acknowledged here is that their novels *Jane Eyre* (1847), *Wuthering Heights* (1847), and *The Tenant of Wildfell Hall* (1848) were initially condemned by reviewers on both sides of the Atlantic as immoral, coarse, and unnatural: these novels were not merely "unfeminine," they were regarded as improper. The American reviewer E. P. Whipple, writing in the *North American Review* in 1848, suggested that these novels by "the firm Bell & Co" have caused a national mental epidemic that he named "Jane Eyre fever," which produced a general outbreak of "moral and religious indignation."[4] Referring specifically to *Jane Eyre*, Whipple wondered if the controversy surrounding it was not the result of "some sly manufacturer of mischief [who hinted] that it was a book which no respectable man should bring into his family circle."[5] In a review of *Wuthering Heights*, G. W. Peck, writing in the *American Whig Review*, also in 1848, argued that "if we did not know that this book has been read by thousands of young ladies in the country, we should esteem it our first duty to caution them against it simply on account of the coarseness of the style."[6] The popularity of the Brontës' novels, exacerbated by their notoriety, was also due to the mystery that surrounded their authorship. Reviewers and readers wondered if these novels were written by a man or woman, or if they were the results of a literary collaboration by a man and woman. This latter suggestion was made by Whipple, who described *Jane Eyre*'s "unconscious feminine peculiarities, which the strongest-minded woman that ever aspired after manhood cannot suppress," and the "clear, distinct, decisive style of [the novel's] representation of character, manners, and scenery [which] continually suggests a male mind."[7] In her first reference to *Jane Eyre*, in a December 1849 letter to her friend Elbridge G. Bowdoin, on returning his copy of the novel, Dickinson writes, "If all these leaves were altars, and on every one a prayer that Currer Bell might be saved - and you were God - would you answer it?" (L28). The implication is that Dickinson and Bowdoin would save "Currer Bell," despite the controversy surrounding *Jane Eyre*. At this point, Dickinson would not have known that the Bells were women, a fact that was revealed a year later to the moral outrage of critics who regarded these women as appealing and intriguing but also "vaguely objectionable, troublesome figures."[8] It took Gaskell's aforementioned biography to transform the "reviled and dubious" Currer Bell into the revered Charlotte Brontë, "a saintly icon of female suffering."[9] One reviewer of this biography described it as equivalent to "one hero plac[ing] the laurel upon the dead brow of another. One hearty, religious, resolute woman comes to do womanly justice to another; womanly in its tenderness, its sympathy, and its power."[10] Another American reviewer, Margaret Sweat, suggested that Gaskell had vindicated the Brontës by showing that their novels were "the very outpouring of pent-up passion, the cry of fettered hearts, the panting of hungry intellects, restrained by the iron despotism of adverse and unconquerable circumstance."[11] These culturally isolated women, who experienced much heartbreak, suffering, and hardship, became at once representative female figures and exemplary artists who used their creativity as a means of escape.

Jane Eyre explores female confinement – Jane is "shut up" in the red room, made to stand still at Lowood School, and feels confined within Thornton Hall – and women's concomitant longing to evade the stillness to which they are doomed, voiced by Jane in the following passage:

> Women are supposed to be very calm generally: but women feel just as men feel; they need exercise for their faculties, and a field for their efforts as much as their brothers do; they suffer from too rigid a restraint, too absolute a stagnation, precisely as men would suffer.[12]

Action comes in the form of a romance with her employer, Mr. Rochester, who embodies Jane's desire for travel and adventure. Although curbed by her position as a woman and a governess, Jane demonstrates her freedom and independence of mind and quick imagination, especially in her playful and flirtatious dialogues with Rochester; these characteristics attract him to her. Rochester longs to possess the kind of personal autonomy Jane exudes. Although he has the freedom and wealth to travel, escaping to the continent in times of trouble, he remains psychologically imprisoned by his marital error. The attraction of *Jane Eyre* for women readers like Dickinson stems from its heroine's acquirement of the economic and external resources to complement her inner liberty. By the end of the novel the blind, physically wounded Rochester marries the newly wealthy, able-bodied Jane. Their happiness stems from their nonhierarchical relationship that unites a feminized man and masculinized woman. No longer Jane's "Master," he has truly become her "second self, and best earthly companion."[13] Dickinson drew on such ideas to construct and unsettle hierarchical relationships between the sexes in her hyperbolic "Master" letters (L187, 233, 248), for example, or poems such as "I rose - because He sank - " (F454 J616).

Wuthering Heights contrasts the shared freedom of Catherine and Heathcliff as children on the moors with the restraints imposed on them by the domestic arrangements at Wuthering Heights. In his review of the novel, Peck provocatively connected the protagonists' shared rebelliousness with American insurgence and nonconformity by noting that an entry in Catherine's makeshift diary was made in 1776, the year of the Declaration of American Independence: "Hindley is a *detestable substitute* – his conduct to Heathcliff is *atrocious* – H. and I are going to rebel – we took our *initiatory step* this evening."[14] Catherine's statement reflects her and Heathcliff's desire to evade a hierarchical, class-inflected adult world and instead to exist in an unrestricted realm of childhood friendship. Later in the novel, clarifying all of this to her servant Nelly Dean, Catherine relates her dream about being "extremely miserable" in heaven and feeling that "heaven did not seem to be [her] home," adding:

> I broke my heart with weeping to come back to earth; and the angels were so angry that they flung me out, into the middle of the heath on the top of Wuthering Heights; where I woke sobbing for joy.[15]

Catherine equates heaven with her marriage to Edgar Linton, an upper-class neighbor, but also realizes that her dream of avoiding adulthood is an impossible and transgressive one. After she marries Linton she feels "shut" up in their home, Thrushcross Grange, and longs to be a "girl again, half savage and hardy, and free."[16]

Catherine's predicament is the seed of many of Dickinson's marriage poems, for example, "I'm 'wife' - I've finished that - " (F225 J199), in which the speaker equates heaven and marriage, sarcastically suggesting that neither offers women happiness or fulfillment, despite their promises of security and status. Similarly, in other poems, such as "I never felt at Home - Below - " (F437 J413) and "Why - do they shut me out of Heaven?" (F268 J248), Dickinson evokes Catherine's suggestion that heaven is an oppressive, formal, and dull place compared to the freedom of childhood. In contrast to the hierarchical world associated with adulthood, marriage, and Christianity, *Wuthering Heights*, like *Jane Eyre*, presents the possibility of parity between its heroine and hero, who are twin souls. Catherine tells Nelly that "[Heathcliff is] more myself than I am. Whatever our souls are made of, his and mine are the same," adding "I *am* Heathcliff – he's always, always in my mind – not as a pleasure, any more than I am always a pleasure to myself – but, as my own being, – so don't talk of our separation again – it is impracticable."[17] Just as they experimented with an androgynous style, the Brontës' novels featured characters that blurred and unsettled conventional notions of femininity and masculinity. This recalls not only Dickinson's "little Girl" who equates her imagination with a male bird, but also Dickinson's penchant for gender-blurring constructions, of identities composed of male and female parts: a Queen-page, an Earl-girl, a Woman-boy, a Wife-Czar, an Earl-Bride. The novel ends with the pair's physical defeat but metaphysical victory: like Antony and Cleopatra (two of Dickinson's favorite literary characters) Catherine and Heathcliff become mythical, spectral figures, haunting the moors.

Written in the late 1850s, the first three stanzas of Dickinson's elegy for Charlotte Brontë, "All overgrown by cunning moss," (F146 J148), present Brontë as a well-traveled bird who, having followed other birds, presumably her dead sisters and brother, to "other Latitudes," is now confined to a weed-grown grave at "Haworth," which the speaker calls the "little cage of 'Currer Bell.'" Death has deprived Brontë of the ability to return to her beloved green "Yorkshire hills" – like the ghosts of Heathcliff and Catherine. Inspired by Gaskell's text to visit the moors and Haworth, the speaker, an early literary tourist, does not find any trace of this famous writer: "not in all the nests I meet - / Can Nightingale be seen." Dickinson placed an "Or" between this section of the poem and her more positive fourth and fifth stanzas, in which Brontë's final journey, after a life of "many wanderings" and much Christ-like anguish, ends not in the ground or in a Christian "Heaven" – which Catherine from *Wuthering Heights* associated with unhappiness, and conventional femininity – but in "Eden." Here Eden, which is associated with fluidity and pleasure in other Dickinson poems (F205 J211; F269 J249), is an asphodel-filled

Elysium, which in Greek mythology was the final resting place of the blessed. Referring to Charlotte Brontë by her surname only, the poem ends by drawing attention to "Brontë's" position as a powerful, commanding female author, offering an alternative to the image of the caged male pseudonym "Currer Bell," as well as to Gaskell's image of the dutiful, moralistic, and religious woman. Dickinson apparently aspired to Brontë's reconciliation of masculine authority with feminine power, signing some of her letters to her literary mentor Thomas Wentworth Higginson simply "Dickinson" (L316, 319, 330, 352, 368, 371).

Like the first part of this Brontë elegy, Dickinson's elegy for Elizabeth Barrett Browning, "I went to thank Her - " (F637 J363), emphasizes the devastation felt at the eternal loss of a beloved writer. In the latter poem, a devotee crosses the Atlantic in the hope of meeting her idol, only to discover that the poet has died. Yet just as the second part of the elegy for Brontë imagines the author rewarded in "Eden" for her great art, Dickinson's other elegies for Barrett Browning present her as a poet who, despite her death, remains an everlasting, inspiring figure whose head is "too High - to Crown" (F600 J312), transforming the minds of "sombre Girl" readers and turning them into poets (F627 J593). In an 1861 letter, written after Barrett Browning's death on June 29 of that year, Dickinson notes for her cousins Louise and Frances Norcross the restrictions placed on Barrett Browning and George Sand when they were young: "That Mrs. Browning fainted, we need not read *Aurora Leigh* to know, when she lived with her English aunt; and George Sand 'must make no noise in her grandmother's bedroom.' Poor children! Women, now, queens, now! And one in the Eden of God" (L234). Dickinson then speculates that these "queens" "forget that now," because such confinement has been eclipsed by their subsequent literary achievements and Barrett Browning's new residence in the "Eden" of God (not Brontë's prelapsarian place of joy and possibility). Dickinson encourages her cousins to take comfort from these women's literary fates, provokingly presenting these two often divisive European writers as ultra-feminine. Dickinson would have been aware that *Aurora Leigh* (1856), which explicitly deals with female sexuality, prostitution, and rape, was regarded by many early critics as coarse and unfeminine; and that George Sand, whom Barrett Browning praised as a "large-brained woman and large-hearted man," was famous for her androgynous appearance and scandalous behavior.[18] Moreover, Dickinson connects *Aurora Leigh*, which celebrates female personal and artistic development, with Sand, whose real name was *Aurore Dudevant* and whose fictional heroines were forerunners to Barrett Browning's.

In her tributes to her European female contemporaries, Dickinson was participating in a transnational network of women, valorizing, inspiring, and "crowning" other women, while validating them as artists who were as serious and significant as their male equivalents. It is likely Dickinson read and emulated the strategies of two 1861 articles in *The Atlantic Monthly*: the first was an obituary for Barrett Browning by the journalist Kate Field, and the second a summary of Sand's autobiography, *Historie de ma Vie* (1855), by the American writer Julia Ward Howe. Field describes Barrett Browning as the "world's greatest poetess"; ranks her alongside Galileo, Michelangelo, and Dante; stresses her erudition, genius, moral courage, powers of sympathy, and selflessness; and also notes that although Barrett Browning was "sinless in life," her political views were often controversial.[19] Having been imprisoned in her father's house on 50 Wimpole Street, Barrett Browning found personal and artistic freedom in Florence, Italy; she connected her own personal struggle with that of her adopted homeland, and wrote heavily criticized poems in support of Italian unification. Similarly, Howe, while stressing that Sand's life was "no example for women to follow," charts her personal and artistic struggles as a woman to show that she was not a "monster," but rather a great writer who should be ranked alongside Dante and Virgil, as well as among a "gallery of great women [including Sappho, Cleopatra, Mary Magdalene and the Virgin Mary], great with and without sin."[20] Dickinson imagines a figure such as Barrett Browning or Sand waiting for her and her cousins as they affront their destinies: "Take heart, little sister, twilight is but the short bridge, and the moon (morn) stands at the end. If we can only get to her! Yet, if she sees us fainting, she will put out her yellow hands." This recalls the following sentiment of female solidarity from the Sand article: "Elizabeth Browning's hands were not too pure to soothe [Sand's] forehead, chiding while they soothed; and [Howe's] hands, not illustrious as hers, shall soil themselves with no mud flung at a sister's crowned head."[21]

Like Barrett Browning, George Eliot was a model of cerebral womanhood, who, like the Brontës and Sand, cross-dressed for success, and became a formidable force against which contemporaries of both sexes measured themselves. Henry James, in 1866, called Eliot a philosopher and serious thinker, who surpassed Dickens and Thackeray, and whose style united "the keenest observation with the ripest reflection."[22] Like the Brontës and Barrett Browning, Eliot was concerned with the restrictions placed on women and the realities of their sacrifices and sufferings, but she placed even greater emphasis on the forces that stifled women's energies, fantasies, personal freedom, and development. Whereas Jane

Eyre and Aurora Leigh find happiness in marriages based on equality that will nourish them, Eliot's heroines, such as Dorothea Brooke from *Middlemarch,* are forced to compromise, losing the freedom they crave or desires they pursue. At the end of *Middlemarch*, although happily married to Will Ladislaw, Dorothea's yearnings are defeated by "the conditions of an imperfect social state"; her acts remain "unhistoric," her life "hidden" and her tomb "unvisited."[23]

Although Eliot's novels in the late 1850s and 1860s were popular and critical successes in America, *Middlemarch* (1872) and *Daniel Deronda* (1876) were less enthusiastically received because Eliot's relationship with a married man, George Henry Lewes, was more widely known and her "secular vision clashed with the richly religious character of American culture."[24] In letters, Dickinson attempts to compensate Eliot for such censure by emphasizing her achievement of literary immortality. In 1873, she writes, "'What do I think of *Middlemarch*?' What do I think of glory - except that in a few instances this 'mortal has already put on immortality.' George Eliot is one" (L389). After Eliot's death in 1880, Dickinson is even more explicit, hoping that Eliot, like Brontë and Barrett Browning, will enter into the paradise of great writers: "Perhaps she who Experienced Eternity in Time, may receive Time's omitted Gift as part of the Bounty of Eternity - " (L688). Unlike Brontë and Barrett Browning, Eliot could not easily be recuperated into an image of feminine sainthood and virtue, and so, in 1885, Dickinson, comparing the suspected immorality of Eliot to the assumed suicide of *Hamlet*'s Ophelia, writes, "None of us know her enough to judge her, so her Maker must be her 'Crowner's Quest'" (L979). Equating Eliot's detractors with Shakespeare's clowns, Dickinson reprimands their moral presumptuousness. In her elegy, "Her Losses made our Gains ashamed - " (F1602 J1562), Dickinson presents Eliot as a figure who transformed her losses and deficiencies ("Life's empty Pack") into exotic treasure (equated with "the East"), recalling Dickinson's comment that "[Eliot] is the Lane to the Indes, Columbus was looking for" (L456). Eliot, in a similar manner to the Brontës and Barrett Browning, transforms insufficient provisions into treasure. While Dickinson draws attention to losses in Eliot's life and (perhaps her loss of heavenly salvation), she implies that the criticism and cultural limitations faced by Eliot and women writers more generally make the "Honey" they produce all the sweeter. In this elegy, as in other poems such as "Title Divine - is mine!" (F194A J1072), Dickinson celebrates painful female triumph, connecting it with forbidden desire, unconventional femininity, and artistic vocation.

Dickinson's preference for these British writers need not signify her rejection of the works of her American female contemporaries, but rather indicates that she lived in an Anglo-American culture whose literary works were shared and invested in by readers on both sides of the Atlantic. Other American women writers such as Louisa May Alcott, Elizabeth Stuart Phelps, Constance Fenimore Woolson, Harriet Prescott Spofford, and Elizabeth Stoddard also found in the lives of European women models of ambitious, successful, esteemed high-brow artists who gave priority to their vocation, while engaging with the pertinent dilemma of the woman writer: how to retain femininity and yet participate in high cultural literary pursuits. The careers of these Europeans proved that genius could transcend gender: Barrett Browning, the Brontës, particularly Charlotte, and Eliot were not merely "shining examples of female capabilities," but "the foremost practitioners of [their respective] art[s]."[25] Similarly, these writers created inspirational heroines who asserted their individuality and strove for self-reliance, while protesting against and sometimes triumphing over the social restraints imposed on them as women. In reading this literature, American women could imagine escape, traveling to the Brontës' Yorkshire moors, to Barrett Browning's Italy, and to Eliot's provincial English towns. Whereas many of her female contemporaries traveled to Europe to experience the personal and creative freedom they associated with it, Dickinson made a similar crossing, albeit in her writings, positioning herself among this transatlantic coterie of women writers.

NOTES

1 Páraic Finnerty, "Rival Italies: Emily Dickinson, John Ruskin and Henry James," *Prose Studies 31* (August 2009), 114.
2 Betsy Erkkila, *The Wicked Sisters: Women Poets, Literary History and Discord* (New York: Oxford University Press, 1992), 79.
3 Elizabeth Gaskell, *The Life of Charlotte Brontë* (Oxford: Oxford University Press, 2001), 228.
4 E.P. Whipple, "Novels of the Season," *North American Review 67* (October, 1848), 355.
5 Ibid., 355.
6 G. W. Peck, "Wuthering Heights," *American Whig Review 7* (June 1848), 572–3.
7 Whipple, "Novels of the Season," 356, 357.
8 Cree LeFavour, "'Jane Eyre Fever': Deciphering the Astonishing Popular Success of Charlotte Brontë in Antebellum America," *Book History 7* (2004),126.
9 Lucasta Miller, *The Brontë Myth* (London: Jonathan Cape, 2001), 26.

10 "Charlotte Brontë," *Putnam's Monthly Magazine* 9 (June 1857), 649.
11 Margaret Sweat, "Charlotte Brontë and the Brontë Novels," *North American Review* 85 (October 1857), 316.
12 Charlotte Brontë, *Jane Eyre* (London: Penguin, 2006), 28, 129–30.
13 Ibid., 293.
14 Peck, "Wuthering Heights," 574.
15 Emily Brontë, *Wuthering Heights* (London; Penguin, 2000), 80–1.
16 Ibid. 124, 125.
17 Ibid. 81, 82–3.
18 Quoted in Linda M. Lewis, *Germaine de Staël, George Sand, and the Victorian Artist* (Columbia, MO: University of Missouri Press, 2003), 102.
19 Kate Field, "Elizabeth Barrett Browning," *Atlantic Monthly* 8 (September 1861), 369, 375.
20 Julia Ward Howe, "George Sand," *Atlantic Monthly* 8 (November 1861), 533, 534.
21 Ibid., 531.
22 Henry James, "The Novels of George Eliot," *Atlantic Monthly* 18 (October 1866), 488.
23 George Eliot, *Middlemarch* (Harmondsworth: Penguin, 1994), 838.
24 George V. Griffith, "George Eliot, Realism, and the American Press, 1858–1881," *American Periodicals: A Journal of History, Criticism, and Bibliography* 9 (1999), 40.
25 Anne E. Boyd, *Writing for Immortality: Women and the Emergence of High Literary Culture in America* (Baltimore: Johns Hopkins University Press, 2004), 29.

CHAPTER 11

Immediate U.S. Literary Predecessors

Cristanne Miller

Emily Dickinson was an enthusiastic reader of literature published by her nineteenth-century predecessors and peers in authored volumes, anthologies, popular periodicals, and the *Springfield Republican*, her family's daily newspaper. The primary literary influences on her writing come from the 1840s through the early 1860s: this is when Dickinson was in school, wrote her early poems (largely unpreserved before 1858), and developed her mature style. Although scholars have long regarded both popular and (most) prestigious poets of this period as writing a conventional verse, the last few decades of research have shown this to be far from the case. The 1840s and 1850s were a time of widespread poetic experimentation: with nontraditional subjects; the use of colloquial language to present philosophical, social, and political concerns; and poetic form. Understanding Dickinson's writing in the context of such experimentation helps to distinguish those aspects of her verse that are strikingly original from those that are broadly shared; it also clarifies contextual frameworks for interpreting her poems in relation to contemporary debates and enthusiasms.

Dickinson's letters are full of references to how much she enjoyed her reading. One cannot, however, regard such references as the last word about what she read. At times, the record is clear. She refers or alludes to Ralph Waldo Emerson in several letters, poems, or prose fragments for more than thirty years (1850–84) and to Henry Wadsworth Longfellow for almost as long (1851–79). Among fiction writers, Harriet Prescott Spofford caught her attention: Dickinson asks Susan Dickinson to "send me everything she writes," although she tells Thomas Wentworth Higginson that "Miss Prescott's [1860] 'Circumstance' ... followed me, in the Dark - so I avoided her - " (L261).[1] She and Sue also enjoyed the adventure writer Ik Marvel. Dickinson writes about Edgar Allan Poe, Nathaniel Hawthorne, and Henry David Thoreau, among antebellum American authors. A brief note in 1861 consists in its entirety of the request, "Will Susan please lend

Emily [Rebecca Harding Davis's] 'Life in the Iron Mills' - and accept Blossom" (L231).

Yet other writers Dickinson read closely are barely mentioned. She refers to James Russell Lowell first in 1869, but Austin's copy of Lowell's 1848 *A Fable for Critics* contains numerous passages with marks of the kind we know Dickinson made in volumes she owned, such as Emerson's *Poems*. Similarly, she refers only once to Oliver Wendell Holmes but was given a copy of his poems in 1849 and marks both an episode of "The Professor's Story" and later a Civil War poem by Holmes in *The Atlantic Monthly* – to which she subscribed. She also sends Sue a copy of Holmes's "Bill and Joe." On William Cullen Bryant's death Dickinson writes to Elizabeth Holland, "We thought you cherished Bryant, and spoke of you immediately when we heard his fate" (L555) – one of several instances indicating that Dickinson and her friends discuss writers – and she appears to make several marks in his 1849 *Poems*, owned by Sue; this is, however, the sole mention of Bryant in her letters.

Dickinson also apparently wrote particular poems in response to her American predecessors. She composed "It sifts from Leaden Sieves - " (F291 J311) after Higginson published an article called "Snow" in *The Atlantic Monthly*, February 1862, praising Emerson's "Snow-Storm" and Lowell's "First Snow-Flake." Perhaps this challenged Dickinson to try the topic for herself. Longfellow's famous "Psalm of Life," with its reference to hearts "like muffled drums ... beating / Funeral marches to the grave," may have stimulated Dickinson to conceive a "Funeral, in my Brain" (F340 J280) rather than the heart, although her transformation of this metaphor bears no resemblance to Longfellow's optimism.[2] In "Besides the Autumn poets sing" (F123 J131), she more clearly responds to Bryant's "The Death of the Flowers," a poem she marks extensively. Dickinson's poem distinguishes the autumn beauty of "Mr Bryant's 'Golden Rod'" (written "golden-rod" by Bryant) from the bleaker moment of fall she describes, also referring to "a squirrel" that appears in Bryant's poem, but not, like him, writing an elegy that follows autumn into winter in memory of a young woman's death.[3] Other critics have found strong resemblances between Dickinson poems and work by Lowell, Higginson, Holmes, and Josiah Holland. Within a decade of the publication of her 1890 *Poems*, her work had been compared to that of ninety-five writers.

Generally, however, Dickinson responds less to a particular writer or work than to popular idioms and genres. During her youth and young adulthood, Dickinson would have read poems about death, nature, flowers, gothic terror, and orientalism in periodicals and in the books circulating within her family and among her friends, and many of her poems echo what she read. Nature was of widespread interest, from the transcendentalists' philosophical reflections to Frances Sargent Osgood's *The Poetry of Flowers, and Flowers of Poetry* (1841). Dickinson frequently used the popular language of flowers in letters and poems. Longfellow's "Catawba Wine" and Emerson's "Bacchus" are just two of the poems she would have read encouraging her "I taste a liquor never brewed - " (F207 J214) – published as "The May-Wine" in the *Springfield Republican* in 1861. Dickinson also wrote several poems using popular tropes of orientalism or using cardinal points and place names suggestively. Through poems situated in the "East," she criticizes aspects of Western Christian culture idealizing, for example, "my little Gipsey being" more than a proper lady in "damask" in "Tho' my destiny be Fustian - " (F131 J163) – a poem anticipated by Emerson's "The Rommany Girl." Others have written about Dickinson's enjoyment and use of popular gothic and sentimental modes.

Among the most influential aspects of antebellum verse culture on Dickinson's writing was the popularity of the ballad. Although Dickinson makes broad use of elements of hymn structure, understanding her writing as influenced by hymns in isolation from other formal influences leads to misleadingly narrow interpretations of her work. As a writer in hymn forms, Dickinson is perceived in the context of religion. Whether one reads her as challenging church and God, constructing her own spiritual path, or expressing religious conviction, the context of hymnody makes religion central to her aesthetic. Understanding instead that Dickinson was equally influenced by popular secular forms enables readers to perceive more accurately the multiple ways in which she engaged with her culture. Moreover, it clarifies aspects of her experimentation with meter, stanzaic form, and lineation. As a poet of modified ballads as well as of modified hymns, Dickinson can be recognized as writing a verse more narrative, more dramatic, and more responsive to contemporary literary culture than usually imagined.

Ballads and hymns were the two greatest formal influences on Dickinson's poetry. Dickinson grew up singing hymns in church and reading them in poetry anthologies as "lyric" poems; Isaac Watts' hymns were included in poetry anthologies, and the editors of an 1831 psalmody claim that Watts has written "nearly half of all the valuable lyric poetry in the language."[4] Many poems were also called hymns – for example, Bryant's "A Forest Hymn" or "Hymn to Death" – even though both are in iambic pentameter, not a popular hymn meter. Dickinson's dictionary defines a "hymn" as any "song praising God," "honorific poem," or "ode to a mythic hero."⁵ Dickinson also had an extensive sheet music collection and loved singing ballads and playing them on the piano. Ballad influences are rhythmic as much as melodic, and Dickinson may have begun some compositions following a particular rhythm or song in her head. Her first stanzas are often the strongest or most striking part of a poem, and they also tend to be the part she revised least. She wrote three entirely different second stanzas for "Safe in their Alabaster Chambers" (F124B J216), for example, without changing the words of the first. The practice of writing a poem to a tune or to the rhythm of another poem was common at the time. As she would have known, Julia Ward Howe composed the "Battle Hymn of the Republic" because she wanted to give the popular song "John Brown's Body" better lyrics for war time, for example, and James Randall composed the Confederate war poem "My Maryland" to the meter of James Clarence Mangan's "Karamanian's Exile." Longfellow composed his verse novel, *The Song of Hiawatha*, in trochaic tetrameter inspired by a translation of the Swedish epic *The Kalevala*. It would not have been unusual for Dickinson to have composed poems according to the rhythm of a remembered verse or song.

Dickinson learned different things from hymns and ballads. A guiding principle of the hymn is that it is sung communally to a well-known tune. Consequently, hymns must have exact accentual syllabic metrical patterns, and every stanza must be the same. The two most frequently used hymn forms are common meter and short meter. Dickinson writes several poems in both meters – for example, "I reckon - When I count at all - " (F533 J569) in 8686 iambics, and "A Bird came down the Walk" (F359 J328) in 6686. Hymns are written in a great number of stanzaic forms, including subtle variations from these frequently used meters, but all are identical in syllabic count from one stanza to the next in order that they may be sung to a single tune. From hymns, Dickinson learns the use of precisely repeated short-lined metrical patterns. She may also adopt the hymn's typically plain-style language, although she often secularizes its address to God or gives that address an irreverent tone.

In contrast, the ballad was associated with authenticity and untutored wildness, both because of its traditional subject matter and its forms. From the time of the mid-eighteenth-century ballad revival, ballads were understood to be lyrics of the folk, involving highly charged narratives and presenting a simple psychological perspective believed to characterize rural or unsophisticated, intuitive, natural sympathies. They were regarded as products of a community, not of a singular self-conscious crafter of language. The colloquial pungency of ballads was presented in rhythmic forms both simple and rule-breaking: ballad verse did not adhere to accentual syllabic verse forms but instead proceeded according to patterns of beats, without regard to the number of unstressed syllables between beats. Hence the ballad freed craft-conscious poets to vary the rhythms of their poems within a beat-based meter. This emancipation was extolled by British romantic poets such as Wordsworth and Coleridge, who were influenced by its loose simplicity. In the United States, both traditional ballads and English, Scottish, and German experiments with ballad form created an enthusiasm for experimental rhythms and stanzaic forms in short-lined verse. Ballads were written by Bryant, Emerson, Longfellow, Lowell, Poe, Lydia Sigourney, John Greenleaf Whittier, and numerous other poets – many of whom also wrote about this form. Although some uses of the ballad involved a strict 8686 form, most included at least occasional lines containing additional or fewer syllables. Moreover, many poems in forms distinctly different from the traditional 4343 balladic rhythm were called ballads if they related a tale or had a ballad-style speaker.

Longfellow wrote and translated several ballads, many of which play with the looseness of beat-based meter – such as "The Village Blacksmith," which varies the syllabic manifestation of its 4/3-beat rhythm in stanzas:

	syllables	beats
Week in, week out, from morn till night,	8	4
You can hear his bellows blow;	7	3
You can hear him swing his heavy sledge,	9	4
With measured beat and slow,	6	3
Like a sexton ringing the village bell,	10	4
When the evening sun is low.[6]	7 or 8	3

The Atlantic Monthly, a magazine Dickinson read avidly, published several contemporary ballads using a beat-based measure, including Whittier's "Skipper Ireson's Ride" (1857), Longfellow's "Catawba Wine" (1857), Lowell's "The Relief of Lucknow" (1858), and Holmes' "The Deacon's Masterpiece: Or the Wonderful 'One-Hoss-Shay'" (1858), which Holmes playfully refers to as a "rhymed problem" because of its highly irregular rhyming.

This looseness in accentual measure in ballads apparently led to more radical kinds of formal irregularity in the 1840s and 1850s in the United States, by both anonymous and highly respected poets in venues from school readers to daily newspapers. Emerson's "The Visit" provides an example of such deviation and was heavily marked in Dickinson's edition – both by a page folded in half and by lines in its margins. This mostly 4-beat poem is metrically irregular throughout, beginning with a

3-beat line in dactyls ("Askest, 'How long thou shalt stay'"), followed by an irregular alternation of 8-syllable trochaic with 7-syllable catalectic lines, but occasionally including lines that are markedly iambic – some 7 and some 8 syllables long. Dickinson marks a trochaic then catalectic sequence of lines ("Say, what other metre is it / Than the meeting of the eyes") and then pencils double lines by the poem's final couplet, which is iambic then catalectic: "If Love his moment overstay, / Hatred's swift repulsions play."[7] The poem also has no regular rhyme scheme and includes two slant rhymes (glance/covenance and state/that) – a kind of rhyming Emerson and other antebellum poets use in many poems (in "Threnody," Emerson rhymes power/mourn and restore/return).

Emerson's "Merlin" shows even more radical variation of beats and lines, altering line and stanza lengths, and varying metrical patterns from iambic to anapestic to trochaic (again often catalectic). Because there is not even a general rising or falling accentual pattern it is at times difficult to say how many beats a line may have. For example, near the poem's beginning Emerson writes:

	Syllables	beats
Nor tinkle of piano strings,	8	4
Can make the wild blood start	6	3
In its mystic springs.	5	2 or 3
The kingly bard	4	2
Must smite the chords rudely and hard,	8	3 or 4
As with hammer or with mace;	7	2 or 3 or 4[8]

Similarly, Longfellow's "The Monk Felix" begins with no pattern of rhythm, beats, or line length, and the rhyme scheme is irregular, even including a rhyme across both a sentence and stanza division. This poem contains stanzas of from 8 to 29 lines, with line lengths varying from 2 to 10 syllables.

Dickinson would have known such formally irregular poems from her school years' *Rhetorical Reader* (by Ebenezer Porter) and from popular periodicals such as the *Springfield Republican* and *The Atlantic Monthly* as well as from the family library; the *Atlantic* even published an early version of Walt Whitman's "As I ebb'd with the ocean of life," in April 1860. In some ways equally radical, a comic poem in the *Republican* (published April 13, 1860) splits words at the end of some lines and generally throws meter and rhyme to the winds. "Owed to the Charlestown Convenshun" by E. Plewry Bust-on-em begins:

> Now you git out! what upon airth d'you 'spose
> Folks sent you down to Charlestown fur, you old

> Eternal splittin-masheen, you?
> I do know that I'm green, but I had thort
> You was intended fur to represent
> The feelins of the democratic per
> Suasion, as far as tha had any; then, what
> Did you run off the track and bust, like a
> Ingine upon the Providence and Am
> Boy railroad fur? ...

From marginal x's and lines in books owned by the Dickinsons, like Lowell's *A Fable for Critics*, it is clear that Dickinson enjoyed comic verse – and often comic verse allowed greater variation in rhyme and rhythm than poems with a serious tone. For example, Lowell's satirical *Fable* contains rhymes like "know it's" with "poets" and "philosopher" with "loss of her" in its 4-beat lines. And Dickinson wrote several comic poems of her own.

Dickinson's experiments with stanza structure, meter, beat-based rhythms, and rhyme schemes closely resemble those of her predecessors in the 1840s and 1850s. Understanding the range of formal irregularity with which she would have been familiar during her youth and young adulthood dramatically calls into question the assumption that Dickinson would not have been able to publish her poetry without severe editorial revision in her lifetime. Most of the irregularities of her poems were familiar to contemporary readers. We see this in the fact that such irregularity was not edited out of those poems Dickinson did publish during her lifetime – most of which contain some deviation from an accentual syllabic or balladic norm. For example, "Nobody knows this little rose" (published August 1858 in the *Republican*) has a 4343 beat structure (8686 syllables) in stanza one but moves to a 3-beat structure in stanzas 2 and 3, varying line lengths from 5 to 7 syllables (F11 J35). "Flowers - Well - if anybody" (published in *Drum Beat* March 1864 and then reprinted in the *Daily* and *Weekly Springfield Republican* and the *Boston Post*) uses an 87 accentual syllabic pattern in one stanza of 8 lines (rhyming abcbdefe) and one stanza of 6 lines (rhyming ghihjh); it also includes the slant rhyme define/men (F95 J137). In March 1862, the *Republican* published "The Sleeping" ("Safe in their Alabaster Chambers - "[F124 J216]), which has a long first line (9 syllables) followed by two shorter lines (5 syllables each) and a second stanza that begins with two short lines (4 and 6 syllables) followed by a 9-syllable line. This poem is irregular in both number of beats and syllables per line, even if one regards the two shorter lines of both stanzas as split metrical lines. It also rhymes "noon" with "stone." Because we cannot know precisely what transcript of the poem was sent to the *Republican*, it is impossible to know whether its editors or the friend who submitted the poem changed any aspect of Dickinson's inscription of the poem. We can know that the poem printed by the *Republican* manifests irregularity in several features and that this irregularity echoes that of other poems published there and in other periodicals.

Dickinson frequently changes stanza structures within a poem, as in "Nobody knows this little rose," or more famously in "After great pain, a formal feeling comes - " (F372 J341), where the opening quatrain's iambic pentameters lead to a 5-line second stanza of 84648 – where the only clear rhyme occurs in the final two lines, of dramatically different length – and then to a final quatrain of 6688 syllables. Dickinson also splits metrical lines – writing, for example, "Of Bronze - and Blaze - / The North - tonight - " (F319 J290) and "They dropped like Flakes - / They dropped like stars - " (F545 J409) in two lines where an 8-syllable line would more logically begin these poems' otherwise consistent 8686 pattern. Again, one can see this in poems not just by famous predecessors such as Longfellow and Emerson but also in popular poems: "Popping Corn" (*Springfield Republican*, September 24, 1860) begins with 2-beat lines rhyming abcb but ends with two couplets of 4-beat lines (rhyming aabb), and contains one 4-beat line midway through the poem. Like the anonymous author of "Popping Corn" and other predecessor or contemporary poets in the 1850s and early 1860s, Dickinson often maintains a rhyme pattern even when varying how she writes out her lines – or rhymes irregularly, or occasionally eschews rhyme altogether.

Like her predecessors, Dickinson typically begins each poetic line with a capital letter and makes the end of the line its strongest point: this is where the rhyme comes, and most of her verse does rhyme. Although in copying poems Dickinson often changes line-internal capitalization and punctuation and varies how she writes a line on the page, she rarely changes the meter of a poem and does not end poetic lines with articles or other function words. As with the writing out of songs, the rhythm of her poems is clear from such features and from their meter, not their look on a page. In fact, the least consistent aspect of Dickinson's poetry is in the way she writes out a poem. No one has determined whether her American predecessors or contemporaries similarly varied the writing out of copies of their poems.

Dickinson's poetry did differ radically from that of her predecessors and contemporaries in its extreme compression. It also differed in the density and intensity of her metaphors and the extent of the disjunction caused by its compressed syntax, punctuation, and juxtapositions. Although Victorians (including Dickinson) loved verse novels and dramas, and long poems generally, her verse was uniquely concise, avoiding detailed descriptive and narrative shading and often even omitting parts of a sentence's grammar. She also eschewed poeticisms, making her language colloquial, pithy, and very much "alive" – the quality she hoped Higginson would affirm she had achieved when she first wrote him in 1862 (L260), perhaps borrowing the conceit from his own "Letter to a Young Contributor": Higginson praises language "so saturated with warm life and delicious association that every sentence shall palpitate and thrill with the mere fascination of the syllables .... Charge your style with life."[9] In contrast, Dickinson's metrical and stanzaic irregularities, slant rhymes, and variant lineation were unusual only because she used them more frequently and at greater extremes than her contemporaries.

The question we perhaps should be asking, then, is not why Dickinson wrote poetry of extraordinary rhythmic diversity in the late 1850s and 1860s, but instead what changed that made such verse seem potentially unacceptable to readers by 1890, when Higginson and Mabel Loomis Todd first edited her poems for book publication. Here a comment by Harriet Prescott Spofford may be useful. Spofford wrote antebellum poetry and fiction in a style of lush or provocative imagery, extreme mental states, sudden transitions, and intense immediacy. After the war, Spofford claimed that "the public taste changed. With the coming of Mr. Howells as editor of the *Atlantic* [in 1866], and his influence, the realistic arrived. I doubt if anything I wrote in those days would be accepted by any magazine now."[10] David Cody speculates that because Dickinson was not attempting to publish after the war she would not have felt any compunction to change her writing habits, developed in the 1850s).[11] This is possible. At the same time, Dickinson's poems written after the war do become at least somewhat less experimental in their metrical and stanzaic forms, in part because she writes a higher percentage of poems containing five or fewer lines. It remains for scholars to determine whether Dickinson in other ways alters her primary style beginning around the late 1860s. The large majority of her poems written before the end of 1865 bear a striking resemblance in several topical and formal features to those of her predecessors writing in the 1840s and 1850s.

NOTES

1 Susan Dickinson, "Harriet Prescott's Early Work," published as a letter to the editor of the *Springfield Republican* (January 1903).
2 Henry Wadsworth Longfellow, *Poems* (Boston: Ticknor and Fields, 1863 [1856]), 10.

3 William Cullen Bryant, *Poems* (Philadelphia: Carey and Hart, 1848), 153–4.
4 Isaac Watts, *Church Psalmody: A Collection of Psalms and Hymns Adapted to Public Worship*, ed. Lowell Mason and David Greene (Boston: Perkins and Marvin, 1831), viii.
5 Noah Webster, *American Dictionary of the English Language* (Amherst, MA: J. S. & C. Adams, 1844). *Emily Dickinson Lexicon*. Available at: http://edl.byu.edu/lexicon/term/200231.
6 Longfellow, *Poems*, 127.
7 Ralph Waldo Emerson, *Poems* (Boston: James Munroe & Co., 1847), 25.
8 Ibid., 180.
9 Thomas Wentworth Higginson, "Letter to a Young Contributor," *Atlantic Monthly* (April 1862), 403, 404.
10 Quoted in David Cody, "'When one's soul is at a white heat': Dickinson and the Azarian School," *EDJ 19.1* (2010), 56.
11 Ibid., 78 n. 5.

CHAPTER 12

U.S. Literary Contemporaries: Dickinson's Moderns

Mary Loeffelholz

Who are Dickinson's contemporaries? At the point of reception, perhaps we all are. From the 1890s through the early 1980s, Emily Dickinson was more often compared by critics to the literary modernists of the era in which her writings were first printed than to her own immediate nineteenth-century contemporaries. Decades after the modernist poet-critic Amy Lowell claimed Dickinson as "a precursor of the Imagists," the grafting of Dickinson into modernism was still generating vital critical work: David Porter's 1981 bid for Dickinson as an early practitioner of "the modern idiom" was met and raised by Susan Howe's ringing claim of 1985 that "Emily Dickinson and Gertrude Stein are clearly among the most innovative precursors of modernist poetry and prose," pioneers of modernism's "linguistic decreation."[1] The late twentieth-century return of historicism to the center of U.S. literary scholarship remanded Dickinson for a time to the company of her nineteenth-century culture – a culture far more rich in women writers, feminist critics observed, than traditional literary histories had fully acknowledged. At the same time as the nineteenth-century Dickinson was ascending, however, modernism was inexorably losing its claim on the leading edge of the present; a Dickinson who can remain our contemporary must increasingly be pried away from modernism and affixed to practices more au courant. In Joy Ladin's summary, "Dickinson has attained the distinction of becoming the only poet to be characterized as a nineteenth-century Romantic or Victorian, a precocious twentieth-century modernist, and a postmodernist 'graphemic' poet whose use of the page is still years beyond that of most twenty-first century poets."[2]

Who were Dickinson's contemporaries, though, in her own eyes? What did the leading edge of the present look like to Dickinson as she was writing? She maintained a lively sense of such an edge, both early and late in her career. In an often-cited lette of 1853 to Austin Dickinson, she crows that her father "gave me quite a trimming about 'Uncle Tom' and 'Charles

Dickens' and these 'modern Literati' who he says are *nothing*, compared to past generations, who flourished when *he was a boy*. Then he said there were 'somebody's *rev-e-ries*,'" – referring to Ik Marvel's 1850 *Reveries of a Bachelor* – "he didn't know whose they were, that he thought were very ridiculous, so I'm quite in disgrace at present" (L113). In the year before her death, Dickinson reported herself as "watching like a vulture" for the appearance of a biography of George Eliot (L962) and recalled a friend joking, about a visit to California, that "the Highwayman did not say your money or your life, but have you read Daniel Deronda" (L974) – the secular version of a test she had posed to a friend many years earlier, about another writer whose new novel, *Jane Eyre*, had electrified her: "If all these leaves were altars, and on every one a prayer that Currer Bell might be saved - and you were God - would you answer it?" (L28, ca. 1849). Salvation or damnation, your money or your life: the capacity to recognize and respond to the new, Dickinson both warns and invites, might be a matter of life and death.

In these epistolary exchanges Dickinson personalizes the contemporary as an intimate drama of challenge and recognition. Modernity for her does not lie in a determinate literary form or content so much as in the challenge and response passed from reader to reader, hand to hand. Dickinson's sense of the contemporary is mediated through her recruitment of print publication into personal correspondence. Persistently, she implicates her correspondents and their shared reading in forms of sociality that run athwart of settled heterosexual domesticity – from the solitary fireside of *Reveries of a Bachelor*, the American bestseller that so vexed her father, to the adulterous or otherwise compromised relationships of George Eliot's life and major novels. Such mediations were for Dickinson both the medium and the matter of modernity, especially when it came to her American contemporaries.

Two figures of many in Dickinson's life stand out as especially important for mediating Dickinson's sense of the contemporary among American writers: Susan Gilbert Dickinson and Thomas Wentworth Higginson. It was with Susan, in 1851, that Dickinson dreamed of having "a 'Reverie' after the form of 'Ik Marvel,' indeed I do not know why it would'nt be just as charming as of that lonely Bachelor, smoking his cigar - and it would be far more profitable as 'Marvel' *only* marvelled, and you and I would *try* to make a little destiny to have for our own" (L56). It was Susan (by her later report) who alerted Dickinson to the appearance of Harriet Prescott Spofford's thrilling story "Circumstance" in the May 1860 *Atlantic Monthly*, and to whom Dickinson responded: "That is the only thing I ever saw in my life I did not think I could have written myself. You stand nearer the world than I do. Send me everything she writes."³

Spofford was among the many women writers professionally championed by Thomas Wentworth Higginson, who helped broker Spofford's introduction to the *Atlantic* in 1859, so it is perhaps not surprising that Higginson apparently asked Dickinson about Spofford in "sound[ing] her on certain American authors" at the beginning of their correspondence; nor that Dickinson's response, though more evasive than in her note to Susan, paid tribute to Spofford's power: "I read Miss Prescott's 'Circumstance,' but it followed me, in the dark - so I avoided her - " (Dickinson tended to disavow the professionalism of her reading habits in her correspondence with Higginson, but not with Susan).⁴ Higginson's efforts to interest Dickinson in the work of his acquaintance Julia Ward Howe met with silence, although likely not complete indifference. When, however, he put Dickinson's poems into the hands of Helen Hunt, Higginson's widow-turned-poet neighbor at Newport, Rhode Island, Hunt's enthusiastic outreach to Dickinson initiated a three-way correspondence that became one of the major anchors of Dickinson's post–Civil War writing life. Higginson, "a firm disciple of 'The Newness' in whatever form it chose to manifest itself," throughout his career identified modernity itself with the emergence of women's writing.⁵ "Ought Women to Learn the Alphabet?" he asked *Atlantic* readers in 1859, and answered: "There can be no question that the present epoch is initiating an empire of the higher reason, of arts, affections, aspirations; and for that epoch the genius of woman has been reserved."⁶ "Have you read Daniel Deronda?" asks Dickinson's imagined California highwayman, more conversationally, with the cutting edge of literary history not far from his victim's purse, or throat. Dickinson's correspondence with Higginson (and with other men of letters in her life, including Samuel Bowles and Josiah Holland), as much as with Susan Gilbert Dickinson, both mediated her engagement with her American contemporaries and increasingly, from the mid-1860s onward, defined the contemporary through the figure of the woman writer.

Higginson was thoroughly self-conscious about his efforts to connect Dickinson with models among contemporary American women writers – and to direct her understanding of what kind of modernity they represented. In a letter written after what would prove to be his final visit to her in December 1873, he counseled his "eccentric poetess" (as he called her in a letter to his sisters) to "cultivate" the more conventionally sociable, outward-facing, healthy modernity represented to him by Julia Ward Howe and Helen Hunt:

> I wish you could see some field lilies, yellow and scarlet, painted in water colors that are just sent to us for Christmas. These are not your favorite colors, & perhaps I love the azure & gold myself – but perhaps we should learn to love & cultivate these ruddy hues of life. Do you remember Mrs. Julia Howe's poem "I stake my life upon the red."
>
> Pray read the enlarged edition of Verses by H.H. – the new poems are so beautiful. She is in Colorado this winter, & enjoys the out-door climate. (L405a)

The poem Higginson recalls for Dickinson in this letter, Julia Ward Howe's "Rouge Gagne" (literally, "Red wins"), daringly presents its speaker at the gaming table (like Gwendolen Harleth, a few years later, in *Daniel Deronda*), playing for her life:

> The wheel is turned, the cards are laid
> The circle's drawn, the bets are made;
> I stake my gold upon the red.
> ....
> Now, Love is red, and Wisdom pale
> But human hearts are faint and frail
> Til Love meets Love, and bids it hail.
>
> I see the chasm, yawning dread;
> I see the flaming arch o'erhead;
> I stake my life upon the red.[7]

The modern woman poet of "Rouge Gagne," unlike the poetess of earlier literary generations, cultivates the "red revealment" of her embodied passions as a public sign of vigorous health rather than suffering it as a private wound; even more, she wagers her economic all on this display. For Higginson, Howe's modernizing riff on the poetess tradition in "Rouge Gagne" apparently summed up the position of an entire generation of women writers who, as Cheryl Walker observes, "had to come to terms" with "the type of the poetess as a cultural phenomenon."[8] Not only did he recommend Howe's poem to Dickinson at a point when he was concerned for her well-being; he also later published, under titles stolen from Howe, two of Dickinson's early poems featuring wagering – "'Tis so much joy!" (F170 J172), titled by Higginson "Rouge Gagne," and "Soul, Wilt thou toss again?" (F89 J139), titled "Rouge et Noir" – in his first selections of Dickinson's work to meet the public eye in 1890. Assimilated by their titles to Howe's emphatically public career, the central place given to these two poems in Dickinson's debut seems intended to justify Higginson's decision to publish Dickinson's writings – as if to say that, like Howe, Dickinson had always put her money on her eventual "revealment."

At the time of his visit in 1873, however, Dickinson probably had already shared with Higginson a poetic riposte to his recommendation that she "cultivate the ruddy hues of life."⁹ Like Howe's "Rouge Gagne," Dickinson's poem riffs on the poetess tradition of bleeding self-expression (as well as on another precursor, Henry Wadsworth Longfellow's manly, didactic "The Village Blacksmth" [1839]), but in Dickinson's poem, red doesn't win:

> Dare you see a Soul *at the White Heat?*
> Then crouch within the door -
> Red - is the Fire's common tint -
> But when the vivid Ore
> Has vanquished Flame's conditions,
> It quivers from the Forge
> Without a color, but the light
> Of unannointed Blaze.
> Least Village has it's Blacksmith
> Whose anvil's even ring
> Stands symbol for the finer Forge
> That soundless tugs - within -
> Refining these impatient Ores
> With Hammer, and with Blaze
> Until the Designated Light
> Repudiate the Forge -
>
> (F401A J365)

For Dickinson, white is the color not of innocence or frailty, but rather of labor, experience, and power. Next to this, the red and the gold of Howe's worldly language of experience in "Rouge Gagne" are, as Dickinson names them with precision, "common" tints that this poem "decreates" (to borrow Susan Howe's locution) in the service of making something new. Where Howe's red Love seeks and finds its passional counterpart, Dickinson's unanointed, unpaired Soul scorches readers who come too close (a thematic difference underlined formally in the contrast between Dickinson's off rhymes of ring / within, Ores / forge versus the closure of Howe's repetition of "Love" and her full rhymes of pale / fail / hail).

In its aggression toward its readers and against genteel or sentimental poetic models, "Dare you see a Soul *at the White Heat?*" shares something with Howe's "A New Sculptor" (published in *The Atlantic Monthly* in September 1862). "A New Sculptor" presents a self-consciously modernizing account of aesthetic value as difficult, labored, challenging, and destructive of previous aesthetic regimes. In Howe's poem, an aristocratic female speaker's "gallery of Gods, / Smoothly appointed" is invaded by a "rude," hammer-wielding visitor, his "sturdy form" begrimed with toil, who lays waste to the speaker's marbles and then calls for clay to build up, in their place, a mighty statue "Of a new feature – with the power of birth / Fashioned and wielded," which the sculptor inscribes "To-day." Both moved and appalled, the female speaker rejects the statue as "a form of all necessities," an affront to the "symmetry and song" of her marbles, only to be instructed in its meaning by the invader:

> "Behold," he said, "Life's great impersonate,
> Nourished by Labor!
> Thy Gods are gone, with old-time faith and Fate;
> This is thy Neighbor."[10]

The explicit class moral drawn in Howe's poem has no counterpart in Dickinson's; it comes, however, at the expense of the female speaker, whose second-hand relationship to culture (she is not the creator of her marbles, only their cultivated consumer) and retrograde classicism define the cutting edge of the present by contrast – as what slashes her. "A New Sculptor" denies her every kind of power, critical and creative, as even the power of birth accrues to the male sculptor (and the poem's rigid alternation of masculine and feminine rhymes underscores the predictability of these roles). By contrast, "Dare you see a Soul *at the White Heat?*" does not find the leading edge of the contemporary by polarizing the identities of its speaker and addressee along gender or class lines; it seizes its indeterminate reader (you, whoever you are, as Whitman also demanded) – offering its challenge, demanding recognition of the new.

Howe's "A New Sculptor" may have been inspired by Rebecca Harding Davis's story "Life in the Iron Mills," published in *The Atlantic Monthly* in April 1861, which also centers on a powerful statue created by a working-class artist that is contrasted, at the story's end, with the more conventional artworks and Aphrodites it overshadows. "Life in the Iron Mills" drew Dickinson's attention as well: "Will Susan please lend Emily 'Life in the Iron Mills' - and accept Blossom," she asked when the story appeared (L231), mediating her engagement with contemporary writers as she so often did through her intimate relationship with Susan Gilbert Dickinson. Perhaps the iron mills made their way into her poem's white heats? Whatever she made of Davis's story, compelling evidence has accumulated that Dickinson, like Howe, translated into poetry some of the contemporary fiction that particularly struck her, especially the sensational, florid tales of Harriett Prescott Spofford and other writers of what Henry James christened the "Azarian School" – characterized, in James' famous review of Spofford, by excessive description, an "almost morbid love of the picturesque," and "an unbridled fancy."[11]

David Cody, the most thorough reader of Dickinson's relationship to the Azarians, suggests that Spofford's story "The South Breaker" (1862) may have provided Dickinson with the first line of "Dare you see a Soul *at the White Heat?*" and with that poem's language of "an incandescent soul" refined by experience: "[I]s it better to lie in the earth with the ore," asks one of the story's characters, "than to be forged in the furnace and beaten to a blade fit for the hands of archangels?"[12] Spofford's "Circumstance," Cody argues – the tale of a frontier woman snatched up by a panther and forced to sing for her life through a long night in the panther's hot grasp, nearly succumbing to exhaustion and despair before her husband arrives to shoot the beast – informs Dickinson's "'Twas like a Maelstrom, with a notch":

> As if a Goblin with a Guage -
> Kept measuring the Hours -
> Until you felt your Second
> Weigh, helpless, in his Paws -
>
> And not a Sinew - stirred - could help
> And Sense was setting numb -
> When God - remembered - and the Fiend
> Let go, then, Overcome -
>   (F425 J414, ll. 10–17, around Autumn 1862)

As Cody observes, "In both tale and poem the protagonist lies helpless in the grasp of a "Fiend" until a providential rescue/awakening occurs,"[13] and in both works the victim's last-minute rescue awakens her to a kind of posthumous life, wondering "Which Anguish was the utterest - then - / To perish, or to live?"

As Cody and other critics have suggested, Dickinson's strategy of writing poems from the perspective of a posthumous speaker may be connected to her reading of another Spofford story, "The Amber Gods," whose first-person protagonist, Yone Willoughby – a narcissistic, warmly exotic "Cleopatra" linked with the Caribbean – struggles with Louise, her more recessive cousin, for possession of a painter, Vaughn Rose, whom they both love, as well as for possession of the talismanic jewelry of the story's title. The protagonist of this tale bears some resemblance to "that torrid spirit" with "depths of Domingo" (L855) in Dickinson's life, Susan Gilbert

Dickinson; and the ultimate focus of the story's murky, diffused eroticism ("not polarized, not organized, without centre," as Yone says of herself) on the straitened deathbed bond of Yone and Louise perhaps added to its fascination for Dickinson.[14] Watched on her deathbed by Louise, visited by Rose who calmly observes her disintegration, the narrator wakes up alone and makes her way through the house, waiting for the clocks to strike, before realization strikes her: "And ah! what was this thing I had become? I had done with time. Not for me the hands moved on their recurrent circle anymore" – and she concludes: "I must have died at ten minutes past one."[15] A great string of Dickinson poems of the early 1860s with posthumous speakers – "'Twas just this time, last year, I died" (F344 J445); "I felt a Funeral, in my Brain" (F340 J280); "I heard a Fly buzz - when I died - " (F591 J465); and "Because I could not stop for Death - " (F479 J712) – may have taken their inspiration from Spofford's story.

From one angle, the ending of "The Amber Gods" uncannily makes literal the question of how to locate the leading edge of the contemporary: what if becoming modern means realizing we have already died? Died without seeing either God or the posthumous family reunion promised by popular nineteenth-century Christian theology? From another angle, the ending of "The Amber Gods" asks a related, equally contemporary question: is it possible to tell the difference between marriage and death? Spofford's answer to this question is radical: "The Amber Gods" represents bourgeois marriage and the production and circulation of art as equally and interchangeably vampiric, requiring blood to sustain them. Vaughn Rose drains Yone's colossal vitality – her willingness to monopolize every form and object of circulation in the story – without changing her nature or reconciling her to the sacrifice.

Even more conservative writers among Dickinson's American contemporaries, such as Helen Hunt Jackson, found ways of posing this question. Jackson's sonnet "Found Frozen" presents a dead woman who "died, as many travellers have died, / O'ertaken on an Alpine road by night"; the opening line's "as" remains suspended between literal comparison and figurative simile until the sonnet's sestet declares that it was "in the place she called her home" that this woman froze to death, while "they who loved her with the all of love / Their wintry natures had to give, stood by / And wept some tears." Unlike Spofford's Yone, Jackson's victim seems to go willingly to the sacrifice, "Patient and faithful to the last," but the poem's final line, asserting that "I, who loved her last and best, – *I* knew," tips the poem toward uncertainty again. *Who* knew what this woman's "soldered mouth could tell" (F238 J187)? Dickinson's "How many times these low feet staggered - " poses this question, from a similarly unspecified observer's perspective, of a housewife worked to her unloved death. Another Jackson sonnet, "A Woman's Death-Wound," explicitly represents unhappy marriage as a posthumous existence: inwardly maimed by "but a word," the woman fronts the world with "nothing missed / In her, in voice or smile," while "each day she counts until her dying be complete."[16]

Read in the light of these contemporary works, some of Dickinson's best-known marriage poems take on a posthumous coloring. The wife of "She rose to his Requirement" who leaves behind the "Playthings of her Life" in entering her new state: does she, "In using, wear away" (F857 J732)? "I'm 'wife' - I've finished that - / That other state," muses the speaker of an earlier poem:

> How odd the Girl's life looks
> Behind this soft Eclipse -
> I think that Earth feels so
> To folks in Heaven - now
> (F225 J199, about Spring 1861)

No less numb, but more pleasantly so, than the toiling wife of "Found Frozen," Dickinson's speaker tentatively tries to attach conventional labels to her current and former states (if this is comfort, that was pain) before giving up the attempt. Her internal monologue blurs the difference between a metaphorical and a literal understanding of being "finished" with Earth. "Title divine - is mine!" (F194 J1072) by contrast seems to claim the title of "Wife - without the Sign" for Dickinson herself, but only on posthumous terms. "Born - Bridalled - Shrouded - / In a Day - ," the posthumous Dickinson, like Spofford's Yone Willoughby, is fully alive to her pain, wedded both *by* it and *to* it.

As he had with Julia Ward Howe's "Rouge Gagne," Higginson forged a posthumous connection between Spofford and Dickinson in his titling of her poems. Recycling the Latin motto that headed the final section of "The Amber Gods" – *Astra Castra, Numen Lumen* (the stars my camp, and God my light) – Higginson titled Dickinson's poem "Departed - to the Judgment" (F399 J524) "Astra Castra," while "I live with Him - I see His face" (F698 J463) became "Numen Lumen." Whatever there is to regret in Higginson's editorial meddling with Dickinson's manuscripts, the network of contemporary women writers he mediated played a vital role in defining Dickinson's own sense of what it meant to be modern: probing for the deathliness at the heart of domesticity, prizing an aesthetics of difficulty and danger – "Dare you see a soul *at the White Heat?*" – and wagering everything on a bid, at once erotic and writerly, for recognition of the new.

NOTES

1. Amy Lowell, "Emily Dickinson" (1918), in *Poetry and Poets: Essays* (1930; New York: Biblo & Tannen, 1971), 107; David Porter, *Dickinson: The Modern Idiom* (Cambridge, MA: Harvard University Press, 1981); Susan Howe, *My Emily Dickinson* (Berkeley, CA: North Atlantic Books, 1985), 11–12.
2. Joy Ladin, "'Where the Meanings, are': Emily Dickinson, Prosody, and Post-Modernist Poetics," *Versification* 5 (2010), n.p. Available at: http://www.arsversificandi.net/current/Versification%205%20(2010)%20Ladin.pdf. (Accessed December 1, 2011).
3. [Susan Gilbert Dickinson,] "Harriet Prescott's Early Work," *Dickinson Electronic Archives* http://www.emilydickinson.org/susan/shdcpb31.html (Accessed November 25, 2011).
4. Thomas Wentworth Higginson, "Emily Dickinson's Letters," *Atlantic Monthly* 68 (October 1891), 446; L261.
5. Barton Levi St. Armand, *Emily Dickinson and Her Culture: The Soul's Society* (Cambridge: Cambridge University Press, 1986), 184.
6. Thomas Wentworth Higginson, "Ought Women to Learn the Alphabet?" *Atlantic Monthly* 3.16 (February 1859), 146.
7. Julia Ward Howe, *Later Lyrics* (Boston: J. E. Tilton, 1866), 195–6.
8. Cheryl Walker, *The Nightingale's Burden: Women Poets and American Culture before 1900* (Bloomington: Indiana University Press, 1982), 87.
9. The surviving manuscripts of "Dare you see a soul at the 'White Heat'?" date from about 1862, but the one sent to Higginson is lost.
10. Julia Ward Howe, "A New Sculptor," *Atlantic Monthly* 10.59 (September 1862), 282–3.
11. Henry James, "Miss Prescott's Azarian," *North American Review* (January 1865), 270–7.
12. Quoted in David Cody, "'When one's soul's at a white heat': Dickinson and the 'Azarian School,'" *EDJ 19*.1 (Spring 2010), 46.
13. Ibid., 41.
14. Harriet Elizabeth Prescott [Spofford], "The Amber Gods," in *The Amber Gods and Other Stories* (Boston: Ticknor and Fields, 1863), 50.
15. Ibid., 80.
16. "Found Frozen" and "A Woman's Death-Wound," in *Poems by Helen Jackson* (Boston: Roberts Brothers, 1897), 19, 205.

CHAPTER 13

Periodical Reading

Joan Kirkby

In 1932 Allen Tate wrote that "All pity for Miss Dickinson's 'starved life' is misdirected. Her life was one of the richest and deepest ever lived on this continent."[1] To a large part this was due to her reading, particularly the newspapers and magazines that brought to her "the living language of nineteenth-century America" and "contributed to the variegated array of subjects and ideas that she could treat knowledgeably in letters and poems" (Capps, 43). The periodicals to which the Dickinsons subscribed were urbane and high-minded, keenly aware of the importance of keeping their community abreast of the latest thought of the day and attuned to the significance of the local and the everyday, fully aware – like Dickinson – that the unknown is at its richest in the most familiar things. Hence a notice that the orioles have returned to Amherst sits alongside columns about the Civil War and the proceedings of Congress in the *Hampshire Franklin Express*. In effect the periodicals offered their readership a vibrant intellectual community, and for nearly fifty years these newspapers and magazines formed a crucial part of Emily Dickinson's mental landscape. The newspapers and magazines shared the quality that she found in letters: "A Letter always feels to me like immortality because it is the mind alone without corporeal friend" (L330).

Among the periodicals that came to the Dickinson household were the daily and weekly newspapers the *Springfield Republican*, established in 1824, and the *Hampshire and Franklin Express*, later the *Amherst Record*, established in 1843. In addition, there were three monthly magazines, *Harper's* (established in 1850), *The Atlantic Monthly* (established in 1857), and *Scribner's* (established in 1870). The Dickinsons had close connections with the editors of three of these journals. The *Republican* was edited by beloved family friend Samuel Bowles. The editor of *Scribner's* was Dr. Josiah Holland, whose wife Sophia was a particular friend of Emily's. In 1862 Dickinson initiated a lasting friendship with T. W. Higginson, the literary editor of *The Atlantic Monthly*, to whom she wrote in 1862 asking if her "Verse is alive" (L260). To a large extent it was a magazine age, and there was a great optimism about what the periodicals might achieve. When Alexis de Tocqueville came to America in search of the ideal of democracy in 1831, he found "a triumph of the local": "Not only were the tastes and habits of republican government first created in the townships and provincial assemblies," but in America every hamlet had its newspaper, and its influence was "immense."[2] These journals covered the wide-ranging concerns of the day, from the changing view of the natural world and of human nature, studies of the mind and consciousness, the great evolutionary debates in the words of the key figures in the controversies, and the nature of the Deity and whether He was best studied through his works (nature) or his words (the Bible). There were essays on "American Free Religion," "The Talmud," "Brahmanism," "Buddhism," "Zoraster and the Zend-Avesta," "Confucius and the Chinese," "Mohammed and His Place in Universal History," and "The Intermingling of Religions" by eminent writers such as James Freeman Clarke, Lydia Maria Child, and John Fiske. In the 1850s and 1860s spiritualism was widely regarded as a new religion that demonstrated the truth of immortality and dispelled the terrors of theology, though by the 1870s it had become part of the new study of the mind. As one column in the *Republican* asserted, each age has a "distinguishing genius" and "the genius of the present age is DISCOVERY."[3]

The *Springfield Republican*, edited by Dickinson's beloved Samuel Bowles from 1851 to 1878, was widely regarded as the leading regional newspaper in America; Amherst's own *Hampshire and Franklin Express* was "one of the best country newspapers in New England" (Whicher, 9). Under the editorship of Bowles the *Republican* aimed to present "the fruit of all human thought and action" and to be "the Daily nourishment of every mind."[4] Its pages are full of lively commentary on contemporary issues, with special attention to new books. It prided itself on being sensible, judicious, and balanced. Dickinson said in 1853, "I read in it every night" (L133). Dedicated to the general welfare and the moral and intellectual improvement of the community, the *Hampshire and Franklin Express* was particularly hospitable to local poetry. In a weekly column entitled "Amherst Matters" there were regular reports on Amherst Academy, Mt. Holyoke Female Seminary, Amherst College, and the Agricultural College as well as summaries of lectures by distinguished visitors such as Emerson, Bronson Alcott, and Twain. There were many references, both serious and whimsical, to Darwinian themes.

Of the monthlies, *Harper's* mission was "to place within the reach of the great mass of the American people the unbounded treasures of the

Periodical Literature of the present age."⁵ In "A Word at the Start" in the first issue the editor states that "the wealth and freshness of the Literature of the Nineteenth Century are embodied in the pages of its Periodicals" and that "the best writers in all departments and in every nation, devote themselves mainly to the Reviews, Magazines, or Newspapers of the day."⁶ The Editor vows to bring to the American people "the best of current writing on politics, science, invention, fine art, the speeches of statesmen, and all the varied intellectual movements of this most stirring and productive age."⁷ *Harper's* featured long essays on historical topics and nineteenth-century writers, frequently recounting visits to authors' homes. It included material previously published in British periodicals and reprinted works by Dickens, Mrs. Humphrey Ward, Henry James, Thackeray, Bulwer Lytton, and others. There were essays entitled "Dreams," "New Discoveries in Ghosts," the "State of the World Before Adam's Time," "A Story of the Daisy," "What are the Nerves," "Insect Wings," "Birds – Their Migrations and Sojournings," and "Apian Psychology and Sociology."

The Atlantic Monthly was established in 1857 – after a meeting of Emerson, Longfellow, O.W. Holmes, and J. R. Lowell – as a journal of literature, politics, science, and the arts and a transmitter of American ideas. There were essays on Darwin, Carlyle, Leibnitz, Holbein, Burke, Byron, Keats, the Brownings, Thoreau, Baudelaire, Gautier, Swedenborg, and topics such as "Cerebral Dynamics," "Individual Continuity," "Do Animals Have Souls?," "The Origin of Religion," and "Can a Bird Reason?" Dickinson's friend Higginson wrote frequently for the journal, as did Henry James, Thoreau, Emerson, Nathaniel Hawthorne, Holmes, Louisa May Alcott, Robert Dale Owen, Julia Ward Howe, Bret Harte, and Sarah Orne Jewett. *Scribner's*, under the editorship of Dickinson's friend Josiah Holland, set out to obtain "the best reading that money will buy" and "to furnish the finest illustrations procurable at home and abroad."⁸ It featured literary and scientific essays such as "A Day with the Brownings," "George Sand," "Was Adam the First Man?," "The Great Want of Woman," "Observations on Insect Life," "The Fly," "Modern Skepticism," "Christ's Resurrection Scientifically Considered," "Embalming the Dead," and "Mr. Tyndall's Address to the British Association," as well as an early illustrated account of Yellowstone Park. The monthlies also carried regular sections devoted to local and national news, new developments in science, new publications, and religious matters.

The editors of the periodicals had a clear sense of their "brilliant mission." Samuel Bowles wrote in 1851 that the newspaper had brought about "a new era," a "wonderful extension of the field of vision," and the "compression of the human race into one great family."

> The brilliant mission of the newspaper is not yet, and perhaps may never be, perfectly understood. It is, and is to be, the high priest of History, the vitalizer of Society, the world's great informer, the earth's high censor, and the circulating life blood of the whole human mind. It is the great enemy of tyrants, and the right arm of liberty.[9]

In 1853 he observed that "In no department of American literature has there been such a manifest advancement, within the last five years, as in the periodicals.... The finest minds of the country are busy in their pages." Moreover, their readership has swelled from thousands to hundreds of thousands: "Five years ago *Harper's Monthly*, which now numbers 115,000 subscribers and half a million of readers had no existence"[10] In 1854 Bowles argued that "the foremost of the agencies now molding, swaying, educating, impelling and leading the American mind is the newspaper.... It forms in the United States the daily intellectual food of millions."[11] In Henry Ward Beecher's words:

> No other element of power has such a sphere. The pulpit, the court, the lecture, compared with the newspaper, touch society in but few places.... All the libraries of Europe are not of as much service in the nations of Europe as the newspaper is to this American nation.... Already the chair is more influential than the bench or the platform. No brain can act upon so many as that which speaks by the printing press of the daily newspaper. Ink beats like blood in the veins of the nation.[12]

The newspaper was hailed as "the dominant form of literature now."[13] The energy and exhilaration inspired by these early newspapers is remarkable. As one columnist wrote: "To cultivate and establish a taste for reading is an attainment of the highest order.... We often hear of those who are fond of reading called recluses – hermits. Nothing can be further from the truth. Can he be a recluse who has it in his power to hold converse at any moment with the choice spirits of the world?"[14]

The impact of the periodicals on Dickinson's writing and thought was immeasurable. The establishment of American periodicals was accomplished in less than half a century, and it was the half century in which Dickinson dwelt. She was participating in a very American enterprise; she was reading, interacting, and dialoguing with the best minds of her day. In the constant valorization of reading, and thought, and of writing as an expansion of the intellect, in the pages of the periodicals, she would have found ample validation of her own project. The periodicals were both friends and interlocutors; as she wrote to her friends, the Hollands, "The

Republican seems to us like a letter from you, and we break the seal and read it eagerly" (L133). Like books, the periodicals were friends; in Sewall's words, "She chatted, or argued, or agreed with these friends, it seems, quite as she did with those of flesh and blood. Many of her poems appear to be her end of conversations struck up with what she found on printed pages" (Sewall, 670).

Dickinson's style was inevitably impacted by periodicals; indeed, she might be said to have begun her writing career on her school newspaper at Amherst Academy, the aptly titled *Forest Leaves*, for which she was responsible for the humor columns. Dickinson's writing style was particularly influenced by *The Springfield Republican,* which George Whicher has said was "next in importance to the Bible in determining the mental climate of Emily Dickinson's formative years" (Whicher, 170). More than a newspaper, it was "an epitome of the region" that reported national and foreign events, the happenings in nearby towns, agricultural and industrial progress, and "the beauties of rural scenery through all the changes of the seasons" (Whicher, 170). The *Republican* was the "lengthened shadow of a single man, the second Samuel Bowles, who gave his lifeblood to the paper"; Bowles wrote editorials, prepared copy, and read proof (Whicher, 170). In terms relevant to Dickinson, Whicher points out that Bowles

> ... was remorseless in his war on excess verbiage. "Put it all in the first sentence," was his favorite admonition. Editorials must be condensed to paragraphs, paragraphs to two-line items. He had no use for phrases that did not "make a hole in the target." The *Republican* became famous for its epigrammatic sentences that snapped like a whip and sometimes cut like a knife." (Whicher, 171)

This illuminates Dickinson's style. To catch the explosive spontaneity of thought, she evolved a concise, epigrammatic, elliptical style; her poems work like lightning, with "Flash - / And Click - and Suddenness" (F901 J974). There is an extraordinary rapidity of execution; her first lines "make a hole in the target": "Before I got my eye put out" (F336 J327), "It was not death, for I stood up" (F355 J510). Moreover, the newspapers regularly featured short lists of witty or pithy statements in columns entitled variously "Scrapbasket," "Gleanings," "Paragraphs," "Thoughts of Great Thinkers," and "A String of Pearls." Many of these are reminiscent of Dickinson's aphorisms and epigrammatic statements in her letters, her poems, and her "Prose Fragments."

Of the echoes, correspondences, analogies, and homologies between Dickinson's writing and that of the periodicals, one of the most prominent is the representation of the great nineteenth-century Darwinian debates, which involved the relation between science and theology, the transformed view of nature, and the emotional toll of Darwinian theory; I have examined Dickinson's engagement with these debates in another context.[15] There are countless other examples of the impact of the periodicals on Dickinson's thought. Sometimes it is a resonance, or a complex of ideas that she shares with the periodicals, and sometimes it is a "habitation," as though she inhabits an idea or a motif and then distills it into her own vocabulary and gives it a voice. De Certeau has suggested that a reader is like a tenant who occupies a space for a time, decorates it to his or her liking, and then moves on.[16] Temporarily occupying the space of another is liberating, particularly in the pages of periodicals like Dickinson's, which themselves depicted so many voices and ideas.

A rather obvious example might be seen in Dickinson's transformation of the poem "Nobody by Somebody" in the *Express,* April 4, 1856. The *Express* poem begins: "If nobody's noticed you – you must be small / If nobody's slighted you – you must be tall / If nobody's bowed to you – you must be low / If nobody's kissed you, you're ugly we know." It continues for four stanzas and ends: "If nobody's slandered you here is your pen / sign yourself 'nobody,' quick as you can."[17] In F260/J288 the speaker seems to inhabit the position of being nobody: "I'm Nobody! Who are you? / Are you Nobody - Too?" Dickinson then reverses the subject position; she valorizes the idea of being a nobody, enlists the nobody as a comrade, and asserts their superiority over the somebodies: "How dreary - to be Somebody! / How public - like a Frog."

There are hundreds of thematic and verbal echoes and parallels and correspondences between Dickinson's writing and that of the periodicals, suggesting that her themes were not idiosyncratic and that she was deeply immersed in her culture's preoccupations. One of these themes is death as memorialized in startling poems like F591/J465, "I heard a Fly buzz - when I died," or F479/J712, "Because I could not stop for Death," or F431/J577, "If I may have it, when it's dead." In these poems Dickinson exhibits her affinity with her times; death was a favorite topic in the periodicals. There were reflections on burial practices, curious dying scenes, ways of committing suicide, premonitions of death, premature burial, mummies, embalming, cemeteries, and tombstone inscriptions. An 1851 essay entitled the "Phenomena of Death" offers a series of quaint reflections on ways of dying that maintains that to be shot is "one of the easiest modes of terminating life; yet, rapid, as it is, the body has leisure to feel and time to reflect," while Lord Byron has observed that "in death from a stab wound the countenance reflects the traits of natural character – of gentleness or ferocity – to the last breath."[18] In 1853 a column is devoted to "SINGULAR DEATHS": "Hannibal committed suicide by drinking bull's blood. The Duke of Clarence was drowned by the order of Richard the Third, in a butt of Malmsey wine."[19] There are countless poems about the death of friends, a baby's grave, dreams of the dead, hours with the dead. The July 18, 1844 *Express* features a poem called "The Dead" that warns: "Wrong not the dead, / Lest they Rise in their might / And terrors confound thee / In visions of night."[20] In the "Valley of Death," the poet imagines his kindred underground: "their bodies are couched with the vilest of creatures / And the clod-worm is eating the flesh from their bones."[21] Dickinson shared with the periodicals the prominence of death as a topic as well as the often surprising whimsical or sardonic tone, but for her these poems offered a space for reflection, thinking through this "most profound experiment / Appointed unto men." (F817 J822). Sitting by the dead, as in F78/J88 – "As by the dead we love to sit" – brings a sense of expanse as the dead grow more luminous. As she wrote to Higginson on the death of his baby daughter, "These sudden intimacies with Immortality, are expanse - not Peace - as Lightning at our feet, instills a foreign landscape" (L641).

There are also many analogs in the periodicals for Dickinson's bride poems. The early bridal poems in the *Express* and the *Republican* are poems of sacrifice and loss, compromised autonomy and early death. An essay in the *Republican* January 25, 1845 reads:

> Marriage is to woman at once the happiest and the saddest event of her life; it is the promise of future bliss raised on the death of all present enjoyment. She quits her home, her occupations, her amusements, everything on which she depends for comfort, for affection, for kindness, for pleasure.... The parents by whose counsel she had been guided, the sister to whom she has dared to impart every embryo thought and feeling; the brother who had played with her ... all to be resigned at one fell stroke.[22]

In "The Bride," "The purest hopes her bosom knew / When her young heart was free / And these and more she now resigns / To brave the world with thee."[23] "The Bride's Departure" is a sad farewell to brother, sister, and mother.[24] In "The Home Angel," the gentle young woman dies shortly after marriage, "as dies a flower in Spring," and we are told that "hundreds like her live and die / in England's household bowers."[25] The bride in "Resignation" has "gone into that School / Wherein she lays aside our fond protection / To own a husband's rule" and lives the "same as Dead."[26]

Whereas the bride poems in the periodicals are full of pathos, Dickinson ironizes the limited gender roles assigned to women in her culture. In F330/J273 marriage is a kind of colonization of the bride: "He put the Belt around my Life - / I heard the Buckle snap - / And turned away, imperial / My Lifetime folding up - ." Her brides are acutely aware of their unimportance, as in F280/J493: "The World - stands - solemner - to me / Since I was wed - to Him - / A modesty befits the soul that wears another's - name." However, in F332/J275 the woman is in attack mode. The man is a dim caviler: "Doubt Me! My Dim Companion! / Why, God, would be content / With but a fraction of the Life / Poured thee, without a stint - / The whole of me - forever - / What more the Woman can / Say quick, that I may dower thee / With last Delight I own" (F332 J275). Dickinson's F957/J732, "She rose to His Requirement," brilliantly encapsulates the motifs of the bride poems in the periodicals. It is a profound poem about the loss experienced by the woman in marriage; she loses "Amplitude," "Awe," "first Prospective," and "Gold."

However striking the many verbal and thematic correspondences between Dickinson and the periodicals, it is the connection with the overall tenor of thought that is the most significant: the shared love of learning, the excitement about new ideas and discoveries, the sense of the mind's expanse in relation to the world. Dickinson once said that the Intellect was the "Native Land," "the only Bone whose Expanse we woo" (L888), and she determined from an early age to live as large a life as possible. "Awe," she wrote, is "the first Hand that is held to us ... though there is no Course, there is Boundlessness - " (L471). The periodicals shared this mission and provided an ideal environment for a philosophical poet whose main task was thinking. In 1857 the *Express* extolled the immortal mind and "the wonderful powers of intellect ... as 'a spark of Deity'": "Now it contemplates scenes of earth ... Now it transports us to the Arctic snows ... It soars among the stars .... Its spiritual eye looks into Eternity ... Then let it spread its buoyant, ethereal wings and soar through boundless regions of the universe, and let it freely bathe in the pure invigorating fount of knowledge."[27]

NOTES

1 Allen Tate, "Emily Dickinson," *Emily Dickinson: A Collection of Critical Essays*, ed. Richard B. Sewall (Englewood Cliffs, NJ: Prentice-Hall, 1963), 20.
2 Alex de Tocqueville, *Democracy in America*, ed. Richard Heffner (New York: The New American Library, 1956), 84, 94.
3 "The Distinguishing Genius of the Age," *Springfield Republican* (February 2, 1856).
4 Georgiana Strickland, "The *Springfield Daily Republican*" *An Emily Dickinson Encyclopedia*, ed. Jane Donahue Eberwein (Westport, CT and London: Greenwood Press), 270.

5 "A Word at the Start," *Harper's Monthly* (June 1, 1850).
6 Ibid.
7 Ibid.
8 "Topics of the Times," *Scribners* (November 1870), 106.
9 "The Newspaper," *Springfield Republican* (January 4, 1851).
10 "Periodical Literature," *Springfield Republican* (April 1, 1853).
11 "Newspapers," *Springfield Republican* (June 19, 1854).
12 "Henry Ward Beecher on Newspapers," *Springfield Republican* (April 12, 1859).
13 "The Newspaper the Dominant Form of Literature Now," *Springfield Republican* (August 13, 1875).
14 "The Lecture of President Stearns," *Springfield Republican* (January 19, 1856).
15 Joan Kirkby, "'[We] thought Darwin Had Thrown the "Redeemer" away': Darwinizing with Emily Dickinson." *EDJ 19*.1 (2010), 1–29.
16 Michel de Certeau, *The Practice of Everyday Life* (Berkeley: University of California Press, 1984), 171.
17 "Nobody," *Hampshire and Franklin Express* (April 4, 1856).
18 "The Phenomena of Death," *Springfield Republican* (February 3, 1851).
19 "A Column," *Springfield Republican* (February 15, 1853).
20 "The Dead," *Hampshire and Franklin Express* (July 18, 1844).
21 "The Valley of Death," *Hampshire Franklin Express* (February 1, 1861).
22 "Marriage," *Springfield Republican* (January 25, 1845).
23 "The Bride," *Springfield Republican* (August 22, 1845).
24 "The Bride's Departure," *Hampshire and Franklin Express* (June 15, 1848).
25 "The Home Angel," *Hampshire and Franklin Express* (June 19, 1857).
26 "Resignation," *Hampshire and Franklin Express* (February 21, 1858).
27 "What Is Mind?" *Hampshire and Franklin Express* (August 14, 1857).

PART III

Social, Cultural, Political, and Intellectual Contexts

CHAPTER 14

Religion

James McIntosh

Emily Dickinson had perhaps a purer upbringing in orthodox New England Congregationalism than any nineteenth-century writer of comparable stature. As is well known, the Amherst she grew up in belonged to the orbit of Connecticut Valley Puritanism, made famous by Solomon Stoddard and Jonathan Edwards. If by the 1830s religion in the Valley was more ordered, staid, and genteel than it had been during the Great Awakening, it held on pervasively to its Calvinist inheritance. Only Congregational churches existed in Amherst during Dickinson's formative years. Amherst College, which her grandfather helped establish, was already a center of intellectual evangelical enthusiasm. Her chief figures of early influence come out of this cultural matrix: her mother, a member of Amherst's First Church by profession of faith; her father, head of the Church's parish committee and treasurer of Amherst College; Aaron Colton, the charismatic and kindly minister of the First Church; Heman Humphrey and Edward Hitchcock, presidents of the College; her youthful teachers at Amherst Academy; and Mary Lyon, founder of Mt. Holyoke Female Seminary. As a child and adolescent Dickinson read what was expected at home and at school, learned the Bible and the New England Primer more or less by heart, and heard sermons every Sunday.

One should be careful not to oversimplify or rigidify the effects of this thorough indoctrination. Dickinson benefitted from it as well as chafing at it. She drew strength and comfort from her religious education and would never have been a poet without it. Moreover, as Jane Donahue Eberwein suggests, the religious discipline Dickinson got at home may well have been gentler than is conventionally imagined.[1] For example, the handbook on parenting used by her family, Abbot's *The Mother at Home*, emphasized that a child brought up in a Christian home like the Dickinsons' could herself become a sanctified Christian without undue strain. It is possible that she felt an early assurance of salvation and resented the implication that she was lost and needed to be saved in a revival or at Mt. Holyoke, especially if it meant surrendering her integrity and exposing herself in public. In her early twenties her religious thinking was strongly influenced by the "Theology of the Feelings" preached by Edwards A. Park and Horace Bushnell. Within the Valley Christian community there were plenty of voices urging "a piety of love rather than of conquest," as Bushnell put it.[2] The mature Dickinson expressed such a piety in her own individual ways, in many poems on Jesus and in letters of consolation to believers.

Nevertheless, when she looked back on her childhood in her thirties and forties, she sometimes remembered her religious education as resonant with dread. In one poem, she recalls Calvinist teaching concerning "the Father and the Son" as "portentous" and "appalling" to a sensitive child (F1280 J1258). This is her usual line in testimony about early church experiences in her letters also, however contradicted by her practice as a poet of comfort. She resisted doctrines such as Total Depravity – all humans since Adam are born depraved and sinful – and Limited Atonement – Christ died to atone for the sins of the elect only, not for anybody else. Her family may well have been nurturing, her community respectable, and her schooling encouraging, but she still sensed a menace in her Calvinistic religious instruction. The context of nineteenth-century Connecticut Valley Calvinism supplied her with mixed messages, with a Christianity both trustworthy and appalling.

Dickinson's first significant contact from outside the orbit of Connecticut Valley evangelical culture was Benjamin Newton, her "Father's Law Student" (L750) and a Unitarian. (Unitarians, largely from eastern Massachusetts, worshipped God as one, not as a Trinity, and had a more optimistic view of human nature than Calvinists.) Newton was extremely significant to her as an unofficial teacher of literature and human values. In a commemorative letter after his early death, she wrote, "Mr Newton became to me a gentle, yet grave Preceptor, teaching me what to read, what authors to admire, what was most grand or beautiful in nature, and that sublimer lesson, a faith in things unseen, and in a life again, nobler, and much more blessed - " (L153). Dickinson, it seems, not only learned sentiments not stressed in her Calvinistic education from Newton, such as a hopeful reverence for the sublime and the beautiful in books and nature, but also felt key Calvinist sentiments reinforced, such as "a faith in things unseen" and in the afterlife. Her spirituality was not to be circumscribed by "doctrines" (L200), and she took her spiritual nourishment wherever she found it, including from Newton. Through the openings he made for her she came to Emerson, Parker, Thoreau, and George Eliot. Yet she also kept the religious teaching she had absorbed already as a storehouse of ideas for poetry.

In 1862 she initiated her correspondence with Thomas Wentworth Higginson, a former Unitarian minister, who she claimed, "saved [her] Life" (L330) when he read her poems and in his own way took her seriously as a poet. At first, his status as an outsider seems to have spurred her to indulge in impish skepticism and scoff at her family's orthodoxy: "They are religious - except me - and address an Eclipse, every morning - whom they call their 'Father'" (L261). As her relationship with Higginson developed, however, she confided in him more seriously, experimenting with religious and poetic speculation for his benefit until the end of her writing life.

Unitarian and liberal Protestant ideas were in the air in the Valley, despite the orthodox establishment, and helped Dickinson to think about religion idiosyncratically and flexibly when the Civil War and the Darwinian revolution shook the assumptions she had grown up with. With her wide reading, she was open to all intellectual currents within her ken, from Catholicism to Darwinism. Her thinking has affinities with the Christ- and woman-centered Protestantism she found in Elizabeth Barrett Browning's *Aurora Leigh*. She was aware of the higher criticism stemming from Germany that questioned the literal truth of the Bible, and already in the 1860s she allowed for the possibly legendary character of the Old Testament. Her poems based on Bible stories can have a labile unpredictability to them because she invents the stories while she adopts them. Her reader may ask (as her correspondents may sometimes have asked), "What will this woman say next?"

In her mature thinking on religious questions Dickinson comes to an idiosyncratic synthesis. Necessarily, it contains contradictions. Her response to her heritage and her education was complex, and she made it part of her business to set forth her truths without being caught in fixed intellectual positions. Yet her very open-mindedness has given her significance for later readers coming upon her religious thinking. She was a poet, not a systematic thinker; she used her religious intimations experimentally to create miniature dramas, each with its own orientation. As Fred D. White puts it, "Dickinson is not merely a spiritual poet but a poet who devises scenarios in which spiritual conflicts are played out, thus allowing us to acquire a deeper understanding of the interplay between the supernatural and the natural."[3]

Here then are some tendencies in her treatment of religious issues. First, she focuses on death and suffering, not just as occasions for tragedy but as a stimulus to human courage and community. Dickinson projects and addresses a human community of sufferers especially in her correspondence, a community of those like her who love life and must bear the deaths of those close to them before they die themselves. One of the claims she makes for poetry is that it relieves suffering and gives renewed life. Because of the silent struggles of the "Martyr Poets" and "Martyr Painters," their readers and viewers are encouraged to "seek in Art - the Art of Peace - " (F665 J544). Dickinson's concern for the "Woe" of friends and neighbors struggling against "The Frost of Death" (F1130 J1136) stems in part from her own knowledge of psychological horror in imagined encounters with madness and death, as dramatized in famous poems such as "I felt a Funeral, in my Brain" (F340 J280) or "It was not Death, for I stood up," (F355 J510). But in other poems she finds a religious answer for this pain and bewilderment in Jesus Christ. The archetype of courage in suffering for her was Jesus, who braved death so that others could face it and perhaps conquer it. Dickinson departs from orthodox teaching, however, in that she hardly ever suggests that human sin causes suffering or death and requires forgiveness. Instead, the God who causes all causes death as well.

Second, Dickinson's work contains a long celebration of God's created world, the "Eden, always eligible" (L391) she observed from her study window. While she objected to the God who approves of death, she was also glad to celebrate Him as the God who made the world. She had a good scientific education from disciples of Edward Hitchcock, president of Amherst and ardent advocate of a Christian synthesis of science and religion. She learned both life-long habits of precise observation and a reverential attitude toward nature as a whole while she grew up with his teaching. Yet the turns she sometimes gave this scientific-religious synthesis might have shocked the orthodox Hitchcock. As early as 1859, her answer to Nicodemus's question, "How can a man be born again when he is old?" is not that a man has a conversion experience in church but that he welcomes the spring with all his senses on (F90 J140). Her reverent this-worldliness, a reverence not only for nature but also for her beloved family and friends, remains a key feature of her religious orientation to the end.

Third, she has a poetic investment in the Trinity, a Trinitarian imagination. As Roger Lundin points out, she differs in this respect from writers nurtured primarily in Unitarianism, starting with Emerson.[4] Indeed, as a dramatist of the Trinity she is unique in her age of transition from assumed shared Christian belief to uncertain conviction. It is difficult to know if or how much she "believed" in the persons of the Trinity because she conjures various scenarios for them and adopts different attitudes toward them in different texts. Nevertheless, she imagines Father, Son, and Spirit convincingly and repeatedly. She is most apt to quarrel with a Father God, not only the omniscient and omnipotent God of her late Calvinistic upbringing, but the God of arbitrary Power she found in the Old Testament, as testified in her remarkable poems on Abraham, Moses, and Jacob. Despite her fealty to her family and to "Masters" and "Preceptors," Dickinson has an anti-authoritarian streak that she expresses whimsically or indignantly whenever she contemplates this image of God. Other poems and letters have a different Calvinistic emphasis; in them she hearkens back to an earlier Puritan conception of God as unknowable as well as arbitrary, a God of awe whom her speakers revere as well as dread.

In contrast to her often forbidding image of the Father, the Son is for her a heroic human-divine figure. He is a Jesus drawn from the Bible, especially from the narrative of the crucifixion and resurrection. It was all-important to her that Jesus faced death so that those who came after might have the hope of immortality. He was a "Tender Pioneer" (F727 J698) whose courage made a reunion with Dickinson's lost loved ones at least poetically conceivable. Because in most of her poems about him she assumes he is a stand-in for the Father, his dramatic presence implicitly softens her conception of a God she sometimes quarrels with.

Dickinson's idea of the Spirit is less often articulated, but no less important. It is the human spirit fused with the Holy Spirit. She associates it with artistic creation.

> This is a Blossom of the Brain -
> A small - italic Seed
> Lodged by Design or Happening
> The Spirit fructified -
> (F1112 J945)

Because the blossom flowers from an "italic Seed," it is implicitly likened to a text. A poem or other imaginative expression is "a Blossom of the Brain" fructified by Spirit. Like any "Flower of the Soul / It's process is unknown - ." Dickinson stresses repeatedly that the Spirit cannot be known but can be experienced. When this spiritual Blossom "is found," however, it is cherished as if promising other such encounters. Yet the poem continues by allowing for a frightening doubt. "When it is lost, that Day shall be / The Funeral of God." The possibility that the Spirit can be lost is posed as unlikely, but here if it should happen it would lead to the death of God and "our Lord" as well – all the persons of the Trinity.

Especially toward the end of her life, Dickinson nearly always assumes that "the Spirit lasts" (F1627 J1576). In one of her 1883 letters to her sister-in-law Susan after the death of her son Gilbert, Dickinson assures her, "Hopelessness in it's first Film has not leave to last - That would close the Spirit, and no intercession could do that - " (L871). In a poem sent to Sue that is a profession of faith in the Spirit as well as in the human imagination, Dickinson writes:

> A word that breathes distinctly
> Has not the power to die
> Cohesive as the Spirit
> It may expire if He -
> (F1715 J1651)

The Spirit is "cohesive" and not likely to "expire." Yet in an undertone the poem raises the possibility that it just might, as if once again to complicate faith with doubt. Still, she implies that the Spirit is overpoweringly present in this life and may well survive in an afterlife.

Fourth, Dickinson was preoccupied with immortality, "the Flood subject" as she called it in a letter to Higginson (L319). Her reflections on the Spirit focus on this preoccupation. As with other "subjects of which we know nothing" (L750), she believed and disbelieved in immortality at different times. A belief in immortality came with her upbringing, reinforced by preceptors such as Benjamin Newton. Not surprisingly, the speakers of her poems often assume its reality. One of her speakers looks forward to a reunion with an imagined lover in heaven ("There came a Day - at Summer's full - " [F325 J322]), while another laments that such a reunion cannot happen because in heaven she would prefer her lover to Jesus ("I cannot live with You - " [F705 J640]). Both poems assume a poetic belief in immortality. Yet she could also imagine the afterlife fearfully as the vast chaotic emptiness of "Eternity," in three poems from her most productive years: "Behind Me - dips Eternity - " (F743 J721), "Our journey had advanced - " (F453 J615) and "Because I could not stop for Death - " (F479 J712). This uncertainty about the afterlife persists through letters and poems of her later years. Yet especially in her letters Dickinson is a great consoler. For all her moments of doubt, she could reassure her correspondents that "we are mentally permanent" (L555), even that "Twas Christ's own personal expanse / That bore him from the Tomb" (L776). She offers her faith in immortality to her correspondents as a flower of her religious thinking. She may cast doubt on orthodox certainties even when she consoles, but with a residue of eschatological conviction.

Finally, implicit in her writings on the Trinity and on immortality is the idea that Dickinson included doubt in the experience of faith. As Roger Lundin puts it, she "searched for a way of encompassing the experience of unbelief within that of belief."[5] Her blending of faith and doubt may be her most daring and original experiment in her thinking about religion. She did not hide such a subversive idea. In a lovely letter-poem to her sister-in-law, the professed Congregationalist Susan Dickinson, she wrote, "Faith is *Doubt*" (L912). To the Unitarian Samuel Bowles she recalled "the Balm of that Religion / That doubts - as fervently as it believes" (L489). As Lundin, following James Turner, suggests, she embraced the possibility of doubt within faith in a new historical context. After the Civil War, for the first time in American intellectual history, unbelief became a plausible option for the educated.[6] But Dickinson never entertained it without reaffirming her faith, either immediately or in subsequent texts.

Since her work became publicly known, Dickinson has been placed in many other religious and irreligious contexts than those with which she was familiar. She brought such interpretive speculation on herself by being at once so hermetic, so open-minded, and so inventive in using what she knew. Jane Donahue Eberwein writes eloquently:

> Emily Dickinson's religious experience must be grasped in terms of her Calvinist heritage but ... she performed her characteristic art of distillation to extract from that tradition a spirituality that shatters sectarian boundaries to link her with many different Christian and non-Christian ways of sustaining the soul.[7]

Eberwein argues that Dickinson not only reached out to the various intellectual formations available to her, however suspect – Unitarianism, Transcendentalism, Catholicism – but she also explored the interstices of Calvinism to allow for broader interpretations of religious issues and texts. More than that, she brought new life to great words from her tradition such as "Glory," "Grace," and "Omnipresence," so that later readers attracted to her might be nurtured by them. Eberwein's nuanced argument suggests how Dickinson still speaks to a time of spiritual longing such as ours.

Dickinson has been compared to nineteenth-century religious questioners she could hardly have known, such as Melville, Dostoevsky, and Søren Kierkegaard, a maverick Protestant philosopher and theologian who explored the interaction of doubt, dread, and faith. According to Elisa New, Kierkegaard's "answer to a dogmatic Christianity is a *lyrical* Christianity."[8] He writes of the solitary experience of the man of faith encountering the unknown, an experience that Reason cannot explain but poetry can intimate. New connects his sense of humankind's existential loneliness to Dickinson's in poems of bafflement in the face of whatever "stands beyond" our world (F373 J501). Dickinson uses "a language of disorientation" to represent either unknown psychic terrors or the unknown in religious experience.[9] For example, in one poem her speaker "escap[es] backward" and "forward" only to confront "the Sea" all around her. Yet though she then retreats "blinded" only to touch the sea again with "undermining feet," the disorienting experience "Instructs to the Divine" (F969 J867). New sees Dickinson's Calvinist heritage as unconsciously conditioning her to imagine such a scene of spiritual instruction, where one is powerless and awe-struck in the face of the divine. She singles out Kierkegaard as a theorist of the psychology of faith and the uncertainty of existence who can illuminate Dickinson's quest to represent her experience of the inexplicable. Dickinson's poems of isolated psychic uncertainty represent only one side of her work, but a side not often associated, as in New's study, with her religious disposition.

Since the 1950s, Dickinson's writings have been interpreted in relation to several contemporary approaches to religion. One that seems especially plausible and promising is that of feminist Christian theology. In a suggestive essay, Roxane Harde shows how Dickinson's reverent this-worldliness foreshadows such a body of thought. "Like today's feminist theologians, Dickinson refuses to look past Earth in order to focus only on the end of things."[10] Harde sees no conflict between Dickinson's love of God's earth and her affectionate poems and comments on Jesus Christ. Harde argues that Dickinson emphasizes Jesus's embodied humanity rather than his divinity. The Dickinson who felt a kinship with the human Jesus who was "acquainted with Grief" (L932) "predates ... Christian feminist theologians like Dorothy Soelle and Kristine M. Rankka ... by recognizing that Jesus suffered, and suffers, with the oppressed."[11] But Dickinson's love of the suffering Jesus on the cross does not lead her to accept the doctrine that he died to atone for human sin. Like the contemporary theologian Rosemary Ruether, she "reject[s] notions of the human soul as radically fallen and the human body as inherently corrupt."[12] Harde also touches on how Dickinson entertains doubt as part of the experience of faith. In a subtle reading of "Going to Heaven!" (F128 J79), a sprightly early piece of this-worldly heresy, Harde interprets, "because of the wonder of this life on Earth ... one must doubt God's eternity, yet because of this same wonder God and eternity must surely exist."[13] Dickinson is by no means always such a liberal feminist theologian in embryo. She lacked abstract affection for "the oppressed" if she did not know them. Yet Harde's liberal emphasis balances New's reading of Dickinson's quest through the unknown, guided by a Calvinist unconscious; and Harde provides a surprising modern instance of Eberwein's argument that Dickinson worked through her Calvinist education to feed the spirit of later seekers and believers.

Finally, while we consider how Dickinson has been placed in these intellectually exalted contexts, we might remember that she worked through her religious thought in a domestic setting. When her mother died, she wrote a narrative of this crucial domestic event for her cousins Louise and Frances Norcross. In it she expresses a moment of her faith and doubt clearly, skeptically, reverently, and thoughtfully.

> She slipped from our fingers like a flake gathered by the wind, and is now part of the drift called "the infinite."
> We don't know where she is, though so many tell us.
> I believe we shall in some manner be cherished by our Maker - that the One who gave us this remarkable Earth has the power still farther to surprise that which He has caused. Beyond that all is silence. (L785)

NOTES

1 Jane Donahue Eberwein, "'Earth's Confiding Time': Childhood Trust and Christian Nurture," *EDJ 17.1* (2008), 1–24.
2 Ibid., 6.
3 Fred D. White, *Approaching Emily Dickinson: Critical Currents and Crosscurrents since 1960* (Rochester, NY: Camden House, 2008), 145.
4 Roger Lundin, *Emily Dickinson and the Art of Belief* (Second Edition: Grand Rapids and Cambridge: William B. Eerdmans, 2004), 171.
5 Roger Lundin, "Nimble Believing: Dickinson and the Conflict of Interpretations," in *There Before Us: Religion, Literature, and Culture from Emerson to Wendell Berry*, ed. Lundin (Grand Rapids and Cambridge: William B. Eerdmans, 2007), 84.
6 James Turner, *Without God, Without Creed: The Origins of Unbelief in America* (Baltimore: Johns Hopkins University Press, 1985).
7 Jane Donahue Eberwein, "'Where - Omnipresence - fly?' Calvinism as Impetus to Spiritual Amplitude," *EDJ 14.2* (2005), 13.
8 Elisa New, *The Regenerate Lyric: Theology and Innovation in American Poetry* (Cambridge: Cambridge University Press, 1993), 159.
9 Ibid., 169.
10 Roxane Harde, "'Some are like my own!' Emily Dickinson and the Christology of Embodiment," *Christianity and Literature 55* (2003), 317.
11 Ibid., 319.
12 Ibid., 324.
13 Ibid., 317.

CHAPTER 15

Death and Immortality

Joan Kirkby

We do not think enough of the Dead as exhilarants - they are not dissuaders but Lures - Keepers of that great Romance still to us foreclosed...[1]

The most striking of Dickinson's poems are those about death. There are the simple, homey poems such as "The last Night that she Lived" (F1100 J1100), or "The Bustle in a House / The Morning after Death" (F1108 J1078), or the child-like "I'll tell you how the Sun rose" (F204 J318). There are poems that calibrate the complex emotional states that accompany loss and grief, the magisterial "After great pain a formal feeling comes" (F372 J341) or "I measure every Grief I meet" (F550 J561). There are death poems of acerbic social observation such as "There's been a Death, in the Opposite House," which ushers in the Minister, the Milliner and "the man / Of the Appalling Trade" (F547 J389). There are poems wryly commenting on the Victorian death bed scene, like the wonderful F591/J465, in which the onlookers are waiting for God or Jesus to be witnessed in the room, but the dying person can only hear the erratic buzzing of the fly. There are witty confrontations with death, as in her most famous poem "Because I could not stop for Death - / He kindly stopped for me - " (F479 J712) and the later "Death is the supple Suitor," whose "stealthy wooing" wins at last (F1470 J1445). Then there are those speakers who are so tormented by the riddle of death that they just want to find out what lies beyond and race headlong towards it: "What if I say I shall not wait! / What if I burst the fleshly Gate" (F305 J277). In some poems there is a desire to be close to the corpse and to understand that strange borderland that separates the dead and the living: "As by the dead we love to sit" (F78 J88) or "If I may have it, when it's dead" (F431 J577). Dickinson acknowledges throughout her work that because "it will not come again / Is what makes life so sweet" (F1761 J1741). Ultimately, death is a riddle: "And through a Riddle, at the last - / Sagacity must go - " (F373 J501).

Critics have long recognized that when Dickinson "dipped her 'fingers in the frost,' ...she took full possession of her genius," that "the most gripping of her poems are those centered around the questions *what is death? why is death? and what is it like to die?*"[2] British poet laureate Ted Hughes argued that Dickinson's Holy Trinity was Death, the beloved Creation, and some terrible, intense vision of the final reality of the Soul; "in her devotion to this Trinity," she became "the greatest religious poet America has produced."[3]

What are we to make of Dickinson's interest in death? Was it purely idiosyncratic? What were the discourses of death that were circulating in Dickinson's culture? Prior to the nineteenth century, considerations of death were by and large accommodated in a traditional religious context. However, in the nineteenth century there was a kind of crisis of death, "an intrusion into society of an asymbolic death, outside of religion, outside of ritual, a kind of abrupt dive into literal death" that Roland Barthes has called "*flat Death.*"[4] Death was cut loose from its theological moorings and people encountered death without the promise of an afterlife. Written in 1817 when William Cullen Bryant was only seventeen years old, his poem "Thanatopsis" articulated flat death in the American context. The poem insists that a few days after death "thy image" shall utterly vanish from the earth:

> Earth, that nourish'd thee, shall claim
> Thy growth, to be resolved to earth again
> And, lost, each human trace, surrendering up
> Thine individual being shalt thou go
> To mix for ever with the elements.

The only consolation is that you will not be alone: "All that breathe will share thy destiny," "All in one mighty Sepulchre."[5] It is no wonder that "The *Bareheaded life* - under the grass - worries us like a wasp" and that the theme of the democracy of death recurs in Dickinson's poetry (L220).

In response to this desacralised death, there emerged a variety of discourses of death articulated by philosophers, spiritualists, scientists, and poets, all searching for alternative forms of continuity. Some were trying to reconcile the decomposing corpse in the grave with the literal account of resurrection in the Bible. Others were arguing that the ether that encircles the globe is the key to immortality, and that death in this world is the awakening to life in the unseen world. Some argued that the living and the dead could communicate through mediums, while others insisted that the mind would survive the dissolution of the body and live forever. These writings offer a heady cocktail of ideas and representations of death that resonate with Dickinson's writing. This is not to say that each one bears a direct relation to a specific poem, but that, taken together, they constitute the rich discursive context in which Dickinson wrote. Her poetry animates the various configurations of death and immortality of her culture.

For more than a century, Edward Young's nine-volume poem *Night Thoughts on Life, Death and Immortality* (1742) was one of the most highly regarded poems in the English language. Young was one of the five authors most studied at Amherst Academy and Mount Holyoke; what was meant by English at Amherst Academy was analysis of Cowper's *The Task* and Young's *Night Thoughts*, along with composition based on Porter's *Rhetorical Reader* and the New Testament (Sewall, 349). Although Young's poem was didactically Christian, it was distinctive in turning to darkness and death for illumination: "*Darkness* has more Divinity for me; / It strikes Thought inward, it drives back the Soul / To settle on Herself."[6] The mind is "By *Death* enlarg'd, ennobled, Deifi'd."[7] Whereas life is but "the Triumph of our mouldering Clay," death is the triumph of "the Spirit Infinite!"[8] In Young's poem, death was figured as an impetus to thought, a prerequisite for imaginative reverie. For Dickinson the poem offered corroboration of her sense of death as a mind-expanding subject for philosophical contemplation. As she once remarked, "the unknown is the largest need of the intellect, though for it no one thinks to thank God" (L471).

Dickinson refers to *Night Thoughts* a number of times from 1846 through 1885. In an early letter to her friend Abiah Root she confides her own declining faith: "the world allured me & in an unguarded moment I listened to her syren voice. From that moment I seemed to lose my interest in heavenly things by degrees" (L11). However, she is delighted that Abiah has decided "in favor of Christ": "Surely it is a fearful thing to live & a very fearful thing to die ... I feel when I seriously reflect upon such things as Dr. Young when he exclaimed, O! what a miracle to man is man - " In another letter she tells Abiah about her recent visit to Mount Auburn Cemetery and muses how swiftly the summer has fled, recalling Young's admonition that we should consult those on their death beds for advice on the worth of our pursuits while living: "Pay no moment but in just purchase of it's worth & and what it's worth, ask death beds. They can tell" (L13).

Edward Hitchcock, Professor of Geology and Theology at Amherst College, was an enabling presence in Dickinson's life, providing a model of bold, forthright and fearless speculation. In *Religious Lectures on the Phenomena of the Four Seasons* delivered to Amherst students between 1845 and 1849, Hitchcock tackles the mechanics of resurrection, addressing

Corinthians xv: "How are the dead raised up? And with what body do they come?" He graphically observes that "Men deposit the bodies of their friends in the grave; but do they remain there? The chemist knows full well that they suffer entire decomposition":[9]

> Go to their burial place, and see if among the great congregation that lie side by side beneath the soil, you can discover any signs of life ... you remove three feet of earth; but you shrink back horrified at the corruption that riots there upon all ages and all classes.[10]

To explain by what body they come, he supposes a kernel of wheat "placed in the earth, where it seems for a time to be dying; and indeed, everything does decay except the minute germ which springs forth from, and is nourished by the decaying cotyledon."[11] This is the process by which the resurrection body arises from that which was laid in the grave. Very few particles of the seed enter into the composition of the plant that springs from it, but "if only a millionth part, or a ten thousand millionth part, of the matter deposited in the grave, shall be raised from thence, it justifies the representations of scripture that there will be a resurrection of the dead."[12] However, what about the issue of individual identity? How are we to recognize our dead on resurrection day? Hitchcock is genuinely puzzled but insists that people will be able to recognize each other in the eternal world, and that the spiritual body will be beautiful and glorious, "a contrast to the loathsome and deformed mass which is deposited in the grave."[13] Hitchcock devotes a chapter to "Death in the Current Organisation of Things" in his later book *The Religion of Geology*, arguing that the idea of perpetual change is the grand conservative principle of material things: "though it is inevitable that bodies are sometimes subject to violent disarrangements and destruction...the chemical powers inherent in matter, soon bring forth new forms of beauty from the ruins."[14] Both texts witness Hitchcock as theologian and man of science puzzling out the antimonies of death and resurrection. There are echoes in Dickinson's writing of similar conundrums in poems such as "Do people moulder equally" (F390 J432), "The Spirit lasts - but in what mode" (F1627 J1576), and "The Chemical conviction / That Nought be lost" (F1070 J954). Hitchcock's boldness and freedom in addressing difficult topics, including the grotesque aspects of Death, provided a model for Dickinson to pursue her own questions about death, the grave, and what comes afterwards. It freed her to talk about death in all sorts of unconventional ways in poems like "It was not Death, for I stood up" (F355 J510), "If I may have it, when it's dead" (F341 J557), and "Twas warm - at first - like Us" (F614 J509).

Ultimately Hitchcock provided Dickinson with a sustaining image of continuity. As she wrote to Higginson: "When Flowers annually died and I was a child, I used to read Dr. Hitchcock's Book on the Flowers of North America. This comforted their Absence - assuring me they lived" (L488).

Another discourse of death was offered by spiritualism, which argued for the possibility of communication between the living and the dead and was taken up by religious as well as scientific thinkers. Indeed spirits and spirit rappings, séances, and conversations with mediums and with the dead fill the pages of the periodicals to which the Dickinsons subscribed from the 1850s on. Dickinson's friend Thomas Wentworth Higginson delivered a number of lectures on spiritualism in New York in the late 1850s. In "The Results of Spiritualism," printed in tract form and reported in the *Republican* in 1859, he maintained that "the principal results of the new phenomena, are the demonstration of immortality and the removal of the fear of death and the terrors of theology."[15] Higginson was a harsh critic of the gloom surrounding death and burial in Christianity, arguing that "the world has never seen an inconsistency greater than that between Christian doctrines and Christian words, in connection with death."[16] Not only do Christian writers do their utmost to "annihilate all actual faith in immortality," but they also "deny all relation between the other world and this."[17] Sepulchral gloom is the traditional phraseology of theology, literature, and art. He cites Gray and Dryden writing of departed friends, "Each in his narrow bed forever laid" and "withering in the grave ... never more to see the sun, / Still damp in a damp vault, and still alone."[18]

Spiritualism comes to save men from a religion like this, bringing us out of the gloom and making life "sublimer, not sadder – more rich and vast and beautiful."[19] Higginson insists that God did not mean us to shrink from death, and if we could only experience it, "simple, pure, free from gloom, it would give us hope." There would be "light and air, brightness, and flowers, freshness and peace."[20] Life "is a progression; it does not end here, it begins here;.... Life is the bud, Death the opening."[21] The 1859 version of Dickinson's "Safe in their Alabaster Chambers" (F124A J216) presents a contrast between the Christian and the natural responses to Death. The "meek members of the Resurrection" are "safe" under the "Rafter of satin and roof of stone - " which forever cuts them off from the natural world. By contrast the Bees are babbling and the Sweet Birds are singing above them. "Ah! what sagacity perished here!" is the final comment of the poem.

A scientific essay published in *The Atlantic Monthly* in 1876 offered another concept of death and continuity. In "The Unseen World" John

Fiske notes that although "contemporary theologians seem generally to believe that one necessary result of modern scientific inquiry must be the destruction of the belief in immortal life," it is not so: scientists, "while upholding the doctrine of evolution, and all the so-called 'materialistic' views of modern science ... not only regard the hypothesis of a future life as admissible, but they even go so far as to propound a physical theory as to the nature of existence after death."[22] Scientists suggest that the vast store of expended energy that drives the universe may be an arrangement by which our universe keeps a memory of the past:

> Each particle of existing matter must be a register of all that has happened.... The air itself is one vast library, on whose pages are forever written all that man has ever said or even whispered.... And as there is a continual transfer of energy from the visible world to the ether, the extinction of vital energy which we call death must coincide in some way with an awakening of vital energy in the correlative world; so that the darkening of consciousness here is coincident with its dawning there. In this way death is for the individual but a transfer from one physical state of existence to another.[23]

This vision of the unending cycle of energy no doubt appealed to the poet, who in her cosmic speculative mode sometimes found herself "Beyond the Dip of Bell - " (F633 J378) or watching the world drop away as she finds herself experiencing a kind of physical evaporation "Of one that leaneth from Balloon / Upon an Ether Street" (F573 J1053).

These were among the discourses of death by writers who were part of Dickinson's intellectual circle. However, there were others who were part of the wider discursive field within which she wrote. One important strand of thought was the idea of the "continued existence of the thinking principle."[24] For instance, John Abercrombie, whose *Inquiries Concerning the Intellectual Powers* was set for study at Amherst Academy in the 1840s, stated that "our whole experience is opposed to the belief that one atom which ever existed has ceased to exist"; in "Our Knowledge of Mind" he wrote: "To conceive then, that any thing mental ceases to exist after death, when we know that everything corporeal continues to exist, is a gratuitous assumption, contrary to every rule of philosophical inquiry."[25] This line of thinking was taken up some twenty years later by Boston philosopher and pastor Hubbard Winslow, who devoted a chapter to "The Immortality of the Human Mind" in his *Elements of Intellectual Philosophy*, arguing that the "dissolution of the body is not a cause adequate to destroy the mind," and that "when we are fully convinced that the death of the body does not necessarily destroy the mind – that we may be as truly living and conscious beings beyond the grave as here – we find no difficulty in believing ourselves immortal. The Rubicon is passed; – we are on the other side of death – the king of terrors is vanquished."²⁶

Dickinson's culture, then, was permeated by these restless, persistent, and varied explorations of death and continuity. All this energy of scientific and spiritual speculation was devoted to the intuition that some kind of life does persist, as does the mind and perhaps identity, even in death. There are echoes of these various discourses of death in Dickinson's writing. In the 1860s she wrote in a letter to Perez Cowan that "Dying is a wild Night and a new Road. I suppose we are all thinking of Immortality, at times so stimulatedly that we cannot sleep. Secrets are interesting, but they are also solemn - and speculate with all our might, we cannot ascertain" (L332). In June 1878 she writes to Mrs. Holland about the death of Bryant, saying "We thought you cherished Bryant, and spoke of you immediately when we heard his fate - if Immortality *be* Fate":

> Dear friends - we cannot believe for each other. I suppose there are depths in every Consciousness, from which we cannot rescue our selves - to which none can go with us - which represent to us Mortally - the Adventure of Death - How unspeakably sweet and solemn - that whatever await us of Doom or Home, we are mentally permanent. "It is finished" can never be said of us. (L555)

In another letter to Mrs. Holland she confides that "Austin and I were talking the other Night about the Extension of Consciousness, after Death and Mother told Vinny, afterward, she thought it was 'very improper'. She forgets that we are past 'Correction in Righteousness' - I don't know what she would think if she knew that Austin told me confidentially 'there was no such person as Elijah'" (L650).

I will close by looking at poem F337/J607, "Of nearness to her sundered Things," which resonates with a number of these discourses.

> Of nearness to her sundered Things
> The Soul has special times -
> When Dimness - looks the Oddity -
> Distinctness - easy - seems -
>
> The Shapes we buried, dwell about,
> Familiar, in the Rooms -
> Untarnished by the Sepulchre,
> The Mouldering Playmate comes -
>
> In just the Jacket that he wore -
> Long buttoned in the Mold
> Since we - old mornings, Children - played -
> Divided by a world -

> The Grave yields back her Robberies -
> The Years, our pilfered Things -
> Bright Knots of Apparitions
> Salute us, with their wings -
>
> As we - it were - that perished -
> Themself - had just remained till we rejoin them -
> And 'twas they, and not ourself
> That mourned -

In this poem the dead are all around us and there is a sense of intimacy, familiarity, and restoration. However, the harmony is broken – the beloved playmate is "Mouldering." It is a sudden intrusion of decay, a reminder of the putrefaction of the grave recalling Young's "mouldering clay" and Hitchcock's "decomposing corpse." And yet the mouldering playmate is recognizable; he wears the same clothes he wore when we last played together. Yet we are divided by a world, the unseen world perhaps; he is a denizen of the ether. Nevertheless there is a momentous sense of homecoming and celebration; the beloved dead have been restored to us. The grave gives us back our dead. Is it a resurrection of sorts? Or is it a séance where those who were held dear can come back to us? The bright knots of apparitions suggest a spiritualist gathering. The apparitions also have wings like angels, for whom death is a birth into Immortality. Or perhaps we are the ones who are dying; perhaps the apparitions are coming for us; perhaps it is our time. Perhaps it is we who have perished and the playmate has come to take us, or perhaps we died before and are now being joined by the more recently dead. It is difficult to know who is dead and who is alive, for the truth of the poem is that it is both. Although not without a macabre touch, it is a poem of love and restoration. If only for a time we are reunited with our beloved dead, and whether it is the dead who are coming back or we who are joining them, it is a homecoming. It is a return to and by our loved ones; we are a community again.

NOTES

1 Emily Dickinson, "Prose Fragments," *The Letters of Emily Dickinson*, Vol. III, 919.
2 Conrad Aiken, in *Selected Poems of Emily Dickinson*, ed. Aiken (London: The Riverside Press, 1924), 21; Clark Griffith, *The Long Shadow: Emily Dickinson's Tragic Poetry* (Princeton, NJ: Princeton University Press, 1964), 112.
3 Ted Hughes, *A Choice of Emily Dickinson's Verse* (London: Faber, 1968), 14.
4 Roland Barthes, *Camera Lucida* (London: Vintage, 1993), 92.
5 William Cullen Bryant, "Thanatopsis," *Poems* (Philadelphia, 1848).

6 Edward Young, *The Complaint: or, Night-Thoughts on Life, Death, & Immortality*, ed. Stephen Cornford, 6 vols. (Cambridge: Cambridge University Press, 1989), Vol. V, lines 128–30.
7 Ibid., Vol. III, line 457.
8 Ibid, Vol. III, lines 467–8.
9 Edward Hitchcock, *Religious Lectures on Peculiar Phenomena in the Four Seasons ... delivered to the students in* Amherst *college, in 1845, 1847, 1848 and 1849* (http://www.archive.org/stream/religiouslectureoohitcrich/religious), 3.
10 Ibid., 12.
11 Ibid., 5.
12 Ibid., 6.
13 Ibid., 10.
14 Edward Hitchcock, *The Religion of Geology and Its Connected Sciences* (Boston: Sampson, 1851), 470.
15 *The Republican*, March 21, 1859.
16 Thomas Wentworth Higginson, *The Results of Spiritualism: A Discourse Delivered at Dodworth's Hall, Sunday, March 6, 1859* (New York: S.T. Munson, 1859). http://higginson.unl.edu/writings/twh.wri.18590306.html, 2.
17 Ibid., 5.
18 Ibid., 6.
19 Ibid., 6.
20 Ibid., 7–8.
21 Ibid, 8.
22 John Fiske, "The Unseen World," *Atlantic Monthly* (Vol. 37, 1876), 267.
23 Ibid., 268–9.
24 John Abercrombie, *Inquiries Concerning the Intellectual Powers* (Boston: John Allen & Co., 1835), 35.
25 Ibid., 35.
26 Hubbard Winslow, *Elements of Intellectual Philosophy* (Boston: Hickling and Swan, 1854), 57–8.

CHAPTER 16

Gendered Poetics

Shira Wolosky

Gender has been as defining of Dickinson, and in many ways as confining, as her room in Amherst. After the seduction of early Dickinson biographies, the first generation of Dickinson criticism largely saw gender as a personal psychology of madness and broken heartedness.[1] The next generation of feminist-minded criticism continued to interpret gender through biography, but in a far broader historical and ideological frame. Dickinson's reclusion was recast into a wider net of female domesticity, anxieties of authorship, and bids for empowerment.[2] Dickinson's gender now stood for both self-doubt and self-assertion, in a broad literary historicity made possible through the recovery of works that had been buried with the death of their female authors – a fate Dickinson had avoided by resisting publication altogether, choosing instead a more private circulation of manuscript poems in letters. Poems previously ignored or slighted as trivial began to receive intense scrutiny.[3] The notions of the "domestic"' and "sentimental" underwent a revolutionary upheaval, from privatized and trifling interests to political and ideological critique.[4] Further ideological reassessments of sexuality challenged earlier stereotypes of Dickinson's spinsterhood in terms of lesbian and queer theory.[5] The latest phase of criticism has expanded these directions, with a firmer shift from private to public spheres so as to place and explore Dickinson's work in the historical and cultural contexts of the Civil War, slavery and race, class, contemporary technologies, and publication practices.[6] Integral to such historicist contexts is Dickinsonian religion in ways that have not yet been fully considered, not only as personal sensibility or theological (non)-alignment but within the cultural-political histories of America and specifically of American women.

A gendered poetics, I will argue, would draw on each of the interests and concerns this variety of approaches has pursued, defining Dickinson's texts as in fact a site of intersection among them.[7] This goes beyond recommending a pluralism of critical approaches.[8] It is a critical claim with rigorous lines of argument and analysis. Such a gendered poetics begins in the reassessment of public and private spheres that has been a major topic of feminist theory, from philosophy and political philosophy to anthropology and historical studies. Carole Pateman, Jean Bethke Elsthain, Michelle Zimbalest Rosaldo, Mary Ryan, and many others have contested traditional assignments of women to the private as against a male public sphere. "Public" and "private" themselves emerge as unstable, and indeed ideological categories, in which whatever women do, even when outside the home, is categorized as "private," and whatever men do, even when for private interest (such as making a living or profit) is categorized as "public." But women, certainly in the American context, have been active participants in public life, if not in the official electoral politics of voting and holding office, then in many civic arenas, from abolition to moral reform to suffrage to sanitation to urban planning to libraries and other community initiatives and institutions.[9]

Such direct participation in public life cannot be claimed for Dickinson, although her reclusive habits mask her considerable contact with an array of public figures: from her father, a longstanding Amherst community leader who served as a U.S. Congressman and Representative to the General Court of Massachusetts; to Samuel Bowles, editor of the *Springfield Republican*; to Thomas Wentworth Higginson, who not only was editor of *The Atlantic Monthly* when he advised Dickinson to keep her verse private, but also was the colonel of the first black regiment in the Civil War when Dickinson first wrote to him to ask his advice on her publishing; to Josiah Holland, biographer of Lincoln. Dickinson's public engagements remain textual, and often only oblique, as is so much of what and how she writes. But it is just this obliquity that suggests contours for a gendered poetics.

Such a poetics would first of all consider gender as an inevitable and foundational category of textual analysis. This applies to the gender of the author, the speaking persona, other figures in the text, and the auditor or reader. Gender, that is, immediately penetrates two basic poles of textual constitution, identified by Roman Jakobson as "addresser" and "addressee."[10] These, however, he wished to bracket out of what for him defined the text's aesthetic dimension, what he called "message," but what functions in fact as pure aesthetic form: the composition of the work in its material components. Jakobson also bracketed out what he called "context," meaning all external references; "contact" as the medium through which the text was transmitted; and "code" as lexical definition.

But a gendered poetics challenges just these exclusions, both as to their possibility and with regard to their implications for aesthetic experience.

As against a self-standing, self-referring formal autonomy, a gendered poetics would approach each dimension – addresser and addressee, context, contact and code – as all entering into an aesthetic event, in complex relationships that may be complementary but also contradictory, mutually affirming but also mutually critical. This emphatically pertains to gender itself. Gender cannot in fact be bracketed aside from other modes or areas of experience. Gender instead penetrates into every mode and area. This ironically pulls against the traditional role of gender, in criticism as well as social-political histories, which was to separate and isolate female experience as "private," domestic, constrained. Indeed, such sequestering has largely been the fate of "women's writing" itself. Gender refuses such segregations. Gender as a literary category penetrates address and reception, as well as imagery, topoi, and topics. It is also an historical category, a political and social category, a psychological and anthropological formation, and a religious positioning. Many of these dimensions enter into each artwork, which becomes not a closed form but a scene of intervention among these different areas, whether in conflictual or confirming, critical or harmonizing ways.

In Dickinson, the ways turn out to be mostly, although not only, conflictual and critical. Owing to her reclusive practices in life and writing, it is easy to overlook how many strands of cultural trajectory enter into her compressed texts, which become scenes of their intense confrontation and mutual interrogation. This occurs through the syntactic breakage and slippage, puns, and metaphorical strains that constitute her poetic;[11] and through the intensities of word choice, which almost always include, often quite surprisingly, economic terms that open the texts into the social worlds contemporary to her, including, as economics so intensely does, gender roles.[12] Politics and history likewise make their sudden, often stabbing appearances. Her texts thus address broad and fundamental questions of American culture and self-definition. Religion, too, emerges as persistently, pressingly confronted in Dickinson texts, in complex relation to the other dimensions active within them – gendered, historical, political, social, economic, cultural. This is not to eliminate the poems' aesthetic dimension, but in fact to constitute it. The aesthetic emerges as exactly the site in which these multiple trends of experience come into contact, in multiple ways. This interrelational contact comes to define not only textuality – what a poetic text is – but also, perhaps particularly for a woman, selfhood and authorship. The "addresser," both as poet and persona, takes on particular modes of self-representation that profoundly shape all the other textual forces and composition.

To illustrate this argument for a gendered poetics I take as my text the poem "I play at Riches - to appease" (F856 J801):

> I play at Riches - to appease
> The Clamoring for Gold -
> It kept me from a Thief, I think,
> For often, overbold
>
> With Want, and Opportunity -
> I could have done a Sin
> And been Myself that easy Thing
> An independent Man -
>
> But often as my lot displays
> Too hungry to be borne
> I deem Myself what I would be -
> And novel Comforting
>
> My Poverty and I derive -
> We question if the Man -
> Who own - Esteem the Opulence -
> As We - Who never Can -
>
> Should ever these exploring Hands
> Chance Sovereign on a Mine -
> Or in the long - uneven term
> To win, become their turn -
>
> How fitter they will be - for Want -
> Enlightening so well -
> I know not which, Desire, or Grant -
> Be wholly beautiful -

This text stretches across a multitude of arenas, with gender both a fulcrum and a prism. The speaker of the poem first seems, as recurs in Dickinson, to be male, exactly because of its economic reference. This "I" tries to constitute himself through what was just emerging at the time of writing as an increasingly dominant American self-definition: "Riches." This becomes explicit in the lines "And been Myself that easy Thing / An independent Man - ." But such cultural definition of the self in economic terms is what the poem goes on to examine and complicate, with peculiar gender shifts along the way. "The Clamoring for Gold" casts "Riches" as something restless and desperate. It is, as the poem pursues, a form of lack, of "Want," tempting to "a Thief" or to a kind of negative "Opportunity," or even, as the poem continues, a temptation to "Sin." Perhaps this is a reference to religious suspicions of material wealth as betraying inner spirituality, even as, in traditions of Puritan America famously explicated by Max Weber, wealth is also spirit's outward sign. Or perhaps "Sin" registers Dickinson's own suspicion against her culture's increasing turn to materialist measures of selfhood. "Riches" as the American dream of independent Manhood is here almost dismissed as too "easy," in contrast to genuine achievement, and threatens reduction to a "Thing."

In a manuscript variant, however, instead of "easy" Dickinson writes "distant."[13] To be an "independent Man" is indeed distant from her because she is a woman. Her approach to "Riches" remains mere "play," in part because her "lot" is one not of overabundance but of dearth, a "Poverty" "Too hungry to be borne." "Riches" is denied her, not least as a female who, at the time of writing, had at best very limited property rights. Yet there is also "novel Comforting" derived in her "Poverty." Here Dickinson enters into her persistent practice of weighing, and recasting, gain against loss. "Riches" seems obvious gain. Yet the "Man / Who own" does not in the end sufficiently "Esteem the Opulence" he seeks. As to the speaker, if he or she "never Can" attain such opulence, then he or she also more fully takes its measure, not only because unable to achieve it, but also through questioning its value.

The poem thus characteristically oscillates between the problem of exclusion from riches as if these are desirable but unattainable and a denial of the value of wealth against its increasing force in American culture. To be the "Man / Who own" is to be reduced to an "easy Thing." The fifth stanza of the poem turns on a pun recurrent in Dickinson, "Mine," coupled with a further political/economic pun, "Sovereign." "Mine" is the economic resource of buried precious metals, but also a possessive pronoun by which, in the framework of what has been called possessive or economic individualism, the (male) self is defined, constituted, and derived in his autonomy and status of self-ownership.[14]

But the poem questions whether selfhood's sovereignty can be reduced only to ownership, even as it registers the power ownership claims on the self. The conclusion of the poem remains rigorously ambivalent. On the one hand, it continues to weigh, in explicitly economic and competitive language, the "long - uneven term to win," which may result in the speaker's own "turn" on the wheel of fortune. On the other hand, the last stanza retracts such gain into further fitness for "Want." It remains unclear, that is, whether "Want" or "Riches" are of greater value; whether, as the poem directly states, "Desire, or Grant - / Be wholly beautiful." "Grant" interestingly appears as "Right" in Fascicle 38, the key term of male liberal selfhood. In the poem, however, the self is not exhausted in possession.[15]

Almost any Dickinson poem that seems to assert the power, completeness, and sufficiency of self also questions, exposes, and subverts such assertions. In this, Dickinson both offers a critique of American notions of selfhood and explores a gendering that American ideologies of selfhood, without acknowledging it, fundamentally assume. Dickinson's poems communicate at times a heady sense of power and autonomy of the self, by itself, without need or dependence. But they also project such American, Romantic, or liberal self-definitions as distressed, incomplete, and male. This skepticism of the autonomous self no doubt reflects in part Dickinson's womanly exclusion from its paradigm as well as from the freedom to pursue its promises. But she also questions the paradigm. Her gender may allow her a critical stance on ideologies of the self that dream of releasing it from social, cultural, or religious constraints: constraints that, however, in other ways are constitutive of identity and, although on one level limit, on others extend the self beyond its own boundaries. Dickinson's poetry contests the American model of self-reliance not only in its male gendering, but as partial, untrue to experience, and morally troubling. The power of her poems of selfhood is the way they often point, not toward this dream of American selfhood, but away from its model, whose fissures she exposes.

In Dickinson's work the autonomy of the self is a riveting center, seductive and yet also delusive, a promise of strength that resides on false premises, with hidden costs. In this, she finds firm place within patterns of nineteenth-century American women's concerns. Alexis de Tocqueville had observed in *Democracy in America* that "Americans are restless in the midst of their prosperity," pursuing with "feverish ardour ... their own welfare" and "forever brooding over advantages they do not possess." Yet this restlessness he characterizes as male. In his discussion of "Religion considered as a political institution," he notes that religion cannot "check that passion for gain which [for men] everything contributes to arouse; but its influence over the mind of woman is supreme, and women are the protectors of morals." He continues with an early outline of what was emerging as the ideology of the separate spheres: "To despise the natural bonds and legitimate pleasures of home is to contract a taste for excesses, a restlessness of heart, and fluctuating desires. ...[But] when the American retires from the turmoil of public life to the bosom of his family, he finds in it the image of order and of peace."[16] Home as haven in a heartless world reads female domesticity as retreat from restlessness. But women's own self-representation and writings launch not a retreat from, but a critique of the "passion for gain" and the selfhood it both presumes and constructs. This is a characteristic stance of much nineteenth-century women's writing, in poetry as in prose.

"I play at Riches" offers an intersection between economic and social constructions, with some allusion to religion ("Sin") and to gender ("independent Man"). In the poem "The World - stands - solemner - to me - " (F280 J493) gender and religion are more central, but still within intersecting economic/social constructions.

> The World - stands - solemner - to me -
> Since I was wed - to Him -
> A modesty befits the soul
> That bears another's - name -
> A doubt - if it be fair - indeed -
> To wear that perfect - pearl -
> The Man - opon the Woman - binds -
> To clasp her soul - for all -
> A prayer, that it more angel - prove -
> A Whiter Gift - within -
> To that munificence, that chose -
> So unadorned - a Queen -
> A Gratitude - that such be true -
> It had esteemed the Dream -
> Too beautiful - for Shape to prove -
> Or posture - to redeem!

Dickinson, as unmarried, clearly stands at a disjuncture from the poem's speaker. This is a gap that the poem widens. The speaker begins by expressing all the appropriate postures of bridehood: solemnity, "modesty," the relinquishing of her "name" for someone else's. But then, in Dickinsonian fashion, conventions, both social and linguistic, begin to unravel. The poem's grammar becomes conditional. The speaker's "Doubt if it be fair" points "fair" – a term of fairy-tale romance – toward a very different sense of justice that brings into question the poem's marital transaction. The woman herself not only "wears" the "perfect - pearl" (an ancient image of female – and especially sexual – purity) but is herself projected as this jeweled object: like a necklace, the Man "binds" the woman "to clasp her soul." This reification into costly object stands in contrast to the possibility of choosing some "whiter Gift - within," which would signal an "unadorned" Queenship; but this inner state seems at odds with marriage itself. The poem, as so often in Dickinson, concludes in intense ambiguity. Is the "Prayer" to be "more angel" the woman's own, or the man's about her? Invoking "Gratitude" which, in the context of the religious language in the text, also puns on grace, the poem then revokes it as a conditional "that such be true." The marriage apparently celebrated at the opening, by the end dissolves as a "Dream Too Beautiful - for Shape to prove"; or, in a very concrete material image that unites a woman's body with her status, "posture - to redeem."

Dickinson's poetics of retraction, of calling into question whatever she seems to be offering, here is directed to a set of intercrossing concerns: the gendering of marriage in economic and legal contract, which also carries strong religious implications. The same gendered hierarchy obtains in all these arenas, in ways the poem shows to be mutually enforcing. The institution of marriage as the "legal death" of the femme couvert, in which women lost (as was still the case in Dickinson's time) their legal, economic, and even national identity, is signaled here in bearing "another's - name" upon her marriage - the sign of transfer of the woman, with any rights and properties, from father to husband. The "modesty" invoked in the text is almost an emblem for this feminized social status. In proliferating etiquette books, magazine articles, and images circulated throughout the discourses of culture, modesty sums up the proper feminine "posture," in body and dress, in voice and its muting, in all public comportment – strictures which Dickinson, for all her critical vision, obeyed. Indeed, the "whiter Gift" of this text evokes Dickinson's own habit of white dress. Yet modesty itself emerges in this text as double-edged, invoking the norm that would keep women in restricted place, while they also employed it, especially in their writing, as a mode of self-representation specifically from a feminized viewpoint and stance.

Many feminist commentators argue that Dickinson withdrew from society in order to gain control over her self, her life, and her work; in this way, she resisted just the sort of ceding of personhood that marriage entailed in her period. There is, however, a profound ambivalence in Dickinson's reclusion, which conformed to as much as it resisted gender norms, an ambivalence fully enacted in this poem. One powerful effect of the poem is to show how legal, economic, and religious norms construct and enact gender in mutually enforcing ways. The poem interweaves and overlays religious with gendered experience, implicating theological as well as social and economic constructs that all operate through gendered hierarchy. Social, economic, religious, and gendered levels are both corollary and convergent. The wedding is at once social and religious, from its note of solemnity and its hymnal metrical echoes, to the "soul" in the poem as wed "to Him" – a social contract that parallels religious order. The "pearl" image links female (sexual) purity with economic value. "Munificence" takes the place of love in the poem's language of exchange. Even "Dream" is "esteemed," which, like "to redeem," has both religious and market senses. Women are among what (male) possessive individuals possess. But this threatens to reduce all relationship to possession and exchange – a core concern of many nineteenth-century women writers.

"The World Stands Solemner" clearly makes gender a central topic through tropes of marriage that then expand outward into economic and religious systems, exposing their implicit gendering. "I play at Riches" is more obliquely gendered, but gender still acts as an axis for the economic and cultural values it more directly engages. In these and other ways gender is revealed as a fulcrum of culture and as an indelible dimension in aesthetic representation. Gender, then, and poetry itself, emerge not as sequestered private concerns but as foundational public engagements.

NOTES

1 For example, John Cody, *After Great Pain* (Cambridge, MA: Belknap Press of Harvard University Press, 1971).
2 Sandra Gilbert and Susan Gubar, *The Madwoman in the Attic* (New Haven, CT: Yale University Press 1979); Suzanne Juhasz, *Naked and Fiery Forms* (New York: Harper and Row, 1976).
3 Joanne Fiet Diehl, *Dickinson and the Romantic Imagination* (Princeton, NJ: Princeton University Press, 1981).
4 Jane Tompkins, *Sensational Designs* (New York: Oxford University Press, 1985); Joanne Dobson, *Dickinson and the Strategies of Reticence* (Bloomington: Indiana University Press, 1989).
5 Early works on Dickinson's gender include Vivian Pollak, *The Anxiety of Gender* (Ithaca, NY: Cornell University Press, 1984); Paula Bennett, *My Life, A Loaded Gun* (Boston: Beacon Press, 1986). For arguments regarding Dickinson's sexuality, see Martha Nell Smith, *Rowing in Eden* (Austin: University of Texas Press, 1992).
6 See, e.g., Shira Wolosky, *Emily Dickinson: A Voice of War* (New Haven, CT: Yale University Press, 1984); Paul Crumbley, *Winds of Will: Emily Dickinson and the Sovereignty of Democratic Thought* (Teuscaloosa: University of Alabama Press, 2010); Karen Sanchez-Eppler, *Touching Liberty: Abolition, Feminism and the Politics of the Body* (Berkeley: University of California Press, 1993).
7 For fuller discussion, see Shira Wolosky, "Relational Aesthetics and Feminist Poetics," *New Literary History* 41.3 (2011), 571–92.
8 Annette Kolodny "Dancing through the Minefield: Some Observations on the Theory, Practice, and Politics of a Feminist Literary Criticism," in *New Feminist Criticism*, ed. Elaine Showalter (New York: Pantheon, 1985), 144–5; 159–63 argues for such pluralism of feminist critical practices.
9 For example, Lori Ginzberg, *Women and the Work of Benevolence* (New Haven, CT: Yale University Press, 1990). For a fuller discussion, see Shira Wolosky, "Public Women, Private Men: American Women Poets and the Common Good," *Signs* 28.2 (Winter 2003), 665–94.

10 Roman Jakobson, "Linguistics and Poetics," *Style in Language*, ed. Thomas Sebeok (Cambridge, MA: MIT Press, 1960), 350–77.
11 Compare with Cristanne Miller, *Emily Dickinson: A Poet's Grammar* (Cambridge, MA: Harvard University Press, 1987).
12 See Thorstein Veblen, *Theory of the Leisure Class* (New York: A. M. Kelley, 1965) for the gendering of economic roles.
13 R. W. Franklin, ed. *The Manuscript Books of Emily Dickinson* (Cambridge, MA: The Belknap Press of Harvard University Press, 1981), 936.
14 C. P. Macpherson, *The Political Theory of Possessive Individualism* (London: Oxford University Press, 1962). For how women are not, see Linda Kerber, "Can a Woman Be an Individual?" *Toward an Intellectual History of Women* (Chapel Hill: University of North Carolina Press, 1997), 201–23.
15 R. W. Franklin, ed. *The Manuscript Books*, 935.
16 Alexis de Tocqueville, *Democracy in America* Vol. 2, Chapter 13; Vol. 1, Chapter 17. Available at: http://xroads.virginia.edu/~HYPER/DETOC/ (Accessed March 23, 2013).

CHAPTER 17

Democratic Politics

Paul Crumbley

Scholarly interest in the political significance of Dickinson's writing is a relatively recent development, in large part stimulated by a late-twentieth-century theoretical shift away from formalist criticism that brought with it an enhanced appreciation for the interconnectedness of literature and culture. In Dickinson's case, the new attention to public dimensions of her writing has been impeded by a persistent and longstanding myth about the poet: that she was an eccentric genius whose reclusive lifestyle reflects an artistic temperament disengaged from her historical moment. Research now demonstrates that the walls of the poet's home were more porous than previously thought. Her careful reading of newspapers, periodicals, and current authors, together with her participation in cultural discourses of the public sphere – such as her poetic responses to the Civil War – all provide evidence that situates her poetry within a vibrant intellectual world much concerned with politics. Dickinson's poetry is no longer studied only for what it tells us about her withdrawal from the world, but also for the ways it helps us understand how she engaged it. One example of that engagement is suggested by the political activism of the men in the family, particularly the poet's father, Edward, and brother, Austin, whose participation in civic life Coleman Hutchison has described as making the Dickinson home a "*political* house ... one in which the politics of the day were ... discussed with some regularity."[1]

Despite the critical inclination to magnify Dickinson's detachment from worldly concerns, not every early reader associated Dickinson with the myth of the recluse, or immediately judged her stylistic innovations as the eccentric outpourings of an isolated genius. William Dean Howells presented a notable departure from this view in a January 1891 review that rejected the tendency to dismiss her poems as stylistically crude, proposing instead that Dickinson "meant this harsh exterior to remain," adding that "no grace or smoothness could have imparted her intention as it does." Even more impressive is Howells's recognition that Dickinson's writing reflected the economic and political currents of her American moment. "If nothing else had come out of our life but this strange poetry," he writes, "we should feel that in the work of Emily Dickinson America, or New England rather, had made a distinctive addition to the literature of the world ... and the interesting and important thing is that this poetry is as characteristic of our life as our business enterprise, our political turmoil, our demagogism, our millionarism."[2] What now seems most perceptive about Howells's review is his recognition that Dickinson's writing was cut from the same cloth as democratic politics and capitalism, a position that today's scholars are examining with renewed vigor, in effect picking up where Howells left off.

Building on Howells's perceptions has been a slow process, due in part to the critical inclination to view Dickinson's poems about interior experience as windows into a solitary self. Even when scholars take Virginia Jackson's advice and replace the fictive lyric subject required by twentieth-century forms of lyric reading with a real, historically grounded subject, the political content can still be hard to see. This is because, as Jackson so accurately notes, Dickinson "tended to take all kinds of public and private, artificial and natural materials into the everyday life of a private person."[3] What this means is that Dickinson's poems about the interior life do indeed explore subjective experience but in a manner that looks outward as well as inward; they turn out to be the best place to look for political content precisely because in them Dickinson shows readers how particular speakers position themselves in the world around them. Once reader attention focuses on the decision-making processes of particular speakers, the poems take shape as commentaries on the citizen's independent exercise of free will that is crucial to the democratic principle of individual sovereignty. Readers then evaluate these decisions through a close scrutiny of speaker choices, a process that enacts on a small scale the critical habit of thought so essential to the democratic citizen's passive or active consent to the decisions that shape the larger political world. Because Dickinson wishes to preserve and strengthen the independent thought of readers, she does not prescribe specific actions; instead, she makes it clear that action of some sort is necessary. Geoffrey Sanborn has this aspect of Dickinson's writing in mind when he argues that Dickinson should *not* be viewed "as someone whose self-gratifying isolation is essentially at odds with democratic sociality." Rather, he contends, despite the fact that Dickinson did not engage in openly political discourses, "she does model a practice that is a precondition of those discourses."[4] She was never a reformer, a dedicated progressive, or a consistent partisan of any stripe, yet the fierce independence so consistently communicated in her poems is fundamentally democratic in its insistence that authority derives from individual consent.

What is most democratic, then, about Dickinson's political writing is her concern with choices that take place in the realm of epistemology, not the development of a consistent political ideology. In the 1828 edition of *Webster's American Dictionary of the English Language* that Dickinson's family owned, democracy is defined as "Government by the people; a form of government, in which the supreme power is lodged in the hands of the people."[5] The *Oxford English Dictionary* reiterates the central role of the people when it states, "sovereign power resides in the people."[6] Dickinson correctly understood that for citizens to exercise their sovereign power they had to develop the habit of exercising free will and independent choice. This is the view Alexander Hamilton expressed in the first page of *The Federalist* where he writes that the success of the American experiment with democracy rests on "the important question, whether societies of men are really capable or not, of establishing good government from reflection and choice, or whether they are forever destined to depend ... on accident and force."[7] Once the citizenry develops the habit of "reflection and choice" that Hamilton identifies, governments face the challenge of representing multiple points of view. In Harold Laski's words, "the power of a State over its own members is, very largely, a problem of representing wills."[8] Dickinson's poetry shows her appreciation for the citizen's obligation to exercise free will on a daily basis as a means of ensuring that the government never relaxes its efforts to provide effective representation. As a political writer, Dickinson's greatest concern was that the citizenry would become complacent and in doing so cede sovereign authority to a government no longer held accountable to the will of the people. Through her poems, Dickinson relentlessly combats complacency by magnifying the choices implicit in the most mundane as well as the most dramatic of human experiences. In Katha Pollitt's words, "every line she wrote is an attack on complacency and conformity of manners, mores, religion, language, gender, thought."[9]

Of the many Dickinson poems that touch on the interconnectedness of free will and choice, none do so with greater clarity than "A Deed knocks first at Thought" (F1294 J1216). As the first line makes clear, the triggering event is the mind's consideration of a deed. The article "A" indicates that the deed is one of many potential deeds and not "the" deed, suggesting that thought is aware of alternative actions that it is not selecting at this moment. Holding alternatives at bay in turn implies resistance, a notion reinforced by the "knocks" metaphor that suggests admission is not automatic. If acceptable to "Thought," the deed then travels to the will, where it once again "knocks" for admission, implying yet another form of resistance that must be overcome. This time the resistance means that a deed approved by thought may be rejected by the will, signifying the speaker's recognition of the familiar gap separating thought from action, a gap that must be overcome by an exertion of will if an approved deed is to enter the world as an "Act." The final step is the will's transfer of the deed to the outside world: if the "Will [is] at Home and well," the deed "goes out an Act." In other words, even if the will is present it may not be well enough to assist with the deed's passage into the world as an act. By stating that a healthy will coordinates with thought and enables the deed's passage from its "Home" in the mind to the world outside that home, the poem advocates a deliberate union of thought and action that is achieved through exercise of the will. The final three lines of the poem tell us that if the actions approved by the mind do not pass into the world, they enter an "entombment" so complete that only God is aware of their "Doom." The obvious political message is that individual health depends on the ability of the citizen to translate private contemplation of potential deeds into actions that take place in the real world. Deeds that are approved by the self but remain private and known only to God are of no use to anyone.

Dickinson further develops the political significance of the will in "Revolution is the Pod" (F1044 J1082), where failure to exercise the will threatens liberty by disconnecting it from the spirit of revolution. As was the case with "A Deed," Dickinson here concentrates on the central role the will performs in maintaining overall health; she even uses a variant of the word "entombed" that appeared in that poem to describe the death of revolution and liberty brought about through a failure of will. A distinctive democratic feature of both poems is Dickinson's presentation of the will as a faculty that must be exercised to achieve positive change. In this poem, though, the speaker focuses on the essential role the will plays in securing liberty by perpetuating revolution. Using terms such as "Revolution," "Systems," and "Liberty," Dickinson pushes the scope of the poem beyond the individual citizen so that we consider what might be thought of as the collective political will of the people that directs the ship of state. Read in this light, the passive construction of the third line, "When the Winds of Will are stirred," embodies the central democratic axiom that the nation is stirred to action by a citizenry accustomed to the exercise of individual sovereignty. Just as in "A Deed," the poem traces a logical sequence of events that forms the foundation for productive political action; in this instance, liberty thrives when the will is activated. By describing revolution as a "Pod" that achieves an "Excellent … Bloom" when the "Winds of Will are stirred," the speaker clearly advocates revolution. The metaphoric reference to "Winds" suggests both an active exertion of will and the notion that the spirit is involved, drawing on the idea that revolution perpetuated by the will of the people is essential to the spirit of a nation whose liberty is founded on democratic principles.

The line of reasoning that unites resistance with sovereignty is wonderfully productive across Dickinson's oeuvre and central to her political epistemology. The poem "A Prison gets to be a friend - " (F456 J652) presents the loss of liberty as a direct result of diminished resistance. This particular speaker goes so far as to state that without resistance liberty ceases to be a realistic possibility: "The Liberty we knew / Avoided - like a Dream - ." In "No Rack can torture me - " (F649 J384), the speaker situates liberty specifically within the domain of thought, concluding that "Captivity is Consciousness - / So's Liberty - ." Another short poem succinctly reiterates this core principle: "No Prisoner be - / Where Liberty - / Himself - abide with Thee - " (F742 J720). The repeated message that resistance is an essential precondition for liberty appears also in "They shut me up in Prose - " (F445 J613), where the speaker declares, "Himself has but to will / And easy as a star / Look down upon Captivity - ." Dickinson's insistence that liberty requires resistance reflects her recognition that the sovereign self is continuously in danger of accepting confinement, especially if the form of restraint is so comfortable that it becomes hard to detect and therefore resist.

To combat the threat of complacency, Dickinson compels reader scrutiny of decisions that inadvertently restrict personal freedom by foreclosing the possibility of resistance. One notable instance of this is through her use of unreliable speakers whose failures to activate the will serve as cautionary tales that dramatize faulty reasoning. This is the case with "Unto like Story - Trouble has enticed me - " (F300 J295), an overtly political poem in which the speaker aspires to be like those "Brothers and Sisters - who preferred Glory" and bent their "young will" to noble purpose. However, even though she acknowledges that "Feet, small as mine - have marched in Revolution," the speaker postpones taking action for fear that she might "shame" the "sublime deportments" of the predecessors she admires. Readers who see through the speaker's rationalization withhold their consent and independently imagine alternative courses of action. Similarly, the speaker of another poem, who declares "I play at Riches - to appease / A Clamoring for Gold - " (F856 J801), justifies inaction by claiming that her current circumstance is superior to the position of power she desires. The speaker deludes herself into believing that actual achievement is inferior to the dream of attainment she sustains by imagining a future when her own "exploring Hands" will "Chance Sovreign on a Mine." In the meantime, she contents herself with an aesthetic conundrum: "I know not which, Desire, or Grant - / Be wholly beautiful - ." As in "Unto like Story," this speaker expresses resistance by admitting a desire to change her circumstances but fails to mobilize the will and take the action that would bring liberty and health.

To see the political content expressed in poems such as "Unto like Story" and "I play at Riches," readers must be attentive to the many ways speakers surrender sovereignty rather than risk losing the security offered by the status quo. Such reading requires a willingness to resist the conclusions of speakers through independent assertions of will that retain reader sovereignty, in effect mimicking public acts of resistance and choice. This strategy invests the experience of reading with political significance even when the content of poems is not overtly political. Dickinson's famous dashes, her capitalization, and her use of variants are all examples of the way she destabilizes the fundamental structure and syntax of the poems as a means of extending her demand for reader choice even to the smallest and most elemental features of her poems. Doing so draws readers into the creative process itself, democratizing the act of reading by leveling the authority of reader and text. Her multiplication of speakers with conflicting attitudes and her creation of poems that support contradictory views further complicate the reader's decision-making role in a manner that is also of a piece with her interest in democratic thought, where resistance and choice require the intellectual flexibility of nimble minds.

Once it is understood that the independent thought Dickinson requires of her readers is consistent with her aims as a democratic writer, comparison with contemporaries such as Whitman and Emerson becomes unavoidable. In his 1871 essay "Democratic Vistas," for example, Whitman's language describing the mental gymnastics performed by democratic readers might also be applied to Dickinson: "the process of reading is ... an exercise, a gymnast's struggle; that the reader ... must himself or herself construct indeed the poem .... Not the book needs so much to be the complete thing, but the reader of the book does."[10] Dickinson is also a trainer of readers who must develop as mental gymnasts if they are to participate in the revolutionary changes required by democratic culture. Through her emphasis on the power of individuals who resist conformity and instead dedicate themselves to individualized modes of thought and action, Dickinson echoes Emerson's declaration that "a greater self-reliance ... must work a revolution in all the offices and relations of men."[11] For Dickinson, as well as Emerson and Whitman, the spirit of revolution had to be urged precisely because the stultifying influence of conformity was very much in the air; for all three, maintaining the liberty achieved by the founding generation depended on the unrelenting independence of all Americans who succeeded them.

Recognition that Dickinson insists on the gymnastic flexibility of her readers has achieved a growing consensus among critics and scholars, but this dimension of her writing has not yet been examined fully in terms of the democratic implications I have just identified. Robert Weisbuch describes Dickinson's writing as composed of "very different notions of what the self can do and what the world allows," all of which "coexist in creative tension" that leaves little room for reader complacency.[12] Alicia Ostriker observes that in Dickinson's poetry "contrary meanings coexist with equal force."[13] Other scholars focus more narrowly on the process of sorting through a proliferation of interpretive possibilities. Cristanne Miller proposes that "the reader must continually stabilize the text by choosing what belongs in it and at the same time repeatedly return to account for the other, unchosen, possibilities of the poem's meaning."[14] In Gary Lee Stonum's words, the reader "becomes a writer – part poet, part recording auditor."[15] Jed Deppman identifies a "profoundly conversational, other-dependent conception of poetry" through which Dickinson "collaborate[s] or compete[s] with real or implied readers."[16] Commenting specifically but not exclusively on Dickinson's manuscripts, Martha Nell Smith also describes reading as a form of collaboration: "reading is a dialogic drama, always a matter of editing, of choosing what to privilege, what to subordinate."[17] All of these approaches acknowledge the process of resistance and choice that I have associated with a democratic political orientation but assess that process in nonpolitical contexts.

The closest approach to an openly political discussion of Dickinson's writing has come through the recent wave of interest in Dickinson's responses to the Civil War. Shira Wolosky's groundbreaking *Emily Dickinson: A Voice of War* that first appeared in 1984 is now heralded as a seminal text that paved the way for an important emerging subfield of Dickinson scholarship. John Shoptaw effectively captures this sea change in his 2010 essay, "Dickinson's Civil War Poetics: From the Enrollment Act to the Lincoln Assassination," when he opens with the following sentence: "That the Civil War has a part to play in Dickinson's poetry is no longer in dispute, though what part it plays is a more complicated question."[18]

Critics no longer need to justify discussions of Dickinson's poems about the Civil War, or – I would argue – politics in general, and can instead devote their attention to her work as a writer dedicated to all facets of human experience, including what it means to be a female citizen in the democratic republic that is nineteenth-century America.

Dickinson scholarship has not yet reached the point where it is possible to say that the part democracy plays in her writing is beyond dispute, but it *is* possible to affirm that recent explorations of Dickinson's political commitments have opened a new field of study within which her democratic sensibility will be a subject of increased scholarly interest. Wolosky announces her participation in this emerging field of scholarship in *Poetry and Public Discourse in Nineteenth-Century America* when she describes Dickinson as voicing a distinctly "American identity consisting of economic, political, and cultural images and references." In language reflecting Dickinson's demand for gymnastic readers, she proposes that her poetry "be seen as a battlefield of ... clashing and conflicting impulses and commitments, with each text offering its own configuration and contest among them, as do poems against and with each other in the ongoing project of her work."[19] Echoing Howells in presenting Dickinson as an expression of American democratic culture, Wolosky goes on to argue that the contests staged in Dickinson's texts reflect a dynamic process of national self-definition that each citizen experiences on a personal level. The challenge that lies ahead is that of connecting new critical insights about the unique demands Dickinson places on her readers to the distinctly democratic impulses that ultimately define her as one of America's most powerful democratic writers.

NOTES

1 Coleman Hutchison, "'Eastern Exiles': Dickinson, Whiggery, and War," *EDJ* 13.2 (2004), 10.
2 William Dean Howells, "Editor's Study," *Harper's New Monthly Magazine* 82 (January 1891), *Reception*, 77, 78.
3 Virginia Jackson, *Dickinson's Misery: A Theory of Lyric Reading* (Princeton, NJ: Princeton University Press, 2005), 92, 53.
4 Geoffrey Sanborn, "Keeping Her Distance: Cisneros, Dickinson, and the Politics of Private Enjoyment," *PMLA* 116.5 (October 2001), 1345.
5 Noah Webster, *An American Dictionary of the English Language*, 2 vols. (New York: S. Converse, 1828).
6 *The Oxford English Dictionary: Complete Text Reproduced Micrographically* (Oxford: Oxford University Press, 1971).

7 Alexander Hamilton, "'Publius,' *The Federalist* I, October 27, 1787," *The Debate on the Constitution: Federalist and Anti-Federalist Speeches, Articles, and Letters During the Struggle over Ratification*, ed. Bernard Bailyn, Vol. 1 (New York: Literary Classics of the United States, 1993), 3.
8 Harold Laski, *A Grammar of Politics: Democratic Socialism in Britain*, Vol. 6 (London: Pickering & Chatto, 1996), 66.
9 Katha Pollitt, "Poetry Makes Nothing Happen? Ask Laura Bush," *The Nation* (February 24, 2003): Online 2. Available at: www.thenation.com./doc.html?I=20030224&s=pollitt (Accessed March 23, 2013).
10 Walt Whitman, *Walt Whitman: Complete Poetry and Collected Prose* (New York: Literary Classics of the United States, 1982), 992.
11 Ralph Waldo Emerson, "Self-Reliance," *Emerson's Prose and Poetry*, ed. Joel Porte and Saundra Morris (New York: W. W. Norton, 2001), 132.
12 Robert Weisbuch, "Prisming Dickinson; or, Gathering Paradise by Letting Go," *Handbook*, 220.
13 Alicia Ostriker, *Stealing the Language: The Emergence of Women's Poetry in America* (Boston: Beacon Press, 1986), 40–1.
14 Cristanne Miller, *Emily Dickinson: A Poet's Grammar* (Cambridge, MA: Harvard University Press, 1987), 49.
15 Gary Lee Stonum, *The Dickinson Sublime* (Madison: University of Wisconsin Press, 1990), 11.
16 Jed Deppman, *Trying to Think with Emily Dickinson* (Amherst: University of Massachusetts Press, 2008), 28.
17 Martha Nell Smith, *Rowing in Eden: Rereading Emily Dickinson* (Austin: University of Texas Press, 1992), 53.
18 John Shoptaw, "Dickinson's Civil War Poetics: From the Enrollment Act to the Lincoln Assassination," *EDJ 19*.2 (2010), 1.
19 Shira Wolosky, *Poetry and Public Discourse in Nineteenth-Century America* (New York: Palgrave, 2010), 16.

CHAPTER 18

Economics

Elizabeth Hewitt

Given that one of Emily Dickinson's best-known poems, "Publication - is the Auction" (F788 J709), seemingly reviles the commodification of art, it comes as no surprise that generations of scholars have seen the poet as, in the words of an early critic, "above economics" (Whicher, 200). Her comparison of publication to, at best, a mercenary and "Disgrace[ful]" marketplace, and, at worst, a slave auction has given corroboration to the mythology of Dickinson as private and abstemious – as a woman who chose not to participate in the growing market and commercial culture of mid-century New England. Because of her celebrated disdain for fame, Dickinson has been an exemplary case study of the romantic who had no truck with the degradations and prosaic details of economic exchange and of labor for hire. That she resisted publication in conventional literary markets and never married offered still more biographical corroboration for the portrait of Dickinson as contemptuous of the marketplace. Isolated from the world, refusing to consume or consummate, manufacturing only rarified and private poetic products, so the story went, Dickinson epitomized the separation between art and economics.

Increasingly, however, scholars have attended to the poet as a product of, and commentator on, social and economic forces. Even as early as 1964, Robert Merideth instructed readers that Dickinson matured "in the midst of the Age of Enterprise [and] the Rise of Finance Capitalism."[1] Calculating that 10 percent of Dickinson's verse employs "the language of economics," he argued that Dickinson engaged in such appropriation to criticize and condemn the "counterfeit values of her time."[2] For Meredith, Dickinson's poetry was at least partially motivated as resistance to the "men of the 'almighty dollar' who were crowding the Dickinson house daily."[3] The phrase "almighty dollar" was Dickinson's own, written in a letter to her brother, Austin, in June of 1853, the week that rail passenger service arrived in Amherst (L128). Reading this same phrase forty years later in almost precisely the same way, Vivian Pollak argues that

Dickinson reveals her "desire to retreat into an older pastoral order of kinship, status, and love," and that her poetry constitutes "an act of political and social resistance against the disruptive democratic, commercial, and technological forces of her time."⁴ Peter Stoneley also locates Dickinson in an increasingly industrial and commercial economy, and similarly stresses that although Dickinson "displays an unguarded fascination with the operations of business and technology," she does so in order to "imagine herself as a figure whose womanly gentility was dated and uncertain in a newly commercialized environment."⁵ Such examples reveal that even as criticism has become increasingly attentive to Dickinson's placement in the economic world, there remains an indefatigable tendency to read her as essentially critical of a nineteenth-century economic culture that is assumed to be antithetical to poetry. With this assumption, critics continually strive to rescue Dickinson's work from the degradations of capital.

But Dickinson's writing does not corroborate this condemnation of commerce. In the letter to her brother from which the "almighty dollar" phrase is taken, she describes the wide social range of the new visitants: "Our house is crowded daily with the members of this world, the high and the low, the bond and the free, the 'poor in this world's goods,' and the 'almighty dollar'" (L128). And when she contemplates the upcoming commencement at Amherst College, at which she imagines many will use the new rail service to arrive, she confidently announces "[I] don't doubt the stock will rise several percent that week" (L128). Given that citizens of Amherst had purchased more than $50,000 worth of stock and that her father was both a major shareholder and director of the company, she had very good reasons to wish for the venture's success. Far from being dismissive of such investments, Dickinson's letters and poetry reveal her deep awareness and keen appreciation of the details of commercial transactions. She tells Austin that she is so piqued when her regular shopkeeper, Luke Sweetser, refuses to deliver peaches that she vows to boycott his shop, gleefully anticipating Sweetser's annoyance when she will "pass by his goods, and purchase at Mr Kellogg's" (L53). And during the period in which her father was serving in the federal Congress, and the family regularly used his franking privileges to post letters, she proposes that she frank the postage to deliver Austin his forgotten slippers. "It isn't *every* day," she muses, "that we have a chance to sponge Congress" (L145). Or, in an early letter to Austin, she describes her mixed appreciation for the singer, Jenny Lind, but exclaims with admiration that she earned over $4000 in ticket sales. I point to these particular moments – and there are many more – not simply to argue for Dickinson's location in the burgeoning marketplace of nineteenth-century New England, but also to suggest that Dickinson had her own investments in the "Age of Enterprise and the Rise of Financial Capitalism." Just because Dickinson did not publish in a conventional literary marketplace does not mean that she hated commerce or pined for an atavistic economy.

Although there is nothing in her curriculum or library to suggest familiarity with the emerging discipline of political economy, Dickinson seems well aware of its fundamental tenets. She understood that "wealth" meant the possession of objects of value, and that value was always relative to the desire for said objects and the effort to accrue them. As Amasa Walker, a lecturer at Amherst College and author of *The Science of Wealth* (1866), wrote – expressing the conventional wisdom of classical political economy in the nineteenth century – for anything to have "value," it was necessary for it to be "an object of man's desire, and [to] be obtained only by man's efforts."[6] Dickinson's poems regularly account for fluctuating value that is a consequence of the instability and variety of human desire. And like many political economists writing at the time, she reveals the rudimentary dynamics of wealth and exchange. Significantly, then, Dickinson's frequent appeals to economic terms are not, as many critics suppose, simply metaphorical. We should not presume that she turns to tropes of fiscal wealth merely as vehicles to describe the topics that really interested her: nature, death, misery, love, and poetry. Instead, Dickinson's frequent employment of economic vocabulary signifies her abiding concern with, and study of, human need and human commerce. Her poetry carefully reckons profit and loss, abundance and poverty, risk and reward because it is deeply attuned to existence's "market price" (F396 J1725).

"I lost a World - the other day!" (F209 J181) describes, for example, a devastating loss by monetizing it: "Of more Esteem than Ducats - ." The precision by which the poem enumerates the value of the loss stands in notable contrast to its ambiguous identity: we don't need to know what the identity of the deprived thing is, only that it is worth more than ducats. The poem also emphasizes comparative exchange value: although "A Rich man - might not notice" the loss, for the speaker's "frugal Eye," the lost object is like a "World." Much more than simply conveying the magnitude of the loss, the turn to the language of political economy reveals how value is determined by relative desire. Dickinson thus suggests that the logic of financial marketplaces can illuminate other kinds of emotional economies. We see something similar from the vantage of a buyer in "*One life* of so much consequence!" (F248 J270), which precisely enumerates as labor cost what the speaker would spend so as to possess the desired object. The speaker would pay "My soul's *entire income* - / In ceaseless - salary - " for the coveted "*life*." Notably the poem also indicates that cost is directly proportionate to demand and not to supply. After all, even as the speaker compares the precious life to a pearl, she also asserts that there is no scarcity: "The Sea is full" of such pearls. But the abundant supply does nothing to devalue the desired object: "That - does not blur *my Gem*!" Once again, the emphasis is not on *what* or *who* the object of desire is, but on *how much* the speaker wants it.

This is a recurrent pattern in Dickinson's verse. In "What would I give to see his face?" (F266 J247), the speaker details the value of the beloved not by describing the object of desire, but by announcing the "shares," "Banks," "Dowries," "stocks," and "Bags of Doubloons" she would be willing to offer so as to purchase "'*One hour* - of her Sovereign's face'!" The heterogeneous range of financial vehicles the poem lists does not indicate economic nescience, but rather underscores a central argument of economic writing, which is that regardless of whether exchange is being made with paper notes, gold, or wampum beads, such instruments only have value insofar as they are made equivalent to other desired objects. This is why in so many of Dickinson's "accounting" poems, the identity of what is lost or gained is rather beside the point. Whether her speakers describe the purchase of flowers, lovers, gold, or corporate bonds, the fundamental structure of exchange and valuation is the same; her poetry strives to reveal this basic arithmetic or syntax of human wants.

Critics have tended, however, to assume that the poet's habitual rendering of desire by way of financial tropes is facetious. As Joan Burdick argues, Dickinson uses economic metaphors in the service of a project that is essentially critical of the economic world in which the poet lived. Dickinson writes "parodies of the religio-economic language of her social class."[7] But such a reading ignores the ways that Dickinson's poetry argues that social and erotic relations, like monetary or commercial ones, operate similarly: value is not intrinsic, but determined by exchange. Dickinson even implies that what constitutes pleasure is not possession, but the transactions that yield it. "I know not which, Desire, or Grant - ," a speaker asserts, "Be wholly beautiful - " (F856 J801). Or, as another poem succinctly states, "Danger - deepens Sum - " (F865 J807). This assessment of the relationship between risk and value articulates the logic essential to speculative capitalism, which is that the greater the risk of loss, the more potential value should accrue to the investor. This goes some way to explain why Dickinson chooses to map such a wide range of economic positions – from penury to prosperity. She does this not to idealize abstemious frugality or indulgent plenitude, but to reveal the larger economical cycles by which want and possession define each other.

Such fluctuations are a central concern in Dickinson's first fascicle book, which includes a three-line verse that precisely captures the poet's economic logic:

> We lose - because we win -
> Gamblers - recollecting which -
> Toss their dice again!
>
> (F28 J21)

Gamblers – like brokers, merchants, and young women – risk losses so as to accrue gains. And the entire fascicle depicts this dynamic, including poems that describe loss like "I had a guinea golden" (F12 J23), "To lose - if One can find again - " (F30 J22), and "I never lost as much but twice - " (F39 J49); but also lyrics that tally gains, like "As if I asked a common alms," (F14A J323), "It's all I have to bring today - " (F17 J26), and "If I should die - " (F36 J54). The last insists that even if the speaker should die, "stocks will stand," "Commerce will continue," and "Trades as briskly fly." It is worth noting that Dickinson writes this fascicle in 1858, immediately after the Panic of 1857 that, among other things, bankrupted the railroad company in which her father and the town were so deeply invested. It is perhaps, then, not surprising that Dickinson's poems register the ways that bubbles and panics are an index both of desire and belief: exuberant "gamblers" bear higher risks and leverage greater debt in expectation of higher gains.

"Removed from Accident of Loss / By Accident of Gain" (F417 J424), written four years later, likewise describes the logic of financial bubbles: exuberance and frenzy are caused when tremendous gains insulate investors from imagining the possibility of incredible losses. It is not only that Dickinson describes changing value in her lyrics, but also that she explicitly ties the poetic work of speculation - the "power to dream" - to determinations of value. Prices rise or fall, markets bubble or burst, not merely because monetary supplies constrict or grow, but because people no longer believe that debts will be repaid, that goods can be sold, or that value will be sustained. And, thus, language is essential to valuation in the marketplace, precisely because language is the means by which credulity – and credit – is engendered.

"Your Riches - taught me - Poverty." (F418C J299), located in the same fascicle as "Removed from Accident of Loss" as well as in a letter to her sister-in-law, Susan Gilbert, likewise charts the dynamic movement of value. Figuring the beloved as a series of terms metaphorically and metonymically connected to financial wealth – as "Gems," "India," "Golconda" diamond mines, "Gold," and "Pearl" – the speaker deprecates her losses. But if the poem is uttered from the perspective of someone who has sustained both a financial and emotional crash, from the depths of ruin and poverty, then the final stanza proposes that there is a certain profit, or "Treasure," that can come from speculation:

> It's far - far Treasure to surmise -
> And estimate the Pearl -
> That slipped my simple fingers through -
> While just a Girl at school.

The speaker may have lost the object of her desire, but from this emotional bankruptcy can come a profitable speculation that will yield its own "Treasure." The poem's invocation of fiscal language suggests that the psychological equipoise required of an investor might likewise bolster the lovelorn, and thus Dickinson's lyric points to the fundamental congruity between the two systems of speculative desire.

I am not suggesting here that Dickinson's erotic lyrics ought to be read simply as political economic treatises, or that she is engaged in a project to convert the economy of human affection into one of monetary profit margins. But it is equally untenable to imagine that her persistent use of economic tropes to describe economies of affection is a parody. There is clearly nothing satirical in the rendering of erotic contracts offered in "I gave Myself to Him - " (F426 J580). Depicting marriage as a "solemn contract," in which the participants speculate on the possible losses that might accrue after ratification, the poem gestures toward anxieties about lifelong contracts and about property laws for married women. In addition to offering a realistic critique of marriage, the poem theorizes more abstractly about valuation, suggesting that possession or ownership can discount worth: "The Daily Own - of Love / Depreciate the Vision - ." The poem argues here for deferral - of either sexual consummation or commercial consumption - proposing that satisfaction is located not at the moment of possession, but in the "Fable" of speculation:

> But till the Merchant buy -
> Still Fable - in the Isles of spice -
> The subtle Cargoes - lie -

Analogizing one lover as a "Merchant" and the other as a "subtle Cargo," the poem captures not only the economic logic that underwrites erotic exchange, but also the erotic current that saturates financial exchanges.

The poem describes the particular pleasures that accrue for merchants who imagine the possible risks and gains that come with changes in prices. Until the transaction happens, all possible gains and losses are "still Fable." That Dickinson describes such speculation as "Fable" reveals a crucial tenet of her verse: poetry is itself an act of speculation. Even in poems that seem to reject "The Clamoring for Gold," proposing "play[ing] at Riches" as a less despicable choice, the speaker nonetheless anticipates that she might "Chance Sovreign on a Mine" (F856 J801). Playing at riches does not involve the sinful ease of "independent Man," but neither does it aver speculation: in fact, the speaker imagines that she will "Esteem the Opulence" all the more because she has experienced the risks and vicissitudes of the market. This negotiation between divine gains and losses, mutual risks and profits, is the central calculation of Dickinson's poetic economy.

Because Dickinson always modulates her discussion of riches with the possibility of insolvency, critics have long associated her with an abstemious economy, a "Sumptuous Destitution."[8] And it is certainly the case that descriptions of poverty, hunger, and want frequently find their place in her verse. "It would have starved a Gnat - " (F444 J612) and "I had been hungry, all the Years - " (F439 J579) both describe a speaker in the thralls of privation. And her destitute speakers are also said to provide the framework for the economic model of Dickinson's own poetics: the extreme thrift of the speaker celebrating her ability to consume less than a gnat is analogized to the efficient frugality of Dickinson's own poetry. David Porter points to the incredible brevity and economy of Dickinson's figural language, arguing that a "single word must carry all the meaning."[9] In her reading of the fascicle books, Sharon Cameron likewise emphasizes Dickinson's economical tendencies: If Whitman eroticizes meaning, Cameron argues, then Dickinson "economizes it." Cameron observes that if a "cursory understanding of economy would endorse the ideology of leanness as an absolute condition of Dickinson's poems," then such an understanding fails to apprehend the ways that Dickinson always interrogates the "economy according to which poems are written ... endlessly raising questions of relation and magnitude."[10] To speak of Dickinson's economizing, in other words, is not necessarily to assume her abstemiousness.

I am suggesting that Dickinson's speakers, "Low at [their] problem bending" (F99B J69), routinely use poetry to "rais[e] questions of relation and magnitude" so as to reckon credits and debts. To describe poetry as a form of epistemological, moral, phenomenological, and erotic bookkeeping, however, is not to corner Dickinson into the position of petty bourgeois. Yet this is precisely the assessment that critics feel they risk when they attend to Dickinson's economic language. And so the alternatives are to insist on Dickinson as critic of capitalism or to read her as participant in its fundamental inequalities. These positions are sketched neatly in two different readings of "The Malay - took the Pearl - " (F451 J452), a poem that outlines an economic competition between an "Earl" and a "Malay." For Stoneley, the poem mocks the "prideful cowardice" of the Earl who, unlike the Malay, will not take a risk to capture the pearl.[11] For Betsy Erkkila, the poem conversely reveals Dickinson's elitist racism – in which she presumes the pearl, the object of value, to be the property of the wealthy white and not the "Swarthy" Malay.[12] Erkkila's evaluation of Dickinson as a bourgeois woman who possesses the luxury by which to transcend the marketplace is said to be confirmed by Dickinson's turn to racial figures – often Jews – to describe mercantilism. One speaker, for example, accuses the other of striking such a hard bargain as to be a "Shylock" (F266 J247). Another, "pleading at the counter," promises diamonds, rubies, and topaz in exchange for a "single smile," assuring the seller "'Twould be a Bargain for a Jew!" (F258B J223). If Dickinson's anti-Semitism seems to indicate a condemnation of mercantilism, then it is worth noting that even as the speakers cast aspersions at their commercial partners, they also fully participate in the exchanges. In this way, even as Dickinson appeals to the stereotype of the avaricious Jew, her poetry defines itself as engaged in this larger project of assessing value, gauging risk, and making exchanges.

These calculations are also omnipresent in the many poems that illustrate what Dickinson calls "Profound - precarious Property" (F1050 J1090). Indeed, as we have seen, one reason property is so valuable is because it is so precarious. The index of any object's value is related to the intensity of desire for it and the effort required to acquire it. Dickinson's depiction of property's tenuous status does not, then, reflect an intrinsic asceticism so much as it reveals her recognition that any object loses value when it is not desired by others. And this fundamental tenet of political economy may offer a very different explanation for Dickinson's own refusal to publish in print.

Scholars most often read Dickinson's publishing strategy as a rejection of literary capitalism by forging an alternative market of portfolio and epistolary exchange. But what if we were to understand these choices as a means by which to sustain the value of her own literary property? By neither acceding her rights (by giving up copyright) nor retaining them, Dickinson left the status of ownership ambiguous. Indeed, in her epistolary writing, the issue of property is perpetually postponed, as each individual letter or poem is one share of a larger corporate body of work. Rather than read Dickinson's rejection of print as marking her exemption from the economic world, then, it can be seen as a canny strategy for sustaining the value of her work by insisting on it as precarious property. In fact, it is hard to think of a nineteenth-century author for whom the issues of intellectual property are more complicated. The intense feuds over ownership of Dickinson's verse ironically illustrate the economic logic that Dickinson so carefully inscribed in her long poetic career. The many who fought to own her literary property also sustained its value with their desire. And yet, the complex legal issues involving literary property ultimately yielded the exceptional situation in which both Harvard University and Amherst College claim copyright. As Elizabeth Horan describes it, "scholarship on Emily Dickinson has been haunted by the spirit of the 'accord' [between Harvard and Amherst], whose elegant precision is covered over by the ubiquitous banality of the permissions statement."[13] As copyright holders, who receive remuneration from property for which they risk nothing – merely receiving revenue when poems are quoted and republished – their economic position is anathema in Dickinson's verse. This would be a "Disgrace of Price" – but not because art yields profit. The discredit comes not from assessing value, but from fixing price: their copyright obviates risk. Dickinson's desire, conversely, was to provide her readers with the knowledge that "treasures" and "subtle cargo" come only from the dangers and possible privations of surmise, estimation, and speculation.

NOTES

1 Robert Merideth, "Emily Dickinson and the Acquisitive Society," *The New England Quarterly* 37.4 (1964), 436.
2 Ibid., 438, 436.
3 Ibid., 436.
4 Vivian Pollak, *A Historical Guide to Emily Dickinson* (Oxford University Press, 2004), 142–3.
5 Peter Stoneley, "'I - Pay - in Satin Cash - ': Commerce, Gender, and Display in Emily Dickinson's Poetry," *American Literature* 72.3 (2000), 582.
6 Amasa Walker, *The Science of Wealth: A Manual of Political Economy* (Boston: Little, Brown, and Company, 1866), 8.
7 Joan Burbick, "Emily Dickinson and the Economics of Desire," *American Literature* 58.3 (1986), 377.
8 Richard Wilbur, "Sumptuous Destitution," *Emily Dickinson: A Collection of Critical Essays*, ed. Judith Farr (Upper Saddle River, NJ: Prentice Hall, 1996), 53–61.

9 David Porter, *Art of Emily Dickinson's Early Poetry* (Cambridge, MA: Harvard University Press, 1966), 135.
10 Sharon Cameron, "Dickinson's Fascicles," *Handbook*, 147.
11 Stoneley, "Commerce, Gender, and Display," 593 n. 25.
12 Betsy Erkkila, "Emily Dickinson and Class," *ALH* 4 (1992), 16.
13 Elizabeth Rosa Horan, "Technically Outside the Law: Who Permits, Who Profits, and Why," *EDJ* 10.1 (2001), 47.

CHAPTER 19

Law and Legal Discourse

James Guthrie

Born into a family of lawyers, Emily Dickinson inevitably grew to be familiar with legal topics, legal language, and legal thought. Spending her entire life beneath her parents' roof, chiefly at the house the Dickinsons called the Homestead, she must have heard her father expatiate on issues of law affecting his clients' interests. Jack Capps, in *Emily Dickinson's Reading*, wrote that "she learned his legal terms and used them to such an extent in her poems that we can only conclude she must have occasionally read his law books" (Capps, 15). Edward Dickinson maintained a private practice in an office situated on the second floor of the Palmer Block, a brick commercial building constructed by his father, Samuel F. Dickinson, also an attorney, a scant two blocks west of the Homestead. Edward's son Austin followed suit, first by attending law school at Harvard College, and then by becoming a partner in his father's firm. The poet's father made a good living, as did Austin, once his father's death in 1874 left a local legal vacuum. Father and son represented clients, acted as treasurers to the College, sat on boards of trustees, occupied state court offices, and, in Edward's case, served in elected positions in the state and national legislatures.

As a young attorney, Edward could take satisfaction in knowing that Massachusetts was a bellwether among the states in confronting contemporary legal quandaries and developing stellar legal talent. Lemuel Shaw, distinguished judge and Herman Melville's father-in-law, was a national exemplar of legal sophistication and personal rectitude. Other courtroom luminaries included the magisterial Joseph Story, the fiery Rufus Choate (whom Edward Dickinson once faced in court), and the iconoclastic Robert Rantoul. Massachusetts courts deliberated many of the most crucial cases of the antebellum era: *Charles River Bridge v. Warren Bridge* (1837), *Farwell v. Boston & Worcester R. R. Corp.* (1842), and the Anthony Burns case (1854), which tested the Fugitive Slave Act. When he proposed marriage to Emily Norcross, Edward Dickinson could reasonably expect the establishment of a private legal practice to lead to financial security, respectability, and perhaps even a national reputation. His subsequent ascent to becoming the most prominent attorney in Amherst, and perhaps in all of Hampshire County, represents an impressive personal achievement.

Edward Dickinson's legal training was cobbled together from courses taken at Yale Law School and from his experience as an apprentice in an Amherst legal practice, a reflection of the era's emphasis upon training attorneys by having them "read" law. But by the time Austin Dickinson attended Harvard Law School during the early 1850s, an American legal education had, at least in New England, become thoroughly standardized and professionalized. Austin applied himself to a rigorous curriculum that included reading Kent's *Commentaries* and Blackstone, as well as taking required courses in Property, Commercial Law, Civil Law, Constitutional Law, Criminal Law, and Equity.[1] While Austin boarded at Cambridge, he and his sister maintained a lively correspondence that often joked about the law and about his future career as attorney, a brand of sibling humor that probably would not always have amused their sober-sided father. Although Edward was proud that his son had embarked on a rigorous plan of study, he evidently questioned whether Harvard could graduate young men up to the challenge of practicing law on a daily basis, year in and year out. In a letter sent to Austin in April 1853, when he had just commenced his first year of legal study, his sister reported to him of his father's reactions to letters sent home:

> You cant think how delighted father was, with the account you gave of northerners and southerners, and the electioneering - he seemed to feel so happy to have you interested in what was going on at Cambridge - he said he "knew all about it - he'd been thro' the whole, it was only a little specimen of what you'd meet in life, if you lived to enter it." I could'nt hardly help telling him that I thought his idea of life rather a boisterous one, but I kept perfectly still. (L116)

This indirect account of Edward's opinion of Austin's legal education, and of the connection of law to politics, points to a certain degree of rivalry between father and son. The poet's quoting of Edward's somewhat melodramatic and self-aggrandizing description of the arduousness of a life devoted to law may also hint at some resentment of the coherence of Austin's education, in comparison to his own more helter-skelter legal studies. The poet, for her part, appears to be trying to smooth over generational differences by passing on her father's praises (which may have been scant during Austin's visits back home) and by emphasizing similarities between father and son.

Dickinson would also have been compelled, even involuntarily, to turn her thoughts at least occasionally to matters of law and business because some of her poem and letter drafts were composed on scrap paper torn from Edward Dickinson's legal form books.[2] This textual confluence of poetry and law would not, I think, have struck her as being particularly ironic. Ordinarily she did not regard her vocation as poet as a means of parodying or impugning her father's profession, or of his speaking and writing style. On the contrary: usually she held in high regard virtually all legal professionals, whether employed as judges, attorneys, police officers, or lowly bailiffs. In her own fashion, the poet's practice of writing and recopying pencil drafts, carefully editing her work and marking variant words for possible future consideration, demonstrated an approach to the composition of poetry as utilitarian as her father's drafting of legal documents.

Although the poet apparently enjoyed learning about the law vicariously from her father and brother, little evidence exists to suggest she envied them or wished women could also attend law school and enter practice (women would not be admitted to the bar until the late 1870s, not long before Dickinson died). She did complain occasionally, and facetiously, that she should be granted the same freedom of action in law and in politics granted to men. In a letter written to Susan Gilbert in 1852, a year before Austin entered law school, the poet wrote,

> Why cant *I* be a Delegate to the great Whig Convention? - don't I know all about Daniel Webster, and the Tariff, and the Law? Then, Susie I could see you, during a pause in the session - but I don't like this country at all, and I shant stay here any longer! "Delenda est" America, Massachusetts and all!
>
> open me carefully
(L94)

Dickinson's hyperbole here imitates flights of oratory then popular in American politics, while simultaneously removing herself from that arena, literally so, as she threatens to secede from the country completely, or else destroy it, as Cato had recommended his fellow senators eradicate Carthage. Her subscript even seems to suggest that the entire letter be treated gingerly, as if it were a bomb - although of course if it had been, Sue, in breaking the seal, would have been blown to bits, preventing her from reading this playfully ominous closing. Edward Dickinson, a delegate to this same Whig convention held in Baltimore on June 16, 1852, likely discussed with his family his fellow New Englanders' support for Webster as a presidential candidate. While visiting Baltimore, Edward delivered this letter from his daughter to Sue, then teaching mathematics at a local school (L94, note). Knowing that her father is bearing her news, Emily Dickinson lampoons the male-dominated, rhetorically aggressive realm of American politics while signaling indirectly that she misses him, and her best friend, together without her in distant Maryland. That Emily Dickinson did indeed comprehend something about "the Law" Susan Gilbert would have understood, yet it is unlikely that she would have interpreted this particular paragraph as an expression of thwarted ambition, or smoldering resentment over male political and professional prerogatives. Sue appreciated Dickinson's mordant wit, which she compared, in a eulogy published in the *Springfield Republican* on May 18, 1886, three days after the poet's death, to a "Damascus blade gleaming, and glancing in the sun."

Dickinson's acquaintance with the law contributed to some of her keenest displays of wit, and not always in ways complimentary to the legal profession, or to humanity in general. Yet even by writing in this vein Dickinson may have been emulating attorneys she had met or heard about. Seasoned practitioners and jurists who, in their offices and courtrooms, may witness an assortment of human follies such as greed, jealousy, and deceitfulness, are sometimes accused by the lay public of conceiving a cynical or jaundiced opinion of human nature. In Dickinson, so hardened a view may seem at odds with the antebellum nation's then-prevailing mood of optimism and idealism, as exemplified by the writings of the Transcendentalists, such as Emerson and Thoreau. Dickinson admired those writers, but as was true for Hawthorne, and especially for Melville, a latent strain of Calvinistic thought peculiarly hospitable to an attorney's or a judge's gimlet-eyed perspective of human nature informs much of her thinking. Perhaps as a consequence, Dickinson, despite being a recluse, became something of a moralist, reverting to the neoclassical manner of thinking and writing natural to her father, and with a correspondingly satirical edge. Many of Dickinson's writings concerning law exhibit a special delight in what modern attorneys call their "war stories": narratives of contracts gone awry, trials blown up, runaway juries. Late in life, Dickinson particularly enjoyed exchanging such stories with Otis Lord. For example, she retained in her workbox a newspaper clipping on which she had written, "Returned by Judge Lord with approval!"[3] The clipping reads:

> NOTICE! My wife Sophia Pickles having left my bed and board without just cause or provocation, I shall not be responsible for bills of her contracting.
>
> *SOLOMON PICKLES*

> NOTICE! I take this means of saying that Solomon Pickles has had no bed or board for me to leave for the last two months.
> *SOPHIA PICKLES*[4]

Also, during the 1882 Kidder trial in Springfield, Judge Lord presiding, Dickinson enjoyed his account of a juror's apparently discretionary cough that Lord thought "not pulmonary" (L750).

The distinctly human element of legal practice appealed to Dickinson, and the personae in her poems, drawn from the several human types to be encountered in virtually any county court, speak in polyphonic, nearly novelistic, voices. In the final stanza of "Is Bliss then, such Abyss" (F371 J340) for example, which debates the walking around a puddle or right through it, the narrating voice conflates that of a testifying witness, the foreman of a jury, and, possibly, a presiding judge:

> But Bliss, is sold just once.
> The Patent lost
> None buy it any more -
> Say, Foot, decide the point!
> The Lady cross, or not?
> Verdict for Boot!

Besides making a clever legal pun on *patents* and *patent*-leather shoes, the poem's narrative voice alternates between internal and dramatic monologues, assuming in the final line the voice of a judge, or possibly the spokesman for a jury. Another pun may be present in *cross*, for judges may ask attorneys whether they wish to cross-examine a witness, "Does counsel wish to cross?" Dickinson's puns and narrative shifts add comic and ironic complexity to a poem describing a plainly trivial dilemma in which a woman wonders whether she should risk her presumably expensive shoes. Because she, in confronting the puddle, must make up her own mind, it does not seem inappropriate that she may think of herself simultaneously as both a lady-lawyer who may wish to cross-examine a witness, and as a deliberative judge or jury.

References to law in the poet's prose suggest that Dickinson recurred to legal terms and concepts nearly reflexively even in her most informal moments. According to the concordance of the poet's correspondence, Dickinson's letters include twenty-one appearances of the word "law."[5] In a letter written to her cousins Fanny and Loo Norcross concerning the probably accidental removal from their house of a spool of thread, she confesses, "I defrauded Loo of 1 spool of thread; we will 'settle,' however - " (L267). She concluded one letter to Mrs. Holland, wife of Josiah Holland, editor of *Scribner's*, by observing, "Blossoms belong to the bee, if needs be by *habeas corpus* (L227)." In another, she wondered whether Mrs. Holland had been the mysterious donor of a box of candy: "Jacob versus Esau, was a trifle in Litigation, compared to the Skirmish in my Mind - " (L743).⁶ Other letters, perhaps written during her convalescence from an optical illness, make oblique references to feeling as if she were immured in a sort of jail. Two of Dickinson's enigmatic "Master" letters allude to Byron's imprisoned Bonnivard, sealed up in Chillon: letters L233 and L248 deploy characterizations of herself as a "culprit" who pleads, paradoxically, to be "punish[ed]" by her unknown correspondent by being incarcerated, rather than "banish[ed]" from his presence. References to law appear sporadically in Dickinson's correspondence throughout her adult life, including letters sent the year before she died to attorney Benjamin Kimball, cousin to her lover, Judge Otis Lord, and executor of Lord's estate.

Dickinson's diction, poetic subject matter, and rhetorical style all owe a great deal to the legal milieu in which she was raised, and in which she evidently felt herself to be quite literally at home. Legal references are comparatively easy to find in her poems: attorney and Dickinson scholar Robert Lambert cites nearly one hundred different legally related words, leaving aside those to be found in her letters; B. J. Smith wrote, "Legal images or specific legal language can be found in roughly three hundred of her poems."⁷ Such relatively esoteric legal terms as "replevys," "Primogeniture," and "codicil" appear in her verse. Her diction in her poems and her letters is also enlivened by several not necessarily legal terms that nevertheless have commonly understood legal meanings. She developed a practice of substituting legally inflected words for those having more generic denotations, using "arraign" to mean *stop*; "adjourn" to mean *leave*; "abrogate" to mean *prevent*; "perjure" to mean *lie*. Law's influence may also be manifested in her rational, logical, often forensic approach to her subject matter. Dickinson gravitated toward issues involving personal rights and responsibilities, liberties and liabilities, trespasses and defenses of property, petitions and denials. Like her Puritan forebears, whose theology was covenantal, she tended to view the universe legalistically, taking pains to distinguish, for example, what belonged to her versus what fell within the province of a monitoring, and often obstructive, God.

An exposure to legal language may also have influenced the formal and rhetorical architectures of Dickinson's poems. Compression and brevity have long been recognized as hallmarks of her writing style, her succinct four-line stanzas packing a good deal of meaning into a very small space. Brevity itself may have been a stylistic inheritance of her family's involvement with the law. In "A prompt - executive Bird is the Jay - ," for example, a bailiff engaged on official business is compared metaphorically with the blue jay, whose bold posture and raucous call imitate the bailiff's official pronouncement of "Oyez, oyez!" to declare court to be in session (F1022 J1177). Conciseness is intrinsic to the executory success of the bailiff's message, whether delivered in court or on the doorstep of a subpoenaed witness. The blue jay's/bailiff's "Warrant" to deliver his message is reflected in every detail of his face and figure, as well as in every clause of the official message he conveys, so that medium, message, and messenger become nearly inseparable.

The very word *brief* would also have been familiar, of course, to Dickinson from encountering it in a specifically legal context: the briefs her father was continually writing. In a letter to T. W. Higginson, the poet described her family's indifference to literature, saying that her mother "does not care for thought" and that Edward Dickinson was "too busy with his Briefs - to notice what we do - " (L261). Between these parental extremes, the poet needed to stake out her own imaginative terrain, and Dickinson's poems often resemble "briefs" in their own right, "Bulletins ... From Immortality" (F820 J827) that present concise statements of fact, marshallings of evidence, and grounds for argument.

Despite the prevalence of law in Emily Dickinson's writings, the subject has received scant consideration from scholars. Among the major biographers, Richard Sewall provides a prescient emphasis on Edward Dickinson's career as an attorney. Cynthia Wolff, on the other hand, devotes almost no attention to the law's impact on Dickinson's literary practice, suggesting only that the poet's works reveal "a doubting attitude toward the efficacy of laws."[8] Alfred Habegger's biography provides by far the most thorough-going consideration of the law's importance to the poet. Habegger supplies valuable concrete information about Edward Dickinson's law business, and about various ethically dubious legal practices ascribable to Edward and to Austin. The most sustained scholarly treatment of the law's importance to Dickinson's poetry remains Lambert's *Emily Dickinson's Use of Anglo-American Legal Concepts and Vocabulary in Her Poetry: Muse at the Bar*. Lambert compiles and indexes the various terms and concepts in Dickinson's poems without delving very deeply into how the poet deploys them in figures of speech. Still, his study is invaluable in spelling out how important the law was to the poet. Betsy Erkkila and Domhnall Mitchell have commented insightfully on how the Dickinsons' practice of law contributed to the family's sense of class entitlement. For discussions of specific legal issues raised in Dickinson's poems such as trespass, inheritance, and bankruptcy, I refer interested readers to my own work.

NOTES

1 The Harvard Law School curriculum in effect while Austin was a student there is reproduced in Robert G. Lambert, *Emily Dickinson's Use of Anglo-American Legal Concepts and Vocabulary in Her Poetry: Muse at the Bar* (Lewiston: Edwin Mellen Press, 1997), 116–23.
2 See, e.g., manuscript A754, reproduced photostatically in Marta Werner, *Emily Dickinson's Open Folios: Scenes of Reading, Surfaces of Writing* (Ann Arbor: University of Michigan Press, 1995), n.p. A rough draft of a letter probably intended for Judge Lord is penciled on the back of what looks to be a legal form setting forth the requirements for disposing of property.
3 Martha Dickinson Bianchi, *The Life and Letters of Emily Dickinson* (Boston: Houghton Mifflin, 1924), 70.
4 Ibid., 70.
5 Cynthia MacKenzie, ed., *Concordance to the Letters of Emily Dickinson* (University Press of Colorado, 2000).
6 Dickinson likely refers to *Genesis* 32–3, in which Jacob sends placating gifts to his brother Esau.
7 Lambert, *Legal Concepts*, i–ii. B.J. Smith, "Vicinity to Laws," *Dickinson Studies* 56 (1985), 38.
8 Cynthia Griffin Wolff, *Emily Dickinson* (New York: Alfred A. Knopf, 1986), 173.

CHAPTER 20

Slavery and the Civil War
Faith Barrett

"The name - of it - is 'Autumn' - / The hue - of it - is Blood -" Dickinson begins in a poem that Franklin dates late in 1862 (F465 J656). The poem offers a peculiar description of a New England landscape, using metaphors that turn autumn color into flowing blood. Struggling at the time she wrote the poem with an acute personal crisis of indeterminate origin, Dickinson is here preoccupied with the disjunction between aesthetically pleasing surfaces and the viscera that subtend them. She may have feared that her own witty and brilliant surfaces might suddenly give way to the despair and anxiety that lay beneath. Many poems from this period point toward an experience of mental breakdown or acute depression. Letters to family and close friends are often taut with emotional intensity, with the pressure of feelings only partially expressed. During this turbulent year, Dickinson was extraordinarily productive as a writer, producing more than two hundred poems according to Franklin's dating of the manuscripts.

The fall of 1862 was also a turbulent time in the American Civil War. The battle of Antietam, fought on September 16, became a turning point for American expectations about the conflict. At the outbreak of hostilities in April of 1861, Northerners and Southerners alike had hoped that the war might be relatively brief. With its staggering rate of casualties – 23,000 wounded and dead in a single day of fighting – Antietam shocked Americans into recognizing that the war might be both long and costly. Though the battle was effectively a draw, McClellan succeeded in preventing Lee's incursion into western Maryland, and this outcome enabled Lincoln to make public a preliminary version of the Emancipation Proclamation that would go into effect on January 1, 1863.

Thus the era of Dickinson's personal crisis coincides with a critical turning point in the Civil War. Read in relation to contemporary events, "The name - of it - is 'Autumn'- " offers a vivid rejoinder to the bloodshed at Antietam: in the poem, the "Blood" spills along the hill and road, spreads to the more urban "Alleys," where the war was also fought, and eventually fills the "Basin" of the military hospital. With this vision of spreading blood, Dickinson responds to Julia Ward Howe's image of a righteous God "trampling out the vintage where the grapes of wrath are stored."[1] Whereas Howe's "Battle Hymn" envisions God redeeming the American nation from the sin of slavery, Dickinson's image of bloodshed is far more ambivalent: no divine authority intervenes to bring meaning to the violence of war.

Yet, as this essay argues, Dickinson uses her Civil War poems to test out opposing ideological positions, sometimes skeptically questioning wartime ideologies and sometimes endorsing them. Reading pairs of poems that take opposing stances, I will suggest that Dickinson finds extraordinary imaginative freedom in poetry, with the possibilities it offers for equivocation, ambivalence, and reversal. Thus while "The name - of it - is 'Autumn' - " offers no image of a divine redeemer saving fallen soldiers, in another battlefield landscape poem, Dickinson suggests that God will recognize each of the dead. Probably written in the spring of 1863, "They dropped like Flakes - " (F545 J409) cycles through the change of seasons, likening falling soldiers to flakes of snow, falling stars, and flower petals. But whereas "The name - of it - is 'Autumn'- " threatens to turn autumn beauty into gory bloodshed, "They dropped like Flakes - " insists on the loveliness of its own metaphors. Though the first poem presents war as an explosion of the violence inherent in nature, the second presents war as an inevitable part of nature's cycles of death and rebirth. "The name - of it - is 'Autumn'- " refuses to attribute meaning to battlefield deaths; by contrast "They dropped like Flakes - " closes with an image of God identifying each fallen man: He "can summon every face," though the fallen are as numerous as blades of grass. "They dropped like Flakes - " thus seems to endorse wartime ideologies that argue that death in battle is a form of Christian martyrdom, a theological view widely held in both North and South.

Read in relation to the Civil War, each of these two poems seems laden with battlefield imagery. Remarkably, however, the first generation of scholars who approached Dickinson's work in the mid-twentieth century for the most part argued that she had little interest in the war. Schooled by New Criticism to value the metaphoric complexity and semantic ambiguities of Dickinson's poems, these critics relied on methods that emphasized reading Dickinson's work in relation to the private ties of family and friendship and the timeless themes of nature, God, and mortality. These reading methods removed Dickinson's poetry from its political context and isolated her work from that of her contemporaries. Such methods almost inevitably presented Dickinson as an innovative eccentric who was years ahead of her time in her fracturing of the lyric self and her radical compression of syntax. If we resituate Dickinson in the context of the Civil War, however, two important features of her project come sharply into focus. First, Dickinson does respond to events taking place during the war years; second, she also responds to writing by her American contemporaries, including journalism, newspaper poetry, and popular song. If we resituate Dickinson in the context of the American Civil War, it becomes apparent that she is *both* an innovator *and* a writer with profound connections to the political debates of the nineteenth century.

It would be a mistake, then, to read Dickinson's reclusiveness as a retreat from engagement with the world. An avid reader of several newspapers and magazines, Dickinson also maintained friendships with Samuel Bowles, editor of the *Springfield Republican*, and with Thomas Wentworth Higginson, a prominent man of letters and the commander of the first African American regiment of the Union Army. Dickinson corresponded frequently with friends during the war. Thus she remained vitally connected to the world in spite of her increasing reluctance, from the early 1860s onwards, to go beyond the boundaries of her father's property. Franklin's dating of Dickinson's manuscripts suggests that she wrote more than 900 poems between 1861 and 1865, effectively half of her total body of poetic work. Clearly the violence of the national conflict served as a catalyst for Dickinson's imagination.

Even scholars who suggest that Dickinson had little interest in the war note the intensity of her response to the death of Frazar Stearns, son of the president of Amherst College and a close friend of Dickinson's brother. Stearns joined the Union Army in 1861 at the age of twenty. When he died in battle at Newbern, North Carolina on March 14, 1862, all of Amherst mourned, and Dickinson responds to his death in several letters and poems. Writing to Samuel Bowles in late March of 1862, Dickinson describes how her brother Austin's "Brain" keeps repeating the phrase "Frazer is killed" – "Frazer is killed" as he grapples with the news of "Frazer's murder" (L256). One month after Stearns' death, Dickinson initiated contact with Thomas Wentworth Higginson and sought his opinion of her poetry. From the spring of 1862 through the end of 1863, Dickinson was thinking with feverish intensity about soldiers' deaths, the ideologies that fueled the Civil War, and her own vocation as a writer.

In "It don't sound so terrible - quite - as it did - " (F384 J426), which Franklin dates in the fall of 1862, Dickinson strongly echoes the phrasing of her March 1862 letter to Bowles. These echoes suggest that the poem may be a response to Stearns' death:

> It dont sound so terrible - quite - as it did -
> I run it over - "Dead", Brain - "Dead".
> Put it in Latin - left of my school -
> Seems it dont shriek so - under rule.
>
> Turn it, a little - full in the face
> A Trouble looks bitterest -
> Shift it - just -
> Say "When Tomorrow comes this way -
> I shall have waded down one Day".
>
> I suppose it will interrupt me some
> Till I get accustomed - but then the Tomb
> Like other new Things - shows largest - then -
> And smaller, by Habit -
>
> It's shrewder then
> Put the Thought in advance - a Year -
> How like "a fit" - then -
> Murder wear!
>
> (F384 J426)

In this poem, the representation of death is wholly divorced from any wartime context in the speaker's intense focus on her own state of shock and grief. She stammers out a response to an unthinkable, self-shattering loss, repeating the news of the death again and again in a vain attempt to absorb it. She repeats to herself the platitudes that are used to comfort the mourning. The threat that lies just beneath the surface of the poem, however, is that the speaker will never be able to accept this death. Here Dickinson resists wartime ideologies that called on families to understand the death of a soldier as a sacrifice necessary to national reunion. By calling the death – whose cause and context the poem refuses to explain – a "Murder," the poem refuses to ascribe to it a compensatory meaning.

In still another poem that Franklin dates in the fall of 1862, however, Dickinson seems to perform an about-face, representing the Christian's ascent to heaven as a military parade and endorsing the idea that fallen soldiers are martyrs for a Christian cause. The imagery in this poem echoes some of the language in the memorial volume Stearns' father published, which emphasizes the family's perception of their son's death in battle as a form of Christian martyrdom:

> Over and over, like a Tune -
> The Recollection plays -

> Drums off the Phantom Battlements
> Cornets of Paradise -
>
> Snatches, from Baptized Generations -
> Cadences too grand
> But for the Justified Processions
> At the Lord's Right hand.
>
> (F406 J367)

While the repetition that opened "It dont sound so terrible - quite - as it did - " represents the numbing shock of the speaker's response to the death, the repetition that opens "Over and over like a tune - " suggests that memories of the dead can be consoling. Here it is not one soldier's death but rather a whole gloriously dying army that the poem presents. In the logic of the poem, the dead soldiers are united in heaven just as their mourning loved ones are united and comforted by the understanding that their grief is shared. As the contrast between these two poems suggests, Dickinson's decision not to publish her work via conventional print media frees her from the obligation of consistency, allowing her to take opposing positions in different poems to explore a range of political and aesthetic stances. Although we have no evidence that Dickinson circulated either of these poems in correspondence, if she did, those in her Amherst circle would surely have understood them as expressing the complex mix of private emotions – shock, grief, anger, acceptance – that many felt on learning of the death of Stearns and other young soldiers from Amherst.

If "It dont sound so terrible" and "Over and over like a tune - " offer two opposing perspectives on the meaning of soldiers' deaths, a poem that Franklin dates in the spring of 1863 synthesizes these two positions, suggesting that the conflict might have both staggering costs and enormous benefits. The poem focuses on civilian-survivors and considers their relationship to the war dead:

> It feels a shame to be Alive -
> When Men so brave - are dead -
> One envies the Distinguished Dust -
> Permitted - such a Head -
>
> The Stone - that tells defending Whom
> This Spartan put away
> What little of Him we - possessed
> In Pawn for Liberty -
>
> The price is great - Sublimely paid -
> Do we deserve - a Thing -

> That lives - like Dollars - must be piled
> Before we may obtain?
>
> Are we that wait - sufficient worth -
> That such Enormous Pearl
> As life - dissolved be - for Us -
> In Battle's - horrid Bowl?
>
> It may be - a Renown to live -
> I think the Men who die -
> Those unsustained - Saviors -
> Present Divinity -
>
> (F524 J444)

Writing one year after Stearns' death, Dickinson now has a far more nuanced understanding of war's consequences. As the conflict continued into its second and then third year, the Northern press offered extensive coverage of its costs, not only in terms of lives lost, but also in terms of the drain on Union finances. The range of references in "It feels a shame to be Alive - " suggests that Dickinson was well-informed about recent financial and legislative developments. In February of 1862, Lincoln signed the Legal Tender Act, creating the first viable paper currency system in the United States. In March of 1862, he proposed that any state willing to emancipate slaves should be compensated, arguing that the costs of the conflict would far exceed the costs of compensating slave-owners, and in March of 1863, he signed the first conscription legislation in the North, requiring all men between the ages of twenty and thirty-five to enlist, unless they could afford to pay $300 for a substitute. The conscription act would have been of particular concern to the Dickinson family because Austin turned thirty-four just a month after it became law. When Austin was drafted in 1864, he opted to pay for a substitute. Given his close friendship with Frazar Stearns, that decision may have been fraught with conflicting emotions.

In "It feels a shame to be Alive - ," Dickinson faces head-on the moral complexity of the noncombatant's position. The poem opens with the speaker's declaration of survivor's guilt. Though the speaker notes that the fallen have given their lives "In Pawn for Liberty - ," she wonders aloud if the living are worthy of this sacrifice. The poem emphasizes that war wastes both human lives and money. Gesturing toward the "greenbacks" whose production Lincoln had authorized, the poem's second stanza likens the printing of dollar bills to the corpses rapidly accumulating on battlefields and in cemeteries. Balancing dollars spent and lives lost against the greater good of "Liberty," the poem gestures toward the expense of feeding and housing soldiers, of munitions and transport, of compensating slave-holders, and of buying a substitute. Having opened up these dilemmas, however, the poem sidesteps them in part by insisting on the "divinity" of the fallen. Reiterating the idea that the living are not worthy of such a great sacrifice, the speaker insists that the dead are "unsustained - Saviors - ." The poem suggests that though the soldiers may have been sustained financially, they have not been sustained by the moral or spiritual worth of the civilians whose "Liberty" they died to save. Ultimately the poem reads as a biting condemnation of the hypocrisy of those who stay at home in wartime.

Rereading Dickinson with attention to the Civil War brings to the fore the military metaphors that abound in many poems from this period; references to slavery and racial difference are, however, fewer and typically more oblique. Just as many Northern soldiers did not believe that they were fighting to end slavery during the early years of the war, so too does Dickinson's poetry suggest that she did not at first link the war directly to slavery. By late 1863, however, that seems to change. In one poem from late 1863 and another from early 1864, Dickinson responds to the rhetoric of abolition and also to newspaper coverage of African American soldiers. The first of these two poems, "Publication - is the Auction - ," abounds with Dickinson's trademark equivocation, that kind of syntactic compression that enables her to propose in a single poem both an argument and its opposite:

> Publication - is the Auction
> Of the Mind of Man -
> Poverty - be justifying
> For so foul a thing
>
> Possibly - but We - would rather
> From Our Garret go
> White - Unto the White Creator
> Than invest - Our Snow -
>
> Thought belong to Him who gave it -
> Then - to Him Who bear
> It's Corporeal illustration - Sell
> The Royal Air -
>
> In the Parcel - Be the Merchant
> Of the Heavenly Grace -
> But reduce no Human Spirit
> To Disgrace of Price -
>
> (F788 J709)

Often mined by critics for its exploration of the perils of entering the literary marketplace, the poem likens the slave on the auction block to the writer who must sell her soul – or at least her mind – in order to see her work in print. At first glance, this argument might seem to link the suffering slave with the writer exposed to critical scrutiny. The second stanza disassembles this association, however, through its adamant linking of purity to whiteness and its insistence that a select few writers – evoked through an elitist royal "We" – should ascend to heaven without having soiled their work with the black ink of literary commerce. Though the poem uses color imagery in a secondary role in support of its primary claims about publication, that imagery seems both to endorse an ideal of white racial purity and to link that purity with divinity. The poem perversely appropriates abolitionist rhetoric for purposes of declaring the speaker's refusal to participate in the literary marketplace. The freedom that the poem's speaker embraces is above all the freedom to hold herself above the literary fray, outside of the kind of commerce that might compel her to assume fixed ideological positions.

In the logic of Dickinson's Civil War–era poetics, however, this poem too must have its opposing reaction. In "Color - Caste - Denomination," which Franklin dates early in 1864, Dickinson makes color imagery central to her concerns. This poem argues without equivocation that the hierarchies of race and class will be erased in the grave:

> Color - Caste - Denomination
> These - are Time's Affair -
> Death's diviner Classifying
> Does not know they are -
>
> As in sleep - all Hue forgotten -
> Tenets - put behind -
> Death's large - Democratic fingers
> Rub away the Brand -
>
> If Circassian - He is careless -
> If He put away
> Chrysalis of Blonde - or Umber -
> Equal Butterfly -
>
> They emerge from His Obscuring -
> What Death - knows so well -
> Our minuter intuitions -
> Deem unplausible -
>
> (F836 J970)

The immediate historical context is particularly illuminating in the case of this poem. Though Lincoln first authorized African Americans to serve in combat positions in January of 1863, it took some time for Northern public opinion to endorse black enlistment. Although a staunch opponent of slavery like Higginson might volunteer to serve as the commander of a black regiment, moderate Northern newspapers came around more gradually to the idea that blacks might make good soldiers. In the summer of 1863, the white-on-black violence of the draft riots that raged in New York City for four days beginning on July 13 resulted in an outpouring of white Northern sympathy for those African Americans who had been killed or wounded. When Robert Gould Shaw died while leading the all-black 54th Massachusetts in a charge on Fort Wagner on July 18, Northern newspapers were quick to praise not only Shaw's heroism but also that of the black soldiers who fell around him. Shaw was buried behind enemy lines in a mass grave with his soldiers, an incident that was widely publicized in the Northern papers, including the *Springfield Republican*. Because Dickinson was regularly corresponding with Higginson, Shaw's death might have registered with particular force.

Central to "Color - Caste - Denomination" is the image of a mass grave in which the blood of different races is mingled. Written when accounts of Shaw's burial would have been fresh in Northern minds, Dickinson's poem reflects on the ethical dilemmas raised by the enlistment of men from different racial, class, and religious backgrounds. The word "Denomination" also reminds readers that wealthy white men such as Dickinson's brother could buy themselves a substitute instead of serving. With its central image of the mixing of races in one grave, "Color - Caste - Denomination" points to the violent division of the American nation along the fault-lines of race, class, and religion and argues that racial and class hierarchies are earthly constructs that will be erased in the afterlife. The poem reads as an oblique elegy for Shaw and his men, celebrating the ways that their burial in a mass grave prefigures this higher heavenly order. The poem thus gestures both toward the reuniting of the nation that is the goal of the Union war effort and toward an ideal of interracial and ecumenical harmony; at the same time, however, it acknowledges that national reunion and ideal harmony can be achieved only through death.

During the Civil War years, Dickinson responds with extraordinary intensity to battlefield violence, wartime ideologies about Christian martyrdom, economic and legislative developments in the North, the rhetoric of abolition, and racial and class hierarchies. Though her approaches to the war may seem oblique or nonreferential, when we resituate the poems in their immediate historical contexts, what comes into sharper focus is the conflicting array of political stances the poems offer – some radical, some conservative, and some quite conventional in their theological or nationalist commitments. As this essay has suggested, Dickinson's perspectives on wartime patriotic ideologies are not always skeptical and critical, and some of the conventional pieties the poems express may echo some of her own beliefs or feelings. Indeed the contradictions that Dickinson explores are those we see in the viewpoints of many nineteenth-century Americans, who needed to believe that their loved ones had died for a good cause, even though they might also question the ideologies that drove the nation to a long and costly civil war. It would be a mistake, then, to read Dickinson's resistance to assuming fixed political positions as a resistance to engaging with the events of her day. In her divided responses to the war, Dickinson explores the divided perspectives of Americans – both Northern and Southern – who celebrated fallen soldiers as Christian martyrs, mourned the meaninglessness of wartime deaths, lamented the rising human and financial costs of the conflict, reasserted arguments about white racial superiority, or dared to imagine a nation undivided by differences of race, class, and creed. In Dickinson's divisions, we find many of the same fault-lines that divided and subdivided the Union, the Confederacy, and the United States both during the Civil War and in its long aftermath.

NOTES

1 Julia Ward Howe, "Battle Hymn of the Republic," *Atlantic Monthly* (February 1862).

CHAPTER 21

Popular Culture

Sandra Runzo

Attention to popular entertainments and to an Emily Dickinson who loved the circus, the masquerade, and the popular song not only places her solidly in the social world but also fortifies a view of her as engaged with key conversations and struggles of her time. Noticing the pervasive presence of popular amusements in her time also prompts questions regarding possible affiliations of the images and meanings of these cultural forms with her verse.

One of the primary sites of public entertainment in the nineteenth century was the dime museum, a kind of building-sized cabinet of curiosities. The wealth of unpredictable and exciting attractions lured people of all classes and ages through its doors; dime museums flourished in the Northeast and Midwest in the second half of the century, although they opened in cities and towns across the nation. The prominent place of P. T. Barnum in American popular culture relates to the importance of his American Museum – the most famous of the dime museums – which opened in New York City in 1842. Barnum's collection of wonders included live animals, waxworks, mummified bodies, "missing-link" exhibits, so-called freaks and living curiosities (such as little people, giants, and conjoined twins), fortune-tellers, ventriloquists, contortionists, magicians, musical entertainers, and theatrical performances, all of which was promoted as educational and fashionable family entertainment. In her *Weird and Wonderful: The Dime Museum in America*, Andrea Stulman Dennett records that Boston had eight dime museums in the nineteenth century, including Moses Kimball's Boston Museum and Gallery of Fine Arts, which opened six months before Barnum's American Museum. While offering attractions similar to those exhibited by Barnum, the Boston Museum eventually became particularly known for its theatrical productions.

Mobile versions of the dime museum, traveling circuses and menageries moved about the countryside in the spring and summer, transporting grand assemblages of exotic animals – elephants, lions, tigers, leopards, zebras, monkeys – as well as trained horses and dogs, acrobats, jugglers, rope-walkers, equestrian daredevils, contortionists, and clowns. Most circuses had side shows, that is, entertainments and exhibitions in small canvas tents near the "big show." The side show also displayed the kinds of "curiosities" seen in dime museums, such as people with bodies of extraordinary physical variation, "missing links," "monstrous" animals, and novelty acts such as sword-swallowers. Blackface minstrel entertainers also performed in the side show, Carl Wittke among those noting that "there was scarcely a circus, a street fair or a patent medicine show which did not carry one or more blackface performers among its entertainers."[1]

Some of the biggest circuses and menageries of the times passed through Amherst. When George F. Bailey and Co.'s Great Quadruple Combination! was in town in 1866, Dickinson wrote to Mrs. J. G. Holland: "Friday I tasted life. It was a vast morsel. A circus passed the house - still I feel the red in my mind though the drums are out" (L318). In a letter to cousin Frances Norcross a few years later, Dickinson mentions watching the cavalcade of The Great North American Circus into the early morning hours as it made its way through the streets of Amherst on its way out of town (L390). The extravagance of the grand procession into town (and the chance for last glimpses of its extraordinary sights as it departed) undoubtedly drew many townspeople to windows and streets. The arrival of Raymond and Waring's Menagerie at 10 o'clock on a Wednesday morning in August 1847 was heralded by a "Gorgeous ROMAN CHARIOT literally covered with Gold!! and drawn by Ten Magnificent Black Horses!" An advertisement in the *Hampshire and Franklin Express* declared that "The Chariot will be followed by THIRTY CARRIAGES, Containing VARIOUS ANIMALS IN THIS EXHIBITION, drawn by ONE HUNDRED HORSES!" (July 29, 1847). Van Amburgh's Great Golden Menagerie claimed to offer "The Largest, Most Varied and Comprehensive Collection of Rare and Curious Beasts and Birds in America."[2]

Dickinson directly referred to or alluded to traveling shows, menageries, circuses and theatricals in several poems (for example, F321/J228 "Blazing in Gold and quenching in Purple," F257/J243 "I've known a Heaven, like a Tent - ," F1270/J1206 "The Show is not the Show"). Although references to popular entertainment might initially seem out of keeping with a less worldly view of Dickinson, the trope of the circus or theatrical – the "show" – registers her attentiveness to earthly wonders and to the otherworldly. To the extent that a circus or traveling show conjures another reality – something fantastical, enigmatic, elusive – it stands as a fitting conceit for Dickinson's concerns with transcendent states and spiritualized spaces. In poem F212/J184, Dickinson directly draws on circus imagery in her depiction of sacred mystery:

> A transport one cannot contain
> May yet, a transport be -
> Though God forbid it lift the lid,
> Unto it's Extasy!
>
> A Diagram - of Rapture!
> A sixpence at a show -
> With Holy Ghosts in Cages!
> The *Universe* would go!

With the carnivalized image of "Holy Ghosts in Cages," Spirit is diminished (even if made spectacular) through its rendering as a circus curiosity or an exhibition of wild animals. The peculiar image of Holy Ghosts elicits the same sorts of queries as do the "curiosities" in museum shows and circuses: are they dangerous or harmless, aberrant or ordinary? The nineteenth-century circus itself augmented the spectacle of its processions with depictions of biblical narratives. The side panels of circus cages and wagons would sometimes be decorated with painted illustrations of some of the more astonishing Bible stories, such as Jonah and the Whale or Daniel in the Lions' Den. While the combination of religious drama and community amusements is clearly not novel to the nineteenth century, and the overlay of religious iconography would have had business purposes (dressing the circus as moral entertainment would likely draw larger crowds), the mixing of circus fantasticalness with stories of religious faith still raises a provocative question: What unexpected wonders might the circus reveal? Possibly, Dickinson laughs at the affiliation of the circus with biblical narratives, relishing the apparent joke that ricochets between sacred texts and a carnival world that celebrates the variousness of earthbound creatures and human ingenuity. The poem, however, conveys an excited wonder through its vocabulary of "transport," "Extasy," and "Rapture," and through its four exclamation points, as if the speaker (and Dickinson) were bedazzled by the marvels before her and enjoying the ironic display that would pretend to "capture" the divine in order to reveal it.

Music offered another form of mass popular amusement, heard in many venues including the circus, the museum, the dance hall, the public concert, the political assembly, the minstrel show, and the home. In the early decades of the nineteenth century, new technologies, such as in the construction of the piano, expanded the possibilities for musical family recreation. By the mid-nineteenth century, the piano had established its place in the parlors of the middle-class (Dickinson acquired her first piano at the age of fourteen), and the abundant production of affordable sheet music brought all types of music into the home. Attention to Dickinson's personal collection of sheet music reveals that she was aware of musicians and music tied to the reform movements of her day; she was also curious about songs that were part of the repertoire of minstrel entertainment.

Dickinson's personal album of sheet music makes evident her interest in popular music.[3] While the Dickinson family library contained such songbooks as *The Psalms, Hymns, and Spiritual Songs of the Rev. Isaac Watts* (1834 edition) and Lowell Mason's *The Boston Academy's Collection of Church Music*, her personal collection includes many marches, polkas, and quicksteps; individual songs from Thomas Moore's much-loved *Irish Melodies*; and Henry Bishop's and John Howard Payne's phenomenally successful "Home, Sweet Home," a song that in the early 1850s became linked to the celebrated Swedish singer Jenny Lind; it was identified as her trademark piece on her American tour in 1850–1. Dickinson possessed the sheet music to many songs tied to the web of American social and political movements of her century, songs such as "Old Dan Tucker," "The Girl I Left Behind Me," and "Yankee Doodle." She owned several songs of the Hutchinson Family Singers, one of the most popular of the nineteenth-century family singing groups and, starting in 1843, regular performers at abolitionist meetings and other political assemblies. Described variously as patriots or rabblerousers, the Hutchinsons presented forceful political voices, continuing, in various configurations, to sing in the causes of emancipation, temperance, women's rights, and peace throughout the century. In addition, Dickinson owned the music to some of the biggest hits of nineteenth-century blackface minstrelsy: "Lucy Neal," "Dandy Jim," "Lovely Fan" (later known as "Buffalo Gals [Won't You Come Out Tonight?]"), "The Blue Juniata," "Who's That Knocking at the Door," "Old Dan Tucker," and "The Jolly Raftsman." Other songs in Dickinson's album, such as folk dances like "Fisher's Hornpipe" and "Durang's Hornpipe," became part of the minstrel dance repertoire in the 1840s and 1850s. In addition to the songs written and performed by Dan Emmett and William Whitlock (both of the original Virginia Minstrels) and by Cool White (of the Virginia Serenaders), another in her collection – Marshall Pike and L. V. H. Crosby's "Oh Give Me a Home if in a Foreign Land" – was performed by the Harmoneon Family, also a blackface minstrel group. That Dickinson knew this music suggests that she had metrical models in addition to the commonly cited Protestant hymn for her own verse; these songs also illustrate ways that social critique and commentary as well as many types of human struggle could be dramatized in lyric form

By the late 1840s, the minstrel show was well established, its evolution characterized by the growing variety of entertainments included in its programs: musical numbers, dance, comic skits, jokes and riddles, mock oratory, and short plays. Generally recognized as "the chief American popular entertainment of the nineteenth century," the blackface minstrel show offered a stage for satires and parodies of high culture (such as opera and Shakespeare's plays) as well as of popular culture (such as musical performers such as the Hutchinson Family or Jenny Lind).[4] Like the musical acts of individual minstrel troupes, the minstrel show was built on the premise of masquerade: impersonations of characters or real people for comic or satiric effect; caricatured or sentimental portrayals of race and gender (which relied on blackface makeup, flamboyant or exaggerated costumes, and cross-dressing); and burlesques of preachers, politicians, and reformers and their views on topics such as women's rights, temperance, and current scientific or technological developments.

Although historians disagree on nineteenth-century purposes and perceptions of the minstrel show, many scholars emphasize two key qualities: (1) that the minstrel show was a performance and (2) that it depicted social conflicts of the nineteenth century and presented social satire. Whereas some scholars are primarily attentive to minstrelsy's role in the evolution of racial caricatures and stereotypes and stress the exploitation of African Americans and African American culture in minstrelsy, others emphasize minstrelsy's role in nineteenth-century class formation. Eric Lott demonstrates how transgressions in blackface performances mediated and directed the establishment of a self-consciously white working class: minstrelsy's "languages of race so invoked ideas about class as to provide displaced maps or representations of 'working-classness'."[5] Dale Cockrell, too, sees performance as the key to the blackface show, and, like Lott, credits minstrelsy with serious class critique and class satire.[6] William J. Mahar concludes that the theatrical entertainment of minstrelsy addressed "the unfairness of privilege" through the burlesque of American elitism and the ridiculing of people of all classes.[7]

Blackface performance was seen everywhere in nineteenth-century America: on the serious theater stage as well as in circuses, traveling menageries, dime museums, and Ethiopian opera houses. Blackface performance was frequently part of Christmastime theatricals in the nineteenth century.

Articles, stories, and advertisements related to blackface minstrelsy appeared in the pages of newspapers and magazines such as *The Atlantic Monthly*, *Harper's Weekly*, and the *Boston Daily Atlas*, publications that came into the Dickinson household. Moreover, the publication and wide distribution of sheet music brought the minstrel performance right into the home. Although blackface troupes did perform in Amherst as did minstrel troupes comprised of black performers, Dickinson would not have had to attend minstrel performances to be informed of them. In short, blackface minstrel shows were the most popular of entertainments during her lifetime. It would be astonishing if she were not well informed about them.

The origins of minstrelsy are found in dance as well as song. Made famous by his performance of "Jim Crow" and credited with originating its stage presentation, T. D. Rice reputedly copied "Jim Crow" from an older black stablehand (or slave or stage-driver) whom Rice observed singing and dancing an unusual shuffle and jump step around 1830. One of the members of the original Virginia Minstrels, Frank Brower was primarily a dancer. Many other dancers found fame on the minstrel stage, one of the most renowned being William Henry Lane, probably a free born black man, performing under the name Juba, who in his act imitated numerous blackface dancers (such as Brower and John Diamond). Diamond performed as a duo with William Whitlock early in his career and, like Juba, appeared in P. T. Barnum's shows in the early 1840s. Three pieces of minstrel music in Dickinson's personal album have cover illustrations that display dancing figures, the cover to Whitlock's "Who's That Knocking at the Door" apparently depicting Whitlock himself playing his banjo while John Diamond (or possibly another dancer who entertained under the name Frank Diamond) jumps or hops in his accompanying dance. The type of music Dickinson gathered in her sheet music collection suggests that dance appealed to her: her collection contains many pieces of lively dance music – quicksteps, waltzes, polkas, hornpipes, and jigs. A fundamental part of the minstrel show, dance of all of these types was included in minstrel performance, parody, and burlesque, as was the ballet.

In several of Dickinson's poems, a dance – most frequently unspecified, but sometimes a jig or waltz or ballet – is mentioned. In a poem from about 1862, Dickinson's speaker imagines herself on stage performing a minstrel-style comic ballet.

> I cannot dance opon my Toes -
> No Man instructed me -
> But oftentimes, among my mind,
> A Glee possesseth me,

That had I Ballet Knowledge -
Would put itself abroad
In Pirouette to blanch a Troupe -
Or lay a Prima, mad,

And though I had no Gown of Gauze -
No Ringlet, to my Hair,
Nor hopped for Audiences - like Birds -
One Claw opon the air -

Nor tossed my shape in Eider Balls,
Nor rolled on wheels of snow
Till I was out of sight, in sound,
The House encore me so -

Nor any know I know the Art
I mention - easy - Here -
Nor any Placard boast me -
It's full as Opera -

(F381B J326)

Although the speaker protests her skill in the classical art of ballet, her accumulated denials construct a vivid portrayal of her performing the dance, or rather some antic parody of it. Her startling performance renders the poem as a comic skit: in declaring what she has not done (not "hopped" or "tossed" or "rolled") and what she does not have ("no Gown of Gauze," "No Ringlet, to my Hair"), she brings to life the image of herself as the most unconventional of ballerinas, a dancing bird, graceful but untutored and most definitely un-balletlike, hopping before an audience, "One Claw opon the air."

Many Dickinson scholars have discussed this poem, noting its attention to artistic performance and the techniques of the artist as well as addressing the contrast between the speaker's (or Dickinson's) ostensibly modest acknowledgment of her lack of training and the revelation of her complete confidence in her skill and originality as an artist. Perceiving the dance as Dickinson's metaphor for writing, several scholars (such as Charles Anderson, Jane Donahue Eberwein, Suzanne Juhasz, Cristanne Miller, Barbara Mossberg, and Vivian Pollak) have addressed the mood of irony, parody, or satire in the poem.

Recognition of Dickinson's knowledge of popular music adds a plausible dimension to her satire beyond the ironic tension between renunciation and self-promotion or the witty demurrals that display not her amateurism, but her impatience with conventional technique and presentation. In other words, someone so clearly informed about the popular music and popular culture of her time might well parody not only the conventions and status of ballet and other classical arts but also the parodic performances of those arts as presented on the minstrel show stage. There are several examples of words and imagery in "I cannot dance upon my Toes - " that hold specific meanings in the world of blackface performance or that evoke blackface minstrelsy. For example, the "Glee" that "possesseth" the speaker denotes high spirits as well as song, and more specifically, song arranged in parts, a popular style for musical groups like the Hutchinson Family Singers and minstrel players. Minstrel songs were commonly referred to as "Ethiopian glee." In addition, while the word "Opera" immediately calls to mind European opera, the poem itself does not depict the opulence of high opera, rather stressing the comic and parodic, and thus pointing again toward that other opera so popular in nineteenth-century America, the Ethiopian Opera, that is, the minstrel show. Some minstrel entertainers called themselves members of opera troupes or opera companies (such as Palmo's Burlesque Opera Company and Kunkel's Nightingale Opera Troupe), and, particularly in large cities of the Northeast such as New York, Boston, and Philadelphia, minstrel troupes sometimes had their own theaters, called Ethiopian Opera Houses.

Similar to the word "Opera," the word "Troupe" offers double meanings, connoting both a dance ensemble and a minstrel troupe. The speaker's expectation that her pirouettes would "blanch a Troupe" suggests, most readily, the altering effect that her bizarre or extraordinary dance would have on the rest of the dance company: they would turn pale from amazement. The word "blanch" is curious, however, suggesting more than a face turning ashen. The word "blanch" emphasizes the removal of all color or a process of whitening. Dickinson's image is especially potent if the troupe being blanched were a blackface minstrel troupe, their whitening somehow magical as if the transformative effect of her dance went beyond a merely physical reaction, the burnt cork makeup vaporized right off the performers' faces. The reference in line eight to the "Prima" also compresses the "high" and the popular, suggesting not only the prima ballerina or the prima donna of an opera company, but also the female impersonator in a minstrel show, who was called the "prima donna." By 1860 the minstrel show prima donna was a well-established major role.

Such impersonation is central to the speaker's activity in the poem. Drawing from elements of the minstrel show, the speaker concocts a caricature of a ballet dancer: a hopping creature, one "Claw" held high, she is both graceful and clumsy, at the least an unusual figure of feminine artistry. One could view her as a female impersonator, burlesquing conventional ideas of the female and feminine with her visions of a gown of gauze, ringlets, a tutu. But the rendering is more than unusual. It is fantastical, the dancer exposed as a gigantic bird, performing its series of little jumps and pirouettes, sufficiently outrageous to "lay a Prima, mad." The dance steps conjure an entertainer on the minstrel stage. Historians of minstrelsy describe the variety of movements that comprise the minstrel dance, including kicks and spins, slides, posturings, hops, and jumps. As described by Hans Nathan, the placement and movements of arms and hands were also critical in the minstrel dance: "Arms and hands formed a most expressive part of the dancer's performance. According to its character, they were intense or relaxed, held over the head or extended in front, with the fingers usually spread wide apart."[8] Other descriptions and the illustrations in Nathan's study often note one arm or hand posed in the air. In Dickinson's poem, the dancer, likened to a bird hopping with one "Claw" held in the air, mimics the gestures of the minstrel dance, even the famous "Jim Crow" whose chorus ends with the line, "Eb'ry time I weel about, I jump Jim Crow."[9]

Initially an image that purportedly conveys strangeness, the pirouette rolls forward as the prominent metaphor for the many turns of the poem. Within the poem, multiple meanings of "glee," "opera," "troupe," "house," and "prima" are set spinning. Images of the classical arts and the popular arts whirl around each other and turn into each other. This mixing of the "high" and the "low" carries an implicit class consciousness, suggesting the speaker's own divided or mischievous sensibility: she courts the classical arts but identifies with the popular forms. In addition, notions of gender are wheeled around, the regalia and postures of the prima ballerina parodied and replaced with the playful (or earnest) performance of the prima female impersonator. In the burlesque presented in the poem, the speaker names the ballet but her dance seems more suited to the minstrel show stage.

Dickinson's allusions to minstrelsy in her writing connect her to a wide and animated cultural conversation that addressed vital questions of personal and public identity and that debated the social struggles of her day. The minstrel show took on the contentious questions of the nation in ways that were not straightforward; its mix of entertainment and social critique produced a language of crossings and costumings, riddles and ambiguity. Whether the minstrel act connected or converged racial identities out of hate, shame, guilt, curiosity, or other motivation, the blackface minstrel performer demonstrated the permeability of the borders of race, gender, and class. As in any time, the popular entertainments of the nineteenth century dramatized some of its most pressing issues and, through their special powers of enticement and excitement, engaged mass audiences in the contemplation of these issues. Her interest in popular entertainment illumines a Dickinson who is aware of the paradoxes and difficulties connected with comprehending forms of identity – racial, gendered, national, human – in her historical moment; just as popular entertainment expressed these conundrums, Dickinson confronted them in her verse, drawing perhaps inevitably on tropes common to popular entertainment.

NOTES

1 C. Wittke, *Tambo and Bones: A History of the American Minstrel Stage* (New York: Greenwood, 1968), 64–5.
2 Quotation taken from a broadside for Van Amburgh, American Antiquarian Society and Readex Digital Collections, "America's Historical Imprints," *Archive of Americana*, 2005.
3 Dickinson's personal album of sheet music is housed at the Houghton Library, Harvard University ("Music: A Bound Volume of Miscellaneous Sheet Music." Archival Negative 49-1469-F). Carlton Lowenberg identifies the contents of this album in Appendix One of his *Musicians Wrestle Everywhere* (Berkeley, CA: Fallen Leaf Press, 1992).
4 A. Bean, J. Hatch, and B. McNamara, "Editors' Preface" in Bean et al. (eds.), *Inside the Minstrel Mask: Readings in Nineteenth-Century Blackface Minstrelsy* (Hanover, NH: University Press of New England, 1996), xiii.
5 Eric Lott, *Love and Theft: Blackface Minstrelsy and the American Working Class* (Oxford: Oxford University Press, 1993), 68.
6 Dale Cockrell, *Demons of Disorder: Early Blackface Minstrels and Their World* (Cambridge: Cambridge University Press, 1997).
7 W. J. Mahar, *Behind the Burnt Cork Mask: Early Blackface Minstrelsy and Antebellum American Popular Culture* (Urbana: University of Illinois Press, 1999), 353.
8 H. Nathan, *Dan Emmett and the Rise of Early Negro Minstrelsy* (Norman: University of Oklahoma Press, 1962), 75.
9 *Series of Old American Songs: Reproduced in Facsimile from Original or Early Editions in the Harris Collection of American Poetry and Plays*. Cur. S. F. Damon. (Providence, RI: Brown University Library, 1936), no. 15.

CHAPTER 22

Visual Arts: The Pentimento

Alexander Nemerov

In her book *Dickinson's Misery*, Virginia Jackson uses the word "pentimento" to describe the covering over of one day by the next in Dickinson's "On the World you colored."[1]

> Aimless crept
> the Glows
> Over Realms
> Of Orchards
> I the Day
> before
> Conquered
> with the Robin -
>   (F1203 J1171)

As Jackson describes this part of the poem, the "Aimless" new morning replaces the actions of the previous day, when the self had conquered realms with the robin. Yet the poem makes us feel that something of the previous day shows through, the conquered orchards still apparent in the aimless new morning. This is a pentimento, an art-historical word meaning a part of a painting that the artist has painted over but that has reappeared with time. Jackson's choice of the word invites a comparison between Dickinson's poetry and the visual arts. The comparison differs from previous accounts of Dickinson and art that focus on her relation to Hudson River School landscape painting (including her brother Austin Dickinson's collection of such paintings at the Evergreens), John Ruskin's aesthetic theories, and twentieth-century figures such as Martha Graham, Barbara Morgan, and Joseph Cornell.[2] Specifically, Jackson's word recalls the most well-known pentimento in an American painting of the 1860s – indeed, one by an artist accustomed to seeing the world "New Englandly," namely, Dickinson's Boston-born contemporary Winslow Homer (1836–1910).

The painting in question is Homer's *Veteran in a New Field*, which he completed in his New York City studio in summer 1865 (Figure 3). It

Figure 3. Winslow Homer, *The Veteran in a New Field*, 1865. Oil on canvas, 24 1/8 × 38 1/8 in. Bequest of Miss Adelaide Milton de Groot (1876–1967), 1967 (67.187.131). The Metropolitan Museum of Art, New York, New York. Image copyright The Metropolitan Museum of Art. Reprinted with permission. Image source: Art Resource, New York.

depicts a Civil War veteran adapting to his new peacetime "field" or vocation as he threshes the wheat with a single-bladed scythe, turning swords into plowshares. But the remains of another object exist in the painting. As the art historian Nicolai Cikovsky, Jr., notes, just above the long hooked blade extending to the veteran's left we see the ghostly vestige of the cradled scythe Homer originally painted (Figure 4). Homer made the change, Cikovsky argues, because he saw the chance to make his picture say more if he replaced a merely accurate depiction of "agricultural technology" with a symbol of "Death the reaper."[3]

So much makes sense, but how does this pentimento relate to Dickinson? The answer, I think, is not a matter of tracing a kindred working procedure – Dickinson's crossing out of words being like that of an artist regretting an earlier design. Nor is it a matter of the meanings in question, for one can imagine that the most fearsomely realized figures in Dickinson's poems do not carry such unequivocal symbols as the one Homer has made his veteran hold. (Dickinson might actually have liked the cradle in the scythe, and enjoyed the birth-and-death gamut of

Figure 4. *The Veteran in a New Field* (detail).

this sweeping, stroking weapon of war and peace.) Instead the kinship of Dickinson and Homer centering on the pentimento – not just this pentimento, but, as we shall see, others in Homer's art – might relate to "misery" as Jackson describes it.

Jackson's brilliant argument is complex, but a summary for my purposes is as follows. The lyric poet, Dickinson being one, must put her words and herself down on the page, and must thus submit to being read and being normalized as a poet who expresses her feelings in a poem, those two mutually defining entities (poet and poem) accepted as a given. But this poet also knows – and this is the misery – that the very performance of herself, and of the writing enshrining her feelings, actually *erases* the physically and emotionally thick "historical experience" that occasioned the words in the first place. Actually, it *almost* erases that experience, for Dickinson's genius, according to Jackson, is that "'a Life' remains in her writing in excess of the figures of that writing" – that, in other words, ensconced in what have come to be regarded as the poems of this poet are *material traces* – the odd scraps of paper she wrote on, the occasions when she wrote her verse, other vestigial ephemera – of life as lived.[4] *Pentimenti*, we might call these traces, which exist in Dickinson's poems like the trace presence of an earlier day after night and a new dawn have vaporized it.

Homer's pentimento is not exactly of this kind. Like many painters, he simply thought better of one idea and replaced it with another. Moreover, he hardly could have expected that the cradled scythe in *Veteran in a New Field* (see Figure 4) would ever show itself and become, as now, an unavoidable part of what it is to contemplate the painting. Nonetheless, this picture – like other paintings he made, starting in the 1860s but continuing into the last decade of his life – reveals a way that the pentimento and what I will call a "pentimento effect" is a figure in his art. More than that, the pentimento in Homer's art is a figure for what Jackson ascribes to Dickinson's poetry: namely, a sign of all that is missed, all that is half-hidden, when we agree to accept such simple designations as "painter" and "painting" as mutually expressive entities. In Homer's case, what is missed is the lived historical experience (often pertaining to the Civil War) that his paintings acknowledge they do *not* show – except as pentimenti. In what follows, I wonder if Homer, like Dickinson, did not have his own form of misery: namely, a knowledge that his pictures needed to come into being if he was to express himself (of course) but that the weightless-infinite material flux of life as lived might be turned to nothing – or, again, almost nothing – in the act of having been expressed. Only in the pentimento would we find it.

Consider *Veteran in a New Field* a little further. Homer originally painted not just the cradled scythe but the branches of a tree at upper right, visible in an 1867 engraving of the picture above the horizon of wheat and to the right of the veteran's lowered right shoulder, but deleted at some later point (see Figure 3).[5] These branches extended to the left, matching the leftward orientation of the cradled scythe's tines. More than the death-scythe Homer finally settled on, these things that are *not* there most recall the war the veteran cannot erase from his mind. The single-bladed scythe is a convenient sign for sure, a legible indicator of his previous vocation, but it forecloses the more primal and vaporous sense of a war present by not being there, a ghostly understructure of never-to-be-discerned experiences. The veteran's missing face is decisive. The finished painting depends on making us sense what is not there.

The following year, Homer evoked the pentimento in a different way – this time involving two Civil War paintings, inviting us to imagine the way one might cancel out the other. They are one of his most famous paintings, *Prisoners from the Front*, and the obscure *Brush Harrow*, which he exhibited together in 1866 at the National Academy of Design (Figures 5 and 6). Cikovsky, noting that the two pictures were paired at the exhibition, invokes the pentimento in his description of their critical

Figure 5. Winslow Homer, *Prisoners from the Front*, 1866. Oil on canvas, 24 × 38 in. Gift of Mrs. Frank B. Porter, 1922 (22.207). The Metropolitan Museum of Art. Reprinted with permission. Image source: Art Resource, New York, New York.

reception: "The more easy legibility of [*Prisoners from the Front*] generated a torrent of critical commentary that overwhelmed the tenderly subtle and poignant meanings of *The Brush Harrow*."[6] *Prisoners from the Front* shows a heroic Union officer, Major General Francis Channing Barlow, surveying a group of three Confederate prisoners – from left to right, a country private, a wizened old man, and a defiant aristocratic cavalryman. From the first, critics recognized the painting as a grand commentary on the war, "a truly Homeric reminiscence," as one writer put it. By contrast, *The Brush Harrow* attracted the notice of only a single critic. Showing one boy astride a horse and the other seated on the plow, it too is a Civil War painting, as Cikovsky notes, depicting these two perhaps fatherless waifs, perhaps orphaned by the war, "pulling a harrow to smooth the ground for planting."[7] But it largely escaped attention.

The Brush Harrow, to put it another way, feels like a picture superseded by *Prisoners from the Front*. Painted the year before its famous companion, and nearly identical in size, it seems like a failed prototype for the grand heroic legibility Homer would complete in *Prisoners from the Front* the following year. Partly this is because *The Brush Harrow* adumbrates the blocking of forms and figures of its successor. The boy seated on the plow, his head turned to the left, anticipates the figure of Barlow, alike in his

Figure 6. Winslow Homer, *The Brush Harrow*, 1865. Oil on canvas, 24 × 37 13/16 in. Harvard Art Museums/Fogg Museum, Anonymous Gift, 1939.229. Reprinted with permission. Photo: Imaging Department, copyright President and Fellows of Harvard College.

cap. The prominent tree on the horizon at right likewise evokes Barlow's heroic singularity. The boy astride the horse, as well as the blocky form of the horse itself, predicts the massed rectangle of Confederate prisoners and their guards. The array of ground, horizon, and sky in each picture is similar, too. These adumbrations, however, are all partial and inchoate, as if the earlier painting and even the figures within it possessed the secret of their inscrutability – the turning away of the boy on the horse, the charged and awkward gap between the two little farmers – in contrast to the crisp coherence of *Prisoners from the Front*, where even the blank space (that between Barlow and the Confederates, for example) is fully charged with epical significance.

There is, in other words, a pentimento effect between the two pictures. It is as if *Prisoners from the Front* were painted over *The Brush Harrow*, and as if by displaying the two pictures together Homer were allowing this connotation to be clear, even if he did not intend the first picture to be read in these terms. It is not beside the point that the lone critic describing *The Brush Harrow* in 1866 noted the initials "U.S." on the horse but that no such initials are visible now, or that infrared photography has revealed numerous pentimenti in *Prisoners from the Front*.[8] Homer's working method allowed for constant adjustments. But beyond that, he seemingly allowed these alterations and effacements to become a part of the finished look of his individual pictures or, as here, even the look of his pictures in relation to one another. The boy turned away, like the veteran in a new field, becomes a sign of a whole painting given over to a sense of its own eradication – to brushing away, as with plow and paintbrush, the articulation of a previous ground in favor of a smooth new surface. And again what is not shown is what is most important. This is because what is not shown – what consents to be visible only in hunch-shouldered disappearance – is an awkward, illegible, yet manifestly sensed field of broken experience, the scratching of the branches on the dirt instead of the stalwart delineation of battle lines, wherein some unheralded sensation of life-as-lived might be glimpsed. Oblivion is the cradle holding this inscrutable mark, as if Homer worked hard to portray these traces he knew would not be seen.

What is a corresponding Dickinson pentimento from those years? Consider the first version of "It sifts from Leaden Sieves - ," written in 1862, a poem Eliza Richards has related to the Civil War (F291A J311):[9]

> It sifts from Leaden Sieves -
> It powders all the Wood.
> It fills with Alabaster Wool
> The Wrinkles of the Road -
>
> It makes an Even Face
> Of Mountain, and of Plain -
> Unbroken Forehead from the East
> Unto the East again -
>
> It reaches to the Fence -
> It wraps it Rail by Rail
> Till it is lost in Fleeces -
> It deals Celestial Vail
>
> To Stump, and Stack - and Stem -
> A Summer's empty Room -
> Acres of Joints, where Harvests were,
> Recordless, but for them -
>
> It Ruffles Wrists of Poets
> As Ankles of a Queen -
> Then stills it's Artisans - like Ghosts -
> Denying they have been -

The poem creates a series of pentimenti. The snow covers the landscape, leveling the world in sameness, but it also allows us to see the wrinkles and rails it smoothes and obliterates. The things we cannot see somehow remain by virtue of having been covered. These pentimenti make the poem miserable, in Jackson's sense. The snowstorm's leveling describes the poem's own cancellations. As the snow blankets the world in a common fate, as death cancels differences, making an Even Face of mountain and field, an Unbroken Forehead instead of the Wrinkles of the Road, so the poem – another totality – blankets a variety of lived experience, leaving no record that these creased and broken sensations ever existed except, somehow, by virtue of the fact that they are no longer there. What is "recordless" is somehow a record – a record moreover that requires obliteration to be seen, or sensed, just as a pentimento requires a finished painting to be manifest.

Dickinson's revisions to the poem add to this idea. The stanzas she cut in the subsequent versions of ca. 1865, 1871, and 1883 – stanzas two, three, and four – are "the panoramic ones," notes Helen Vendler.[10] These stanzas are beautiful, but because they do nothing but extend our visions of the snow, Vendler notes, they accomplish little except emphasize the complete mastery of the poem's sweeping image, and therefore of the poem itself, as the expression of a world where all succumbs to its soft and unified atmosphere. Although stanzas three and four abound in pentimenti – and therefore help give the 1862 version its panoply of forgotten-erased things – the covering snow, as Vendler puts it, "smoothes out the characteristics of the landscape"; the omitted stanzas, only elaborations "on this conceit of smoothing," "add nothing new." The sense of a world become unified and pretty too quickly – a world without particularity – is maybe what caused Dickinson to find lines for "the sheer unpredictability" of the snow, by contrast, in her 1883 revision, where it scatters, gathers, and curls seemingly without design.[11]

There was another reason Dickinson wished to deny a pleasant unity. Totality was a sign of the national media during the Civil War years and after – a unity that a poem wishing to stress the broken field of private experience would need to avoid. When she first wrote "It sifts from Leaden Sieves - ," Dickinson drew upon Thomas Wentworth Higginson's essay "Snow," published in *The Atlantic Monthly* in February 1862, but she came to realize that Higginson's homogenous lyric flurry was not the effect she wanted in her poem. The sweeping effects of a huge snowstorm, in Higginson's description, suggest mass publication: namely, a national periodical's newly realized powers of covering a land, of making "level and wide-swept meadows" of the same beautiful stuff, the unities of media making everything alike. The sun shining brightly the next morning is likewise a totality, an "undisputed monarch" as much as the storm that made the level meadows it beams on. Even interior mental worlds are made by the unifying storm outside. The storm winds of the night before, swirling around a "household ... vexed by broken dreams," create the empathetic clichés of the inhabitants, their "changing fancies of lost children on solitary moors, of sleighs hopelessly overturned in drifted and pathless gorges, or of icy cordage upon disabled vessels in Arctic seas."[12] The sentimental zephyrs and supple phantoms of a total environment put ideas in the heads of readers inundated by the same material. Even as the new conditions of reading and writing must have struck Higginson with awe – how could he not admire the potential totality of such coverage, of creating widespread effects like a god? – it was still the very point for a literary man, should he observe the world closely and honestly, to pick out the little particulars that no totalizing snow could obliterate.

Dickinson worked within the same frame. Writing her poems in a way that separated them entirely from national publications, she did so also with a sense of her poetry's relation to the sweeping sameness of a journalistic atmosphere. "It sifts from Leaden Sieves - " courts unity, the repetition of smoothness and softness, while keeping an eye out for the small thing that would defy such coverage.[13] "She must not have wanted a panorama" – Vendler's account of why Dickinson revised the poem – speaks alike to the dangers of a poetic and journalistic totality in 1862.[14] When one's poem becomes itself an expression of the world going under, smoothed and softened to melancholic grace, with few obdurate details that truly stick in the mind, the poet must graze against the storm powers of a world she *cannot* arrogate to herself but only accept as the thwarted sense of a truer revelation. When the skies splinter with twigs and broken branches, falling to the snow instead of the snow falling to them, then it is the better part of wisdom to grasp at straws.

Homer was a national artist – *Veteran in a New Field* was reproduced as a wood engraving in *Frank Leslie's Illustrated Weekly* on July 13, 1867 – but he too sought the oddity of an unresolved picture. Maybe a many-bladed farm tool, correctly shown, accurate to the last particular, had the power to resist becoming a symbol – symbols being only another form of totality – and to become instead a catachresis, cocked and slanted, holding us forever at a proper remove. Or maybe, better, the *painting over* of this same farm tool, replacing it with the legibly symbolic single-bladed scythe, made it retire now with the right misery, the shadowed glow of what's not said or ever could be said, the flaking of sunlight on iron. Jackson, describing a central preoccupation of Dickinson, notes the "rhetorical difficulty of pointing to an experience (or an identity) before it becomes metaphor."[15] In that sense, even the cradled scythe is a metaphor. But to see it vanish is to sense the strangeness that defies our terms.

NOTES

1 Virginia Jackson, *Dickinson's Misery: A Theory of Lyric Reading* (Princeton, NJ: Princeton University Press, 2005), 207.
2 On Dickinson, Hudson River painting, and Ruskin, see Judith Farr, *The Passion of Emily Dickinson* (Cambridge, MA: Harvard University Press, 1992); on Dickinson and twentieth-century art, see Susan Danly, ed., *Language as Object: Emily Dickinson and Contemporary Art* (Amherst, MA: Mead Art Museum, 1997).
3 Nicolai Cikovsky, Jr., in Cikovsky and Franklin Kelly, *Winslow Homer* (Washington, DC: National Gallery of Art, 1995), 24–5.
4 Jackson, *Dickinson's Misery*, 222, 228.
5 Cikovsky, *Winslow Homer*, 24–5.
6 Ibid., 54.
7 Ibid., 26, 54.
8 Ibid., 54, 55. Nicole Bass, a Ph.D. student in the history of art at Yale University, notes that on close inspection of the painting no "U.S." is visible on the horse.
9 See Eliza Richards, "Weathering the News in US Civil War Poetry," *The Cambridge Companion to Nineteenth-Century American Poetry*, ed. Kerry Larson (Cambridge: Cambridge University Press, 2011), 123. Richards's reading of the poem called it to my attention for inclusion in this essay.
10 Helen Vendler, *Dickinson: Selected Poems and Commentaries* (Cambridge, MA: The Belknap Press of Harvard University Press, 2010), 108.
11 Ibid., 108–9.
12 Thomas Wentworth Higginson, "Snow," *Atlantic Monthly* 9 (February 1862), 188–9.
13 On the crossings between poetry and journalism during the Civil War, see Eliza Richards, "Correspondent Lines: Poetry and Journalism in the U.S. Civil War," *ESQ: A Journal of the American Renaissance* 54 (2008), 145–69; and Alexander Nemerov, *Acting in the Night: Macbeth and the Places of the Civil War* (Berkeley: University of California Press, 2010), 144–5.
14 Vendler, *Dickinson*, 108.
15 Jackson, *Dickinson's Misery*, 219.

CHAPTER 23

Natural Sciences

Sabine Sielke

The first edition of Emily Dickinson's poems, "creatively" edited by Thomas Wentworth Higginson and Mabel Loomis Todd and published in 1890, sorted the texts into four "books" entitled "life," "love," "nature," and "time and eternity." A heading such as "natural sciences," covering astronomy, biology, chemistry, physics, and the geosciences, was probably far from the editors' minds, but not because poetry and science belonged within two separate cultures. Rather, as the sciences evolved during the nineteenth century, common notions of life, nature, and time transformed as well, yet remained inextricably entwined. As philosophy and the natural sciences separated during the nineteenth century, literature also took new shapes. Therefore if the "natural sciences" constitute a context in which to reposition Dickinson's work, this is at least partly due to the communication gap between scientists and literary intellectuals bemoaned by C. P. Snow in 1959. Since then, a prosperous field of scholarly work called "literature and science" has evolved that recognizes Emily Dickinson as a poet deeply invested in the sciences and its philosophies.

We need to acknowledge that this context of the "natural sciences" is as much our own as it is that of Dickinson, who in her lifetime witnessed fundamental developments in science and technology. Driven in part by a continuous desire to refashion our sense of who Dickinson was, the thriving "Dickinson industry" has recently projected the poet as healer, philosopher, and, as Robin Peel's study *Emily Dickinson and the Hill of Science* does, as "concealed natural philosopher/scientist."[1] Whether we concord with Peel's argument or not, Dickinson took great interest in the science of her time, in part because, like all romantics, one of her main concerns is man's relation to the natural world and its laws. She read nature as "the unfolding of natural law," yet also acknowledged the proximity of nineteenth-century theology, philosophy, and science.[2] "[T]he Supernatural," she wrote in a letter of February 1863 addressed to T. W. Higginson, is "only the Natural, disclosed - " (L280). This explains why any attempt to calculate the number of Dickinson's poems that "touch on scientific themes" and to distinguish specific disciplinary lenses remains a suggestive approximation at best;[3] it also explains why the poet's interrogation of the natural sciences can be discussed as interventions into the history of ideas and (mental) philosophy.[4] The very act of accentuating how science informs Dickinson's poetry therefore bespeaks our own attempt to reassociate literature with the sciences – an attempt that often diminishes the fundamental methodological differences between how literature and science approach "the laws of nature." Dickinson herself was highly aware of these asymmetries. In fact, her take on science is critical and engaged rather than positivist and affirmative; it figures as "an extension of her relationship with all authorities."[5] For the poet, science neither managed to demystify nature nor did it "reveal the handiwork of a divine intelligence" as promised.[6] At the same time, Dickinson presents science, analogous to her own poetic experiments, as challenging established nineteenth-century views and beliefs by "new evidence" hard to be "square[d]" with scripture.[7] Her interrogation of contemporaneous scientific insight thus cuts two ways; it is, on the one hand, welcoming and inquisitive, and on the other, skeptical and ironic, "an indictment of the hubris of science."[8]

If we map the "natural sciences" as a field of knowledge production closely interconnected with Dickinson's work, at issue is not only the question of how science is featured in Dickinson's poetry, but also how Dickinson is featured in science writing. I therefore approach the affiliation of Dickinson's poetry with the sciences from the following three directions. After delineating, in a first step, how the sciences of her day fared in Dickinson's writing, I take a second step to show why Dickinson's interest in the sciences galvanizes around matters of perception and cognition, central facets of both Romanticism and early neurobiology. My final step turns the tables and briefly highlights how both writers in the (cognitive) sciences and authors of literary texts have come to recognize Dickinson as a science writer.

SCIENCE IN DICKINSON

The business of the modern sciences has been to study and elucidate the laws of the natural world. Evolving from natural philosophy's primary concern with the laws of physics and mathematics, their work was subjected to dramatic transformations since the turn of the eighteenth century, when zoologists and botanists began to investigate life forms with theoretical rigor and professionalized nature studies, giving rise to modern biology, with its set of privileged methods.[9] In the process, the nineteenth-century natural sciences offered competing answers to questions that religion, theology, and philosophy pondered in their own, oftentimes intersecting ways. Dickinson could be convinced by neither the religious dogma of her day, nor by Transcendentalist thinking, nor by scientific advances: "Faith," one of her poems bluntly and ironically states, "is a fine invention / When Gentlemen can *see* - / But *Microscopes* are prudent / In an Emergency" (F202 J185). Like religious beliefs, scientific methods and technologies remain crutches that fail to build a bridge to the unknown. "The Chemical conviction / That Nought be lost" may reaffirm pantheism, yet it "Enable[s] in Disaster" only a "fractured Trust." It offers little consolation for lost lives: "The Faces of the Atoms / If I shall see / How more the Finished Creatures / Departed me!" (F1070 J954). Not in spite of, but because of her knowledge of science, Dickinson privileged poetry as the most potently creative medium to ponder and approximate the complexities of life – complexities that, for her, resist scientific and philosophical explanation as well as verbal and visual representation. In fact, some of her poems, mimicking mathematical equations, and thus, like the natural sciences, employing mathematics as an essential tool, pose as experiments *and* crosscut reductive scientific reasoning.

Science education constituted a considerable part of Dickinson's curriculum at Amherst Academy (1840–6) and Mount Holyoke College (1847–8) and included chemistry, physiology, astronomy, and natural philosophy. Dickinson attended classes by geologist and evolutionary theologist Edward Hitchcock, author of *The Religion of Geology* (1851), who is held accountable for a great degree of the poet's interest in the (geo)sciences – an interest that resounds within her lyrics and letters featuring volcanoes and foreign places from Australia and Brazil to Italy and India, Japan and Jamaica, Norway and Russia, and exposes what Paul Giles calls her "global consciousness."[10] In addition, Dickinson created an herbarium with four hundred pressed flowers and plants (preserved at Harvard's Houghton library and published in 2006 in a facsimile edition), which documents her familiarity with cultured plants and wildflowers as well as with the Linnaean system of classification and which, Richard B. Sewall suggests, is deeply related to her practice of writing poetry.[11] Dickinson had an "extraordinary" knowledge of botany;[12] in her poems, she critically reflects on its very methods: "I pull a flower from the woods - / A monster with a glass / Computes the stamens in a breath - And has her in a 'class'!" (F117 J70). Moreover, a considerable part of her texts, including some of her most well-known lyrics, provide a habitat for hummingbirds, bees, butterflies, gnats, crickets, flies, and spiders and are informed by a deep sense of wonder for their organic complexity.[13] Composing most of her poems after Darwin had published *On the Origin of the Species* (1859), Dickinson was well aware of his revolutionary contribution to theories of evolution and the heated debates and "darwinizing" it provoked in New England and its public media.[14] Rendering the bee as both "nation" and "population" (F1764 J1746), speaking of a flower that "bloomed and dropt" as "Species disappeared" (F843 J978), and calling worms "Our little Kinsmen" who – providing "breakfast" for birds – enhance the food chain (F932 J885), Dickinson's poems capture the impact and tenor of these debates with much humor and ironic distance.

Thus "[a]ntebellum science," Peel underlines, "provided Emily Dickinson with a lexicon, source of metaphor, and set of analogies that her more obvious skepticism about science can make us overlook."[15] In fact, as Daniel J. Orsini noted in 1981, Dickinson put science to a "daring and original use."[16] Her poems are replete with tropes from the fields of geology, biology, and meteorology, carefully chosen rhetorical figures that manage to foreground both the materiality of the natural world and the limits of scientific methodology, while at the same time acknowledging that "[i]t is not possible," as zoologist Richard Lewontin has it, "to do the work of science without using a language that is filled with metaphors. Virtually the entire body of modern science is an attempt to explain phenomena that cannot be experienced directly by human beings."[17] Aware of this fact, Dickinson in turn aims to render experiences and phenomena fundamental to human existence, such as sexuality, pain, and death, which resist scientific reasoning and representation. In this enterprise, science thus becomes "useful insofar ... as it reveals the limits of objectivity" and attests to its own inventive creativity.[18]

Although for Dickinson science and poetry overlap in their desire to know "otherness," her writing suggests that no such knowledge and certainty can be attained. With such a view, she courageously positions herself in the middle of a debate of immense cultural scope. In fact, her sense of what science can and cannot do is closely linked to her critique of New England transcendentalism; both positions explain why nature is a crucial, yet not primary concern of Dickinson's poetics. Like Whitman and the English Romantics, Dickinson is preoccupied with the relation of self and nature, the power of the imagination, and the limits of poetry. Unlike Whitman, however, who meant to put Emerson's transcendentalist philosophy into poetic practice and, in his poems, aims to bridge the gap between self and other or nature, Dickinson is highly skeptical of idealist convictions. She strongly resists the notion that nature gains its significance primarily through the perceiving consciousness, that words are directly fastened to visible things, and that the business of the philosopher or poet is to leap over the chasm of the unknown. Instead Dickinson recognizes nature's defiance of human understanding, be it scientific or philosophical, and cherishes perception itself: "Perception of an object costs / Precise the Object's loss - / Perception in itself a Gain" (F1103 J1071). "Nature and God," she writes elsewhere, "I neither knew"; both remain strangers whose secrets are not to be revealed (F803 J835). No matter how close we deem our mind – or our tools and technologies – to be to nature, "nature is a stranger yet; / The ones that cite her most / Have never passed her haunted house, / Nor simplified her ghost" (F1433 J1400). "Split the Lark - and you'll find the Music - ," Dickinson sarcastically suggests in another poem: sound cannot be located physically, and "Music" derives from our perception (F905 J861). Rejecting Emerson's idealism and teleology, she insists on the separation between self and nature as a fundamental condition of human subjectivity. Knowing that nature – and as a consequence, the natural sciences – cannot answer the questions that preoccupy her, Dickinson turns toward the landscape of our psyche, where she locates another version of the division between self and other. With less interest in the psychology of our mental disposition than in the physiology of our senses, nerves, and brains, the poet is way ahead of her time, once again.

RE-COGNIZING DICKINSON

When we acknowledge that the context of the "natural sciences" is as much our own as it is Dickinson's, we need to figure in the recent shift in our common understanding of what these sciences entail. To do this calculation let us recall the "second look" Snow took at his two cultures thesis in 1963. Retrospectively, he "regretted" using as his "test question about scientific literacy, *What do you know of the Second Law of Thermodynamics?*" Instead Snow "put forward a branch of science which ought to be requisite in the common culture": molecular biology.[19] Unlike thermodynamics, he explained, this field "does not involve serious conceptual difficulties" and "needs very little mathematics"; "most of all," it needs "a visual three-dimensional imagination."[20] Snow's change of mind was, on the one hand, prophetic, in that it foresaw the biosciences' increasing significance at the turn of our millennium. This rise to prominence partly results from the fact that, unlike the second law of thermodynamics, which is of "universal physical significance," the new biosciences "deal ... only with microscopic parts of the cosmos" which are nonetheless "of importance to each of us."[21] On the other hand, Snow's shift from physics to biology also counts as a major move from "hard" to historical science. According to Lewontin, biology "is all about unique historical events ... and does not have the kind of universals about which physicists speak." And although no science works without metaphors, only biology offers "grand universals" or "generalizations" that actually work as "governing metaphors."[22]

One metaphor-turned-icon ruling our sense of the sciences as biosciences is that of the brain. Once "wider than the Sky" (F598 J632), the brain has narrowed and shrunk, especially during the 1990s "decade of the brain," and multiplied serially in the diagnostic practice of neuroimaging, which some critics consider a sophisticated extension of phrenology because, once again, types of brains are being distinguished. Dickinson's work evolved when neurophysiologic insights into the work of the brain were developing and, like the poet's modernism *avant la lettre*, interrogating traditional (enlightened) notions of a (full, rational) self. By the 1840s, physiologist Xavier Bichat, for instance, had located memory and intelligence in the brain and situated emotions in various internal organs; Franz Joseph Gall and Johann Gaspar Spurzheim situated the mind and emotions exclusively in the brain and engaged in mental mapping using experiments instead of relying on introspection.[23] Although Dickinson was probably unaware of these findings, as Wilson reasons, she was familiar with Calvin Cutter's popular science textbook *Anatomy and Physiology Designed for Academies and Families* (1847) and took particular interest in this (brain) matter. Taking cognition as her primary subject in several poems, Dickinson voices both her preference of "the word 'brain' to 'mind'"[24] and a "critique of neuroscience," which "shares its terms with that science."[25] Her poems acknowledge the precarious, if privileged position of the inquisitive subject whose very means of inquisition, the brain, turns into the object of inspection. Moreover – and in contrast to the methodological atomism of contemporary (cognitive) science – Dickinson's explorations of anatomy and nature are "cosmic" and of universal relevance, indeed.[26]

Dickinson's poem "The Brain - is wider than the Sky - " (F598 J632) insists on the immense scope of our mental universe and insinuates that this magnitude evolves from neurophysiologic processes, which engage what we now consider "the vast expanse of the cerebral cortex," its "myriad units," and "billions of neurons."[27] Based on what Roland Hagenbüchle called "phenomenological reduction" – a focus not so much on things and phenomena themselves, but on how they affect our body and mind – many of Dickinson's poems are preoccupied with such physiological operations and, more significantly, with their disruption and failure.[28] The "central paradox" of Dickinson's poem, however, "depends," as Otten observes, "on the mind conceived both as substance – and so bounded and measurable – and as simultaneously limitless."[29] Analogously, even if "Perception of an object costs / Precise the Object's loss - ," as Dickinson puts it, "Perception in itself" comes out as "a Gain" and a recurrent motivation of many of her poems (F1103 J1071). For Dickinson, this cognitive surplus escapes science, theology, and language alike as the riddling end of F598/J632 subtly suggests: "The Brain is just the weight of God - / For - Heft them - Pound for Pound - / And they will differ - if they do - / As Syllable from Sound - ." Aligning the act of measuring brain matter ("wider," "deeper") with the desire to render God in material terms ("weight"), this poem at the same time acknowledges and dismisses the attempt of phrenologists to distinguish and quantify the intellectual capacities of different "races" by assessing brain size from the circumference of the human skull.

In part due to developments in (bio)technology we are now able to "weigh" the human brain with more accuracy than Dickinson could ever foresee. We know, for instance, that the brain constructs coherent images of the world from fragments, situating content topographically in space and supplementing missing pieces. "The brain is unity," "[t]he brain is the screen," Gilles Deleuze famously claimed, thus underlining the interdependence of cognition and our sense of the world, on the one hand, and the media that make up significant parts of that world, on the other.[30] Dickinson's work, however, seems to resist the coherence that our brain imposes on our fragmented view of the world – a tendency that is partly due to the poet's dissenting view of the supposed certainties disseminated by philosophers, physicians, and scientists. Troping cognition in hymnody, Dickinson evolves her own neurophilosophy, distinguishing the (im)material worlds both brain and God are capable of producing on the basis of distinct forms of mediation ("Syllable from Sound") and in the process evolving her own "Compound Vision" (F830 J906) from "that Covered Vision - Here - " (F782 J745).

DICKINSON IN SCIENCE (WRITING)

Given Dickinson's complex engagement of the natural sciences in general and in matters of cognition in particular, it comes as no surprise that

Dickinson's writing is in turn echoed by philosophers, neurophysiologists, and (science) writers as well as by authors working at the crossroads of seemingly distant disciplines today. Neuroscientist Miriam M. Goodman opens her research paper on "mutations in the *painless* gene" with Dickinson's line "After great pain, a formal feeling comes" (F372 J341).[31] The studies *Being No One: The Self-Model Theory of Subjectivity* (2003), by philosopher Thomas Metzinger, and *Wider than the Sky: The Phenomenal Gift of Consciousness* (2004), by neurologist Gerald M. Edelman, even appropriate lines from Dickinson's poems to promote their own work.[32] Moreover, Dickinson's poem "The Brain - is wider than the Sky - " serves as an epigraph to both Edelman's argument and Richard Powers's novel *Galatea 2.2* (1995), a narrative on connectionism and artificial intelligence that references Dickinson's writing repeatedly. The same poem reappears in Powers's 2006 novel *The Echo Maker* which, like Metzinger's work, plays on Dickinson's poem "I'm Nobody! Who are you?" (F260 J288) as well. Siri Hustvedt's 2010 autobiographical account *The Shaking Woman, or a History of My Self* (2010) is preceded by the first stanza of Dickinson's poem "I felt a Cleaving in My Mind - " (F867 J937).[33] Withholding the second quatrain, which renders the unraveling of thought processes by way of synaesthesia, Hustvedt's text then goes on to supplement its own exploration of that neurological condition. In this way, writers and scientists alike acknowledge Dickinson's writing as a form of knowledge production and approximate the ways in which the natural sciences and literature make sense of the world. "This world," though, the poet advised, "is not Conclusion" (F373 J501); neither were the "integrating tendencies of her era" that she resisted; nor is our current tendency to grant the natural sciences an increasing amount of prestige and license to truth-telling.[34] Dickinson's interrogation of the natural sciences offers us a warning not to suspend our disbelief too early.

NOTES

1 Robin Peel, *Emily Dickinson and the Hill of Science* (Madison, NJ: Fairleigh Dickinson University Press, 2010), 14.
2 Joan Kirkby, "'[W]e Thought Darwin Had Thrown "The Redeemer" Away': Darwinizing With Emily Dickinson," *EDJ 19*.1 (2010), 18.
3 Fred D. White, "'Sweet Skepticism of the Heart': Science in the Poetry of Emily Dickinson," *College Literature 19* (1992), 121.
4 Cf. Jed Deppman, *Trying to Think with Emily Dickinson* (Amherst, MA: University of Massachusetts Press, 2008).
5 Peel, *Emily Dickinson*, 44.

6 Jennifer J. Baker, "Natural Science and the Romanticisms," *ESQ 53* (2007), 387.
7 Peel, *Emily Dickinson*, 40.
8 Eric Wilson, "Dickinson's Chemistry of Death," *American Transcendental Quarterly 12* (1998), 28.
9 Compare with Baker, "Natural Science," 388–9.
10 Paul Giles, "'The Earth reversed her Hemispheres': Dickinson's Global Antipodality," *EDJ 20.1* (2011), 9.
11 Richard B. Sewall, "Science and the Poet – Emily Dickinson's Herbarium and 'The Clue Divine,'" *Harvard Library Bulletin 3* (1992), 11.
12 Marianne Erickson, "The Scientific Education and Technological Imagination of Emily Dickinson," *EDJ 5.2* (1996), 46.
13 Cf. Louis C. Rutledge, "Emily Dickinson's Arthropods," *American Entomologist 49* (2003), 70–5.
14 On Dickinson and Darwin, see Kirkby "'[W]e thought'" and the chapter on "Dickinson and Darwin" in Peel, *Emily Dickinson*, 287–329.
15 Peel, *Emily Dickinson*, 382.
16 Qtd. in Wilson, "Dickinson's Chemistry of Death," 28.
17 Richard C. Lewontin, *The Triple Helix: Gene, Organism, and Environment* (Cambridge, MA: Harvard University Press, 2000), 3.
18 Wilson, "Dickinson's Chemistry of Death," 37.
19 C. P. Snow, *The Two Cultures: And a Second Look* (Cambridge: Cambridge University Press, 1963), 72–3.
20 Ibid., 73.
21 Ibid., 74.
22 Quoted in Mary Poovey, "The Model System of Contemporary Literary Criticism," *Critical Inquiry 27* (2001), 437.
23 Jonathan Crary, *Techniques of the Observer: On Vision and Modernity in the Nineteenth Century* (Cambridge, MA: MIT Press, 1990), 81.
24 Camille Paglia, *Sexual Personae: Art and Decadence from Nefertiti to Emily Dickinson* (New York: Vintage, 1991), 625.
25 Thomas J. Otten, "Emily Dickinson's Brain: On Lyric and the History of Anatomy," *Prospects: An Annual of American Cultural Studies 29* (2005), 76.
26 Compare with Giles, "The Earth."
27 Antonio R. Damasio, "Modelling the Mind/Brain Relationships," *Exploring the Concept of Mind*, ed. Richard M. Caplan (Iowa City: University of Iowa Press, 1986), 86.
28 Roland Hagenbüchle, "Precision and Indeterminacy in the Poetry of Emily Dickinson," *Emerson Society Quarterly 20* (1974), 34.
29 Otten, "Emily Dickinson's Brain," 58.
30 Gilles Deleuze, "The Brain is the Screen: An Interview with Gilles Deleuze," trans. Marie Therese Guirgis, *The Brain Is the Screen: Deleuze and the Philosophy of Cinema*, ed. Gregory Flaxman (Minneapolis: University of Minnesota Press, 2000), 366.
31 Miriam B. Goodman, "Sensation Is Painless," *Trends in Neurosciences 26* (2003), 643.

32 Thomas Metzinger, *Being No One: The Self-Model Theory of Subjectivity* (Cambridge, MA: MIT Press, 2003); Gerald M. Edelman, *Wider Than the Sky: The Phenomenal Gift of Consciousness* (New Haven: Yale University Press, 2004).
33 Richard Powers, *Galatea 2.2* (New York: Picador, 1995); Richard Powers, *The Echo Maker* (London: Heinemann, 2006); Siri Hustvedt, *The Shaking Woman, or a History of my Nerves* (New York: Holt, 2010).
34 Michael Theune, "'One and One Are One' and Two: An Inquiry into Dickinson's Use of Mathematical Signs," *EDJ 10.1* (2001), 114.

CHAPTER 24

Nineteenth-Century Language Theory and the Manuscript Variants

Melanie Hubbard

At least sometimes, Emily Dickinson found it hard to communicate. We have her poetic meditations on her composition problems, but we also have what one might call the physical evidence of a struggle – the variants in manuscript. Although Sharon Cameron in *Choosing Not Choosing* has attributed to Dickinson a stunning Transcendental language theory that accounts for the variants as the infinite deferral of identity (at the level of the poem, the collection, and finally the self), this theory depends on a formalist reading of the fascicles as an intentional artistic structure; it also depends on an ahistorical reading of the variants as a unique formal fact of the poems.[1] But it is not at all clear that Dickinson's fascicles and variants are unique or artistically intended. Instead of offering a formalist analysis, then, of what the variants are in themselves, my attention to the language theory in Dickinson's rhetoric textbooks and popular treatises historicizes the variants as products of the unresolved tensions implicit in an evolving philosophical-theoretical debate (perhaps first noted by James A. Berlin, in *Writing Instruction in Nineteenth-Century American Colleges*) about the relationship between thought and language – a debate set off by the very skeptical semiotic theory of Locke, which stated that language was a conventional notation system in unmotivated relation to both thought and reality.[2] Samuel P. Newman's textbook, *Practical System* (1827), required at both Amherst Academy and Mt. Holyoke, taught that language was an overlay unfixed to thought.[3] In contrast, Richard Whately's textbook, *Elements of Rhetoric* (1828), still extant in the Dickinson's library, taught that words actually constituted our ideas; "nominalism" integrates language into the act of knowing and nearly identifies language and consciousness.[4] Finally, a mid-century rhetoric, derived from transcendental strains, takes knowledge of the real as common sense, but raises nominalism to the level of religion, with composition its sacrament; it comes to Dickinson through Richard Trench's 1855 popular treatise, *On the Study of Words*, also extant in the Dickinson library.[5] If language constitutes our thinking, says Trench, our very consciousness must be carried, as it were, in the fragile material ark of words. And words have made us what we are in spirit. Body and spirit, human and word, are symbiotic entities, such that humans curate and care for language – or fail to – while language imbues us with our humanity.

Although diction is emphasized as the bedrock of communication in Newman, and even of consciousness in Whately, such a simple thing as word choice becomes fraught with historical and sacramental responsibility in Trench. Each theory implicitly beats back Locke's skepticism by attempting to stabilize conventional references or finesse the gap between terms and experience. Although Dickinson engages all these strains of thought, the seemingly simple act of identifying and communicating experience remained both theoretically and practically complicated. Here it is perhaps worth emphasizing that because Dickinson's education was full of contradictions, the poems are a site where these language theories may compete with, confuse, or complement one another. Dickinson's variants arise in the context of a proposed radical disjunction between thought and language that none of these language theories solves to her satisfaction.

In a relatively early poem about the composition process, the speaker reflects not only on the difficulty of conveying private experience to another, but also on the difficulty of formulating experience as language, even to herself. At base is Locke's skeptical conception of the relation between signifier and signified, as conveyed by Newman. Of Newman, Berlin remarks, "Language is regarded as a mechanical sign system, separate from thought, throughout."[6] Using the example of the Spanish entrada and the fact that pictures of the conquistadors were brought to Montezuma, Newman instructs his readers, "Hence we infer, *that words answer the same purpose as pictures; they bring up to the mind subjects and thoughts which they are designed to represent.*"[7] Further clarifying that the Spaniards and the English use different languages (and therefore a different word) to refer to the same object, Newman remarks, "Hence we infer, *that there is no natural connexion between words and the objects which they represent.*"[8] Newman's textbook recognizes that the conventional relations between signifiers and signifieds are constantly changing. Newman's project is to produce, through arduous instruction in "verbal criticism," a stable but also nimble collective repertoire, so that all agree, contractually as it were, on words and their meanings. But this assumes that both "words" and "ideas" are known quantities simply in need of alignment.

Dickinson's poem detects a problem: she can't identify her "idea" in the first place. No generation of alternatives will solve this problem; it "defies" her:

> I found the ⁺words to every thought
> I ever had but One -
> And that - defies me -
> As a Hand did try to chalk the Sun
>
> To Races - nurtured in the Dark -
> How would your own - begin?
> Can Blaze be ⁺shown in Cochineal -
> Or Noon - in Mazarin?
> ⁺phrase ⁺done
>   (F436 J581, Autumn 1862)

Having had a "thought," or private experience, perhaps even what Locke would call a new "simple idea," she finds there is no public word for it. She occupies the position of the blind, those "Races - nurtured in the Dark - " when she attempts to articulate, to herself as another, her experience. To what shared visual experience can she refer an inexperienced person? How will she match her experience to a word, or even an agreed-on color? Peculiarly, the poem recognizes that even private experience must be processed through a conventional, public language. It would seem that this necessity would lead to a sort of linguistic optimism: any "thought," to be recognized at all, must take its place in language. And she has managed to match "every thought ... but One" to its corresponding word. But in this case, the speaker's imaginative experience eludes her ability to conceptualize it; "thought" and "word" are revealed to be neither the same nor coextensive, and the poem implies that either any chosen term may miss conveying the experience, or the experience, by definition private, cannot publicly be conveyed – even to oneself. The "thought" remains unnamed, except by way of metaphors like "Blaze" and "Noon" that themselves point to a blinding light. She seems to be saying that she cannot even "see" what she saw (much less "say" it). We are left groping for words and definitions, or, in the case of the poem, paint colors. Dickinson's speaker wonders whether it would be possible, as Newman suggests it would be, to convey the experience directly, in pictures, without words – let it be "shown" or "done," not articulated. But even paint is a medium; representation itself is the difficulty. So the poem ends with questions, and, it has to be said, variants.

The variants represent the problem, or even enact it. First, identifying the word that might match the "thought" amounts to its articulation; its articulation would precisely convey it to another. Thus there is uncertainty or openness on both ends of the communication process, and the "right" word is as much a matter of "what other people know" as "what I know." Perhaps one would expect the difficulty to manifest in the crux of naming the experience – that the variants might proliferate around "Blaze" or "Noon"; instead, the poem generates alternatives within itself and resorts to variants for a different sort of crux; the difference between "phrase" or "words" (and even "shown" or "done") stands for the problem of how to convey the experience. But the variants simply displace the pressure. It is clear that, for Dickinson, difficulty articulating the prelinguistic persists late into her career. The 1872 poem beginning "Shall I take thee, the Poet said" (F1243 J1126) even more directly, and perhaps less despairingly, thematizes the generation of variants as insufficient to the "Vision" that supersedes them.

Richard Whately's *Elements of Rhetoric* solves the problem of the disjunction of words and ideas by discrediting the notion that they are ever separable. We *cannot* have a thought without its already being a word. It is a mistake to imagine that "thought" is somehow prior to language. Even Locke had admitted, "I find that there is so close a connection between ideas and Words."[9] Locke suggested that words might actually constitute our "complex ideas" by holding them together, as it were. "Though therefore it be the mind that makes the collection, it is the name which is, as it were, the knot that ties them fast together."[10] Later thinkers such as Hume and Stewart argued that we do not actually call up the original impressions of our experience, but think with words. Dugald Stewart sums up nominalism: "According to these philosophers, there are no existences in nature corresponding to general terms; and the objects of our attention in all our general speculations are not ideas, but words."[11] That is, words don't correspond to particular concrete things at all (they are general tokens), and, beyond our undifferentiated experiencing, our thinking takes place in words.

Dickinson's Whately text sets these ideas out quite clearly:

> There are still ... many ... who, if questioned on the subject, would answer that the use of Language is to *communicate* our thoughts to each other; and that it is peculiar to Man; the truth being that *that* use of Language is *not* peculiar to Man, though enjoyed by him in a much higher degree than by the Brutes; while that which does distinguish Man from Brute, is another, and quite distinct, use of Language, viz. *as an instrument of thought*, – a system of General-Signs, without which the Reasoning-process could not be conducted. The full importance, consequently, of Language, and of precise

technical Language, – of having accurate and well-defined "names for one's tools," – can never be duly appreciated by those who still cling to the theory of "Ideas;" those imaginary objects of thought in the mind, of which "Common-terms" are merely the names, and by means of which we are supposed to be able to do what I am convinced is impossible; to carry on a train of Reasoning without the use of Language, or of any General-Signs whatever.[12]

In the Locke–Newman rhetoric, humans have "ideas" (or "subjects and thoughts") which then get tagged with names or designations – our "terms" or "general-signs." But Whately insists that there is no such thing as thinking without signs. Thus Whately's readers are to understand that language is not simply a representation of thought – it is the medium of thought.

If Dickinson missed this in her Whately, she would have had another opportunity to meet this idea developed at length in Whately's source, used to supplement instruction in philosophy at Amherst Academy, Dugald Stewart's *Elements of the Philosophy of the Human Mind* (1792). Stewart quotes the chemist Lavoisier: "I perceived, better than I had ever done before, the truth of an observation of Condillac, that we think only through the medium of words."[13] Furthermore, Stewart says, recommending the study of the philosophy of mind, "there are some arts, in which we not only employ the intellectual faculties as instruments, but operate on the mind as a subject."[14] Among those arts is "poetry."

In the following poem, Dickinson explores these ideas quite directly, pursuing the analogy of language as the instrument or tool by which we think and even come to know our own minds.

> Myself was formed - a Carpenter -
> An unpretending time
> My Plane, and I, together wrought
> Before a Builder came -
>
> To measure our attainments -
> Had we the Art of Boards
> Sufficiently developed - He'd hire us
> At Halves -
>
> My Tools took Human - Faces -
> The Bench, where we had toiled -
> Against the Man, persuaded -
> We - Temples build - I said -
> (F475 J488, late 1862)

In the poem, the "Carpenter" is confronted with the choice to use her tools for personal monetary gain. But she rejects the offer, in part because, given the chance to reply to the "Builder," the "Tools" and even the "Bench" suddenly take "Human Faces." That is, they are not simply instruments; their "Faces," like Whately's "Names," embody or externalize human consciousness – a humanness they serve and make. "My Plane, and I, together wrought" implies not only the mutuality of tool and user, but also their fusion into the more-than-human "We" which speaks at the end. The poem depicts a living feedback loop. (Think of Escher's hand drawing and being drawn.) If one reads the last line as spoken by the "Bench" (rather than by the "Carpenter"), the speaker's "We" is fused into a new "I," the Bench-human. The human speaker recedes into the other-than-human, even the oracular – for which voice they build "Temples." The Carpenter and her tools do not make a product that could be alienated from their making; reciprocating personhood, they make, in effect, the conditions of their existence. In a poem about the fit of thought and word, word and user – a poem in which the speaker refuses an outsider and even an outside – the lack of variants literalizes nominalist confidence.

This poem's nominalism, raised to the level of religion, owes much to the rich understanding of language available to Dickinson in Richard Trench's *On the Study of Words*. Going far beyond the Common Sense understanding of words as our "instruments," Trench, influenced by Coleridge and Emerson, is explicit that our relationship with words is reciprocal.

> They beat with the pulses of our life; they stir with our passions; we clothe them with light; we steep them in scorn; they receive from us the impressions of our good and of our evil, which again they are most active still further to propagate and diffuse.... Is there not something very solemn and very awful in wielding such an instrument as this of language is, with such power to wound or to heal, to kill or to make alive?[15]

Dickinson's letters and poems reflect such an understanding of this "most active" linguistic power. Words may "heal," but they can also "kill." In fact, the misuse of words explicitly injures the spirit: "There is an atmosphere about them which they are evermore diffusing, a savour of life or of death, which we insensibly inhale at each moral breath we draw."[16] One has only to recall Dickinson's poem, "A word dropped careless" (F1268 J1261), which ends, "Infection in the sentence breeds / And we inhale Despair/ At distances of Centuries / From the Malaria - " to note the influence of Trench's ideas, and perhaps even his phrasing And Trench's sense of words' historical materiality informs a tragic vision of their loss. They may "expire," that is, disappear entirely.[17] But a language also survives its individual users. Trench says it is "an ark riding above the waterfloods that have swept away or submerged every other landmark and memorial ....

Far beyond the written records in a language, the language itself stretches back."[18] Trench emphasizes the historicity and fragility of human intercourse and the therefore sacramental duty of the artist to preserve and use words in their most essential and vivacious senses through the study of etymology.

In an undated poem (F1715 J1651), the speaker explores the idea of language as the carrier of the human spirit by comparing the experience of an essential "Word" with the taking of Communion.

> A Word made Flesh is seldom
> And tremblingly partook
> Nor then perhaps reported
> But have I not mistook
> Each one of us has tasted
> With ecstasies of stealth
> The very food debated
> To our specific strength -
>
> A Word that breathes distinctly
> Has not the power to die
> Cohesive as the Spirit
> It may expire if He -
>
> "Made Flesh and dwelt among us"
> Could condescension be
> Like this consent of Language
> This loved Philology

This poem uses imagery suggestive both of Christ's incarnation and of the sacrament of communion. In it, the thought (a "Word") condescends to its materiality as a word ("Flesh") that nurtures the human as "food." No longer an instrument, language is seen here to be a spiritual requirement, as dear as breath itself. That it is spiritual – that is, imaginary – makes it capable of sustaining relation; taking in the word produces an imaginative relation with a collective self inside the flesh, "strength." This collective, "Cohesive" self is termed "Spirit." The artifact is beneficent because it "breathes" with human power. This sort of word, therefore, "Has not the power to die" – not because it is not alive in first place, but because, as in Trench, it is coextensive with the human meaning-making community; in that sense, "It may expire if He - ."

Despite imagined consummations, the speaker calls the experience of a perfect, even sacramental fit between thought and Word – the "consent" of "Philology" – "seldom." Dickinson was aware that even Stewart and Whately, despite their nominalistic optimism, noted the potential for slippage in the mind's association of thought and word – for mistake. Trench, despite his lingering Emersonian optimism, admitted that "names are not ... coextensive with things," including "the domain of thought and feeling."[19] The poem implies, with words such as "mistook," "partake," and "stealth," that though these slippages exist, you might overlook them, improperly enough, and take a word to be adequate for your own furtive uses. This poem is also variant-free, as were all known poems sent out to others; perhaps the prospect of actual use excused the stealth.

In a poem that we might take as this poem's demonic twin (especially given the echoing of their last stanzas), Dickinson engages in a thought experiment in which the manipulated tool is so fused to the user's intention that there is no mistake, and so effective in its marking that it can make the world speak or "reply" as an echo of itself. Her famous "Loaded Gun" poem presents all three language theories in action at once. The Locke–Newman rhetoric is present as the drive to unite idea and word, word and world, without the loss implied by mediation. Whately's nominalism accounts for the analogical workings of the poem as it explores the relationship between instrument and user. And Trench's tragic word appears at the riddling close of the poem. The presence of the three language theories accounts for its knotty but not necessarily confused set of tensions and its nearly unreadable close, but the nightmare quality of the "solution" to the problem of language, and its irony, is all Dickinson.

My Life had stood - a Loaded Gun -
In Corners - til a Day
The Owner passed - identified -
And carried me away -

And now We roam †in Sovreign Woods -
And now We hunt the Doe -
And every time I speak for Him
The Mountains straight reply -

And do I smile, such Cordial light
Upon the Valley glow -
It is as a Vesuvian face
Had let it's pleasure through -

And when at Night - Our good Day done -
I guard My Master's Head -
'Tis better than the Eider-Duck's
†Deep Pillow - to have shared -

To foe of His - I'm deadly Foe -
None †stir the second time -

> On whom I lay a Yellow Eye -
> Or an emphatic Thumb -
>
> Though I than He - may longer live
> He longer must - than I.
> For I have but the ⁺power to kill,
> Without - the power to die -
> ⁺the - ⁺low ⁺harm ⁺art
>
> (F764 J754, 1863)

The speaker of the poem implicitly compares, through metaphor, its "Life" to that of a "Loaded Gun" the "Owner" "identified - ." The Owner now uses the gun to "hunt" and "kill" his targets, and the gun is precise and deadly. It notes its own deathlessness and dependency on the owner's living. This seems straightforward enough, especially to the speaker, but the reader notes the irony or even contradiction of the gun's uncanny ability to speak, seemingly unprompted, of its own history and existence.

Whately's nominalism, as in the Carpenter poem, sponsors the poem's attention to the relationship between tool and user. The tool is "identified" by (or even with) the "Owner" and made to "hunt" and "speak;" if the tool is language and its owner is thought, then their action together is to identify the objects of thought – the world they hunt. The gun-word's speaking turns out to be so accurate and effective that its targets "straight reply" in echo, or mirror its face's "glow." But all the world can speak is what the gun has spoken, and the world is obliterated in the process. Though the gun-word seems pleased with its effectiveness and power, we can see that it is a killing machine. Sharon Cameron, who in *Lyric Time* explicitly doubts that this poem is about language, nevertheless brilliantly articulates its logic toward the end of her analysis of lyric: "The reification of the word, the breathing of life into it ... is predicated on the detachment of word from life ... that it might survive life. For the other side of language viewed as the loss of being is an immortality of the word that specifies being's death as its first, most urgent requirement."[20] "Language viewed as the loss of being" is precisely Locke's (and Hume's) skeptical position; we know the world only through our own mediations; therefore we never know it. Newman's rhetoric is content to simply stabilize our substitutions, but the poem's speaker carries out the dream of a perfect correspondence between thought, word, and world. In the end, the reified word is all there is. But the final formulation of the poem's speaker, though it may be read as a pat declaration of immortality, a continuation of the gun's self-satisfaction, seems to point to a problem; the gun cannot "die." And the irony of the word's humane ability to address us – its agency as the poem's speaker and its intimate acquaintance, at the end, with the idea, if not the possibility, of mortality – contradicts everything it has told us about itself. It appears that it can speak without killing, that is, in addressing us rather than articulating the objects of consciousness. Much like the "tools" in the Carpenter poem, the gun for a moment takes a "Human Face." Furthermore, not to put too fine a point on it, the poem employs a number of variants which end up being the speaker's; so that its wavering between "power" and "art," for example, directly undermines the story of its accurate marksmanship. Under interrogation, we might say, the gun's story begins to fall apart. And this is because Dickinson is bigger than the poem's speaker; the poem, as a thought experiment, derives from a complex understanding of language that emphasizes its artificiality, its potential for mistake, and its formation of human consciousness. Newman, Whately, and Trench in Dickinson's hands make a satisfyingly skeptical and humane mash-up, one that emphasizes the high stakes and near impossibility of articulation.

NOTES

1 Sharon Cameron, *Choosing Not Choosing: Dickinson's Fascicles* (Chicago: University of Chicago Press, 1992).
2 James A Berlin, *Writing Instruction in Nineteenth-Century American Colleges* (Carbondale: Southern Illinois University Press, 1984).
3 Samuel P. Newman, *A practical system of rhetoric, or, the principles and rules of style inferred from examples of writing, to which is added a historical dissertation on English style.* (Albany, NY: Delmar Scholars' Facsimiles & Reprints, 1995 [1827]).
4 Richard Whately, *Elements of Rhetoric, Comprising the Substance of the Article ....* (Boston: James Munroe and Co., 1839). For information on which texts are in the Dickinson library, see Carlton Lowenberg, *Emily Dickinson's Textbooks* (Lafayette, CA: Carlton Lowenberg, 1986).
5 Richard Chevenix Trench, *On the Study of Words* (Ann Arbor, MI: Gryphon Books, 1971 [1855]). The 1855 edition was owned by Susan Dickinson, Emily's sister-in-law and friend.
6 Berlin, *Writing Instruction*, 38.
7 Newman, *A practical system*, 115.
8 Ibid., 115.
9 John Locke, *An Essay Concerning Human Understanding*. Abridged and edited by A. S. Pringle-Pattison (Oxford: Clarendon Press, 1924 [1690]), 222.
10 Locke, *An Essay*, 240.
11 Dugald Stewart, *Elements of the Philosophy of the Human Mind* (Albany, NY: E & E Hosford, 1822), 169. The 1847 Boston edition is in the Dickinson library at Harvard.

12 Whately, *Elements of Rhetoric*, 20.
13 Stewart, *Elements*, 51.
14 Ibid., 57.
15 Trench, *Study of Words*, 122–3.
16 Ibid., 102.
17 Ibid., 18.
18 Ibid., 124.
19 Ibid., 205, 202.
20 Cameron, *Lyric Time*, 188.

CHAPTER 25

"Say Some Philosopher!"

Jed Deppman

Emily Dickinson was a serious poet, but was she also a serious philosopher? Some readers would answer: of course not. For one thing, generic differences make it impossible: philosophy is systematic and analytical. Philosophers induce, deduce, and write an un-poetic prose that reaches for clarity, accuracy, and objectivity. For another, a long critical tradition confirms that if philosophy is antithetical to most poetry then it is a fortiori remote from Dickinson's sphinx-like, tuneful, imagistic lyrics. In 1923 Herbert Gorman found that Dickinson had become inaccessible because both the "conditions which made" her and "the philosophical atmosphere in which she came to maturity" had "vanished."[1] In 1932 Allen Tate said that Dickinson, great though she was, could not "reason at all."[2] In 1981 David Porter lamented that Dickinson's readers received a "language experience" without a "completed conceptual experience."[3] He described her as "doomed" to move forever away from "understanding" and deeper into "doubt," blaming this condition on her "want of philosophical development."[4]

Other readers would answer: of course. For one thing, if philosophy is not just a logical or analytic method but a love of wisdom and a search for difficult truths, then Dickinson's poetic and epistolary writings on love, death, God, consciousness, ecstasy, identity, nature, and language are full of it. For another, a long critical tradition confirms Dickinson's identity and strength as a thinker. In the nineteenth century Lavinia Dickinson said that her sister Emily "had to think - she was the only one of us who had that to do."[5] In 1965, Albert Gelpi likened her intelligence to the "fierce brightness" of Jonathan Edwards and placed her in a Puritan philosophical tradition in which "the obligation of the individual man strained his stamina to the uttermost" and forced one to live "in the certitude of death."[6] In 1984 Barton Levi St. Armand found that Dickinson had a "magnetic appeal to our own age of anxiety and existential vacuity" and that she anticipated many "current aesthetic and philosophical concerns."[7]

In 1985 Jane Eberwein argued that Dickinson anticipated the "challenges of modern poetry and philosophy" because she was sensitive to "human isolation when nature is essentially estranged from man, as man from God."⁸ Eberwein saw the poet "adopting intellectual rather than emotional forms of expression – even in the presentation of feelings."⁹

The choice is not either–or, for there are many valid ways to think of Dickinson as a philosopher. In school she received training in academic philosophy, which she used throughout her life (not just in poetry) to help think about personal and public events. Indeed by the late 1850s, when she started her most productive period of writing, she had already lived a life of intense thinking. To read her teenage letters to Abiah Root is to see how prompted she was by the deaths of some friends and the evangelical conversions of others to think hard thoughts and form lifelong habits of self-scrutiny. In this she was not unique: historically, the time of her life, 1830 to 1886, was a turbulent one that provoked new thinking across America on many issues, including immigration, suffrage, westward expansion, new technologies, booming industries in publishing, and translation.

Of the myriad cultural transformations of her time, those occasioned by war, science, and religion had especially deep philosophical repercussions. Drew Gilpin Faust notes that from 1861 to 1865 the Civil War, "in its scale," "brutality," and "seeming endlessness," forced Americans to rethink almost every aspect of their experience of death.¹⁰ Thus, although Dickinson's death poems are often considered private meditations, they were also part of a larger national enterprise to test and revise the philosophical apparatus of the traditional ars moriendi. Before the war it was natural to assume that dying souls would be surrounded by loved ones, speak last words on a deathbed, and then ascend to heaven, but the new realities of death – young men dying suddenly, violently, far away, and en masse – forced Americans to develop other explanations and expectations. In another way, the natural sciences introduced new questions, theories, and vocabularies, with geography, geology, botany, astronomy, and chemistry becoming especially valuable for Dickinson.

One can also say that a popular scientific tendency flourished in the 1840s and 1850s that encouraged Dickinson and her contemporaries to think about thinking itself. What seem to us now to be various (pseudo) sciences of mind were burgeoning – psychology, physiology, mesmerism, and phrenology – but were still broadly understood to be within the province of philosophy. One landmark text was Sampson Reed's 1826 *Observations on the Growth of the Mind,* which presented the idea that the mind was something that *grew* and shaped itself.¹¹ By endowing the mind with its own organic history and active powers, Reed challenged the widely accepted Lockean model of it as a tabula rasa and site of passive synthesis. Pursuing the issue, the Transcendentalists inspired more new thinking about thinking, for example, Emerson's descriptions of "Man Thinking" in his 1837 *The American Scholar*: "A great soul will be strong to live, as well as strong to think."¹² Put into these perspectives, Dickinson's many poems about the brain and mental activity seem more culturally engaged than eccentric or narrowly philosophical.

Another key context was religion, which throughout the nineteenth century was aligned more closely with philosophy than it is today. One of the "biggest mistakes we make with Dickinson," argues biographer Alfred Habegger, "is to detach her from the religious currents of the 1850s," of which "the single most important was the growing tendency within orthodoxy to question the primacy, even the necessity, of a rationally articulated faith" (Habegger, 310). To the extent that thinkers with liberal tendencies such as Horace Bushnell and Edwards Park loosened the philosophical underpinnings of religion, aesthetic approaches became an attractive and reasonable way to think about spiritual questions. Habegger notes that both Bushnell's 1849 *God in Christ* and Park's 1850 "The Theology of the Intellect and That of the Feelings" drew attention to the figural nature of language and argued for a poetic, symbolic approach to the expression of religious truth.¹³ Critics today are still discovering which problems, perspectives, terms, and ideas such authors contributed to Dickinson's thinking, but we can already appreciate the impulses they gave her to blend philosophy, religion, and creative writing.

These contexts help us understand why Cynthia Griffin Wolff described Dickinson as an artist in a time of fading transcendence, a thinker in an age of transition when the English language was itself "beginning to be substantially drained of its otherworldly implications."¹⁴ Many critics now also agree with Suzanne Juhasz's judgment that the mind was "the setting for Dickinson's most significant experience," though it is less clear why this was so and what it means for readers of her poems.¹⁵ Juhasz argues that the poet's "move into the mind" is best understood as "occasioned by her social and psychological situation as a woman who wanted to be a poet."¹⁶ Another (not necessarily conflicting) possibility is that she internalized mental habits from her schooling in philosophy and drew on them throughout her life.

Dickinson attended Amherst Academy from 1840 to 1847 and then Mary Lyon's Female Seminary, which later became Mt. Holyoke College, for the fall 1847 and spring 1848 semesters. "We'll finish an education sometime, won't we?" she remarked to Abiah Root at the age of fourteen, "You may then be Plato, and I will be Socrates, provided you won't be wiser than I am" (L5). Three months later she continued the theme as she described the Amherst Academy: "We have a very fine school. I have four studies. They are Mental Philosophy, Geology, Latin, and Botany. How large they sound, don't they?" (L6). Given the levity of these exchanges, one might wonder how serious Dickinson was about her philosophical assignments. Biographers and critics have not much pursued the question. Dickinson neither wrote essays nor quoted philosophers, so the path of least resistance has been to assume that she did not absorb much of it. Maybe her year of post-secondary education was not enough to equip her with academic philosophy, or perhaps she was too young, female, and independent- or poetic-minded for it? One of her earliest biographers, George Frisbie Whicher, cemented these doubts when he said disparagingly that the "'Mental Philosophy' recited by a girl of fifteen from Upham's manual cannot be taken seriously" (Whicher, 47).

But in fact it can. Whicher and others have underestimated not only this particular girl of fifteen but also three other things: the schools, which pushed philosophy; the books themselves, which took pains to be readable; and the general cultural prestige of mental philosophy in Dickinson's time. "Between 1827 and 1860 the number of textbooks on mental philosophy proliferated" in America, points out historian Rand Evans.[17] And it is crucial to know that the subjects of "Mental" and "Moral" Philosophy were not just any subjects in high school and college curricula: they sounded "large" to Dickinson because they were respected, fundamental disciplines with a status far greater than distribution requirements or electives. At Amherst and many other colleges they were required, in heavy doses, because they were the essence and pinnacle of the educational experience. In a majority of universities and colleges during Dickinson's time it was a significant duty of the president to teach them.

Upham's "manual" was his *Elements of Mental Philosophy*, a standard textbook from about 1840 to 1870 "designed chiefly for those who are young, and in the course of education."[18] It was one of a cascade of philosophical books available to Dickinson, many of which were, and remain, more accessible than their titles might now suggest. Today Upham's 1840 *Outlines of Imperfect and Disordered Mental Action* sounds like a recondite treatise, but it was the 100th book published in the "Family Library" series from Harper and Brothers and, as one of the first books in America to discuss mental illness and insanity, may have contributed to Dickinson's serial meditations on mental trauma and disorder.[19] At the very least Upham's lengthy analyses and lively examples of disordered experiences of time and space represent a theoretical articulation contemporary with her poems about mental reactions to great pain. His chapters on "disordered," "divided," and "intermittent" consciousness provide an analytical vocabulary similar to the one Dickinson employed in her poems on fractured subjectivity.

Another crucial text was Isaac Watts's *On the Improvement of the Mind*, which was widely read and cited, taught at the Amherst Academy, and required for admission to Mary Lyon's Seminary.[20] It included exercises to strengthen such powers of the mind as memory, imagination, reasoning, and humility. Extolling the value of carefully observing and analyzing one's own mental phenomena, books like Watts's help us understand not only why Dickinson might have chosen to move "into the mind" but also what she did while she was there. As was noted in a textbook used from the 1850s at Amherst College, the discipline of mental philosophy included "a method of readily reading the lessons from our own inward experience."[21] To become adept at it, a student was directed "to commune with himself; to study himself; to know himself; to live amid the phenomena of his own spiritual being."[22] Dickinson's fame is due in part to the rigor with which she followed these directions: she selected herself as her own society, interrogated the phenomena of her spiritual being, and wrote.

Doctrinally, what Upham, Watts, Thomas Brown, Dugald Stewart, and others offered Dickinson was a sanctioned synthesis of British Empiricist and Scottish doctrines, a philosophy that originated in the writings of Locke and Thomas Reid and came to be known as "Common Sense Realism." Many historians of philosophy have written negatively about this early- and mid-nineteenth-century academic philosophy, suggesting that Common Sense amounted to pedestrian observations dressed up pedantically to buttress religious orthodoxy. Indeed, mental philosophy was usually taught as a propaedeutic to Moral philosophy, which in turn upheld Protestant Christianity.

But other historians, notably Flower and Murphey, argue more positively that the Common Sense Realists formed not a backwater but a complex bridge from the eighteenth-century Enlightenment to the late nineteenth-century pragmatists.[23] They note that Reid's Common Sense followers appealed to nineteenth-century America by cooperating intellectually with religious doctrines and by remaining within the scientific paradigm of Newton, Locke, and eighteenth-century developments such as physiology and chemistry. Holding the line against

Humean skepticism, German speculative metaphysics, and American Transcendentalism, they emphasized psychology, empiricism, the truth of scientific achievements, and the beliefs that they felt made science possible, for example, the existence of one's own self and others, causality, and external reality. Knowledge itself was seen as purposive, cumulative, corrigible, and "sufficient to govern actions successfully."[24] The cumulative evidence from letters and poems suggests that Dickinson spent a good deal of time on the Common Sense bridge. She carefully tested core aspects of the philosophy – its heavy dependence on human intuition as trustworthy, on the regulatory ideal of a well-balanced mind, on the referential stability of language – but was also repeatedly stimulated by the analytical distinctions it made among emotions and mental states and by the attention it paid to the operations of the mind (even as involved in sense perception).

The Massachusetts poet was also well placed to register the impact of the Transcendentalists, and thus to consider the more speculative strains of philosophy emanating from such publications as Emerson's books of poems and essays or the 1840s Transcendentalist journal *The Dial*. As with the sirens of Common Sense, and perhaps again because of her well-learned habits of mental philosophy, here too she was tantalized but ultimately noncommittal. She wrote many poems wrestling with Transcendentalist ideas (self-reliance, nature as the expression and being of deity, the individual soul and moods as the interpretable site of corresponding cosmic activity), but she no more trusted the Transcendentalist version of intuition than that of the Common Sense philosophers; despite real effort, she never could confirm God's immanence in the natural world.

It remains an open question how frequently, and to what degree, Dickinson's poems were motivated by the questions pursued by her philosophical contemporaries. Ultimately, however, the problem is less to identify philosophical concepts, arguments, and vocabularies in her writing than to understand how they have been repurposed and what work they do. It helps to recall a recurring gesture of her thought, one that reflects the Common Sense emphasis on personal experience and observation but also questions the basic value of philosophizing: she experiences something striking, asks a pointed philosophical question about it, and critiques, laments, or laughs at the quality of the conventional answers. Such a sequence efficiently creates a philosophical space of questioning: "So gay a Flower / Bereaves the mind / As if it were a Woe - / Is Beauty an Affliction - then? / Tradition ought to know - " (F1496 J1456). Alas, too often the philosophical tradition could *not* explain such things as why minds could be "bereaved" by beauty or whether beauty itself should be construed as a mode of affliction.

The following poem ironically frames the activity of philosophizing even as it pursues a typical Common Sense inquiry into how much and what kind of control we have over memory. Its relentless manner and know-nothing posture recall Socrates, and its speed, energy, and sharp wording communicate a satire whose targets are hard to identify:

> Knows how to forget!
> But could It teach it?
> Easiest of Arts, they say
> When one learn how
>
> Dull Hearts have died
> In the Acquisition
> Sacrifice for Science
> Is common, though, now -
>
> I - went to School
> But was not wiser
> Globe did not teach it
> Nor Logarithm Show
>
> "How to forget"!
> Say some Philosopher!
> Ah, to be erudite
> Enough to know!
>
> Is it in a Book?
> So, I could buy it -
> Is it like a Planet?
> Telescopes would know -
>
> If it be invention
> It must have a Patent -
> Rabbi of the Wise Book
> Dont you know?
>   (F391B J433)

As is often the case, it is possible to contextualize this poem in the academic philosophy available to Dickinson. If we return to Upham's *Elements*, we find a section treating "the power of the will over mental associations."[25] Part II, Chapter V, titled "Memory," has thirteen subheadings; chapter VI is "Duration of Memory," with seven more subheadings, beginning with "Restoration of Thoughts and Feelings Supposed to be Entirely Forgotten." In a line of thinking that may linger in the background of the poem, Upham argues that although many people think we "cannot be conscious of our whole past life, because it is utterly forgotten," the truth is that "nothing is wholly forgotten," for "the power of reminiscence slumbers, but does not die."[26]

But it was rarely just a matter of academic philosophy for Dickinson. Questions about memory and forgetting recurred throughout her life and were often connected to emotional circumstances. In an 1870 conversation she pointedly asked her longtime mentor T. W. Higginson: "Is it oblivion or absorption when things pass from our minds?" (L342b). From this angle the poem represents the arch-Dickinsonian philosophical problem, so often pressing and practical, about how to use the resources of thought to negotiate an existential or emotional trauma. The first two lines recall the many moments in her youthful correspondence when she assumed the posture of having been forgotten by her correspondent. In fact an earlier draft of this poem was folded into three sections, as if intended for mailing, and had a personal pronoun and two attention-getting dashes in the second line: "Knows how to forget! / But - could she teach - it?" (F391A). "She" suggests an epistolary context, one that would explain the spirited, passive-aggressive tone: *I guess you've forgotten all about me, so maybe I could learn how to be cold and neglectful, too?*

These kinds of contexts simultaneously distract from philosophical interpretations and ramify or intensify them by embedding them in the lives of Dickinson and her readers. They remind us that Dickinson usually had immediate purposes for her thinking, whether we taxonomize its written expression as poetry, philosophy, or something else. The challenge and opportunity for critics is that she often drew from academic philosophy, but instead of remaining within it, took up many of its distinctions, problems, and techniques and blended them with other vocabularies from science, religion, literature, and elsewhere.

Reflecting heterogeneous resources, Dickinson's poems continue to respond to many kinds of philosophy. One interpretive method is thus to identify poems that resonate with specific philosophical ideas or techniques and then explore how far the parallels go. Skeptical Humean questions about the independence of the external world permeate "Perception of an Object costs" (F1103 J1071), "Heaven is so far of the Mind" (F413 J370), and "To hear an Oriole sing" (F402 J526), the last of which includes reported dialogue about where sound really is: "The 'Tune is in the Tree - ' / The Skeptic - showeth me - / 'No Sir! In Thee!'" Heideggerian existentialism shares many of the premises tested in "Of Death I try to think like this" (F1588 J1558) and "Did life's penurious length" (F1751

J1717). Phenomenological attitudes toward consciousness and embodiment are detectable, respectively, in "The nearest Dream recedes - unrealized - " (F304 J319) and "I felt my life with both my hands" (F357 J351). Comparisons to Nietzsche are invited by the unsparing nihilism in "Those - dying then," (F1581 J1551) and "I reason, Earth is short - " (F403 J301), in which "Anguish" is "absolute," and "many hurt, / But, what of that?"

Another method is to examine philosophical elements in Dickinson's vocabulary. She used "Being" as a substantive quite often, but do those uses amount to an ontology? Can philosophers elucidate the meanings she gave to infinity, eternity, immortality? And here's a puzzle: Why does one almost never find the ordinary word "idea" in Dickinson's poems, otherwise chock-full of epistemological worries over brains, minds, thoughts, and knowing? Concordances list only one use of the word "idea" and no "ideas" at all. And yet the 1840s–60s were years of flourishing idealisms in America. In Dickinson's purview were the texts and influences of Plato, Kant, the British and German Romantics, the Transcendentalists, the post-Kantian German metaphysicians, and the St. Louis Hegelians, all of which were saturated with the term and idea of "idea," so Dickinson's resistance is noteworthy.

Perhaps the word had become epistemologically dangerous, too misleadingly Platonist-Idealist or Emersonian-Transcendentalist to risk using. Another possibility is that, having been exposed to controversies over materialism and skepticism, Dickinson came to distrust the roles assigned to "ideas" in the processing of human experience. Perhaps she knew and approved of a specific critique, such as that of Hume provided by Thomas Brown.[27] Flower and Murphey note that Brown understood the operations of mental association to take place "on a much wider base than that suggested by Hume."[28] The issue was that Hume had "emphasized ideas to the neglect of other elements in mental activity."[29] One can generate other possible solutions to the case of the missing idea but the larger point is that many such questions remain to be asked about Dickinson and philosophy.

Because she so often used poetry as a form of creative philosophical writing, Dickinson can be considered a pragmatist *avant la lettre*. From this perspective, her work provides an unlooked-for confirmation and extension of Flower and Murphey's thesis about the vitality of early nineteenth-century philosophy. Long before Common Sense philosophy and Emersonian Transcendentalism helped catalyze the philosophy of Peirce, Santayana, and Dewey, it stimulated the thought and writing of Emily Dickinson.

NOTES

1 Herbert S. Gorman, *The Procession of Masks* (Boston: B. J. Brimmer Company, 1923), 54.
2 Allen Tate, "New England Culture and Emily Dickinson," *The Recognition of Emily Dickinson: Selected Criticism since 1890*, ed. Caesar R. Blake and Carlton F. Wells (Ann Arbor: University of Michigan Press, 1968), 160.
3 David Porter, *The Modern Idiom* (Cambridge, MA: Harvard University Press, 1981), 93.
4 Ibid., 163.
5 Quoted in Millicent Todd Bingham, *Emily Dickinson's Home: The Early Years as Revealed in Family Correspondence and Reminiscences* (New York: Dover, 1967), 414.
6 Albert Gelpi, *The Mind of the Poet* (Cambridge, MA: Harvard University Press, 1965), 57.
7 Barton Levi St. Armand, *Emily Dickinson and Her Culture: The Soul's Society* (Cambridge: Cambridge University Press, 1987), 11.
8 Jane Eberwein, *Strategies of Limitation* (Amherst: University of Massachusetts Press, 1985), 61.
9 Ibid., 145.
10 Drew Gilpin Faust, "The Civil War Soldier and the Art of Dying." *The Journal of Southern History*, 67.1 (2001), 5.
11 Sampson Reed, *Observations on the Growth of the Mind* (Boston: Crosby, Nichols, and Company, and George Phinney, 1859 [1826]).
12 Ralph Waldo Emerson, "The American Scholar," *The Works of Ralph Waldo Emerson*, 5 vols. (Boston: Houghton, Osgood and Company, 1880), V, 84.
13 Horace Bushnell, *God in Christ: Three Discourses Delivered at New Haven, Cambridge, and Andover, with a Preliminary Dissertation on Language* (Hartford, CT: Brown and Parsons, 1849); Edwards Park, "The Theology of the Intellect and That of the Feelings," *Memorial Collection of Sermons*, ed. Agnes Park (Boston: The Pilgrim Press, 1902).
14 Cynthia Griffin Wolff, *Emily Dickinson* (New York: Knopf, 1986), 441.
15 Suzanne Juhasz, *The Undiscovered Continent: Emily Dickinson and the Space of the Mind* (Bloomington: Indiana University Press, 1983), 1.
16 Ibid., 12.
17 Rand B. Evans, "The Origins of American Academic Psychology," *Explorations in the History of Psychology in the United States*, ed. Joseph. M. Brozek (Lewisburg, PA: Bucknell University Press, 1984), 43.
18 Thomas Cogwell Upham, *Elements of Mental Philosophy* (New York: Harper and Brothers, 1842), 14.
19 Thomas Cogwell Upham, *Outlines of Imperfect and Disordered Mental Action* (New York: Harper and Brothers, 1840).
20 Isaac Watts, *On the Improvement of the Mind*, ed. Joseph Emerson (New York: A. S. Barnes, 1849).
21 Laurens Hickock, *Empirical Psychology; or, The Human Mind as Given in Consciousness. For the Use of Colleges and Academies* (New York: S. C. Griggs & Co., 1854), 17.

22 Ibid., 17.
23 Elizabeth Flower and Murray G. Murphey, *A History of Philosophy in America*, 2 vols. (New York: G. P. Putnam's Sons, 1977), I, 204.
24 Ibid., I, 247.
25 Upham, *Elements*, 213 and following.
26 Ibid., 408–9.
27 Thomas Brown, *Lectures on the Philosophy of the Human Mind*, 2 vols. (Hallowell ME: Masters, Smith & Co., 1848).
28 Flower and Murphey, I, 261.
29 Ibid., I, 261.

PART IV

Reception

CHAPTER 26

Editorial History I: Beginnings to 1955
Martha Nell Smith

Since Emily Dickinson's death in 1886 and the publication of her writings in book volumes beginning in 1890, readers have encountered very different presentations of her work in both print and digital form. In the 1890s, readers saw three editions of her poems – *Poems by Emily Dickinson* (First, Second, and Third Series) – and one of her letters – *Letters by Emily Dickinson* – edited by Thomas Wentworth Higginson and/or Mabel Loomis Todd. Having coedited *Poems* in 1890 and 1891, Todd edited a volume of the poet's letters on her own in 1894 and another volume of poems in 1896. From Todd's editions of Dickinson's letters (an enlarged edition was published in 1931), her most addressed correspondent, sister-in-law Susan Dickinson, was omitted, an editorial casualty resulting from Todd's affair with Susan's husband, Dickinson's brother Austin. The affair precipitated the so-called "War Between the Houses," accounts of which are primarily found in "gossipy memoranda" in the Todd–Bingham archive; as biographer Richard Sewall notes, the "historical validity of such material ... is always open to question" (252). But it is clear that Todd's estrangement from her once dear friend Susan Dickinson and the struggle between the other woman and a "*wife forgotten*" spilled over into a contest between camps – Higginson/Todd/Bingham and Dickinson/Bianchi/Hampson – for the first half century of Dickinson's editorial history (L93). That divide persists, informing the two variorums, as well as recent biographies of the poet.

By reviewing the first decades of Dickinson's editorial history, beginning with the writer herself, and ending with the publications that immediately preceded the first variorum edition of her poems in 1955, this essay seeks to reveal why knowing that still largely unfamiliar history is crucial for understanding the legacies that frame receptions and critical understandings today. Occluded for much of the first 120 years of Dickinson scholarship and reception was the role of Susan Dickinson, devoted reader and early editor, whose deep, sustained engagements with Dickinson's writings likely resulted in at least ten poems being printed during the poet's lifetime.¹

Though it might be said that every writer is her first editor, this idea deserves special consideration in Emily Dickinson's case; she published herself coterie-style by sending poems in her letters. The present record shows that more than one-third of Dickinson's poems were sent as mail: as letter-poems, or accompanying or within missives sent via the postal service or courier. As a majority of her letters have been lost, a reasonable conclusion is that half or more of her poems were published in letters to contemporaries. Such distribution practices put editorial control entirely in Emily Dickinson's hands; indeed, her only surviving remark about seeing her work in print voices consternation with editorial interference.

When Dickinson saw "A narrow Fellow in the Grass" (F1096 J986) printed in *The Springfield Republican*, she complained to Higginson, whom she worried might have seen the publication: "Lest you meet / my Snake and / suppose I deceive / it was robbed / of me - defeated / too of the third line / by the punctuation - / The third and / fourth were one - / I had told you / I did not print - " (L316).² Here she declares frustration that editors had inserted a question mark where she had placed none. That such changes would be inevitable when publishing her poems conventionally, in what she called "the Auction" (F788 J709), and that she was not under financial exigencies to publish, may have dissuaded her from joining the popular women writers of her day who enjoyed some financial compensation for their published writings. In any case, her parsimoniousness with Helen Hunt Jackson (she gave Jackson only one poem, "Success is counted sweetest" (F112 J67), to print in the Roberts Brothers publishers' No Name Series), and her firm declaration to her cousin Louise Norcross that she had "replied declining" to another woman writer who had requested that she print more of her poems (observing "perhaps she stated it as my duty, I don't distinctly remember, and always burn such letters" [L380]) indicate that Dickinson had refused overtures from others urging her to print.

Evidence exists, however, that strongly suggests Emily Dickinson's keen interest in seeing her work "before the curtain," as Susan would write to Higginson in December 1890.³ In May 1894, Mabel Loomis Todd wrote to Robert Underwood Johnson, of the *Century Magazine*:

> Emily Dickinson's sister tells me that for some years before her death she [Emily] was accustomed to send off many letters and packages addressed to "Roswell Smith, Century Company." What they were no one knew, but she and her maid remember distinctly mailing such packages very often. (Leyda II, 483).

In spite of Emily Dickinson's "declining" conventional publication at times, this report of her communicating routinely with a particular publisher – "Century Company" published the literary magazine – offers strong evidence that Dickinson pursued the possibility of conventional publication. Along with her twenty-five-year correspondence with Higginson, an influential literary figure who championed women writers, this suggests that her notions of possibilities for publication extended beyond her own efforts through personal correspondence.

During her lifetime, Emily Dickinson edited and circulated poems through epistolary networks, or by reading them aloud to audiences she favored. A March 26, 1904 letter from Dickinson's beloved cousin Louise Norcross to the editors of Boston's *Woman Journal* makes clear that Dickinson's literary work was no secret. Norcross's account provides a rare portrait of the woman poet at work, writing and reading aloud amid the duties of housekeeping:

> ... I know Emily Dickinson wrote most emphatic things in the pantry, so cool and quiet, while she skimmed the milk; because I sat on the footstool behind the door, in delight, as she read them to me. The blinds were closed, but through the green slats she saw all those fascinating ups and downs going on outside that she wrote about."[4]

Susan Dickinson introduced Mabel Loomis Todd to Dickinson's poetry by reading to her in the parlor of the Evergreens; Todd notes in her diary for February 8, 1882 that she "went in the afternoon to Mrs. [Susan] Dickinson's. She read me some strange poems by Emily Dickinson. They are full of power" (Leyda II, 361). Popular writer Jackson seems to have created a booklet of the poems Dickinson had sent her: "I have a little manuscript volume with a few of your verses in it" (L444a). These scenes of localized reading and editing, through handcrafted media and in domestic spaces, shifted dramatically when Dickinson's poems began to be distributed through mechanical reproduction rather than by hand-to-hand and word of mouth.

At least forty manuscript books and scores of poems on loose sheets were found after Dickinson's death; her sister Lavinia wanted poems from that trove incorporated into a printed volume and turned to Susan to accomplish the task. Susan was the logical choice to shape Dickinson's diverse writings into the kind of printed volume that nineteenth-century audiences would recognize as poetry rather than what Sandra Gilbert, writing of both Whitman and Dickinson, calls "not poetry."[5] Susan had received more poems from Emily than any other correspondent, and, according to the written record, she is the only contemporary reader at whose behest Emily Dickinson changed a poem, "Safe in their Alabaster Chambers - " (F124 J216).⁶ She also entertained editors in her home and was probably responsible for the "larceny" (as Susan called it in her obituary for Emily) that had brought Emily's poems to editors' attention, so that individual poems were printed in the *Springfield Republican*, the Civil War publication *Drum Beat*, the *Brooklyn Daily Union*, *Boston Post*, and *Round Table*.⁷ Arguably, beyond Dickinson herself, Susan was Emily's first editor and agent.

Susan's obituary for Emily Dickinson makes legible that she already had a reputation as a writer before any printed volume of her work appeared. That Dickinson was read aloud not only in Amherst parlors but also in the Boston drawing rooms Higginson frequented, and that she circulated her poems to scores of correspondents, account for the localized fame of the writer. The obituary also makes clear that Susan recognized a dilemma – how to portray Emily Dickinson the poet without depicting a cliché fictional character such as "Mercy Philbrick," whom Susan names. The story of Mercy, who became a famous poet only after rejecting two suitors, and who thrives on her secret passion for one, is too usual, Susan claims, to be Dickinson's. Susan's letters to editors also offer valuable information about Dickinson's project and the challenges facing all her editors, not just the early ones.

Susan was the first to declare that Dickinson stayed at home "in the light of her own fire" and "on her own premises," that she was "not disappointed with the world" and that "her talk and her writings were like no one's else."⁸ Memorialized is a strong, loving, brilliant woman writer with serious artistic objectives, who was not writing "for Time," as her primary goal was not achieving "Fame" (F536 J406). Susan was not interested in portraying a woman poet as easily commodified as Lucy Larcom or Maria Brooks, reclusive and always wearing white. More than a century of speculations about Dickinson's private life show that Susan's anxieties were justified; even Higginson's work confirms them. Not long after the first *Poems of Emily Dickinson* appeared, Higginson situated Dickinson among other literary figures he deemed "secondary" such as Lydia Maria Child and Catharine Sedgwick; characterized her as "morbidly sensitive" and "pitifully childlike"; and proclaimed that she "never quite succeeded in grasping the notion of the importance of literary form."⁹

The truism that Susan Dickinson, Emily's most faithful contemporary reader, did not work to get Dickinson's writings printed after the poet's death is in fact false. Within months of Emily's death, Susan outlined her ideas for a volume of her beloved friend's work to Higginson, and she approached editors of *Century Magazine* about publishing one of Dickinson's poems. Between Dickinson's death and the first production of a printed volume of her work four years later, Susan Dickinson began to work on her "Book of Emily," the outline for which is available in *Writings by Susan Dickinson*.[10] An extraordinarily well-read intellectual, acquainted with the conventions of poetry publication, Susan Dickinson nevertheless envisioned a volume of Emily's writings that was not only poetry. She wrote Higginson in December 1890 that she would have fashioned a book using "many bits of her prose – passages from early letters quite surpassing the correspondence of Guderodie with Bettine – quaint bits to my children &c &c".[11] As Dickinson's primary audience, Susan determined that including writings that were "rather more full, and varied" than the conventional presentation of discrete lyrics by Todd and Higginson was in order. Rather than separating the poems from their original contexts and dividing them into the predictable subjects that audiences expected, Susan wanted to showcase how embedded poetry was in Emily's daily life, as well as the way poetry registered profound emotional and intellectual experiences; she also wished to highlight Emily's humor and her work in multimedia by adding drawings, engravings, and other cutouts to her own words. In spite of these labors, Higginson discouraged the plan; it was his market judgment that the kind of diversified volume she had first imagined was "un-presentable."[12]

Not only in deference to Vinnie's wishes but also bowing to Higginson's market judgment and readers' expectations, Susan struggled with how to make a book from the fascicles, reading through them and marking individual lyrics with initials (D, F, L, N, P, S, W – presumably for topics such as death, love, nature, poetry) and "X's" to categorize and group them. In other words, she tried to make *their* "Book of Emily" but could not, because it went against her better judgment, informed not by consumer preferences but by decades of her creative collaboration with Emily. Conflicted, distracted, and grieved by the losses, all within a few years, of Emily, her sister, and her youngest son Gilbert, Susan moved slowly. Vinnie grew impatient and demanded that the manuscript books be returned so that another editor could get the job done more quickly. Though she was to work on her "Book of Emily" for the rest of her life, on plans that would become *The Single Hound* published within a year of her death, Susan returned those poems that had not been sent to her directly.

Mabel Loomis Todd, herself a writer whose poetry had been rejected by publishers, seized the opportunity of a loving sister's impatience and offered her services as an editor. Lavinia would later testify that Todd had asked to edit the poems because she thought it would be good for her literary reputation, and that "it made her reputation."[13] To get her sister's poems into print, Lavinia turned to Higginson, Dickinson's correspondent for nearly a quarter of a century, who had power in the world of American letters. As Susan had sought his counsel, so did Todd, which resulted in Higginson's coediting. Though he had discouraged Susan from publishing the more varied volume of Dickinson's writing she imagined, he wanted to use her perceptive obituary as the introduction to the 1890 *Poems*. Though Todd refused, she mined it for the introduction to the 1891 *Poems*. Borrowing Susan's phrasing, Todd says that Dickinson "was not an invalid," nor was she "disappoint[ed]" with the world, and that her withdrawal was a result of her "nature." Susan wrote that Dickinson "seemed herself a part of the March sky" and that immortality made "her life ... aglow."[14] Following her lead, Todd in turn mentions the poet's intimacy with the "March sky" and says that "immortality" was "close about her."[15] Though Todd repeatedly tried to excise traces of early editorial and readerly roles, Susan Dickinson ghosted these first editions. Because Todd received few letters from Dickinson, her editorial work was primarily with the poems in the manuscript books, textual bodies that Dickinson assembled and that Todd completely dismembered. In spite of the painstaking work of R. W. Franklin, those manuscript bodies will never be reliably restored exactly as Dickinson left them, a casualty of editorial practices of which readers and critics should be mindful. More than 19,000 copies of the first *Poems by Emily Dickinson* sold on both sides of the Atlantic; the book was widely reviewed, and introduced the Amherst poet to the world.

In a lawsuit over a piece of land that Todd claimed Austin Dickinson had bequeathed her, Lavinia allied herself with Susan Dickinson. Todd's fury over losing the lawsuit resulted in her locking hundreds of poems away and making them inaccessible to the reading public. No poems or letters of Emily Dickinson were published between 1896 and 1914, when, in the wake of her mother's death, Susan's daughter Martha Dickinson Bianchi published six editions of her aunt's writings between 1914 and 1937, with the early editions produced mostly from poems, letters, and letter-poems that Susan had in her possession. She also published two additional volumes, *The Life and Letters of Emily Dickinson* (1924) and *Emily Dickinson Face to Face: Unpublished Letters with Notes and Reminiscences* (1932), edited according to the vision articulated by her mother Susan. Indeed, Bianchi's *The Single Hound: Poems of a Lifetime* (1914), dedicated "as a memorial to the love of these Dear, dead women," restored Susan as a primary player in Dickinson's writing life, at least for a few decades.[16]

The earliest four editions, even that by Bianchi, were all shaped by conventional notions of what a book of poetry should look like. The Higginson and Todd volumes were divided into the conventional subjects often found in presentations of poetry ("Life," "Love," "Nature," "Time and Eternity"); Bianchi's edition is divided into six sections designated only by roman numerals, leaving the nature of the groupings up to the reader. By 1896, Todd had had experience with audiences wondering about the eccentric Amherst woman poet who was "indifferent to all conventional rules" and exhibited "scornful disregard of poetic technique," but whose "flashes of wholly original and profound ... thought" showed that she had "fine insight into life." Reviews characterized her poems as "original," "compelling," "terse," "powerful," "suggestiferous," "weird," "enigmatical," "Delphic," "erratic," "tough," "rugged," and "fragmentary."[17] Todd's editing suggests that she believed that Higginson's "eccentric poetess" needed normalizing in order to appeal to a wider audience. So when Todd published "A solemn thing - it was - / I said - / A Woman - white - to be - " (F307 J271) in her third production of Dickinson's poems, she was undoubtedly anxious about how audiences might respond to the last two stanzas in which the female speaker concludes by sneering at "Sages" who would consider her life "small." Todd titled that culturally blasphemous poem "Wedded" and excised the offending final two stanzas. Todd had cut out stanzas before. She edited with an eye toward "market value" and biography – whether protecting the image of Dickinson from presumptions that she challenged cultural norms too boldly or excising the presence and influence of Susan, the "too-much-loved woman friend," as Todd's daughter Bingham characterized her.[18]

By the time Bianchi started publishing her "Aunt Emily," she was likely angry and anxious about her mother being chopped out of Emily Dickinson's personal and literary histories. Thus it is no surprise that her inaugural publication of her aunt's work features the "*Dedicatory poem*," "One Sister have I in our house" (F5A, J14)[19] a poem so clear in its esteem and affection for Susan Dickinson that Todd sliced it up and heavily inked over the version she discovered in one of Dickinson's manuscript books that she likewise more than dismembered; material evidence shows that rather than simply removing the threads that bound the handmade book together, Todd ripped it apart, cutting leaves up and inking over poetic expressions, all in an effort to obliterate Dickinson's love for her sister-in-law.

As Bianchi had been fretful about her mother Susan Dickinson's influence being obliterated, so Bingham, mindful that outliving Bianchi gave her the advantage of the last word, was concerned that her mother Todd's work as an editor not be obscured. After Bianchi died in 1943, Bingham published the withheld poems in *Bolts of Melody: New Poems of Emily Dickinson*, a volume of "over 650 hitherto unpublished poems," in 1945.[20] That same year, she also published *Ancestors' Brocades: The Literary Debut of Emily Dickinson*, an account of the editing and transmission of Dickinson's papers that sought to explain why her mother and then she had withheld hundreds of poems. In 1955, she complemented her narrative of how Dickinson became an author with the heavily biographical *Emily Dickinson's Home: Letters of Edward Dickinson and His Family*. All of the publications by Bianchi and Bingham sought to be the most authoritative and so competed with one another, thereby perpetuating their mothers' struggles. As had her mother, Bingham claimed a closer relationship to the Dickinson family than she had (Emily refused to meet Mabel face-to-face). In publications such as *Face to Face*, Bianchi reminded readers that she and Dickinson were genetically intimate and that the poet imagined herself and Susan Dickinson as carnally intertwined – "when my Hands are cut, Her fingers will be found inside."[21]

Whereas three publications were singly edited, Bianchi coedited most of the volumes of her aunt's poems with Alfred Leete Hampson, who edited *Poems for Youth by Emily Dickinson* in 1934, and who was named beneficiary of Bianchi's estate, which included her aunt's writings; his wife Mary Landis Hampson negotiated copyright of Emily Dickinson's writings after his death in 1952, copyright that extended to the manuscripts Todd had in her possession and that her daughter Bingham donated to Amherst.[22] The volumes Bianchi coedited with Hampson became increasingly professionalized as lyrics, looking like what readers would expect when opening a book of poetry. With the centennial of Dickinson's birth in 1930, Bianchi and Hampson made sure that the author was celebrated in her hometown, and that news of the celebration was broadcast widely. In 1938, George Whicher made clear her authorial stature in the first sentence of his biography's "Preface": "Emily Dickinson's poems, the final and artistically the most perfect product of the New England renaissance, have quietly attained the rank of an American classic."

Though they tried to maintain objectivity, Johnson and then Franklin were influenced by Bingham, who also persuaded Richard B. Sewall to write Dickinson's biography to tell Mabel Loomis Todd's story; in his "Preface" Sewall says he wrote *The Life of Emily Dickinson* at Bingham's behest, so that "'the whole story' of her mother's involvement [with the Dickinsons]" could be told "in the setting of the larger story of Emily Dickinson" (xii). Like her mother, Bingham was concerned to preserve the reputation of the poet to whom she had devoted her talents and energies. So when Rebecca Patterson's award-winning biography *The Riddle of Emily Dickinson* was published in 1951, arguing that Dickinson's passions were lesbian, and making that case during the height of what we now know was the "lavender scare" of the Cold War, Bingham abruptly produced her last editorial act entangled with biography, *Emily Dickinson: A Revelation* (1954).[23] Though by her own admission she could find no evidence other than what she said was her mother's word to confirm that a group of manuscript drafts and scraps belonged together and that they were addressed to Judge Otis P. Lord, Bingham asserts that he was a passionate love interest of Emily Dickinson. Though this assertion contributed nothing to understanding Dickinson's practices as a writer, such a proclamation reinforced cultural presumptions that she must have been heterosexual. After decades of increasingly powerful, pathologizing theories about same-sex passions, Bingham's anxiety is understandable, though not admirable. After all, though she was a geographer who held a Harvard (Radcliffe) Ph.D., her entire life, and even her professional reputation, hinged on Dickinson's. To avoid having her life's work sullied by suggestions that the subject of her editing was a sexual pervert, Bingham occluded, or erased, aspects of Dickinson's life story.

While Bingham was reaffirming Dickinson's status as a heterosexual, Johnson was completing his magisterial variorum edition, *The Poems of Emily Dickinson* (1955) and *Emily Dickinson: An Interpretive Biography* (1955). Johnson's landmark edition brought together poems that had been dispersed throughout separate volumes, providing new opportunities for the study of Dickinson's work. Yet this valiant effort also submerged the gossip surrounding the making of the earlier editions by Higginson, Todd, Bianchi, Hampson, and Bingham, gossip significant because it influenced convictions about what counts as a Dickinson poem or letter, who were her most important contemporary audiences, who were her first editors, and who influenced her literary productions. The advantage and disadvantage of these early editions is that they are not organized by speculations about chronology. Dating Dickinson's manuscripts is guesswork and an art as much as it is a science; dating compositions is nearly impossible with almost all of her poems. For one thing, the date of copying may or may not be close to the date of composition.

As Ruth Stone declared on the centenary celebration of the poet's death, Emily Dickinson "broke the tiresome mold of American poetry," and "we still stand among those shards and splinters."[24] To do her work justice requires breaking tiresome editorial molds and conventions. In the twenty-first century, we still stand among those shards and splinters.

NOTES

1 Chapter 5 of Martha Nell Smith, *Rowing in Eden: Rereading Emily Dickinson* (Austin: University of Texas Press, 1992) discusses Susan Dickinson's direct access to the editors who published Dickinson's poems during her lifetime.
2 The manuscript of this letter can be seen at *Emily Dickinson's Correspondences: A Born-Digital Textual Inquiry* (Charlottesville: University of Virginia Press, 2008). Available at: http://rotunda.upress.virginia.edu/edc.
3 Quoted in Smith, *Rowing in Eden*, 216.
4 Quoted in Gary Scharnhorst, "A Glimpse of Dickinson at Work," *American Literature* 57 (October 1985), 484–5.
5 Sandra Gilbert, "American Sexual Poetics," *Reconstructing American Literary History*, ed. Sacvan Bercovitch (Cambridge, MA: Harvard University Press, 1986), 128.
6 A history of the exchange regarding the composition of "Safe in their Alabaster Chambers" can be found in "Emily Dickinson Writing a Poem," *Dickinson Electronic Archives* (available at: http://www.emilydickinson.org/safe/index.html), and in Ellen Louise Hart and Martha Nell Smith, *Open Me Carefully: Emily Dickinson Intimate Letters to Susan Huntington Dickinson* (Ashfield, MA: Paris Press, 1986), 60, 97–100. Susan Dickinson's transcriptions are in the Houghton Library (MS Am 1118.96, Series I.B, folder 54), and in *Writings by Susan Dickinson*. Available at: http://www.emilydickinson.org/susan/edvoldex.html.
7 Karen Dandurand, "New Dickinson Civil War Publications," *American Literature* 57 (October 1985), 190–2. Susan Dickinson's obituary is in *Writings by Susan Dickinson* in both draft and printed forms. Available at: http://www.emilydickinson.org/susan/edobit1.html.
8 Obituary, *Writings by Susan Dickinson*.
9 Quoted in Smith, *Rowing in Eden*, 213.
10 See "Prefatory Notes" in *Writings by Susan Dickinson*. Available at: http://www.emilydickinson.org/susan/edvoldex.html.
11 Quoted in Smith, *Rowing in Eden*, 215.
12 Quoted in Smith, *Rowing in Eden*, 217.
13 Millicent Todd Bingham, *Ancestors' Brocades: The Literary Debut of Emily Dickinson* (New York: Harper & Brothers, 1945), 358.
14 Obituary, *Writings by Susan Dickinson*.
15 This and the previous quotation of Todd are from the Preface in *Poems by Emily Dickinson*, ed. T. W. Higginson and Mabel Loomis Todd (Boston: Roberts Brothers 1891), 8.
16 Martha Dickinson Bianchi, Preface in Emily Dickinson, *The Single Hound: Poems of a Lifetime*, ed. Martha Dickinson Bianchi (Boston: Little, Brown, and Company 1914), vi.

17 Overview of early reviews in Klaus Lubbers, *Emily Dickinson: The Critical Revolution* (Ann Arbor: The University of Michigan Press, 1968), 23–4.
18 Mabel Loomis Todd and Millicent Todd Bingham, *Bolts of Melody: New Poems of Emily Dickinson* (New York: Harper & Brothers Publishers, 1945), 4.
19 Dickinson, *The Single Hound*. There are two versions of the poem; this version was sent to Susan.
20 Here I quote from the advertising copy for *Bolts of Melody: New Poems of Emily Dickinson*, ed. Mabel Loomis Todd and Millicent Todd Bingham (New York and London: Harper & Brothers Publishers 1945). Bingham listed her mother as an editor though Todd had died thirteen years before.
21 Quoted in Hart and Smith, *Open Me Carefully*, 102.
22 Mary Hampson called the poems at Amherst College the "stolen poems" (personal conversation, Evergreens, March 1984).
23 See Margot Canaday, *The Straight State: Sexuality and Citizenship in Twentieth-Century America* (Princeton, NJ: Princeton University Press, 2011).
24 Ruth Stone, "Breaking the Tiresome Mold of American Poetry," *Titanic Operas, Folio One: A Poets' Corner of Responses to Dickinson's Legacy*, ed. Martha Nell Smith with Laura Elyn Lauth. Available at: http://www.emilydickinson.org/titanic/stone.html.

CHAPTER 27

Editorial History II: 1955 to the Present
Alexandra Socarides

The editorial history of Emily Dickinson's writings took a dramatic turn in 1955 when Thomas Johnson gathered and edited all of Dickinson's then-known poems for publication by Harvard University Press in a magisterial three-volume edition entitled *The Poems of Emily Dickinson*. Although readers at mid-century may have momentarily thought that the editorial project was then complete – that they finally had all of Dickinson there was to have, and all in one place – Johnson's edition in fact spurred subsequent editors to rethink, revise, and remake his work. Johnson's edition had made certain critical conversations possible, as now readers had access to Dickinson's many drafts, to a roughly chronological order of the poems, to descriptions of what the manuscripts looked like, and, in many cases, to knowledge of the persons to whom they had been sent. Perhaps most importantly, his edition urged critics to think about *how* to represent Dickinson's work. Johnson's choices eventually came under scrutiny, as have every editor's since, and with each subsequent attempt to edit Dickinson's poems, readers and scholars learn something new not just about Dickinson but about what is entailed in such an endeavor. In this way, 1955 was the birth of modern Dickinson criticism as we know it. Johnson's greatest legacy is that it is now impossible to imagine a time when the debates inaugurated by his edition did not exist, when you could simply read a Dickinson poem without thinking about how it came into your hands as a readable text.

In this essay I offer an overview of the major editorial projects from 1955 to the present, telling the story of scholars whose insights about and passion for Dickinson have shaped her work in fascinating, and sometimes competing, ways. Embedded in this story are others about the history of twentieth-century reading practices and about the rise and impact of digital media. Throughout, I explain not only how each edition does something new, but how we have come to think in ever more interesting ways about forms of publication and their impact on the study and interpretation of Dickinson's poetry. By the time we get to the digital projects of the present moment, we will have made our way through a series of innovations, discoveries, and methodological shifts, all of which lay the groundwork for the as-yet-to-be-defined editorial practices of the twenty-first century.

Because so many different editions of Dickinson's poems had been published between 1890 and 1955, one might think that Johnson's task was simply to compile all of these poems in one place and to supplement them with the forty-one never-before-published poems. Yet Johnson's work was far more complicated than that, as the subtitle to his book – "Including variant readings critically compared with all known manuscripts" – begins to make clear. Indeed, Johnson did not just publish one version of each of the 1,775 poems, but *all* of them, meaning that the entry under a given poem often included two, three, or four versions, with Dickinson's variant words supplied under each of these poems. Although this kind of variorum had been produced before 1955 – of the Bible, many of Shakespeare's plays, Pope's *The Dunciad*, and Whitman's *Leaves of Grass* – it was exceptional to have one for the poetry of a nineteenth-century American woman. For the first time readers could see different drafts of the same Dickinson poem and understand that she sometimes sent the same poem to more than one person. This allowed Johnson (and his readers) to begin to construct an understanding of Dickinson's compositional method as it applied to the genesis and revision of a poem.

Although this may have been the most productive feature of Johnson's edition for readers and critics, the quieter aspects of his editorial work would later come under attack and would, in turn, guide the editorial efforts that followed. For instance, Johnson was the first to arrange the poems chronologically. To do so, he characterized Dickinson's handwriting for every year between 1850 and 1886, noting everything from the size, slant, and spaces between her letters to the precise way that she looped her "g" and crossed her "t." While Johnson himself admitted that his dates were often "a calculated guess," the impact of having the poems appear for the first time in chronological order (even if that order was sometimes dicey) was profound, in that it allowed critics to visualize the scope of Dickinson's entire career and to map developments across and within it.[1] In addition, Johnson broke with many of Dickinson's earlier editors by retaining her misspellings, reproducing (as closely as he felt possible) her capitals, and refusing to turn her dashes into commas, as had been the practice of previous editors. Despite having produced what he calls a "literal rendering" of her poems, Johnson's commentary on his practice suggests that this would not always be necessary.² For example, of her dash, he writes: "Within lines she uses dashes with no grammatical function whatsoever. They frequently become visual representations of a musical beat. Quite properly such 'punctuation' can be omitted in later editions, and the spelling and capitalizations regularized, as surely she would have expected had her poems been published in her lifetime."³ Johnson's "literal rendering," then, was simply that – not a manifesto on the perfect way to render the poems.

Johnson was the next to issue another edition of the poems and, indeed, he made a series of different decisions this time around. Because *The Complete Poems of Emily Dickinson* (1960) was meant as a "reading text," Johnson was faced with having to select "one form of each poem" as well as choosing between Dickinson's variant words – returning to an earlier editorial practice that erased knowledge of the many drafts of Dickinson's poems, of their circulation in letters, and of the additional words and phrases that she often wrote alongside a poem.⁴ Johnson retained the chronological format of his variorum, this time placing the date "that is conjectured for the earliest known manuscript" and the date of first publication at the bottom of each poem.⁵ Whereas the variorum had foregrounded, in its introduction and notes, the problems with accurate dating, the reading edition silently solidified these dates.

Much as the first edition of Dickinson's letters in 1894 had followed directly on the heels of the publication of her poems, a new (and still the most comprehensive) edition of Dickinson's letters was edited by Johnson and published in 1958, between his variorum and reading editions of the poems. According to Johnson, this edition of Dickinson's letters, which he coedited with Theodora Ward, was not simply a "companion edition" to that of the poems, but a summation: with it, "the task of editing the poetry and prose of Emily Dickinson, undertaken in the spring of 1950, is brought to its conclusion."⁶ With the letters Johnson employs a methodology similar to the one in his variorum edition of Dickinson's poems: he collects all previously published letters and adds "about one hundred" newly found ones; establishes a chronology using, when dates are not given, an analysis of her handwriting; and provides explanatory notes about persons, events, and quotations that appear in each letter.⁷ Although the editorial process seems quite straightforward and is related to his earlier process of editing the poems, Johnson's Introduction leads readers to approach the letters in a specific way; he presses on certain "noteworthy characteristic[s]" of Dickinson's letters, including her "acute sensitivity," her "quest for a guide," and her "self-elected incarceration."⁸ Because he presented the letters as "the expression of her unique personality," Johnson was less interested in the issues of textuality, materiality, and genre that later critics would emphasize.[9] The one suggestion that Johnson is thinking about *how* these letters are written appears when he states that "the letters both in style and rhythm begin to take on qualities that are so nearly the quality of her poems as on occasion to leave the reader in doubt where the letter leaves off and the poem begins."[10] Later critics would return to this sentence over and over again, claiming that Johnson himself recognized that the boundary between poem and letter was not nearly as stable as his regal multivolume set now made them appear to be.

In his Acknowledgments in the *Letters*, Johnson states that with his work on the poems, letters, and the interpretive biography that he had published in 1955, he had now "set forth the story of Emily Dickinson's life and writing as fully as I know how to tell it."[11] This sentence is interesting because it declares "fullness" to be the goal, it implies that what an edition presents depends on the editor's ability to "know," and it positions the editor less as an arranger of someone else's work and more as a storyteller. After almost seventy years of multiple, partial editions, Dickinson's readers were hungry for this kind of comprehensive firmness. For more than twenty years this treatment of Dickinson's texts would suffice, until, in 1981, Ralph Franklin edited *The Manuscript Books of Emily Dickinson*, and everything broke wide open.

This was not Franklin's first attempt to revise Johnson's work: in *The Editing of Emily Dickinson: A Reconsideration* (1967) he had argued against the order that Johnson had established for the poems that Dickinson had copied into the homemade books of poetry that had come to be called her "fascicles." But it took Franklin's two-volume edition of facsimiles of the manuscripts to puncture the authority that Johnson's variorum had established. In *The Manuscript Books of Emily Dickinson*, Franklin not only establishes an internal order for poems within fascicles and an external order of the fascicles themselves (Johnson had only noted which "packet" a given poem could be found in), but in doing so, he puts the manuscripts (or, to be more accurate, copies of the manuscripts) into readers' hands for the first time. Not only did this allow readers to witness aspects of Dickinson's process that they had never before seen (including what her handwriting and revisions looked like), but it made clear that many of Johnson's decisions had been governed by his editorial theory and not by Dickinson's manuscripts. For instance, readers could now see that the variants that Johnson had noted at the end of a poem often were interlined or written in the margins, and that the words Johnson had placed on a single line often encompassed two lines in her manuscript.

On the one hand this watershed moment resulted from the information that Franklin had presented, but on the other hand the information itself (what year a given poem was actually composed, what poems were copied next to each other in a fascicle, etc.) was less important than what Franklin's presentation of such facts suggested. By reproducing the manuscripts, Franklin suggests that this is the more legitimate way to read Dickinson. He states as much in the Introduction when he writes: "A facsimile edition is of particular importance to Dickinson studies, for the manuscripts of this poet resist translation into the conventions of print."[12] Two sentences later he hits this note again when he states that Dickinson "left her manuscripts unprepared for print."[13] Here, then, Franklin raises the problem of print, not for Dickinson (as in, why did she not print) but for us (as in, why do we try to read her in print).

Although in the wake of Franklin's edition many critics simply read the print versions alongside the manuscripts – or, even more problematically, read the manuscripts *as if they were print*, ignoring the questions that physical details raise about a text's identity – a major shift in editorial practice had occurred. Franklin himself signaled this shift by taking the opportunity of his next editorial undertaking to provide both facsimiles of manuscripts and transcriptions. In *The Master Letters of Emily Dickinson* (1986), published five years after *The Manuscript Books*, Franklin presented the three hotly debated letters in the Dickinson canon in this form, arguing that such a presentation would allow readers to see the "stages in the composition of each letter."[14] He primarily takes issue with how previous editors had dated these letters: Millicent Todd Bingham in *Emily Dickinson's Home* (1955), Johnson and Ward in *The Letters of Emily Dickinson* (1958), and Jay Leyda in *The Years and Hours of Emily Dickinson* (1960) had all, according to Franklin, gotten it wrong. Their erroneous dates had depended on faulty transcriptions; by turning to the manuscripts themselves, Franklin would now establish the correct chronology.

The move to treating manuscripts as texts that readers could encounter for themselves, rather than material the editor has to work with behind the scenes to produce transcriptions for a reading public, gave rise to the practices of the next generation of Dickinson's editors. Although the most obvious shift was the tendency of later editors to present readers, as Franklin had, with copies of manuscripts to consider for themselves, this was only the beginning. In subsequent editions of Dickinson's texts, attention to the manuscripts produced a different kind of Dickinson editor and reader. For one thing, editorial projects ceased to strive for comprehensiveness, as can be seen in Marta L. Werner's edition of forty late manuscripts in *Emily Dickinson's Open Folios: Scenes of Reading, Surfaces of Writing* (1995) and in Ellen Louise Hart and Martha Nell Smith's edition of the correspondence between Dickinson and her sister-in-law, Susan Huntington Dickinson, in *Open Me Carefully: Emily Dickinson's Intimate Letters to Susan Huntington Dickinson* (1998). Just as it was before Johnson's landmark attempt at a comprehensive edition, these editorial projects are partial, but not because we did not have access to materials. Instead, these editions focus on what the reader can see for him or herself, insist upon more open-ended readings of Dickinson, and deemphasize the editor's authority. In these editions the theoretical problems of editorial practice themselves become central.

Although the editorial undertakings of Werner and Hart/Smith have some things in common – they emerged at the same time, are products of (if acts of resistance to) earlier attempts at authoritative editing, and treat relatively small pieces of the Dickinson canon – they are also very different. Werner's goal was largely "archival," informed by her argument that "the spectacular complexity of the textual situation circa 1870 ... has been all but erased by the editorial interventions and print conventions of the past century," so that "access to Emily Dickinson's late writings will only be gained by attending to the textual specificities of the holographs themselves."[15] Werner reproduces an eclectic assortment of texts (poems, jottings, cancelled writing, notes to self) written on a diversity of materials (envelopes, advertisements, letter-writing paper, torn and cut paper), all of which present readers with a different Dickinson than they had seen before. Although Johnson had published transcriptions of these manuscripts as poems, letters, or prose fragments, readers had never seen the materials on which these words and lines appeared. *Open Me Carefully*, meanwhile, pursues a twofold goal, allowing readers to see something both biographical (the intimacy of Emily and Susan) and generic (that the "letter-poem" was a form that Dickinson regularly worked in). To do this, Hart and Smith do not foreground manuscripts in the way Werner does, but rely on transcriptions that are informed by their work with manuscripts. For instance, they use Dickinson's manuscript lineation throughout, producing poems, letters, and the hybrid "letter-poem" – texts that look different from anything we have encountered before. Both editions not only deepen our understanding of aspects of Dickinson's work, but also show how representing and contextualizing textual details are significant for the editorial enterprise.

At the close of the twentieth century, editorial projects dealing with Dickinson's work were dominated by an interest in the manuscripts, which raised certain questions. Are the editorial options of print and manuscript that have emerged over the twentieth century fixed and central? Will there be (or, can we already sense) a backlash to the growing insistence that Dickinson be read in manuscript form? What lies beyond the manuscript? Although this could have been a moment to explore such questions, Franklin's return to the scene in 1998 with a new variorum edition of Dickinson's poems instead made it clear that the major, Harvard-published editorial projects were not pushing forward into the unknown, but were returning to the old forms. Although different in several elements of content – poems were added and more details about the manuscripts appear in the notes – Franklin's *The Poems of Emily Dickinson: Variorum Edition* (1998), published in a three-volume set and followed the next year by a reading edition, worked within the parameters that Johnson's earlier variorum and reading editions had established. Franklin, like Johnson, published transcriptions of all extant manuscripts in his variorum and then chose one version of each poem and, without variants or explanatory apparatus, published these in his reading edition. Given that Franklin had been working with the manuscripts since the 1980s, it is strange that he produced editions of the poems that, according to his own assessment, are based on the assumption that "a literary work is separable from its artifact."[16]

Although it is unclear if Franklin wanted to do something other than produce more accurate versions of Johnson's variorum and reading editions, most people today use his numbers and versions of poems when quoting, teaching, and discussing Dickinson poetry. The importance of this is not to be underestimated, for Franklin's chronology and transcriptions are a result of his long work with the manuscripts and the almost half decade in which he wrestled with Johnson's editorial decisions. Franklin's edition is significant for students, in particular, who can now look up any Dickinson poem in his variorum and find a longer and more complicated story of its composition, publication, and editing than Johnson had represented. This is a drastically different situation than earlier students were in, when Dickinson's poems were presented as lyrics isolated from any history. Although it is a boon to have an edition of the poems that is fuller and more accurate in its transcriptions and descriptions, the question remains: What else, besides fullness and accuracy, has the history and development of editorial practice, as it applies to the work of Emily Dickinson, produced? What work remains to be done now that Franklin has produced *another* variorum and reading edition?

One way to answer this is to look at the work on Dickinson that is taking place on the web. The Emily Dickinson Electronic Archives (www.emilydickinson.org) has been around since 1995, houses selected photographs of manuscripts as well as critical articles about electronic archives, and is open to all visitors to this site. More recently, Marta L. Werner's "Radical Scatters: Emily Dickinson's Late Fragments and Related Texts, 1870–1886" (http://libxmlia.unl.edu:8080/cocoon/radicalscatters/default-failed.html), which was first posted in 1999 but was revised and updated in 2007, and Martha Nell Smith and Lara Vetter's "Emily Dickinson's Correspondences: A Born-Digital Textual Inquiry" (http://rotunda.upress.virginia.edu/edc/default.xqy), which was launched in 2008, began taking full advantage of the spaces and tools made available by the web. While both require a username and password and both are, again, selective editions from the Dickinson oeuvre, neither Werner nor Smith replicate the work she did in her earlier print editions, for the point of these digital projects is to make new lines of inquiry possible. For instance, by placing "core texts" (eighty-two documents that carry more than a hundred fragmentary texts) and "trace fragments" (other texts that are in some way associated with the "core texts") together, Werner asks the viewer to "attend to the mystery of the encounters between fragments, poems, and letters, listening especially to the ways in which, like leitmotifs, the fragments both influence the modalities of the compositions in which they momentarily take asylum and carry those leitmotifs beyond the finished compositions into another space and time."[17] In order to help the user do this, Werner provides several ways of viewing each text (a reading view, facsimile, and transcription) as well as information organized under the following categories: physical description, collection, transmission history, publication history, and commentary. Smith and Vetter take a similar approach, with their preferred categories being manuscript description, history, previous printings, digital edition, additional editorial notes, and constellation notes. Even if the print variorum editions had included all of the information that Werner, Smith, and Vetter include, the print format made it impossible to put texts in conversation in the way that these digital projects do. For instance, Werner offers the user a place to see how she has identified a text (for example, "Composed by Dickinson in pencil" or "Text contains stray letters and/or marks"); from there she allows the user to link to all other texts that have been tagged this way. In addition to Smith and Vetter's "Constellation Notes," which makes it possible for the user to link to all previous versions and related texts, their archive allows users to search by categories such as genre and manuscript features. These editors are taking advantage of the kinds of knowledge that are made available when we shift how we read, view, process, tag, cluster, search, and zoom.

Looking toward the future of her online archive, Werner writes that "the fragments in Radical Scatters offer only an entry point into the mass of late, unbound, extra-territorial writings in Dickinson's oeuvre. In the future, some of the documents included in the present archive will fall outside of it, while others, not yet identified as fragments, will enter it, producing not new 'collections' but rather unforeseen and anomalous orders."[18] While here Werner addresses the implications of later editors' decisions about the texts she considers, her words might be used to characterize the future of editorial projects in general, for with digital technologies the need for rigidly defined collections has ceased. Yet as we look back over the editorial history of Dickinson's texts, it should be clear that the web will not be the final context for editorial work. In fact, we do not yet have comprehensive knowledge of the media we will use for the reading, access, and dissemination of Dickinson's texts in the twenty-first century. Perhaps more importantly, we do not yet know what difference those media will make.

NOTES

1 Thomas H. Johnson, ed., *The Poems of Emily Dickinson, including variant readings critically compared with all known manuscripts* (Cambridge, MA: The Belknap Press of Harvard University Press, 1955), lxii.
2 Ibid., lxiii.
3 Ibid., lxiii.
4 Thomas H., Johnson, ed., *The Complete Poems of Emily Dickinson* (Cambridge, MA: The Belknap Press of Harvard University Press, 1960), x.
5 Ibid., xi.
6 Thomas H. Johnson and Theodora Ward, eds., *The Letters of Emily Dickinson* (Cambridge, MA: The Belknap Press of Harvard University Press, 1958), xxiii, xi.
7 Ibid., xxiv.
8 Ibid., xv, xvii, xix.
9 Ibid., xxi.
10 Ibid., xv.
11 Ibid., xi.
12 R. W. Franklin, ed., *The Manuscript Books of Emily Dickinson* (Cambridge, MA: Belknap Press of Harvard University Press, 1981), ix.
13 Ibid., ix.
14 R. W. Franklin, ed., *The Master Letters of Emily Dickinson* (Amherst: Amherst College Press, 1986), 5.
15 Marta Werner, *Emily Dickinson's Open Folios: Scenes of Reading, Surfaces of Writing* (Ann Arbor: University of Michigan Press, 1995), 1–2.

16 R.W. Franklin, ed., *The Poems of Emily Dickinson: Variorum Edition* (Cambridge, MA: The Belknap Press of Harvard University Press, 1998), 27.
17 Marta Werner, *Radical Scatters: Emily Dickinson's Late Fragments and Related Texts, 1870–1886*, University of Nebraska Lincoln, July 8, 2012. Available at: http://libxml1a.unl.edu:8080/cocoon/radicalscatters/default–failed.html.
18 Ibid.

CHAPTER 28

On Materiality (and Virtuality)

Gabrielle Dean

In 1981, Ralph Franklin published *The Manuscript Books of Emily Dickinson*, reproducing the handwritten texts and arrangements of Emily Dickinson's fascicles – the forty booklets of more than eight hundred poems that Dickinson copied, organized, and sewed together, which had been disassembled by her editors Mabel Loomis Todd and Thomas Wentworth Higginson after her death. By "reassembling" the fascicles, Franklin gave critics access to a key feature of Dickinson's writing that had been visible before only to researchers who dug into the Dickinson archives: its material form. *The Manuscript Books* thus initiated a new critical awareness of the importance of materiality to Dickinson's work – an understanding that, in the fascicles and in all her writing, Dickinson's techniques are intimately tied to the physical environments of composition. Ideas about materiality are now embedded in many different critical approaches to Dickinson. Textual critics who examine punctuation and lineation, feminist critics who look at gendered models of authorship, historicist critics who are interested in the economics of the nineteenth-century literary household – all might find it useful to investigate, for example, Dickinson's copying and binding practices, her paper-saving habits, and her family's book-collecting and reading customs. Given the broad range of critical inquiries that materiality motivates, this essay is devoted to airing questions, not to concluding them.

If the reception of Dickinson's work has hinged historically on the interpretation of her fascicles by Todd and Higginson as they prepared the first book versions of her poems, then what did her editors actually see when they encountered these curious aggregations of paper? How did they read their physical features, especially in relation to the book form that the fascicles seem to both imitate and resist? To what extent could they imagine materiality as an important part of her writing practice? How did later editors address it, especially after *The Manuscript Books* made the fascicles visible? These questions beg prior questions about Dickinson's own seeing, reading, and imagining of her fascicle project. The editorial and critical response to the fascicles as objects is difficult to separate from the material circumstances of Dickinson's poetic practice. Moreover, because neither Dickinson nor her first editors recorded their accounts of materiality per se, the choices inherent in Dickinson's poetic production and reception can be investigated only circumstantially – by resort to the material evidence that remains.

Although the forty bound fascicles, with their unusual structure, set into motion the examination of materiality in Dickinson's work, there are other material forms to consider. What about the fifteen "sets" of poems (copied like the fascicles but not sewn), other miscellaneous drafts and copies, and texts written on fragments of paper, which some critics call "scraps"? What about Dickinson's letters, which often contain poems? Do the other gatherings she created – her herbarium, for example – shed light on her views about the poetic potential of materiality? And how did her encounters with the writings of others, always embodied by some medium, influence the horizons of material possibility she saw for her own work?

Given that letters, manuscripts, and books were pervasive constituents of nineteenth-century experience, we must also ask, do Dickinson's critics err in ascribing a special status to materiality in her work? Do we exaggerate the role of materiality because of our reliance on material sources of information, in the absence of the usual editorial authorizations granted by poets who oversee the translation of their manuscripts into print?

Comparing Dickinson's material expressions to those of her peers leads to one additional line of inquiry. What about us? Like Dickinson and her contemporaries, who worked across various manuscript and print platforms, we consume and generate text in a hybrid system: we still read and write in manuscript and print, but increasingly we rely on digital constructs. The digital environment has a materiality (for it is after all grounded in hardware) that we often experience as a simulated reality. What does the transference of Dickinson's texts into virtual settings do to or for the texts – and to or for us, her readers?

These four intersecting contexts – (1) the characteristics of Dickinson's poetic production and critical reception in terms of materiality; (2) the material features of her reading and writing environment, more generally; (3) the material culture of poetic production in the mid- to late nineteenth century; and (4) the questions that virtual representations of Dickinson's writing provoke – are addressed in a different order in what follows. Because the initial interest in materiality in Dickinson's work proceeded from the rather extraordinary fascicles, critics often see her materiality as absolutely unique. Here, I begin instead with the nineteenth-century material culture of poetry, considered very briefly in the work of two of Dickinson's peers, Walt Whitman and Christina Rossetti. This context indicates a very different justification for the critical examination of Dickinson's material forms: because they are historically representative.

MATERIAL CULTURES OF POETIC PRODUCTION

The material variety of the Walt Whitman archive points to his eclectic compositional practices. Whitman had the habit of writing down thoughts, phrases, and early drafts of poems and prose works on scraps, envelopes and letters, as well as in notebooks – both "commercial notebooks ... which he amended at will by cutting out and replacing pages and pasting in clippings, photographs or scraps of manuscripts" and "home-made notebooks which he created by folding and/or cutting sheets of paper and fastening with a pin or ribbon."[1] Whitman, then, offers both a corroborating and counter example to Dickinson. Like Dickinson, he made use of the ephemera that crossed his path as well as gatherings – notebooks – to compose, edit, store, and organize his writings. Moreover, he published *Leaves of Grass* in several expanding editions over several decades, throwing doubt on the identity of "the book" in ways that the fascicles also do. Unlike Dickinson, he had authorial control over the compilation of his fragments in print.

Christina Rossetti presents a different set of resemblances. Born in the same year to prominent, intellectual families, both Dickinson and Rossetti began to circulate poems within domestic and friendship circles in their teen years, lived all their lives in familial households, never married, and outwardly obeyed many social conventions, while confounding aesthetic ones. For both, sisters or sister-figures served as readers and intermediaries. Rossetti's sister Maria was her first copyist, while Dickinson's sister Lavinia, her friend and sister-in-law Susan, and Susan's rival Mabel Loomis Todd were all key to the creation or transmission of her work. In both cases, male friends or family members served as mentors and presided over significant publications that often protected the poet's privacy. Rossetti's grandfather privately printed a collection of her poems in 1847; her brother Dante Gabriel helped her publish her first poems in 1848; seven poems were published pseudonymously in 1850 in a journal under the editorship of her brother William Michael. William Michael also recopied her works and edited two important posthumous collections, but the notebooks he drew from may not have contained the latest versions of

On materiality (and virtuality) 295

some of her poems. Dickinson's first work in print was a valentine spoof that appeared anonymously in 1850 in the Amherst College *Indicator*, edited by Austin's fraternity brother. Of the eleven poems published in her lifetime, anonymously, five appeared in *The Springfield Republican* edited by family friends Samuel Bowles and Josiah Holland. Her correspondence with Thomas Wentworth Higginson was initiated and often carried out in the mode of a private tutorial. For both Dickinson and Rossetti, these private domains of writing engendered poems in multiple states, the products of disjointed and sometimes indeterminate histories. Both poets relied on pseudo-book forms to collect their works – notebooks and fascicles – but also destabilized the finality of these forms.

These comparisons yield two insights with regards to materiality. First, Dickinson's material practices of composition were not atypical. Notable contemporaries engaged, like her, in a poetic process that included paper saving, copying, organizing, and binding. Second, Dickinson's "drafts" were not sifted into "final" book form in her lifetime, as was the case with Whitman and Rossetti. But rather than stabilize the difference between composition and publication, Dickinson's material practices blur this distinction, suggesting that writing cannot always be straightforwardly categorized as public or private. In short, the materiality of Dickinson's writing does merit special critical attention, precisely because it illuminates not just her work but also that of other poets. This fact does not diminish Dickinson's particular poetics of materiality, distinct from that of Whitman, Rossetti, or anyone else.

THE MATERIALITY OF DICKINSON'S POESIS

The fascicles, which have received the most scrutiny of all Dickinson's materials, constitute what critics have called a "private form of self-publication" – a physical manifestation of the textual methodology that has been described as "choosing not choosing."[2] Each fascicle consists of "small sheets of paper folded in two by their manufacturer"; Dickinson "stacked several such sheets on top of one another, threaded a piece of string through the two spaced holes on the left margin of the stack, and tied the whole assembly together."[3] Scholars of the "manuscript school" contend that the orthography, lineation, word-spacing, pagination, order, size, and binding system of the fascicles, not to mention their textual variants and mechanics, all make contributions to Dickinson's poesis, which aims not to establish a total work of art but to explore possible and multiple meanings across boundaries.[4] As collections, the fascicles encourage overlapping interpretations: within the fascicle environment, a poem's connections to other poems may be significant; by itself, the same poem may invite a different reading. As hand-made booklets, the fascicles may be seen as imitations of or alternatives to book publication. As vehicles of text, the fascicle layouts deviate from the familiar arrangements of the book and the page, forcing readers to reexamine the many formal cues we expect such visual displays to provide: cues about unity, order, and completeness.

Indeed, all of Dickinson's material devices – not just the fascicles – contradict conventional expectations about form, sometimes in ways that also bear on genre. Differentiating Dickinson's poems from her letters, for example, can be difficult because she used the same paper for both kinds of writing and frequently copied poems into or enclosed poems with letters. This interchangeability is typified by the exchange of letters and poems between Dickinson and her sister-in-law; it is not really possible to "distinguish between poetic and epistolary texts" in this case, some critics have contended – to do so would amputate and misrepresent the correspondence.[5]

Although the texts in the fascicles and sets are recognizable as poems, and although the texts written to correspondents are often recognizable as letters and/or poems, other Dickinson manuscripts take the play of transactions across words, lines, pages, poems, and bindings to new horizons. Critical examinations of the scraps have prompted two noteworthy observations. First, the scraps are not necessarily drafts; some contain texts that are also incorporated into poems or letters, but others seem to be intact as they are, if generically indeterminate. If the fascicles challenge conventional distinctions between parts and wholes at the macro levels of the book and page, the scraps do so at the micro level of the phrase or passage. Because they are small, the scraps invite close study; as a consequence, critics have remarked the subtle ways in which the orientation of script on these papers is often a response to the paper's shape, texture or prior inscription. This dialogue with paper seems to occur most frequently in scraps that originally belonged to a chance piece of manuscript or printed paper – and in fact the second significant observation about the scraps concerns Dickinson's affinity for ephemera. Dickinson composed texts on "abandoned letters; advertising circulars and flyers ...; bills for the delivery of milk; concert programs; the torn corners of magazines; dust jackets; the insides of slit envelopes ... and envelope flaps; the flyleaves of books; the margins from book pages, legal forms, and magazines; stationery ...; notebook leaves ... bits of wrappers ... and strips of wrapping paper."⁶ What looks like an astounding array of ephemeral papers is simply an accurate reflection of the growth of print culture in the industrial era. Dickinson's response to this abundance, however – to save, reuse, and keep – is perhaps more characteristic of the pre-industrial period, when paper was relatively expensive.

Dickinson's material innovations, which are also textual, formal, and generic innovations, have not made definitive inroads into print editions of her work – nor can they, if the graphic and physical features of the manuscripts are taken at face value. Clearly, in dismembering the fascicles, Todd and Higginson considered their physical construction to be less important than the poems they bore. But for twenty-first-century critics, Dickinson's materiality has been enormously provocative. Ralph Franklin's 1998 variorum edition of *The Poems of Emily Dickinson*, for instance, was greeted both with celebration for its representation of the multiplicity of Dickinson's texts and disappointment in its neglect of the "physical choreography of her poems."⁷ Some critics argue that, although Franklin provides unprecedented access to Dickinson's textual variations, his decisions to organize the poems chronologically and regularize them with regard to typeface and lineation "run contrary to recent assumptions about the primacy of the manuscripts themselves – assumptions which, ironically, emerge historically as responses to his earlier publication of the *Manuscript Books*."⁸

Although there appears to be critical consensus about the importance of materiality to Dickinson's poesis, there is disagreement about the limits of the manuscript paradigm. In the debates that surround "the construction of a 'scriptural' Dickinson," some critics worry that it has led to fetishization, hagiography, and deficiencies in historical perspective.⁹

BEYOND THE MANUSCRIPTS

Given the puzzles that the manuscripts present, some critics have turned to the world beyond the borders of Dickinson's own poems and letters – to the textual artifacts of her household and community – to try to understand the place of her manuscripts in a larger material culture. In fact, awareness of this particular material context pre-dates Franklin's *Manuscript Books*; Higginson himself aligned Dickinson's work with Ralph Waldo Emerson's idea of the "Poetry of the Portfolio," and this association has been followed up by critics who look at Dickinson's writings within the culture of scrapbooks, keepsake albums, and commonplace books in the nineteenth century, particularly among women. It is likely that

Dickinson herself kept "a scrapbook of clippings from national magazines, local newspapers and illustrated books, which she used to ornament some of her own manuscripts."[10] Certainly, she had friends who did. Friends and contemporaries also kept clippings in school notebooks and copied poems into commonplace books – activities that "extended domestic culture into the school" and vice versa.[11] These forms suggest that Dickinson might have devised the fascicle as a way to preserve her texts, not unlike the plant preservation strategy of the herbarium. Whether the texts they carried were poems, clippings, or botanical specimens with labels, personal codices allowed Dickinson's contemporaries to exercise their memories; to extract samples for occasions when they might be needed – letters of condolence or congratulation, for example; or to revive important past experiences.

Another benefit for the compiler of the nineteenth-century scrapbook, keepsake album, or commonplace book was the gateway it provided to author-like invention. Hand-sewing a codex, or filling in a commercially printed bound album, could be seen in relation to public authorship in part because of the explosion in print forms that industrial technology made possible. Commonplace books and albums were situated on a popular print culture continuum that included, for example, literary annuals and gift books: anthologies that combined miscellaneous texts, illustrations, and decorative elements. Because women often contributed to these published volumes, women who generated private manuscript codices could imagine their craftsmanship in public terms if they so desired.

Industrial technology also transformed newspapers and magazines. Between 1840 and 1880, the number of periodicals produced in the United States increased almost sevenfold; many of the new titles were sold at lower prices, due to the cost savings of new methods of mass production and advertising. The expanded price structure made room for a more diverse press. These changes in kind were accompanied by changes in material presentation, as publishers looked for inexpensive ways to package their wares. Folded, sewn, and wrapped serials – the ephemeral sources of clippings that could be immortalized in scrapbooks and albums – proliferated; the pamphlets and broadsheets that Dickinson encountered at home and among friends suggested a range of relationships between authorship and its material instantiations.

BEYOND PAPER

The material common denominator of both Dickinson's texts and the textual culture of her time is paper. Paper as a medium for the inscription of text has many advantages; it is relatively inexpensive, easy to use, and widely available. It can be bound into a codex to facilitate continuous reading, but in this form it also abets discontinuous reading practices, through the use of an index, for example. Nevertheless, paper as an inscriptive device has certain physical limitations. It allows us to travel in a linear fashion – backwards and forwards – but it does not readily serve connections that occur within or across texts.

Digital media, in contrast, facilitates many kinds of connections. It is for this reason that electronic editions and archives of Dickinson's work have such great potential to reveal the profusion of links between and throughout her texts and her culture. The *Dickinson Electronic Archives* prioritizes the person-to-person circulation of manuscripts within Dickinson's circle and "the physical object over the logical lexical content."[12] Consequently, its editors have focused on amassing page images of selected poems, letters, and miscellanies. The *DEA* is evolving into an interactive library of texts and critical responses, with the aim of encouraging the study of connections between Dickinson and her peers. Out of this mission grew a related project: *Emily Dickinson's Correspondences*, a scholarly edition of poems and letters from Dickinson's correspondence with Susan Dickinson.[13]

Radical Scatters: Emily Dickinson's Late Fragments and Related Texts, 1870–1886 is focused instead on the scraps. This archive contains a set of materially discrete and autonomous "core" fragments; "trace" fragments – drafts or versions of other texts; and poems and letters that relate to particular scraps. The collection's principle – giving primacy to the scrap instead of the fascicle, the page, or the poem – offers a new vision of Dickinson's work, replacing teleological assumptions about composition, wherein drafts lead to fair copies which lead to print, with the view of a "constellation." Yet as its editor notes, the restoration of connections between scraps and other texts and the recognition of some scraps as autonomous "fails to effect any lasting closure."[14] *Radical Scatters* offers concrete evidence that Dickinson's work is not easily brought into any kind of corporal order.

Each of these archival projects presents a different subset of Dickinson texts, brought together to highlight aspects of her oeuvre that have been overlooked. Students and critics also long, however, for a comprehensive digital archive of Dickinson's work. That goal is complicated by the practical challenges common to digital scholarship. Digital archivists must contend with the legal complexities of obtaining permission to reproduce copyright-protected texts, the technological challenges of an evolving digital infrastructure, and the uncertainty of hosting arrangements in a changing publishing environment. Both of the university presses that support *Radical Scatters* and the *DEA*, for example, limit all or part of their resources to subscribers. There is a poignant irony that, in this case, such obstacles threaten to make Dickinson's material poesis – only recently recovered as meaningful – obscure once more.

And do they not, these digital archives, again disassemble Dickinson's fascicles? The *texts* may be more accessible, but what happens to the *material* architecture of her work in the digital realm? It would be easy to condemn electronic collections for re-dematerializing Dickinson. It is true that Dickinson's writings draw materiality into their meanings; that certain perceptions are available only through the manuscripts; and that each degree of separation from the manuscripts – whether we read manuscript facsimiles, variorum editions, or the conventionalized versions edited by Todd and Higginson – dilutes some aspects of her work. But digital archives offer in exchange insights into Dickinson's intricate manipulations of materiality that would be otherwise unobtainable.

The many debates surrounding the representation of Dickinson's manuscripts have shown us that there is no ideal way to reproduce them – each attempt results either in a new work or an imperfect copy. Digital renderings do no more harm to the materiality of Dickinson's writing than do print editions and paper facsimiles. Unlike most printed books, however, an electronic archive can be designed to be transparent – to reveal the biases inherent in its construction. With the many pathways they make possible, digital archives also help us read Dickinson's textual networks, by showing the relationships among different versions of a poem, for example, or different genres of writing. And by illuminating the complexities of Dickinson's writing practices, digital archives redistribute textual authority in ways that reiterate the strategies of this author of multiple versions, variants, and material states.

Finally, by making more of Dickinson's "workshop" visible, digital archives can help us see her writing in relation to the wide world of text she inhabited, with its numerous physical forms. The more we know about Dickinson's broader textual culture, the more apparent it becomes that the materiality of writing in her time was as unruly, various, and mutable as it is in ours. The diverse materiality of text in the mid- to late nineteenth century was something Dickinson embraced – along with the diverse practices it enabled.

NOTES

1 Alice L. Birney, "About Whitman's Notebooks," *Poet at Work: Walt Whitman Notebooks 1850s –1860s*. Online. Library of Congress. Available at: http://memory.loc.gov/ammem/collections/whitman/wwntbks.html.

2 Dorothy Oberhaus, *Emily Dickinson's Fascicles: Method and Meaning* (University Park: Pennsylvania State University Press, 1995), 1; Sharon Cameron, *Choosing Not Choosing: Dickinson's Fascicles* (Chicago: University of Chicago Press, 1992).
3 Mary Loeffelholz, "What Is a Fascicle?" *Harvard Library Bulletin 10*.1 (Spring 1999), 23.
4 Domhnall Mitchell's phrase in *Measures of Possibility: Emily Dickinson's Manuscripts* (Amherst, MA: University of Massachusetts Press, 2005), 11.
5 Cristanne Miller, "The Sound of Shifting Paradigms, or Hearing Dickinson in the Twenty-First Century," *A Historical Guide to Emily Dickinson*, ed. Vivian R. Pollak (New York: Oxford University Press, 2004), 204.
6 Mitchell, *Measures of Possibility*, 192.
7 Martha Nell Smith and Ellen Louise Hart, "On Franklin's Gifts & Ghosts," *EDJ* 8.2 (Fall 1999), 29.
8 Domhnall Mitchell, "Emily Dickinson, Ralph Franklin, and the Diplomacy of Translation," *EDJ* 8.2 (Fall 1999), 40.
9 Lena Christensen, *Editing Emily Dickinson: The Production of an Author* (New York: Routledge, 2008), 26.
10 Barton Levi St. Armand, *Emily Dickinson and Her Culture: The Soul's Society* (New York: Cambridge University Press, 1984), 26.
11 Virginia Jackson, *Dickinson's Misery: A Theory of Lyric Reading* (Princeton, NJ: Princeton University Press, 2005), 60.
12 Martha Nell Smith, Ellen Louise Hart and Marta Werner, eds., *Dickinson Electronic Archives*. Online. University of Virginia Press 1997–2008. Available at: www.emilydickinson.org/index.html.
13 Martha Nell Smith and Lara Vetter, eds., *Emily Dickinson's Correspondences: A Born–Digital Textual Inquiry*. Online. University of Virginia Press, 2008. Available at: http://rotunda.upress.virginia.edu/edc/.
14 Marta L. Werner, ed., *Radical Scatters: Emily Dickinson's Late Fragments and Related Texts, 1870–1886*. Online. University of Nebraska–Lincoln, 2007–2010. Available at: http://libxml1a.unl.edu:8080/cocoon/radicalscatters/default–login.html.

CHAPTER 29

The Letters Archive

Cindy MacKenzie

"There seems a spectral power in thought that walks alone" muses Emily Dickinson in a letter to her "Preceptor" and nineteenth-century man of letters, Thomas Wentworth Higginson, adding philosophically that "a Letter always seems to me like immortality because it is the mind alone without corporeal friend" (L330). As readers, our encounter with Dickinson's letters partakes of the haunting quality she describes; we sense the trace of the woman who writes through her correspondents to us. But there are numerous other phantoms haunting the many gaps in the Dickinson archive; phantoms lingering among the more than one thousand extant manuscripts that form a mere fraction of the entire number she likely wrote; phantoms in the missing correspondences to significant recipients, in the lack of specific dating of the letters, and certainly in the gaping hole created by the nearly complete absence of correspondents' letters to Dickinson, most being burned, as was the custom of the day. Complicating these absences is the heavy-handed editorial intrusion and bias in the transcription and editing of the manuscripts. In their wish to protect their privacy, the correspondents themselves or their relatives deleted passages and mutilated the letters which, as Martha Nell Smith asserts, "strip[ped] away information, context, and connections, creating holes in our reading that can never be restored."[1] In addition, with each scholarly analysis, another spectre and its accompanying speculations enter the critical narrative so that "the structure of the archive is spectral," as Derrida argues in *Archive Fever*. He goes on to say, aptly, that "the technical structure of the archiving archive also determines the structure of the archivable content even in its very coming into existence and in its relationship to the future. The archivization produces as much as it records the event."[2] Thus, despite its undeniable importance and usefulness, the broader contextual framework marked by the absences that haunt the archive of Dickinson's letters presents significant – and challenging – interpretive considerations: first, in the process of its construction and its subsequent impact on biographical, editorial, and scholarly interpretations; and second, in its relationship to Dickinson's poetry and to the oeuvre as a whole.

With the posthumous publication of two editions of *Poems by Emily Dickinson* in 1890 and 1891, editors Mabel Loomis Todd and Thomas Wentworth Higginson imposed editorial changes on the manuscripts that reflected their own conventional tastes. At the same time, however, perhaps because of their intervention, they successfully introduced readers to what was an original and idiosyncratic poetry by bringing it into a conventional form. Moreover, because of the poet's frequent use of the lyric "I" as well as descriptions of intense personal experiences without biographical context, the poems piqued readers' curiosity about the life of the mysterious, reclusive woman, dubbed "the Myth of Amherst," who wrote them. Responding to this interest and without the benefit of a journal or notebook that might have been kept by the poet, the vivacious Todd set aside her editorial work on a third volume of poems to undertake, at the request of and with the assistance of Emily's sister, Lavinia, the slow process of collecting and arranging letters from as many recipients as they could identify and locate. But when *The Letters of Emily Dickinson* was published in 1894, the two volumes of 345 letters comprising correspondence of ten recipients left many readers disappointed. As one reviewer for a Boston journal notes: "Four years we have waited for these 'Letters,' hoping to find in their pages a clue to the whole life, and now we are as much at a loss as ever" (*Reception*, 391). Indeed, early readers, expecting to find unmediated access to the life of the mysterious woman who wrote such enigmatic poetry, would not have been satisfied by that first collection of letters even as they may have been enlightened by what it did provide. Questions about sequence remained, as well as more personal questions about whom she loved, about the losses and pain she suffered, about her religious beliefs, literary influences, and artistic aspirations. Despite the collections of letters following Todd's, including Thomas Johnson's 1958 edition, which brought together more than a thousand letters in one collection arranged as closely to accurate dating as possible, today's readers and scholars remain persistent in their efforts to find answers to questions surrounding the poet's life and work.

To a great extent, the problem lies in the legendary "War Between the Houses," the soap-opera-like story through which Dickinson's archive comes to us, as it predetermines our understanding of her life and work. The ongoing debate among scholars is generated not only by the posthumous publication of the poet's works, but also by the competing factions involved in the editing process as each side attempts to "correct" the work of the other. This "war" originated in large part from the adulterous affair between Austin Dickinson and Mabel Loomis Todd, which gave rise to the creation of a compelling narrative that pits Susan, a bereaved mother (her nine-year-old son, Gilbert had died of typhoid fever) and a betrayed and angry wife, against the passionate, energetic, and free-wheeling Mabel. The tension between the two women resulted in powerful biases that exerted a distorted and distracting influence on the biographical, editorial, and scholarly interpretation of Dickinson's life and work. Played out in the publishing history, interpretive differences between archival houses began with Todd's first edition of the poet's letters in 1894, followed by Susan and Austin's daughter Martha Dickinson Bianchi's publication thirty years later of *The Life and Letters of Emily Dickinson* (1924) and *Emily Dickinson Face to Face: Unpublished Letters with Notes and Reminiscences by Her Niece* (1932). The enmity between the mothers erupted for many more years through their daughters when Mabel and David Todd's daughter, Millicent Todd Bingham, edited both *Emily Dickinson: A Revelation* (1954), featuring letters to Judge Otis Phillips Lord, and *Emily Dickinson's Home: Letters of Edward Dickinson and His Family* (1955). In 1951, Theodora Van Wagenen Ward, granddaughter of the Dickinsons's close friends, made available *Emily Dickinson's Letters to Dr. and Mrs. Josiah Gilbert Holland*. Ward then collaborated with Thomas Johnson on the magisterial three-volume edition of *The Letters of Emily Dickinson* published in 1958. All the phantoms housed in these earlier archives, along with Johnson's and Ward's, are now placed under the same archival roof.

Although on its face, then, Dickinson's epistolarium conveys the impression of an authoritative stability, that appearance is far from fact. In the process of its compilation, power struggles arose among the letters' recipients as familial pride in Emily's literary accomplishments and her burgeoning fame increased their sense of entitlement to the manuscripts. As Millicent Todd Bingham notes in her account of her mother's editing project: "The search for her letters, which had been going on intermittently for at least two years, presented problems in human relationships rather than perplexities of a literary nature."[3] In particular, Todd encountered difficulties with the poet's cousins, Frances and Louise Norcross, who would not consent to full publication of their letters from Emily. Instead, they transcribed them, omitting passages they considered too private to publish; when they died, in accordance with their wishes and with the custom of the time, all letters in their possession were burned. In addition, as Bingham notes, biases and distortions in the Norcross collection occurred simply by virtue of the arbitrary numbers of documents in each recipient's possession so that "the Norcross sisters have occupied a place among Emily's correspondents out of proportion to their importance and solely because all of her letters to them had been preserved."[4] As Austin's lover, Mabel herself created a problem for an objective editing of the letters, as Dickinson's friends and family members, aware of the affair as well as of the growing hostilities between Mabel and Lavinia, began to resent her participation in their relative's legacy.

These hostilities have continued to influence the positions taken by editors and scholars. One such case pertains to textual problems revealed in the letter drafts Emily wrote to Judge Otis Lord. The rough and fragmentary state of this collection has generated skepticism regarding the legitimacy of the correspondence and suspicions about the effects of excessive tampering in general. In part, the dispute has led to extensive scholarly discussion of textual problems inherent in the Johnson and Franklin editions with the resulting increased focus on original manuscripts as sources of a potentially unmediated access to textual meaning. This trend is evident in Marta Werner's *Emily Dickinson's Open Folios: Scenes of Reading, Surfaces of Writing* (1995), which houses and rigorously discusses the forty or more pencil drafts of the Dickinson-Lord archive. In general, the erotic nature of this "correspondence" has frequently attracted scholarly attention that perpetuates the tenacious stereotype of Emily as a heartbroken and reclusive spinster as well as the wish to name the person who rejected her, Lord being one of those speculations. Similarly, the inordinate critical attention paid to the three "Master" letters is evidence of the strength of this desire to situate the drama of unrequited love at the center of her life. Even R.W. Franklin's publication of *The Master Letters of Emily Dickinson* in 1986, in a slim volume, with an accompanying envelope that enclosed folded facsimiles, gives the impression that the letters were sent, while, in fact, they exist only in draft form and may not have been sent at all. Fraught with gaps that cannot be restored and editorial biases that distort interpretation, the "Master letters" continue to provoke persistent efforts to name the "Master"; possible candidates such as Judge Otis Lord, her father's friend, Charles Wadsworth, minister in Boston, and Samuel Bowles, editor of the *Springfield Republican*, are among the numerous speculations. Challenges to this approach are evident in the wide range of interpretive possibilities for these letters, questions such as Roland Hagenbuechle raises in *The Emily Dickinson Handbook* (1998): "Is the Master a biographical person? And if so, who is it? Is it really the same person in each of these poems? Or is it perhaps the poem's Oversoul? The mind's male animus? The self's creative alter ego? Is it in some sense Christ or Dickinson's appropriation of Christ?" (*Handbook*, 382). In *A Vice for Voices: Reading Emily Dickinson's Correspondence*, Marietta Messmer makes a case for textual rather than biographical interpretation, arguing that "rather than sites for self-disclosures to an intimate friend," these drafts were instead "rhetorical performances ... deliberately tailored toward a specific recipient."[5] Finally, in response to speculation about the man who might have inspired Dickinson's art, Martha Nell Smith and Ellen Louise Hart propose that Susan Dickinson, Emily's sister-in-law and lifelong friend, was the poet's central erotic and literary inspiration. Compiling the significant correspondence between the two women in *Open Me Carefully: Emily Dickinson's Intimate Correspondence with Susan Huntington Dickinson* (1998), the editors aim to persuade readers away from longstanding views derived from misinterpretation and censorship of the poet as a lonely, unmarried woman toward an image of Dickinson as a passionate and vibrant woman. Feminist scholarship in general moved the discussion of Dickinson's relationships to those with female friends such as Elizabeth Holland and Catherine (Kate) Anthon.

Although speculations about the poet's life are useful in providing a broad contextual framework, Melissa White raises a cautionary point in "Letter to the Light: Discoveries in Dickinson's Correspondence," in which she demonstrates that such speculations can be completely inaccurate, yet highly influential in their impact, stating that in the end, "the received version of a text determines the critical tradition."[6] Exemplifying her point, she refers to the discovery of the omitted portion of a beautiful letter (L785) Emily wrote to her Norcross cousins on the death of her mother, a letter that reveals new biographical information promoting fresh insight into the circulation of Dickinson's manuscripts, and a reconsideration of past and present editing practices. Specifically, the missing portion of the letter, despite inviting all kinds of speculation regarding Dickinson's relationship with her mother, reveals more about nineteenth-century attitudes toward privacy than anything else.

Dickinson's privacy was a concern not only for the recipients of letters, but for Todd herself, who, though stating her reluctance to expose Dickinson unfairly, declared her intention to portray Dickinson in a more positive light, as she and "some of Emily's friends ... were troubled by what they considered the failure of Amherst people to understand her."[7] Whatever Todd's true ambitions, and whatever editorial practices she carried out to honor her intentions, it would appear that Dickinson herself succeeds in protecting her privacy through her unique epistolary style, described by Agniezska Salska in "Dickinson's Letters" as an achievement that "quite radically and experimentally, put[s] to her own use a pervasive cultural habit" of letter writing (*Handbook*, 166). Throughout all of the letters, Dickinson demonstrates that her correspondents played an important part in the development of her writing so that the traces of their presence are evident in her own words; letters, for Dickinson, are collaborative works that forge relations between individuals. Exhibiting an acute sensitivity to each of her recipients, she conveys a variety of poses that, although derived from her own experience, points away from specific events in her life. Critics Suzanne Juhasz and Cristanne Miller demonstrate the way in which this epistolary technique provides her with control in the various roles she adopts with each recipient: while disguising, she paradoxically reveals her "self."[8] Further, many of the roles she assumes, says Judith Farr in *The Passion of Emily Dickinson*, are derived from artistic and aesthetic representations of her time, so that, for example, "in her allusions to herself as a nun, by her assumption of white and her repeated association of herself with lilies, Emily Dickinson was participating in a finely articulated iconographic tradition."[9]

Farr considers Dickinson's letters as "works of art" in their own right, thus closing the gap between poem and letter as generic forms.[10] Similarly, Martha Nell Smith regards the boundaries between the genres as nonexistent, noting that Dickinson's "self" was not a faithful representation, but rather a performance made up of both fact and fiction.[11] Agnieszka Salska emphasizes the continuous relationship between poem and letter in which each genre informs the other, claiming that the letters "became the territory where she could work out her own style, create her poetic voice, and crystallize the principles of her poetics" (*Handbook*, 168). Messmer's *A Vice for Voices* was the first book-length exploration of her correspondence "as an interpretive unit that can shed fresh light on many aspects of her highly innovative poetics"; Messmer advances "an argument for 'correspondence' (rather than 'poetry') as Dickinson's central form of public artistic expression."[12]

As the generic distinctions between poems and letters have been destabilized, additional resources have emerged. Editorial projects such as the *Dickinson Electronic Archives* promise to challenge early editing practices in a way that embraces manuscript as well as print editions. Cynthia MacKenzie's *A Concordance to the Letters of Emily Dickinson* (2000) provides a useful tool for word and phrase searches; and recently, a collection of essays, *Reading Emily Dickinson's Letters: Critical Essays* (2009), edited by MacKenzie and Jane Donahue Eberwein, take advantage of new resources to offer revisionary interpretations of questions about Dickinson's relationships, views, and art.

Characterized by a dynamic multivocality and an extensive cultural imaginary, then, Dickinson's letters provoke unanswerable questions in a way that reflects the poet's intellectual personality, as her niece Martha Bianchi insightfully observes: "her impatience with detail and what she termed 'mere fact' grew upon her, in her search for truth. It was the principle beyond the truth that she was after, the source of light beyond the pine trees and not only the principle, but its ultimate significance."[13] In Dickinson's famous letters to T. W. Higginson, rich with the poet's oblique statements regarding her poetics, we find significant clues to understanding her rationale for the elliptical quality of her work. In her response to what must have been Higginson's request for a daguerreotype, we see the poet's capricious love of riddle at play, but we also observe her belief that such representative forms risked a loss of vitality, as she states that she does not have a mold because "the Quick wore off those things in a few days" (L268). She offers instead, an impressionistic "word-picture": "I had no portrait, but am small, like the Wren, and my Hair is bold, like the Chestnut Bur - and my eyes, like the Sherry in the Glass, that the Guest leaves - " (L268). Dickinson's letters foreground the haunting effect evident in this example and, as such, demonstrate her aesthetic, as another passage to Higginson signals: "Nature is a Haunted House - but Art - a House that tries to be haunted" (L459A). While a letter attempts to "compensate for corporeal absence,"[14] metonymically, the letter is a representation of the self, the trace of the writer and of the recipient inscribed in a communication with "not only the spectre of the addressee but also with one's own phantom which evolves underneath one's own hand in the very letter one is writing or even in a series of letters, where one letter reinforces the other and can refer to it as witness."[15]

Disappearing into the word, Dickinson haunts her own House of Language, inhabited by her poems and letters. After the death of Charles Wadsworth, reading something by or about him, Dickinson said, "I have had a Letter from another World."[16] As William Decker notes, for Dickinson, a letter need not be sent from the afterlife to assume such a spectral quality, for "so miraculous to her were the communications that traversed the forbidding distances between individuals that she represents the epistolary act as always potentially a species of divine visitation."[17] Offering a related insight, Christopher Benfey notes that Dickinson included the riddle poem "A Route of Evanescence" (F1489 J1463) in seven different letters, suggesting the poem's importance to her.[18] The hummingbird metonymically represents a letter, the exotic "mail from Tunis," of the poem's last line; we, the observers and the readers, can only partially understand its innate mystery in its after-effect, the evanescence of its flight. Indeed, the play between absence and presence that epistolary communication enacts "articulates and substantiates the central paradox of epistolary discourse: that the exchange of personally inscribed texts confirms even as it would mitigate separation."[19] In her consolatory letters, some of the most beautiful in the archive, absence informs the text, yet for Dickinson, language can mitigate the sense of loss and offer a compensatory solace for a letter's recipient. Such is the case in a letter to her sister-in-law, Susan, after the death of Gilbert where she expresses the child's dynamic essence, his "Route of Evanescence," in brilliant images: "He knew no niggard moment - His Life was full of Boon - The Playthings of the Dervish were not so wild as his - No crescent was this Creature - He traveled from the Full - Such soar, but never set - I see him in the Star, and meet his sweet velocity in everything that flies - His Life was like the Bugle, which winds itself away, his Elegy an echo - his Requiem ecstasy - " (L868). Spirit and word converge in a way that, at least temporarily, denies the reality of death. The beauty of this letter arises, as Decker so beautifully states, from Dickinson's awareness "of the absence that letter writing creates in spite of its intention to extend presence ... thereby affirm[ing] the compensatory value of language as well as, more specifically, the motive generosity of epistolary discourse, which she identifies as love and regards as the agent of immortal life.[20] As a brilliant theoretician of letter writing, Dickinson's poetic transformation of its conventions establishes their distinctiveness.

So when Dickinson ends her letter of self-description to Higginson asking, "would this do just as well?" (L268), her question is rhetorical. He - and we - must read in a way that makes this mode of representation sufficient, by accepting the unknown as part of the meaning. Would the emergence of new letters satisfy our desire to "know" the poet and her work? Probably not: scholars and archivists circulate their own letters to the world by interpreting and reinterpreting Dickinson's words that changing contexts, like the spinning wheel of "Circumference," generate. Any move to declare a conclusive "truth" regarding the Dickinson archive is impossible, though we may become convinced for a time, through repetition and empirical argument, of the veracity of a specific fact. But the "truth" lies in our ongoing pursuit, as the meanings we derive from the traces of meaning in Dickinson's letters offer us a glimpse of the woman as well as of the poet who saw the hummingbird as a "Route of Evanescence," a letter as a bulletin from "Immortality." The collaborative nature of epistolarity, based as it is on sequential messages, parallels the reader's part in the creation of meaning of a poem as Dickinson sees it. By extension, the circulating "letters" of scholars and readers continue to add to the archive as they generate possibilities of interpretation and thereby enrich our understanding of Dickinson's epistolary project. For in the end, the "archive is not something done and dusted, a thing of the past. On the contrary, the archive is never closed."[21] Dickinson's archive remains a haunted house that by its very nature ensures her immortality.

NOTES

1 Martha Nell Smith, *Rowing in Eden: Rereading Emily Dickinson* (Austin: University of Texas Press, 1992), 148.
2 Jacques Derrida, *Archive Fever*, trans. Eric Prevowitz (Chicago: University of Chicago Press, 1995), 17.
3 Millicent Todd Bingham, *Ancestors' Brocades: The Literary Debut of Emily Dickinson* (New York: Harper and Brothers, 1945), 247.
4 Ibid., 248.
5 Marietta Messmer, *A Vice for Voices: Reading Emily Dickinson's Correspondences* (Amherst: University of Massachusetts Press, 2001), 77.
6 Melissa White, "Letter to the Light: Discoveries in Dickinson's Correspondence," *EDJ*, *16*.1 (2007), 6.
7 Millicent Todd Bingham, *Emily Dickinson's Home: Letters of Edward Dickinson and His Family* (New York: Harper, 1955), 374.
8 Summarized in Messmer's critical overview, *Vice for Voices*, 12–13.
9 Judith Farr, *The Passion of Emily Dickinson* (Englewood Cliffs, NJ: Prentice-Hall, 1966), 39.
10 Judith Farr, quoted in Messmer, *Vice for Voices*, 15.
11 Summarized in Messmer, *Vice for Voices*, 15.
12 Messmer, *Vice for Voices*, 7.
13 Martha Dickinson Bianchi, *Emily Dickinson Face to Face: Unpublished Letters with Notes and Reminiscences* (Boston: Houghton Mifflin, 1932), 68.
14 Elizabeth Hewitt, *Correspondence and American Literature, 1770–1865* (Cambridge: Cambridge University Press, 2004), 155.
15 Janet Altman, *Epistolarity: Approaches to a Form* (Columbus: Ohio State University, 2007), 2.
16 William Merrill Decker, *Epistolary Practices: Letter Writing in America before Telecommunications* (Chapel Hill: University of North Carolina Press, 1998), 173.
17 Ibid., 173.
18 Christopher Benfey, *A Summer of Hummingbirds: Love, Art, and Scandal in the Intersecting Worlds of Emily Dickinson, Mark Twain, Harriet Beecher Stowe, and Martin Johnson Heade* (New York: Penguin Press, 2008), 208.
19 Ibid., 46–7.
20 Ibid., 175.
21 Derrida, *Archive Fever*, 10.

CHAPTER 30

Critical History I: 1890–1955

Theo Davis

In the Preface to the 1890 *Poems by Emily Dickinson*, Thomas Wentworth Higginson urged readers not to be taken aback by Dickinson. Her work's "seemingly whimsical or even rugged frame" offered "flashes of wholly original and profound insight" and "words and phrases exhibiting an extraordinary vividness."[1] Plenty of reviewers took Higginson's assurance and lauded Dickinson as an eccentric whose verse had a "weird power and even fascination," but stern ones such as Thomas Bailey Aldrich could not forgive her for "set[ting] at defiance the laws of gravitation and grammar."[2] Although Dickinson received some attention in the early twentieth century from critics interested in imagist and symbolist poetry, including Conrad Aiken and Amy Lowell, it was the work of R. P. Blackmur, Allen Tate, Yvor Winters, and George Whicher that established her as a major poet in the 1930s. They set the terms that would characterize criticism through the 1940s and 1950s.

The story of Dickinson's march to acclaim is the focus of critical histories of this period by Caesar Blake and Carlton Wells, Klaus Lubbers, and Richard Sewall.[3] They cast that story as the rise of modern academic critical methods capable of understanding Dickinson's greatness – as those enchanted by "weird power" were not – and make critical history a labor of critical legitimation. More recent considerations by J. Willis Buckingham, Marietta Messmer, and Virginia Jackson read the same story as a fall: academic criticism delegitimated nonprofessional readers while erasing the network of personal affiliations in which Dickinson's manuscripts circulated.[4] In Jackson's influential view, academic criticism foisted on Dickinson an ideal of the lyric poem as a disembodied, timeless voicing of the soul – without links to the author, her paper and handwriting, or her social and historical context. But even these critiques partake of critical history as critical heritage, as their interest in critical history lies in its ability to reveal problematic concepts that remain essential to the discipline. Contrary to the story of the development and solidification of academic criticism that previous histories assess, I argue that signal critical problems persist from the 1890s into the 1930s and beyond. Moreover, the canonical New Critical readings of Blackmur, Tate, and Winters do not contain the exclusive focus on close textual analysis of the lyric poem that is so regularly attributed to them. In the criticism this essay considers, the boundary between linguistic analysis and historical inquiry is barely meaningful, and academic and public criticism intersect with ease, as do close reading and critical flights of fancy. Rather than tracing a developmental trajectory, this essay suggests that praiseful and harsh treatments of Dickinson, from the 1890s through the 1950s, continually struggle to contact and engage with Dickinson's writing. The terms of that struggle indicate an essential breakage between thought and sensory experience brought on in and by Dickinson. In making this argument, I suggest that the interest of critical history need not be as the origin story of our discipline: the unfamiliarity of other intellectual contexts can help us see Dickinson differently, and force us to reconsider our own time's critical frameworks.

In the 1890s, an industrious metaphoricity cuts across different estimations of Dickinson. *The Christian Intelligencer* had it that "Most of our diamonds, opals, emeralds, being polished and set after the best manner of art, how unwontedly one enjoys a handful of them in rough … just such jewels by the handful Miss Dickinson has left us."[5] To Arlo Bates it seemed "as if this gentle poet had the blood of some gentle and simple Indian ancestress in her veins still in an unadulterated current."[6] Lilian Whiting "contemplat[ed] the beautiful idea enshrined like a diamond in its shattered matrix of discolored quartz."[7] Even Aldrich groused via imagery: her "ideas totter and toddle, not having learned to walk."[8]

The metaphoricity is part of a criticism that works through assertion and quotation, linked by image and outburst ("What a strange and gnomelike presence lurks in all her lines!").[9] Developing a more rigorous method was the point of the New Criticism's turn to textual analysis (also called formalism) in the 1930s. As Wimsatt and Beardsley wrote, "[t]he more specific the account of the emotion induced by a poem, the more nearly it will be an account of the reasons for the emotion, the poem itself."[10] Sighing over "a strange and gnomelike presence" would be, to the New Critics, avoiding the work of "account[ing]" for a poem. And yet, the emergent formalist criticism of Dickinson does not entirely abandon the earlier mode of quotation followed by expostulation or metaphoric redescription.

Yvor Winters's title, "Emily Dickinson and the Limits of Judgment" may sound austere, but Winters is not doing very close reading. He notes that a poem has "a number of terms representing familiar abstractions" but trusts us to see them for ourselves, and elsewhere asserts "There is great power in the phrasing of the remainder of [a] poem" – and then just quotes it.[11] "Farther in summer than the birds" is, he writes, "one of the most deeply moving and most unforgettable poems in my own experience; I have the feeling of having lived in its immediate presence for many years."[12] To be in the poem's "immediate presence," Winters turns not to close reading but to testimony about his experience.

New Criticism's famous ideal of a poem conjoining thought and language in a self-sufficient work is linked to a broader principle that can, ironically, cut against that poetic ideal. This is a principle that thought must be deeply connected to character and world. An instance of that principle at work is Winters's appeal to the moral clarity that Dickinson's "New England heritage" bequeathed her, with a "natural[ness]" that finesses genetic and contextual determinism.[13] It is also why he rejected Dickinson's poems on experience after death: they imply that poetry could be severed from human experience, both actual and possible. He finds such poems "forced and somewhat theoretical," worked in the vein of "an idea, not as something experienced."[14] On the same principle, Allen Tate's notorious comment that her work contained "no thought as such at all" was meant as praise (he says the same of Shakespeare).[15] Tate argues that Dickinson's "is a poetry of ideas" embedded in culture and identity, not taken as objects of detached assessment such as an "opinion of the New Deal."[16] Like Winters, Tate saw the United States of the 1930s as a culture of relativism, lacking in essential beliefs. Both critics opposed such relativism with an account of beliefs that are lodged in one's identity: Tate celebrates Dickinson for "an ingrained philosophy which is fundamental."[17] Such fundamentalism – Winters uses the term absolutism – is, however, a kind of relativism because for each critic it entails an unbreakable bond between belief and a specific personal and cultural identity. Whereas the New Critics have been taken to task for claiming an objectivity without ideological taint, these essays are actively calling for ideology. This is ideology not as a misrepresentation of reality, but as a climate of beliefs that one experiences *as* reality, rather than one in which beliefs are things among which one can pick and choose, or even argue. To the New Critics, seeing thought as wedded to concrete experience is what it means to see poetry as historical. In classic New Critical fashion, Tate praises how in one poem, "Every image is … fused with the central idea."[18] But this did not sever the poem from history, as art does not "rise in a vacuum."[19] Rather, Dickinson's ability to "fuse[]" idea and image is grounded in how "deeply" her beliefs are "imbedded in her character."[20] Here, the ideal of the poem fused to itself stands in the service of an argument for the fusion of beliefs to geographical, cultural, and historical location.

In "Emily Dickinson: Notes on Prejudice and Fact" (1937), R. P. Blackmur counters Tate by averring that one can never say exactly how a context informs a poem. But for Blackmur experience and a version of history remain relevant, as when he notes that among her poems, "what differs is the degree or amount of experience actualized in the verse."[21] "Renunciation / Is a piercing virtue" "rises ... out of a whole way of life ... felt suddenly at what can be called nothing less than a supremely sophisticated level."[22] That feeling for life persists into a feeling for language, as the "directly physical" quality of "piercing" makes the poem's first lines work.[23] Blackmur continues, "Some function of the word *pierce* precipitates a living intrinsic relation between renunciation and virtue; it is what makes the phrase incandesce."[24] It is strange to see Blackmur use the figurative "incandesce" because he mocks the metaphoricity of earlier criticism by invoking a reader who so loves Dickinson that he sees no need to understand her: "here is great poetry – we know what *that* is! A chalice, a lily, a sea-change."[25]

The New Critics do make more specific attempts to locate why Dickinson compels attention, but we still have Winters's feeling of having lived with a poem: Tate's aside that "after Emerson New England literature tastes like a sip of cambric tea,"[26] and Blackmur's "incandescence." Stranger still is Winters's use of quotation without discussion, or Blackmur's insistence on the physicality of the word "pierce," in which a repetitive deictic gesture unwittingly betrays the difficulty of locating effects in the words that produce them. The New Critics may have been right to lament their predecessors' fast and loose way of writing around literature, with judgment and opining interspersed with quotations, and little to cast a line between them. But how is that line to be cast?

New Criticism had no strong answer to that question because it was not really a theoretical position. It was pragmatic and prescriptive, urging critics to spend more time looking at the words before writing about them. Part of the pragmatism is that it never rejected thinking historically, biographically, ethically, politically, or even personally. (Even the avowedly theoretical framing of New Criticism in Wimsatt and Beardsley's "The Intentional Fallacy" and "The Affective Fallacy" is countered by a pragmatic flexibility at the heart of each essay.) But the lack of a strong account of the ability of language to speak for itself is most profoundly evident when the readings bring us right to the gap between word and analysis:

the gap looks even more daunting when one seeks to bridge rather than to leap it.

The pragmatism is also implicit in the fact that increased textual analysis was not solely the domain of the New Critics. For example, Genevieve Taggard's *The Life and Mind of Emily Dickinson* initiates a dual plea for biographical study and textual analysis through a poem by Taggard herself:

> Go to her verse, reader,
> ...
> Read her own page, reader.
> Wait ... read the great verse. Do not look up if you think you hear her.
> Do not for a moment stir.
> She will come near, confidently nearer,
> Even as I write this, she is here.[27]

Taggard is a very close reader: at one point she delineates how "'Inebriate of air am I' plays with the delicate *i* sound in the first word, repeats it in 'air' and then grounds it in the word '*I*.'"[28] But she pivots right into a rhetorical invitation: "Will my reader read the rest of the poem with analytical eyes?"[29] A sign of the lack of boundary between popular and academic literary criticism in this period, and of the New Critics' openness to mixing close reading with other methods, is that Tate called this an "excellent book."[30]

Another instance of the combination of close reading and biography is George Whicher's *This Was a Poet*. Whicher traces how Dickinson "discar[ded] in effort after effort what was too personal and poignant until only the pure quintessence of impassioned thought remained" (Whicher, 284). This is peculiar: an intentionalist account of how the author came to write poetry that did not speak of herself. Whicher believes a poem ought to be complete in itself, and yet he needs to know if Dickinson's love poems were "figments of the imagination" or "reports ... of what she had actually experienced" in order to judge them (Whicher, 81). Is this just theoretical incoherence, failing to see that biographical and historical explanations are opposed to textual ones, or is the mistake in thinking such methods are theoretically opposed? Although I take it to be the latter, the question must be settled elsewhere; here I will turn to how Dickinson's work resisted the very union of thought and experience (whether in life or in poetry) that made it seem important that her work be based in lived experience, and that the poem's thought be fully embodied in the word.

We can see this resistance in Dickinson through Whicher's own reading. He deems her an empiricist relentlessly attending to "the hard facts of experience" – but she's also uninterested in external reality, "hardly notic[ing] trees at all." (Whicher, 297, 257). Noting the jarring between mind and world in her work, Whicher observes, "It was vital to her method to bring fact into paradoxical conjunction with thought, not so much to merge or reconcile the two as to establish their dramatic interplay" (Whicher, 291). This suggests that Dickinson was acutely interested in thought's relation to sensory experience, but less invested than the critic in cementing that relationship.

In the 1890s, critics felt that something powerful came out of Dickinson's poetry, but it was not quite locatable in its rough words and form. In contrast, the New Critics argued that when she went awry it was in her willingness to take words beyond what she knew (Winters censured her "distressing" "lightness," and Blackmur frowned at her "irresponsible" uses of language).[31] The first generation found a potent reading experience that could not be entirely justified by the poetry, and a thought in the poetry that seemed poorly connected to its material form. The New Critics found language that could stray too far from the author's experience, and a reading experience that could, again, not always be connected to the language of the poem. These sometimes negative assessments of Dickinson actually bring out the brilliant and disturbing ways that Dickinson does not suture thought to sensation: by not fully connecting her thought to words or her poetry to her life, and by creating poems that prompt experiences that are not fully explicable by analysis of those poems.

But the early critics found the connection of poetry to experience so essential that even Dickinson's seemingly wan life had to be defended for the poetry to be accepted. Tate maintained, "All pity for Miss Dickinson's 'starved life' is misdirected. Her life was one of the richest and deepest ever lived on this continent"; Richard Chase had it that Dickinson's isolated life was "yet one of the notable public acts of our history."[32] Whicher explained that despite her failure to be interested in trees, Dickinson was a poet of rich internal experience, making "field notes" on consciousness (Whicher, 293). Rebecca Patterson's *The Riddle of Emily Dickinson* also stresses the origin of Dickinson's work in a "real" relationship, with Kate Anthon.[33] Seeing Dickinson as a lesbian sets Patterson apart from all other critics in these decades, but so does the way she links the life to the poetry. Patterson observes how the use of direct address obscures the gender of the beloved, and she discusses Dickinson's inversions of gendered pronouns with a highly unusual sense that poetry might successfully break from life experience.

The willful estrangement that Patterson considers may be a version of the apparent incompletion that rankled the earliest critics. Bates wrote that Dickinson could "have enriched the language with lyrics which would have endured to the end of time," but due to her lack of "technical skill" she had only "put upon paper things which" show "what she might have been."[34] Dickinson "put upon paper things" of an uncertain identity, which might be "a new species of art" but were not lyric poems.[35] To Aldrich, "several of the quatrains are curiously touching, they have such a pathetic air of yearning to be poems"; others were "disjecta membra," scattered fragments of ancient pottery.[36] Dickinson's writing seemed at once the ruin of lyric poetry, and its undergrown beginnings. Given the recent discussion of how the editing and typesetting of Dickinson's work mangled it into lyric poetry, it is striking that here even the notorious early editing and printing of Dickinson largely failed to make her look like a lyric poet. Even Higginson could find only "glimpses of a lyric strain."[37]

And as early as the 1891 *Poems*, the uncertain identity of what Dickinson wrote was linked to the manuscripts. In that edition, Mabel Loomis Todd observes that "many" manuscripts "bear evidence of having been thrown off at white heat," without "revision."[38] She mentions their "perplexing foot-notes, affording large choices of words and phrases. And in the copies which [Dickinson] sent to friends, sometimes one form, sometimes another, is found to have been used."[39] Todd frames the problem as one of poems awaiting completion: "They should be regarded in many cases as merely the first strong and suggestive sketches of an artist, intended to be embodied at some time in the finished picture."[40] Here, emphasizing the manuscripts is a way to excuse the work's failure to settle into final, "embodied" form.

But then, observing the changes in the handwriting – "as she advanced in breadth of thought, it grew bolder and more abrupt, until in her latest years each letter stood distinct and separate" – Todd nods to the visual power of the manuscripts.[41] Since "The effect of a page of her more recent manuscript is exceedingly quaint and strong," Todd included a "fac-simile."[42] Here Todd uses the manuscript as if the handwritten paper might be the finished form that the words did not provide. As recent Dickinson criticism often offers the manuscript-object as the privileged opposite to the edited and printed poem, it is worth noticing that here the embrace of the manuscript aligned with the wish for a finely embodied poem.

That connection survives into F. O. Matthiessen's discussion of the manuscripts in the 1940s. He objected that Millicent Todd Bingham printed one poem "without variants, even though the facsimile yields … at least a dozen choices for its final line."[43] He felt that such manuscripts were "not finished," and did not show "what she finally intended."⁴⁴ Recommending a printing "with the variants noted not too distractingly," Matthiessen writes that we "must print each manuscript *in toto* as the special case it is."⁴⁵ Even as he laments the partiality of what she left, he argues that we can use it "to follow her … to her few delicate yet full-blooded marriages between spirit and form."⁴⁶ He opposes the good, "full-blooded" poems to the unmarried fragments, but he also aligns the value of the handwritten page with that of the self-complete poem. Each is a route to grounding thought in a material form.

There is little attempt in Tate, Blackmur, or Winters to promote a poetry circulating in a timeless, disembodied vacuum. Their goal was embodiment, the lodging of thought in the material of life, and of words – the "full-blooded marriage[] between spirit and form." The press to embody Dickinson in manuscript form paralleled the New Critical prizing of lyrical and ideological embodiment. Recent critical insistence that we abandon the printed text and the concept of the lyric poem to embrace the manuscripts may only partake of a continuing critical desire to put Dickinson together in material form, and thus resist that breakage of thought and sensation which is central to her work.

By 1954, deep into the era of New Critical dominance, Donald Thackrey wrote a book committed mostly to close reading of Dickinson. And yet even Thackrey writes that "There's a certain slant of light":

> …is one of those rare poems which are experienced, never completely understood. It seems to me impossible to read the line without feeling a tragic, serene emotion which must be akin to the melancholy about which Keats writes. Emily Dickinson's poem is much less specific than the "Ode on Melancholy" in describing the nature of the emotion, but her poem captures and transmits the experience itself.⁴⁷

He praises Dickinson for conveying an experience that she failed to put into words, and that he apparently cannot analyze. Perhaps the endurance of such arpeggios of critical testimony in Dickinson criticism is a necessary way of talking about what pertains to a poem but cannot be identified with or in it. "What a strange and gnomelike presence lurks in all her lines!" suggests, after all, that what matters does not belong.

NOTES

1 Thomas Wentworth Higginson, Preface, *Poems by Emily Dickinson*, ed. Mabel Loomis Todd and Higginson (Boston: Roberts Brothers, 1890), in *Reception*, 14.

2 "Volumes of Poems," *Book Buyer* 8 (January 1892), in *Reception*, 284 [Thomas Bailey Aldrich], "In *Re* Emily Dickinson," *Atlantic Monthly* 69 (January 1892), in *Reception*, 283–4.
3 Richard B. Sewall, "Introduction," *Emily Dickinson: A Collection of Critical Essays* (Englewood Cliffs, NJ: Prentice-Hall, 1963); Caesar Blake and Carlton Wells, *The Recognition of Emily Dickinson: Selected Criticism since 1890* (Ann Arbor: University of Michigan Press, 1964); Klaus Lubbers, *Emily Dickinson: The Critical Revolution* (Ann Arbor: The University of Michigan, 1968).
4 Buckingham, "Introduction," *Reception*, xi–xxiii; Marietta Messmer, "Dickinson's Critical Reception," *Handbook*, 299–322; Virginia Jackson, *Dickinson's Misery: A Theory of Lyric Reading* (Princeton, NJ: Princeton University Press, 2005), 92–100.
5 [Denis Wortman], "The Reading Room," *The Christian Intelligencer* 62 (May 27, 1891), in *Reception*, 147.
6 [Arlo Bates], "Books and Authors," *Boston Sunday Courier* 96 (November 23, 1890), in *Reception*, 29.
7 [Lilian Whiting], "Emily Dickinson's Poems," *Boston Beacon* (December 13, 1890), in *Reception*, 55.
8 Aldrich, "In *Re* Emily Dickinson," in *Reception*, 283.
9 Bliss Carman, "A Note on Emily Dickinson," *Boston Evening Transcript* (November 21, 1896), in *Reception*, 508.
10 W. K. Wimsatt and Monroe C. Beardsley, "The Affective Fallacy," *The Verbal Icon: Studies in the Meaning of Poetry* (Lexington: The University of Kentucky Press, 1954), 34.
11 Yvor Winters, "Emily Dickinson and the Limits of Judgment," *Maule's Curse: Seven Studies in the History of American Obscurantism* (Norfolk, CT: New Directions, 1938), 156.
12 Ibid., 160. Because all of the criticism considered here refers to pre-Johnson editions of the texts, and inhabits a world before Dickinson's poems were numbered, I refer to the poems by the titles the critics use rather than by subsequent citation systems.
13 Ibid., 165.
14 Ibid., 154.
15 Allen Tate, "New England Culture and Emily Dickinson" (*Symposium*, April, 1932), in *Recognition*, 164.
16 Ibid., 153.
17 Ibid., 153.
18 Ibid., 160.
19 Ibid., 163.
20 Ibid., 162.
21 R. P. Blackmur, "Emily Dickinson: Notes on Prejudice and Fact," *Language as Gesture: Essays in Poetry* (New York: Harcourt, Brace and Company, 1952), 36.
22 Ibid., 35.
23 Ibid., 36.

24 Ibid., 37.
25 Ibid., 27.
26 Tate, "New England," 156.
27 Genevieve Taggard, *The Life and Mind of Emily Dickinson* (New York: Alfred A. Knopf, 1930), viii.
28 Ibid., 269–70.
29 Ibid., 270.
30 Tate, "New England," in *Recognition*, 157.
31 Winters, "Emily Dickinson," 152; Blackmur, "Emily Dickinson," 42.
32 Tate, "New England," 158; Richard Chase, *Emily Dickinson* (William Sloane Associates, 1951), 269.
33 Rebecca Patterson, *The Riddle of Emily Dickinson* (Cambridge, MA: Riverside Press, Houghton Mifflin, 1951), 8.
34 Bates, "Books and Authors," in *Reception*, 33.
35 Ibid., 33.
36 Aldrich, "In *Re* Emily Dickinson," in *Reception*, 283, 284.
37 Higginson, "Preface," in *Reception*, 14.
38 Mabel Loomis Todd, "Preface" to *Poems by Emily Dickinson. Second Series*, ed. T. W. Higginson and Mabel Loomis Todd (Boston: Roberts Brothers, 1891); in *Reception*, 236.
39 Ibid., 236.
40 Ibid., 236.
41 Ibid., 237.
42 Ibid., 237.
43 F. O. Matthiessen, "The Private Poet: Emily Dickinson," *Kenyon Review* II (Autumn, 1945), in *Recognition*, 231.
44 Ibid., 231.
45 Ibid., 231.
46 Ibid., 235.
47 Donald E. Thackrey, *Emily Dickinson's Approach to Poetry* (Lincoln: University of Nebraska Press, 1954), 77.

CHAPTER 31

Critical History II: 1955 to the Present
Magdalena Zapedowska

Thomas Johnson's 1955 edition of *The Poems of Emily Dickinson* began a new era in Dickinson studies. For the first time, Johnson collected all known poems with variant readings and arranged them chronologically by his own dating, preserving Dickinson's unorthodox spelling, punctuation, and capitalization. This edition, followed by *The Letters of Emily Dickinson* three years later, cemented the poet's canonical status and inspired a wave of major critical studies during the 1960s. Since then Dickinson's recognition has continued to grow, leading to a steady outpouring of criticism; new scholarly editions of Dickinson's writings; translations of her work into many languages; and the founding, in 1988, of the Emily Dickinson International Society, which sponsors *The Emily Dickinson Journal* and an academic conference. The critical understanding of the poet has changed dramatically in the past fifty years. The Dickinson of the 1960s was isolated from the world and indifferent to current events. She explored timeless metaphysical questions in a poetry that transcended her culture and did not develop. Albeit influenced by Calvinism and Transcendentalism, she wrote in a fragmented protomodernist style, which made her difficult to situate in American literary history. By contrast, today's Dickinson engages with her historical, political, social, and cultural environments in ways that reflect her gender and class status, is deeply affected by the Civil War, draws strength from her relationships with other women, and absorbs the motifs, sentiments, and forms of nineteenth-century popular American poetry. Not only is she immersed in history, but her views, style, and composition practices change over time. Her place in literary tradition is among other nineteenth-century genteel American women poets and, more broadly, within nineteenth-century transatlantic poetic culture.

My goal in this essay is to trace the evolution of Dickinson criticism since 1955, in particular the shift of emphasis from Dickinson's detachment to her connections with history, popular culture, and other people. I present this movement as a series of critical turns, each of them contributing to a more situated and more externalized image of the poet. The formalist turn of the 1960s focused on Dickinson's poetic technique and the patterns defining her style. With the feminist turn in the late 1970s critical attention shifted to the implications of gender for Dickinson's poetry and life. Building on feminist criticism, the manuscript turn of the 1990s raised questions about the material circumstances of Dickinson's writing and the biographical context of her manuscript circulation, in particular her love for Sue Gilbert. The historicist turn, whose different incarnations draw on cultural history, feminist recovery work, and marxist sociology of literature, has called attention to Dickinson's embeddedness in her cultural milieu, demonstrating how her poetry participates in contemporary cultural trends and how it reflects the historical, political, economic, and social circumstances of her life. It has also inspired interest in Dickinson's development as a poet. Finally, the turn to the reader has focused on Dickinson's connections with her audience, both historical and implied, her forms of poetic address, her demand for reader participation, and the concrete communicative function of her writings. The critical turns in Dickinson studies are reflected in biographical scholarship, discussed in a separate section. Although my approach may overemphasize similarities between critical works, it has the advantage of highlighting the changing direction of Dickinson criticism and the cumulative nature of our understanding of Dickinson's work. Because my essay continues Marietta Messmer's excellent survey of Dickinson criticism through the mid-1990s (*Handbook*, 299–322), the works I discuss in greatest detail are book-length studies published in the last fifteen years. For a thorough overview of criticism until 2007, I refer readers to Fred White's *Approaching Emily Dickinson* (2008).

BIOGRAPHY

Biographical scholarship of Dickinson has developed in tandem with literary criticism. The first authoritative biography, Richard Sewall's *Life of Emily Dickinson* (1974), presents the poet through her relationships with family members and friends rather than telling the story of her life. Sewall's nonchronological approach parallels the critical view that Dickinson's poetry did not change, while his meticulous reconstruction of Dickinson's cultural environment paves the ground for contextual studies of her poetry, and his emphasis on relationships anticipates critical interest in Dickinson's human connections as the subject of her writings and the concrete historical frame for understanding her work. The 1970s and 1980s saw an explosion of psychobiographical studies, including John Cody's influential *After Great Pain: The Inner Life of Emily Dickinson* (1971). These studies tend to have a strong negative focus, interpreting Dickinson's poetry as compensation for loss, frustrated desire, unresolved crisis, or mental illness.[1] Feminist concerns underlie Cynthia Griffin Wolff's *Emily Dickinson* (1986), an intellectual biography that focuses on the poet's rebellion against the patriarchal God of Calvinism. With the historicist turn of the 1990s came renewed interest in the historical circumstances of Dickinson's life, leading to the publication of several biographical studies during the 2000s. The most important of these, Alfred Habegger's *My Wars Are Laid Away in Books: The Life of Emily Dickinson* (2001) highlights the chronological development of Dickinson's life, personality, and poetry as influenced by her environment from family dynamics to cultural milieu, with emphasis on schooling and the family's economic instability. Two recent works extend Sewall's focus on relationships: Brenda Wineapple's *White Heat: The Friendship of Emily Dickinson and Thomas Wentworth Higginson* (2009) and Aife Murray's primarily biographical *Maid as Muse: How Servants Changed Emily Dickinson's Life and Language* (2009), which examines the Irish maid Margaret Maher's influence on Dickinson's class and ethnic attitudes and her composition practices. Lyndall Gordon, in *Lives Like Loaded Guns: Emily Dickinson and Her Family Feuds* (2010), shares many concerns of manuscript scholarship, highlighting the consequences of the Austin and Mabel affair for the posthumous editing, publication, archiving, and biographical representations of the poet.

THE FORMALIST TURN

Following Johnson's variorum edition of the poems, critical studies published in the 1960s, such as Charles Anderson's *Emily Dickinson's Poetry: Stairway of Surprise* (1960), sought to assess Dickinson's poetic project as a whole and understand the influences that shaped her poetic vision. Formal analysis was particularly suited to the first of these goals. The formalist turn, marked by David Porter's *Art of Emily Dickinson's Early Poetry* (1966), called attention to the language, prosody, and poetic structure of Dickinson's work. Extending the New Critical approach, formalist critics treat the poem as an autonomous aesthetic object and rely on close reading to reveal the poem's internal tension. Through the analysis of stylistic and structural features, they aim to identify Dickinson's poetic method (Weisbuch's analogy, Hagenbüchle's metonymy) and the defining quality or theme of her poetry (Weisbuch's scenelessness, Porter's quest for fulfillment, Salska's unresolved confrontation between the mind and the unknown).[2] Most formalist critics see Dickinson as a post-Emersonian poet whose vision originates in fragmentation and loss. This emphasis on fragmentation is especially strong in studies that use formal analysis to deconstruct Dickinson's poetic project: Sharon Cameron's *Lyric Time: Dickinson and the Limits of Genre* (1979) and David Porter's *Dickinson: The Modern Idiom* (1981). Two later studies integrate formal analysis with a feminist or cultural perspective: Cristanne Miller in *Emily Dickinson: A Poet's Grammar* (1987) demonstrates how Dickinson manipulates syntax to achieve compression, a stylistic feature that disrupts patriarchal norms. In *Positive as Sound: Emily Dickinson's Rhyme* (1990) Judy Jo Small examines Dickinson's use of rhyme in the context of her musical culture and literary tradition.

The formalist turn has had an enduring impact on Dickinson studies. Its findings about Dickinson's poetic technique, language, personae, and structural patterns have been assimilated, reinterpreted, and contested by later critics, and its method of formally astute close reading has remained an effective tool for understanding Dickinson's complex poetry. Recent years have seen revived interest in the formal features of Dickinson's poems. Scholarship by Cristanne Miller, Faith Barrett, and Eliza Richards combines the formalist approach with historicist study of nineteenth-century prosody, models of authorship, and Civil War periodical culture.[3] On the other end of the current formalist spectrum stands Helen Vendler's *Dickinson: Selected Poems and Commentaries* (2010) with its New Critical model of reading poems as self-contained aesthetic units.

THE FEMINIST TURN

Heralded by Adrienne Rich's groundbreaking essay "Vesuvius at Home: The Power of Emily Dickinson" (1975) and Sandra Gilbert and Susan Gubar's *Madwoman in the Attic: The Woman Writer and the Nineteenth-Century Literary Imagination* (1979), the feminist turn revolutionized Dickinson studies by demonstrating the significance of gender for the poet's life and art. Feminist investigations of the sources of Dickinson's female creativity, her position as a nineteenth-century woman poet in a patriarchal culture, and her gendered relation to language and literary tradition reinterpret many insights of formalist criticism while amending its neglect of gender issues. The feminist turn occurred in several stages.[4] The first wave, begun by Rich and Gilbert and Gubar, accentuated Dickinson's enraged rebellion against patriarchal structures and the conflict between her conventional identity as a woman and her creative identity as a poet. The second wave shifted attention from biographical reference to questions of language and representation. Following Margaret Homans's *Women Writers and Poetic Identity* (1980), studies by Joanne Feit Diehl, Suzanne Juhasz, Cristanne Miller, and Mary Loeffelholz draw on deconstruction in analyzing Dickinson's manipulation of language to disrupt patriarchal discourse, her gendered pursuit of knowledge in language, and her estrangement from the masculine romantic tradition.[5] Cheryl Walker's *Nightingale's Burden: Women Poets and American Culture Before 1900* (1982) initiated a third stage in Dickinson's feminist reception, which identifies the themes or techniques Dickinson shares with other nineteenth-century American women writers. This feminist-contextual approach, refined by Joanne Dobson in *Dickinson and the Strategies of Reticence* (1989), is extended by later critics who variously situate Dickinson among her female contemporaries. Finally, Paula Bennett's *Emily Dickinson: Woman Poet* (1990) and Martha Nell Smith's *Rowing in Eden: Rereading Emily Dickinson* (1992) reemphasize the biographical reference of Dickinson's writings, exploring her lesbian identity, her relationship with Sue Gilbert, and her gendered manuscript practices. The insights of feminist criticism have become a fundamental component of Dickinson scholarship of the 1990s and 2000s, which integrates questions of gender with literary, cultural, and sociohistorical concerns.

THE MANUSCRIPT TURN

While the first critical study of Dickinson's handwriting was Edith Wylder's *The Last Face: Emily Dickinson's Manuscripts* (1971), manuscript scholarship emerged in the wake of R. W. Franklin's facsimile edition of *The Manuscript Books of Emily Dickinson* (1981). Emphasizing the materiality of Dickinson's texts, scholars such as Martha Nell Smith, Ellen Louise Hart, Marta Werner, and Paul Crumbley contend that Dickinson played with the visual aspects of her manuscripts, such as lineation, calligraphy, and the arrangement of words on the paper, and that, by embedding poems in letters, she undermined the boundary between the two genres. Dickinson's correspondence and manuscript books, Smith argues in *Rowing in Eden* (1992), constituted an alternative form of publication outside the conventions of print. Consequently, manuscript scholars critique standard print editions of Dickinson as inaccurate and propose alternative ways of representing her writings, whether in print or in electronic archives. Manuscript study and historicism converge in Virginia Jackson's *Dickinson's Misery: A Theory of Lyric Reading* (2005), an argument from the late correspondence and drafts that Dickinson did not write lyric poetry but wrote for specific historical recipients, and Alexandra Socarides's *Dickinson Unbound: Paper, Process, Poetics* (2012), which traces the development of Dickinson's manuscript practices over time. By situating Dickinson in the material context of her writing, manuscript scholarship has called attention to her composition and circulation practices and inspired lively debates about the identity of a Dickinson poem. The claims of manuscript scholars have been contested by Cristanne Miller, especially in "The Sound of Shifting Paradigms, or Hearing Dickinson in the Twenty-First Century" (2003), and by Domhnall Mitchell in *Measures of Possibility: Emily Dickinson's Manuscripts* (2005), an empirical study of the manuscripts' visual features. Both critics assert that Dickinson conceived of her poetry in aural rather than visual terms and observed the distinction between poetry and prose.

Franklin's painstaking reconstruction of Dickinson's manuscript books, or fascicles, led to questions about the intentionality of their arrangement. Ruth Miller's *The Poetry of Emily Dickinson* (1968) was the first study to postulate a narrative pattern in the fascicles. Dorothy Huff Oberhaus's *Emily Dickinson's Fascicles: Method and Meaning* (1995) also interprets the fascicles as a coherent narrative, of a Christian spiritual pilgrimage culminating in conversion. From a poststructuralist perspective, Sharon Cameron in *Choosing Not Choosing: Dickinson's Fascicles* (1992) argues that Dickinson's poems are not discrete but that a poem's identity is extended and destabilized by variant words and by the fascicle context, in which poems function as variants of each other. More recently, in *Reading the Fascicles of Emily Dickinson* (2003) Eleanor Elson Heginbotham proposes that Dickinson acted as editor of her own poetry books and examines how poems repeated in a second fascicle acquire different meaning in each fascicle context.

THE HISTORICIST TURN

Barton St. Armand's discussion of Dickinson's immersion in the folk, popular, and elite strands of American Victorianism in *Emily Dickinson and Her Culture: The Soul's Society* and Shira Wolosky's analysis of the poet's response to the Civil War in *Emily Dickinson: A Voice of War*, both published in 1984, anticipated a wave of scholarship that seeks to position Dickinson more firmly in her place and time. Recent essay collections such as Vivian Pollak's *Historical Guide to Emily Dickinson* (2003) and

Martha Nell Smith and Mary Loeffelholz's *Companion to Emily Dickinson* (2008) demonstrate the poet's immersion in the fabric of history, including her deep engagement with the Civil War – a major topic in the criticism of the past few years. On one end of the historicist spectrum are the marxist approaches that focus on the economic, material, and political contexts of Dickinson's poetry, demonstrating how it reflects the systems of power embodied in class and cultural hierarchies. In "Emily Dickinson and Class" (1992), Betsy Erkkila asserts that Dickinson's poetry was politically conservative and grounded in class privilege. Building on Erkkila, Domhnall Mitchell in *Emily Dickinson: Monarch of Perception* (2000) analyzes Dickinson's engagement with social and political issues in the rich context of local material history, concluding that Dickinson resorted to poetry as a site of stability in a world of social change that threatened her. Murray extends Mitchell's focus on class in *Maid as Muse*, where she links Dickinson's productivity to the presence of servants and argues that Dickinson's relationship with the Irish maid Margaret Maher not only lessened the poet's class and ethnic prejudice but also inspired her late poetry. Sharing Murray's interest in the materiality of daily life, Daneen Wardrop's *Emily Dickinson and the Labor of Clothing* (2009) examines the role of clothes in Dickinson's poetry and life from the combined perspective of labor, class, and fashion histories. Opposing the scholars who stress the poet's conservatism, Paul Crumbley in *Winds of Will: Emily Dickinson and the Sovereignty of Democratic Thought* (2010) discusses Dickinson's poetry in relation to Whig political culture with its emphasis on personal choice; he argues that the undecidability of her poems constitutes their democratic dimension.

The sociohistorical approach represented by Mitchell and others seeks to amend the dominant focus on religion as the context for Dickinson's poetry. Since Albert Gelpi's *Emily Dickinson: The Mind of the Poet* (1965), critics have variously presented Dickinson as a religious rebel oppressed by the patriarchal structure of Calvinist Christianity (Wolosky, Wolff), an agnostic in an era of growing metaphysical uncertainty (Porter, Salska), or a committed if unorthodox believer who draws strength from her religious faith (Eberwein, Oberhaus). The past fifteen years have seen renewed scholarly interest in Dickinson's religious themes. Jane Donahue Eberwein's scholarship continues to explore the inspiring and liberating influence of late Calvinist culture on Dickinson's imagination.[6] In *Nimble Believing: Dickinson and the Unknown* (2000) James McIntosh argues that Dickinson oscillates between faith and doubt and is fascinated with the unknown as the ground of encounter with God. According to Linda

Freedman in *Emily Dickinson and the Religious Imagination* (2011), theology provided Dickinson with a vocabulary to think about poetry and her poetic vocation. Other scholars emphasize the empowering potential of religion for women and situate Dickinson in female religious traditions. For Beth Maclay Doriani in *Emily Dickinson: Daughter of Prophecy* (1996), the poet continues the tradition of female prophecy as she draws on the Bible and American female religious writers of her time for an authoritative poetic voice. Victoria Morgan's *Emily Dickinson and Hymn Culture* (2010) draws connections between Dickinson's poetry and nineteenth-century American women's hymnody, which gave women privileged access to God outside of masculine theology. The influence of science and its changing relationship with religion on Dickinson's poetry is the focus of Robin Peel's *Dickinson and the Hill of Science* (2010).

Another group of historicist studies seek to establish Dickinson's place in the history of American literature by comparing her with other authors. Karl Keller's *The Only Kangaroo Among the Beauty: Emily Dickinson and America* (1979) began to revise the perception of Dickinson as culturally isolated. Following Keller, studies by Walker, St. Armand, Dobson, and Bennett examine Dickinson's affinities with a range of nineteenth-century popular American women writers from cultural and feminist perspectives. Later critics set Dickinson in more specific traditions of women's literature: Doriani relates Dickinson's poetry to female prophecy, while Marianne Noble in *The Masochistic Pleasures of Sentimental Literature* (2000) reads Dickinson's writings as a culmination of nineteenth-century sentimentalism and contends that the poet found opportunities for erotic pleasure in the dominant discourse of female submission. Elizabeth A. Petrino's *Emily Dickinson and Her Contemporaries: Women's Verse in America, 1820–1885* (1998) shifts attention to Dickinson's connections with nineteenth-century women poets, demonstrating Dickinson's indebtedness to and divergence from the popular poetry of Frances Osgood, Lydia Sigourney, and Helen Hunt Jackson. In *Dickinson's Misery*, Virginia Jackson elaborates on Walker's approach, presenting Dickinson as a sentimental poetess immersed in the female poetic discourse of pain and self-abasement. These studies have resulted in a new conception of Dickinson's place in literary history, encapsulated by Mary Loeffelholz's *From School to Salon: Reading Nineteenth-Century American Women's Poetry* (2004), which presents Dickinson not as a central or unique figure but as a participant, alongside Helen Hunt Jackson and others, in a shared post–Civil War literary field of aesthetically ambitious poetry.

Loeffelholz's approach marks the shift of focus from Dickinson's affinities with her female contemporaries to her historically situated reading of male and female writers. The importance of reading as a context for Dickinson's poetry was first highlighted by Jack Capps in *Emily Dickinson's Reading, 1836–1886* (1966). Building on Capps and Sewall, formalist and feminist critics assumed Dickinson's familiarity with Emerson and the Romantic tradition. More recently, critics have examined Dickinson's reading of books, periodicals, and textbooks in an effort to understand how she absorbed and reworked elements of her culture. In *Emily Dickinson's Shakespeare* (2006), Páraic Finnerty reconstructs the social and cultural assumptions about Shakespeare in the nineteenth-century United States as the context for Dickinson's reading of the English bard. Besides influencing her ideas of fame, death, friendship, and love, Shakespeare may have provided Dickinson with a model of authorship which achieves "literary renown but also authorial disappearance" (14). Jed Deppman emphasizes reading in *Trying to Think with Emily Dickinson* (2008) as he sets the poet among the philosophical and lexicographic debates of her time and discusses the influence of Dickinson's favorite novels on her poetry, which questions the metaphysical foundations of her culture in ways that anticipate postmodern philosophy. The special issue of *The Emily Dickinson Journal* on the poet's reading, edited by Daniel Manheim and Marianne Noble (2010), includes essays on Dickinson's use of literary allusion and her responses to contemporary scientific, poetic, and journalistic writings. Most recently, in *Reading in Time: Emily Dickinson in the Nineteenth Century* (2012), Cristanne Miller demonstrates how Dickinson's reading of periodicals, schoolbooks, and books from the family library encouraged her to write formally innovative poetry.

THE TURN TO THE READER

Critical attention to Dickinson's reading has been accompanied by increased scholarly interest in Dickinson's readers. Helen McNeil's *Emily Dickinson* (1986) and Gary Lee Stonum's *The Dickinson Sublime* (1990) were the first critical studies to emphasize the rhetorical, reader-oriented character of Dickinson's poetry. Later critics have argued that Dickinson wrote for a specific historical audience, aimed to evoke a particular response in her readers, and demanded readers' participation in the creation of meaning.[7] Recent studies examine the poet's rhetoric, correspondence, and reception, extending the scope of Martin Orzeck and Robert Weisbuch's pioneering collection *Dickinson and Audience* (1996).

Studies with a rhetorical focus emphasize Dickinson's address to the historical or implied audience. Robert McClure Smith in *The Seductions of Emily*

Dickinson (1996) and Noble in *Masochistic Pleasures* analyze Dickinson's rhetorical strategies in relation to erotic and textual desire. Smith argues that Dickinson's poetry simultaneously provokes and frustrates the reader's desire for meaning, while Noble discusses Dickinson's sentimental masochism as rhetorical manipulation. Focusing on the rhetorical function of genre, Jackson in *Dickinson's Misery* contends that Dickinson texts are not lyrics, or expressive private poems without historical reference, but are addressed to specific recipients and refer to concrete historical circumstances. The situation of address, Jackson argues, determines the genre of a given text.

The turn to the reader has inspired closer study of Dickinson's letters, the most explicitly reader-oriented genre, as biographical and cultural documents, literary artifacts, vehicles for exchanging ideas, and objects of editorial intervention. In *Vice for Voices: Reading Emily Dickinson's Correspondence* (2001), Marietta Messmer claims that the letters, not the poems, are at the center of Dickinson's oeuvre; Dickinson constructs them as a performance, using multiple voices to critique patriarchal discourse. The essays in Jane Donahue Eberwein and Cindy MacKenzie's *Reading Emily Dickinson's Letters* (2009) discuss Dickinson's correspondence from biographical, literary, and editorial perspectives.

Finally, interest in the poet's historical audiences across time and space has led to several studies of Dickinson's reception. Two monographs examine Dickinson's influence on later authors: Thomas Gardner's *A Door Ajar: Contemporary Writers and Emily Dickinson* (2006) discusses Dickinson's legacy in American literature at the turn of the twenty-first century, and Vivian Pollak's work in progress investigates premodern and modern American women poets' ambivalent responses to Dickinson. Two recent essay collections discuss Dickinson's reception on the large scale of national literatures and the small scale of individual readers' experience. Domhnall Mitchell and Maria Stuart's *The International Reception of Emily Dickinson* (2009) reflects the movement to expand the context for Dickinson study beyond the United States, discussing critical and creative responses to Dickinson in Europe, Asia, Australia, and South America. Cindy MacKenzie and Barbara Dana's *Wider than the Sky: Essays and Meditations on the Healing Power of Emily Dickinson* (2007), comprising a mix of scholarly essays and testimonies, foregrounds readers' personal responses to Dickinson's work.

NEW DIRECTIONS

New directions in Dickinson criticism are informed by the view of the poet as steeped in the tradition of American literature and embedded in the fabric of history. Besides topics like the Civil War, reading, religion, and audience, several intersecting trends will be shaping the near future of Dickinson scholarship. One is the focus on Dickinson's development, exemplified by Cristanne Miller's and Socarides's new books. Another trend, which Miller's book also encapsulates, is renewed interest in the formal features of Dickinson's poetry, accompanied by study of its genres. Meanwhile, the contexts of Dickinson poetry continue to expand as scholars investigate the poet's philosophical affinities, study her responses to science and technology, and begin to look at her work from a transatlantic perspective. The emphasis on Dickinson's connections with the external world will likely result in more studies of her nature poetry. We can also expect greater interest in the affirmative, playful, and joyous aspects of Dickinson's work.

NOTES

1 See also, e.g., Vivian R. Pollak, *Dickinson: The Anxiety of Gender* (Ithaca, NY: Cornell University Press, 1984).
2 Robert Weisbuch, *Emily Dickinson's Poetry* (Chicago: University of Chicago Press, 1975); Roland Hagenbüchle, "Precision and Indeterminacy in the Poetry of Emily Dickinson," *ESQ 20.1* (1974), 33–56; Agnieszka Salska, *Walt Whitman and Emily Dickinson: Poetry of the Central Consciousness* (Philadelphia: University of Pennsylvania Press, 1985).
3 See, e.g., Faith Barrett, "'Drums Off the Phantom Battlements': Dickinson's War Poems in Discursive Context," *A Companion to Emily Dickinson*, ed. Martha Nell Smith and Mary Loeffelholz (Malden, MA: Blackwell, 2008), 107–32; Eliza Richards, "'How News Must Feel When Traveling': Dickinson and Civil War Media," in Smith and Loeffelholz, *Companion*, 159–79.
4 The four stages of the feminist turn are adapted from Margaret Dickie, "Feminist Conceptions of Dickinson," *Handbook*, 342–55.
5 Joanne Feit Diehl, *Dickinson and the Romantic Imagination* (Princeton, NJ: Princeton University Press, 1981); Suzanne Juhasz, *The Undiscovered Continent: Emily Dickinson and the Space of the Mind* (Bloomington: Indiana University Press, 1983); Mary Loeffelholz, *Dickinson and the Boundaries of Feminist Theory* (Urbana: University of Illinois Press, 1991).
6 See, e.g., Jane Donahue Eberwein, *Dickinson: Strategies of Limitation* (Amherst: University of Massachusetts Press, 1985); Eberwein, "'Is Immortality True?': Salvaging Faith in an Age of Upheavals," *A Historical Guide to Emily Dickinson*, ed. Vivian Pollak (Oxford: Oxford University Press, 2004), 67–102.
7 See, e.g., Suzanne Juhasz, Cristanne Miller, and Martha Nell Smith, *Comic Power in Emily Dickinson* (Austin: University of Texas Press, 1993).

CHAPTER 32

Dickinson's Influence

Thomas Gardner

Emily Dickinson's influence is most readily apparent in what we might think of as conversational interchanges unfolding between her poems and the work of other writers. Her poems and letters speak, and, making out what they can, writers respond back, often in versions of her voice, if only, as Charles Wright puts it, to inquire "Can you hear me?" and "What?"[1] A powerful early example of this interchange can be found in John Barry's account of an evening in 1893 in which William Dean Howells read some of the poems in the first collection of her work, *Poems by Emily Dickinson* (1890), to the novelist Stephen Crane. Overwhelmed, Crane responded by producing, over the next three days, thirty poems which would form the core of his book *The Black Riders* (1895).[2] Judging by the darkly riddling texture of his verse, what spoke to Crane was the oracular, if only half-understood, authority of her voice, liberating him to speak likewise.

As we move forward to writers of the Modernist generation, the demand for a response posed by Dickinson's poems comes much more sharply into focus. Hart Crane, for example, begins his "To Emily Dickinson" (1927) with a plea to be heard:

> You who desired so much – in vain to ask –
> Yet fed your hunger like an endless task,
> Dared dignify the labor, bless the quest –
> Achieved that stillness ultimately best,
>
> Being, of all, least sought for: Emily, hear![3]

Dickinson posed a distinct challenge for Crane. Like him, she "desired so much," pursuing vision "like an endless task." Yet somehow, she was able to be content with the "labor" itself, coming to rest, finally, in a condition of "stillness" with an end never fully achieved. What Crane hears, he continues, is silence itself – "Eternity possessed / And plundered momently" in each attempt to grasp it.[4] The poet Jorie Graham speaks of these moments in Dickinson as "great failures of human speech," her voice coming to a halt before something that makes language bend and fall away.⁵ Crane sees these moments as the "flower" that "withers [not] in your hand," but he understands that the achieving of such stunned silences is the task of a lifetime:

> The harvest you descried and understand
> Needs more than wit to gather, love to bind.
> Some reconcilement of remotest mind – ⁶

Not just wit, not even love – what Dickinson urges him to access is his "remotest mind": the mind out upon circumference, stunned before and momentarily "reconcile[d]" with what is beyond its ability to possess. In F466/J657, Dickinson pictures this act of gathering as "spreading wide my narrow Hands / To gather Paradise - ." Crane echoes that image, some years later, in his vision of Brooklyn Bridge, traffic lights "beading [its] path" like an "immaculate sigh of stars," "condens[ing] eternity" as it lifts night in its "arms."⁷ It was an achievement both visible and tantalizingly far from him.

The conversation deepens when we turn to Robert Frost, another Modernist, who responds not just with stunned amazement but a version of Dickinson's own voice. Dickinson was for Frost "one of the great American poets," and what he heard in her was a voice that had peered into immensity and returned, with "Odd secrets of the line to tell!" (F132 J160).⁸ One senses, because of the piecemeal publication of her work across Frost's lifetime, voices engaged in almost parallel projects. Dickinson's image of the snow in "It sifts from Leaden Sieves - " (F291 J311), for example, published in 1891, resonates quite powerfully with Frost's "Desert Places," published in 1936. Dickinson's steady snowfall erases the landscape's features, making "an even Face / Of Mountain, and of Plain - / Unbroken Forehead from the East / Unto the East again - ," an unreadability echoed and intensified in Frost's account of snow and night falling across another blank field:

> And lonely as it is that loneliness
> Will be more lonely ere it will be less –
> A blanker whiteness of benighted snow
> With no expression, nothing to express.⁹

How strange it must have been for Frost who, in 1928's "Acquainted with the Night," paced his way into a darkness beyond "the furthest city light," starting and stopping, unable to articulate what had darkened his heart, suspended in a time "neither wrong nor right," to encounter Dickinson's

"We grow accustomed to the Dark - " (F428 J419), a poem not published until 1935 but clearly anticipating his.[10] We turn from a world lit and familiar and solid in much the same way we turn from a neighbor's lamp, Dickinson writes. We pause, take an "uncertain step," and then, as either "Darkness alters" or our eyes do, move forward as "Life steps almost straight." Frost would have heard the "odd secrets of the line" recorded in the word *almost*, understanding that they were both working their way through similar blank landscapes, what Dickinson's poem calls "Evenings of the Brain - ."

We see yet another way of responding in a third Modernist, Marianne Moore. As a number of critics have recently shown, Moore found in Dickinson a key female precursor rather than a direct influence. Moore knew Dickinson's poems and was aware that reviewers often linked their names, but as Linda Leavell argues, by the time Moore published her single piece on Dickinson, a 1933 review of Todd's *Letters of Emily Dickinson*, her striking way with language was already fully established.[11] What we see in the review is Moore placing Dickinson within the contours of her own poems, drawing her in as an ally and support.

In Todd's edition of the letters, Moore finds a version of herself – "that rare thing, the truly unartificial spirit – flashing like an animal, with strength or dismay."[12] In the naked confidence of Dickinson's questions and affirmations, Moore discovers a voice still sounding despite "the ruses and dust-obscured emulations of ambitious biography" that had steadfastly and scandalously attempted to make "idiosyncrasy out of individuality" in the poet.[13] Idiosyncrasy can be dismissed or pitied, but individuality lives on. The markings of Dickinson's voice – the poems' "daring associations of the prismatically true," "the swerve to a pun or the quoting of a familiar phrase in a new connection" – are, Moore suggests, not "defects" but, "for the select critic, attractions."[14] These, of course, are markers of Moore's voice as well, an idea that she encourages us to explore by alluding, in these phrases, to her great poem "In the Days of Prismatic Color" (1919). There, Moore argues that, unlike the days before the fall, "when Adam was alone" and color, in its prismatic display, was "fine" not because of "refinement" but because of "originality," "complexity [now] is not a crime."[15] It is simply part of the fallen world. The problem, Moore continues, is with complexity that is murky and not plain, complexity "committed to darkness." True art, she insists, would rest neither in darkness nor in the formal simplicities of an earlier period. Rather, much like the flashing originality of Dickinson and Moore, it would revel in its own "daring associations of the prismatically true." Though the wave of time crashes over such work, it will "be there when the wave has gone by," Moore concludes her poem.[16] She must have taken great comfort in seeing the assertions of this earlier work confirmed in Dickinson's ever-rising reputation.

When we turn to the generation of writers after the Moderns, we turn to writers who had Johnson's 1955 edition available to work with. Significantly expanding the Dickinson canon and bringing into coherence a mind developing over time, Johnson's edition spoke with startling directness to poet after poet. Elizabeth Bishop, for example, knew Dickinson's poems and letters before the Johnson edition, praising, in a 1951 review of an edition of Dickinson's letters to the Hollands, the exposed strength of her sentences: "It is the sketchiness of the water-spider, tenaciously holding to its upstream position by means of the faintest ripples, while making one aware of the current of death and the darkness below."[17] But it was not until the 1955 edition that Dickinson's power became fully apparent to her. She wrote to Robert Lowell that year that "I like, or at least admire, her a great deal more now – probably because of that new edition, really. I spent another stretch absorbed in that, and think ... that she's about the best we have."[18] In fact, as she mentioned to Lowell in another letter, she began drafting "a complicated poem about Hopkins and E. Dickinson – after reading the new edition."[19] That poem, begun in 1955 and returned to in the 1970s, was never finished, but one of the things Bishop seems to have been thinking about was the fragile linguistic structures each writer wove, becoming, in their retreat from the marketplace, self-caged birds, having it out there, alone, with God. The peeled willow stems of the cages in the drafted poem – "one – the other – made by hand / peeled withies" – recall the strong yet flexible water-spider's legs, both making visible, in their fragile arcs, the powers above which they are suspended.[20]

One can see clearly how fully Bishop absorbed this lesson if we juxtapose her late masterpiece "In the Waiting Room" with Dickinson's F633/ J378. Dickinson begins, "I saw no Way - The Heavens were stitched - / I felt the Columns close - ," linking her failure to reach a closed-off, unresponsive heaven to an abandoned, claustrophobic tightening of the senses. Bishop describes an oddly similar experience – herself as a child, reading *The National Geographic* while waiting for her aunt in the dentist's office, feeling herself pulled under by its strange world of dead bodies, spurting volcanoes, and naked women with "horrifying" breasts.[21] Dickinson's stitches are echoed in the volcano's winding "rivulets of fire," the explorer's "laced boots," the binding by which the "dead man [is] slung on a pole," and the pointed heads of babies and the necks of women "wound round and round" with string and wire. The child soon finds herself tightly wound into this world as well, "too shy to stop" and pull back.

Like Frost, Bishop speaks back by dramatizing Dickinson's essentially sceneless abstractions, feeling them out with her own body.[22] Her aunt's scream, mysteriously felt in her own throat, could be Dickinson's scream as well. Whatever the case, both poets react to the collapse of self and the senses in the same way. Dickinson writes:

> The Earth reversed her Hemispheres -
> I touched the Universe -
>
> And back it slid - and I alone -
> A speck opon a Ball -
> Went out opon Circumference -
> Beyond the Dip of Bell -

And Bishop answers:

> I said to myself: three days
> and you'll be seven years old.
> I was saying it to stop
> the sensation of falling off
> the round, turning world
> into cold, blue-black space.
> . . .
> I knew that nothing stranger
> had ever happened, that nothing
> stranger could ever happen.

Dickinson's influence, I have been arguing, is that of a voice awaiting an answer. Bishop's "I," giving way and then reestablishing itself as something forever strange to itself, poised against "cold, blue-black space," is a profound restatement of Dickinson's "speck opon a Ball - ," the self most alive in the moment it is undone, the moment it is reversed.

Adrienne Rich's response to Johnson's Dickinson, quite consciously revised a number of times, was several-sided and instructive. It begins with the poem "I Am in Danger - Sir - ," written in 1964, after an extended period spent with what the poem calls Johnson's "variorum monument."[23] As the title suggests, the poem focuses on Dickinson's quietly confident response to Higginson's charge that her verse was "uncontrolled." Rich addresses Dickinson directly. "Who are you?" she asks, thinking particularly of Higginson's description of her as his "partially cracked poetess."²⁴ Being "half-cracked" was "more / than a symptom - / [it was] a condition of being," Rich writes. It was a condition Dickinson "chose to have ... out at last / on [her] own premises," cracked or split between domestic routine and the pulsing dangers of thought.

Twelve years later, in her groundbreaking essay "Vesuvius at Home," Rich refines this idea, identifying so deeply with Dickinson that she travels to the poet's house in order to have it out on her own premises. What she hears now is the measuring and careful release of a volcanic, inward power: "To recognize and acknowledge our own interior power has always been a path mined with risks for women; to acknowledge that power and commit oneself to it as Emily Dickinson did was an immense decision."²⁵ Dickinson possessed "a mind capable of describing psychological states more accurately than any poet except Shakespeare"; she "seemed to tell me that the intense inner event, the personal and psychological, was inseparable from the universal" and far beyond "mere self-expression."²⁶ But, as in "I Am in Danger - Sir - ," Dickinson also gave voice to the "dangers and risks of such possession if you are a woman." The crucial expression of this warning, for Rich, is the much commented on "My Life had stood - a Loaded Gun - " (F764 J754). Rich argues that the owner in this poem is the poet's active side, releasing, in the gun, a "possibly unacceptable, perhaps even monstrous" power.²⁷ What the poem wrestles with is the split between one's "publicly accessible persona" and this "essential, creative and powerful self," with all its dangers and risks. Simply by voicing this tension, Dickinson emboldens Rich to say "yes" to her own explosive powers.

How interesting, then, in 1980, to see Rich respond one last time to Dickinson within a larger poem entitled "The Spirit of Place" and this time let her go, allowing her to remain the "stranger" she had always seen herself as. Now, Rich vows to "cover [her] / from all intrusion," to "ask no more of who or why or wherefore," and to "close the door / ... and silently pick up my fallen work."²⁸ That work, as has been increasingly clear since the early 80s, is with those "*with whom ... your lot is cast*," the marginalized and silent.²⁹ It involves embracing "the world / as it is / not as we wish it," not just releasing one's inner powers but applying them, putting them into action: "staying cognizant," "honor[ing] with grief with fury with action" "those who did not / survive what was done to them."³⁰ Rich honors Dickinson's voice in this last poem, then, by pushing off from it and moving out on her own.

As we draw nearer to the present time, the aspects of Dickinson's voice responded to become more and more specific, more and more individualized. Susan Howe's insistence on naming and claiming *My Emily Dickinson* (1985) is perhaps the most forceful example of this. Howe's Dickinson, in this extraordinary work of poet's prose, "built a new poetic form from her fractured sense of being eternally on intellectual borders, where confident masculine voices buzzed an alluring and inaccessible discourse .... Pulling pieces of geometry, geology, alchemy, philosophy, politics, biography, biology, mythology, and philology from alien territory, a 'sheltered' woman audaciously invented a new grammar grounded in humility and hesitation."[31] Lost in a sort of linguistic wilderness, Dickinson found herself free to use whatever fragments she was able to gather, drawing forth what Howe calls a powerfully expressive "undervoice" from the dominant discourse buzzing about her: "Forcing, abbreviating, pushing, padding, subtracting, riddling, interrogating, re-writing, she pulled text from text."[32] It is this voice and its revolutionary grammar that Howe both unfolds and employs, pulling texts from the texts Dickinson used, creating something utterly original in American letters. As her work has continued, in both essays and book-length poems, Howe has wandered more and more deeply and richly into this wilderness Dickinson opened up for her: "Here are unmown fields unknown inhabitants other woods in other words: enigma of gibberish unwritten wife."[33] Howe offers the reader what she was first offered in Dickinson: "a threshold at the austere reach of the book."[34]

Charles Wright describes Dickinson as "the only writer I've ever read who knows my mind, whose work has influenced me at my heart's core, whose music is the music of the songs I've listened to and remembered in my very body."[35] The music he is talking about, that of A. P. Carter and the Carter family, gives voice to what he calls a "surreal simplicity and ache" for something beyond this world. What Dickinson gave him was a powerful series of images, many of them having to do with light, to return to and release that childhood music. Dickinson's "certain Slant of light," appearing and disappearing, leaving in its wake "Heavenly Hurt," is, for Wright, one of the most resonant versions of this image (F320 J258). As light draws near and then retreats, another world is made momentarily visible and then withdrawn, for both writers. It is a process neither of them can control: "None may teach it - Any - / 'Tis the Seal Despair - ." And yet its presence is everywhere sought. Wright's *Zone Journals* (1988) is a sustained unfolding of this image, associating it with the momentary traces of memory, light, shadow, and music, accessed through the open hands of a contemplative, flexible concentration, letting go of what can never be held:

> Something about a dark suture
> Across the lawn,
>   something about the way the day snips
> It open and closes it
> When what-comes-out has come out
>   and burns hard in its vacancy,
> Emerging elsewhere restructured and restrung,
> Like a tall cloud that all the rain has fallen out of.[36]

One sees this fleeting trace of some other world everywhere in both Wright and Dickinson.

Kathleen Fraser, in "re:searches" (1987), develops Dickinson's vacancies in quite another way. Studying the "eee face ment" of Dickinson's work she attributes to Dickinson's brother's mutilation of some of her poems and letters after her death, Fraser finds in those gaps a sort of charged "radial activ- / ity" that frees her own language to move in new ways – creating what she calls "this lyric forever error, this / something embarrassingly clear, this / language we come up against."[37] Ironically, the damage done to Dickinson's language produces for Fraser a language newly responsive to "one's own at-oddness with the presumed superiority of the central mainstream vision," a language capable of giving words to the "uncertainty and multiplicity in female experience."[38] Working from a less experimental tradition, Alice Fulton, in *Sensual Math* (1995), focuses on Dickinson's dash and hears in it another way of articulating uncertainty and multiplicity. For her, "The dash is an empty space, but Dickinson's syntactical deletions often ask to be filled in; they exist to be recovered .... You feel like you're building the poem with her as you read. Sometimes you can't recover the deletions. The phrases on either side of the dash remain non sequiturs."[39] Reaching for that open-ended potential in her own work, Fulton developed what she calls "a bride" or "a seam made to show," which she prints like this: "= =." The device is particularly useful for displaying the expressive power of hesitation, as in this response to her sister, who had asked whom her recently deceased twenty-one-year-old daughter most resembled: "I think she = = you, I said / in some wrong tense."[40]

Probably the most striking recent response to the freeness of Dickinson's expression can be found in Lucie Brock-Broido's *The Master Letters* (1995). There, beginning with the basic rhetorical framework of Dickinson's three so-called Master Letters – "gracious, sometimes nearly erotic, worshipful documents, full of Dickinson's dramas of entreaty & intimacy, her distances" – Brock-Broido creates "a series of latter-day Master Letters, echo[ing] formal & rhetorical devices from Dickinson's work," but speaking to her own obsessions.[41] Dickinson's unreachable Master become "a composite portrait, police-artist sketch" and her speaker becomes "a brood of voice – a flock of women with Dickinson as mistress of the skein, the spinning wheel, the Queen Domestic, composed and composing, as she did, from her looms & room & seclusion."[42] Consider, for example, the beginning of a poem whose title is drawn from another Dickinson letter – "I Don't Know Who It Is, That Sings, nor Did I, Would I Tell":

November

Master -
You say I have Misenveloped & sent you something Else. In the middle of it all, my mind went blank, all the red notes of terror, blinking. Please to tell me - have I unsettled you by this?[43]

Springing off of Dickinson's letter L187 ("You ask me what my flowers said - then they were disobedient - I gave them messages"), Brock-Broido's address to the one she eventually calls "*My Apparition - Lord*" combines recognizably contemporary language and imagery with Dickinson's aggressive, pleading tone. Teasingly unsettled in its directness, intimate in its breathiness, the poem stammers its way towards some unnameable "it," revealed only in its effect on the language surrounding it. It changes a straightforward apology into "something Else," creating a blankness blinking with the "red notes of terror." Here once again, Dickinson's influence is almost palpable, calling yet another new voice to the surface.

The intimacy of exchange is, for all of these writers and many others who could have been examined, the most notable feature of any engagement with Dickinson. Whether prompted by an image, a tone of voice, a pause or a dash, an erasure, voices in Dickinson's wake inevitably move in tandem with hers, producing a music both hauntingly private and deeply shared. There would seem to be no limits to the ways her voice draws other voices out.

NOTES

1 Charles Wright, "Italian Days," *The World of the Ten Thousand Things* (New York: Farrar, Straus and Giroux, 1990), 92.
2 Paul Sorrentino, ed., *Stephen Crane Remembered* (Tuscaloosa: University of Alabama Press, 2006), 142.
3 *The Complete Poems and Selected Letters and Prose of Hart Crane*, ed. Brom Weber (Garden City, New York: Anchor Books, 1966), 170.
4 Ibid., 170.

5 Jorie Graham, "Some Notes on Silence," *19 New American Poets of the Golden Gate*, ed. Philip Dow (New York: Harcourt, Brace, Jovanovich, 1984), 411.
6 Crane, *The Complete Poems*, 170.
7 Crane, "To Brooklyn Bridge," *The Complete Poems*, 46.
8 Karl Keller, *The Only Kangaroo Among the Beauty: Emily Dickinson and America* (Baltimore: Johns Hopkins University Press, 1979), 309.
9 Robert Frost, "Desert Places," *Robert Frost: Collected Poems, Prose, & Plays*, ed. Richard Poirier and Mark Richardson (New York: Library of America, 1995), 269.
10 Frost, "Acquainted with the Night," *Collected Poems*, 234.
11 Linda Leavell, "Marianne Moore's Emily Dickinson," *EDJ* 12.2 (2003), 12–13.
12 Marianne Moore, *The Complete Prose of Marianne Moore*, ed. Patricia C. Willis (New York: Viking Penguin, 1986), 291.
13 Ibid., 293.
14 Ibid., 292.
15 Marianne Moore, "In the Days of Prismatic Color," *The Complete Poems of Marianne Moore* (New York: Macmillan, 1967), 41–2.
16 Ibid., 42.
17 Elizabeth Bishop, *Prose*, ed. Lloyd Schwartz (New York: Farrar, Straus and Giroux, 2011), 263.
18 Quoted in Victoria Harrison, *Elizabeth Bishop's Poetics of Intimacy* (Cambridge: Cambridge University Press, 1993), 35.
19 Ibid., 35
20 Ibid., 35–6.
21 Elizabeth Bishop, "In the Waiting Room," *Poems* (New York: Farrar, Straus and Giroux, 2011), 179.
22 The term "sceneless" is Robert Weisbuch's in "Prisming Dickinson; or, Gathering Paradise by Letting Go," *Handbook*, 200.
23 Adrienne Rich, "I Am in Danger - Sir - ," *The Fact of a Doorframe: Poems Selected and New 1950–1984* (New York: Norton, 1984), 70–1.
24 Quoted in note to L481.
25 Adrienne Rich, *On Lies, Secrets, and Silence* (New York: Norton, 1979), 166.
26 Ibid., 167, 168.
27 Ibid., 175.
28 Rich, "The Spirit of Place," *The Fact*, 300–1.
29 Ibid., 298.
30 Ibid., 299, 302–3.
31 Susan Howe, *My Emily Dickinson* (Berkeley: North Atlantic Books, 1985), 21.
32 Ibid., 29.
33 Susan Howe, *The Birth-mark* (Hanover: Wesleyan University Press, 1993), 2.
34 Ibid., 2.
35 Charles Wright, *Halflife: Improvisations and Interviews* (Ann Arbor: University of Michigan Press, 1988), 54.
36 "A Journal of True Confessions," Wright, *The World*, 145.

37 Kathleen Fraser, *il cuore: the heart (Selected Poems 1970–1995)* (Hanover: Wesleyan University Press, 1997), 82.
38 Kathleen Fraser, *Translating the Unspeakable: Poetry and the Innovative Necessity* (Tuscaloosa: University of Alabama Press, 1997), 31, 135.
39 Alec Marsh, "A Conversation with Alice Fulton," *TriQuarterly 98* (1996–97), 31.
40 Alice Fulton, *Sensual Math* (New York: Norton, 195), 61.
41 Lucie Brock–Broido, *The Master Letters* (New York: Knopf, 1997), vii, viii.
42 Ibid., viii.
43 Ibid., 62.

CHAPTER 33

Translation and International Reception
Domhnall Mitchell

One of the few welcome effects of the competitive and partial aspects of Emily Dickinson's posthumous publication was that, from 1890 onwards, her poetry was kept in the public eye, with separate American editions appearing in 1891, 1896, 1914, 1924, 1929, 1930, 1935, 1937, and 1945. Four editions of her *Poems*, First Series, were sold out between October and December of 1890, and by the end of the decade the combined sales of her first, second, and third series of poems, as well as a selected edition of her letters, amounted to almost 20,000 copies (*Reception*, 557–8). With reissues appearing in 1901, 1902, 1904, 1906, 1908, 1910, and 1912 (in addition to anthology inclusions), the poet's work received renewed attention and evaluation almost continuously for decades after her death in 1886. Dickinson's delayed arrival on the literary scene extended the initial period of her reception well into the twentieth century: unseen and major poems were still being newly released as late as the 1929 *Further Poems of Emily Dickinson* and 1945 *Bolts of Melody*. Improvements in the facility and frequency of transatlantic travel and communications meant that such attention spread abroad. With each publication, the circumference of reception widened, sometimes very quickly: the first British review of the 1890 *Poems* appeared in January 1891, for example, while in 1898 German translations of four of her poems were published along with a critical commentary in the *Illinois Staats-Zeitung*, constituting "the earliest translation of Dickinson's poetry into any language and most probably the first introduction to the author that was not in English."[1] At other times, the connections were more oblique: non-English speakers could read Dickinson's F1788/J1763 "Fame is a bee" in Norwegian as early as 1914 because a translation of the American theologian James Russell Miller's devotional writings included his quotation of this poem – though the first record of a literary translation into Norwegian was not until 1935.[2] And in 1917, only three years after their original English publication in *The Single Hound*, Spanish versions of F557/J308 "I send Two Sunsets - ," F592/J674

"The Soul that hath a Guest," and F1686/J1687 "The gleam of an heroic act" appeared simultaneously in Madrid and Buenos Aires in a collection by the poet Juan Ramón Jiménez – making his the first Spanish versions to circulate in Latin America.³ In what follows, we look more specifically at the international aspect of Dickinson's reception, offering a brief overview of trends within criticism, adaptations, and translations, and tracing some of the ways in which Dickinson's writing has been assimilated within different cultures, as well as the versions of the poet that emerge from these encounters.

"Tell all the truth but tell it slant, success in circuit lies," a fictionalised version of Queen Elizabeth in Alan Bennett's novella *The Uncommon Reader* quotes from Dickinson's poem – after having first misattributed the lines to E. M. Forster.⁴ At one level, the joke relates to certain preconceptions about the Queen's personality and interests, but it also implies readers who know better: in twenty-first century England, Ireland, Scotland, and Wales, Dickinson's poems are familiar. And indeed they are: a year earlier, in an interview with *The Guardian*, controversial musician Pete Doherty admitted lifting lines from another of Dickinson's poems (F396 J1725) "I took one Draught of Life") for his song "At the Flophouse," and described her as a "hardcore" poet.⁵ Doherty had studied Dickinson at secondary school, where *A Choice of Emily Dickinson's Verse* is part of an optional unit in the English literature curriculum for the final exams: in Ireland ten of Dickinson's poems are on the 2011–14 syllabus for the corresponding Leaving Certificate examination. Dickinson's poetry is well represented on several modules for undergraduate studies at universities throughout Britain and Ireland.

Emily Dickinson's reputation in Great Britain was not always subject to play. The British publication of the 1890 *Poems: First Series* in August 1891 sold disappointingly (five hundred copies, as opposed to four thousand during the same period in the United States), so much so that the 1905 Methuen reprint claimed to be "the first issue in England" and itself garnered only a tiny number of reviews, most of which described her as "unknown" (*Reception*, 559–63). In fact, Dickinson's initial reception was a contentious one. For Andrew Lang (1844–1912), the Scottish critic and fiction writer who commented more than once on Dickinson in the immediate aftermath of her American printing, her poetry was less important than its consideration by William Dean Howells (1837–1920), the influential American novelist and literary critic, who claimed that if "nothing else had come out of our life but this strange poetry we should feel that in the work of Emily Dickinson America, or New England rather, had made a distinctive addition to the literature of the world."[6] Lang's first response to Dickinson appeared in the *Daily News* of London in January 1891; Howells is mentioned three times more often than the poet herself. Quoting this passage, Lang accuses Dickinson of being remote "from meaning, from music, from grammar, from rhyme [and from] articulate and intelligible speech."[7] Although there are suspicions of literary nationalism here – of using Dickinson to argue that America was culturally incapable of producing great poetry – the truth is less straightforward, as Lang did in fact acknowledge the greatness of other, male, American writers in separate reviews. In attacking Howells through Dickinson, Lang was opposing the idea that literature produced in America was separate from literature in English generally, and insisting that there were universal standards to evaluate all writers. At stake in Lang's response to Howells, then, were contesting definitions of literary history and practice. And though early British responses to Dickinson appear xenophobic, they repeated criticisms that had first surfaced in America: "it would be easy to make fun of the lady's rhythmic and rhyming methods," wrote one reviewer, while another pointed to an "an entire waywardness of form" and a third complained of rhymes that "are sometimes very dreadful."[8]

Certainly the 1920s and 1930s saw the consolidation of Dickinson's reputation not only in England but internationally, prompted in part by Martha Dickinson Bianchi's *Complete Poems* and Conrad Aiken's *Selected Poems of Emily Dickinson* (both in 1924).[9] Aiken's introduction, and his selection of poems for an edition published by Jonathan Cape in London, were crucial to the process of Dickinson's transmission in England: his description of her commitment to "concise statement in terms of metaphor" developed an association with Imagism first established by Amy Lowell, and his inclusion of Dickinson in an anthology of *Modern American Poets* (1922) helped prepare the way for her later (and still ongoing) reception as a pre-Modernist writer.[10] Promoting her as "among the finest poets in the language," he even went as far as suspecting that the technical "lapses and tyrannies" so bemoaned by other critics "were deliberate."[11] Critics who attacked or supported Dickinson, then, were not simply intent on evaluating her individually as a poet, but were using her to help define and promote certain ideas about what constituted acceptable poetry. The formlessness that made Dickinson enemies in the nineteenth century gained her important allies in a Modernist era when formal improvisation was more highly regarded. The English poet and critic Susan Miles argued in *The London Mercury* of December 1925 that Dickinson's "irregularities [of meter and rhyme] have a definite artistic significance," noticing her strategic deployment of near- and half-rhymes in particular.[12] And in 1934 the Swedish critic Margit Abenius published an influential article on Dickinson that cited Aiken, and approvingly noted that "years before the modernists [Dickinson] goes unconcernedly past rules, rhymes and syntactic laws."[13]

A sea-change had occurred in Dickinson's reception: new editions – culminating in the standard 1955 Harvard Variorum – promoted her formal structures as motivated and innovative. In his introduction to *A Choice of Emily Dickinson's Verse* (1968), the English poet laureate Ted Hughes (1930–98) denied that her use of the dash was "capricious and arbitrary," while in his 1995 acceptance speech for the Nobel Prize in Literature Seamus Heaney grouped her with Paul Celan and John Keats as practitioners of an extreme version of the pursuit of truthfulness through the form of "cadence and tone and rhyme and stanza."[14] Dickinson was an early influence on Hughes, who taught at Amherst in the spring semester of 1958, and on Sylvia Plath, another writer who combined New England and British allegiances.[15] That *A Choice of Emily Dickinson's Verse* was commissioned by Faber, then the preeminent outlet for poetry in Britain, shows how firmly assimilated Dickinson had become by the late sixties within an Anglo-American canon of poetry that included Auden, Eliot, Lowell, MacNeice, Moore, and Pound, as well as Heaney, Hughes, and Plath.[16] And the virtues that Hughes identified in an earlier essay – of skeptical attention to "Nothingness," of "doubt and ironic query" – placed her very much in the New Critical tradition of a poetry defined by tension and ambiguity that still surfaces in more recent interpretive attention to her opaque indeterminacies.[17]

It is precisely such ambiguity, together with extreme compression and nonstandard syntax and punctuation, which present particular kinds of challenges to different languages – especially (as with the Slavic languages, Chinese, and Japanese) when there is a shift into grammatical systems and alphabets that are distinct from English. Even the morphology of Finnish, though, is such that pronouns appear at the ends of verbs, and no distinction is made on the basis of gender: the identification of "Death" as masculine in F479/J712 "Because I could not stop for Death - " would then have to be made lexically – by using additional words. This is part of a more general problem identified by Sirkka Heiskanen-Mäkelä: "While Dickinson's own abstractive – or elliptic – diction calls for only a few words, the Finnish tongue – by nature very concrete and descriptive – demands a great many of them to translate the same idea."[18] Viktor Finkel makes a similar point about Russian: "Dickinson's short lines are so expressive that in order to retain their sense and figurativeness the translator must make the poem longer and bulkier."[19] And Nabil Alawi writes that the gender of nouns is also a complication in Arabic, where "the sun is always feminine" (as indeed it is in Irish), making it difficult to translate instances in some of Dickinson's poems where the sun represents a specifically masculine force.[20]

But translation also presents obstacles – and opportunities – that are *culturally* as well as linguistically specific. Alawi, for instance, goes on to report that one of the main challenges to Arabic speakers is religious: "Biblical words do have equivalences in Arabic, but they do not represent the psychological and emotional meanings that are associated with them in a Christian (or Western) context."[21] In an interesting discussion of F320/J258 "There's a certain Slant of light," Marvin Zuckerman points out that the word "Cathedral" can have a very different set of negative meanings for a speaker of Yiddish with roots in eastern Europe than it might for someone whose culture is western and Christian.[22] Commenting again on "Because I could not stop for Death - ," Chanthana Chaichit offers the insight that in Thai culture "'Death' [cannot be] described as a gentleman; nor can 'Death' be conceived in a romantic, optimistic way. If there were any image of 'Death' as a person, it would not be a mortal person, and not a kind of genteel Dickinson lover."[23] And one of the reasons it has been suggested that Dickinson's poetry has not been as popular in France is "the relative unfamiliarity of Dickinson's biblical and Shakespearean references" as well as the absence of a collected edition of the poems in translation.[24]

Dickinson scholarship is nevertheless very well-established abroad – particularly so in Germany, the United Kingdom and Ireland, Italy, Japan (where the first responses can be traced back to the end of the nineteenth century), and Scandinavia. And translations of the complete poems have appeared in Japanese, Italian, and Norwegian: substantial editions have also been published in French (of the fascicles, by Malroux, in 1998) and in German.[25] Without question, these works owe their existence in part to perhaps the single most important event in the twentieth-century history of Dickinson's international reception – Thomas H. Johnson's 1955 three-volume variorum edition of the poems. The first fully comprehensive edition that was chronologically ordered and rigorously edited, with a good scholarly apparatus, its impact has been acknowledged by readers of many nationalities.[26] The (German) scholar Roland Hagenbüchle's lifelong study of Dickinson's technique and (Swedish) Brita Lindberg Seyersted's analysis of her poetic style depend a great deal on the cumulative impression made possible by a collected edition – as does (Indian) Mansoor Khan's analysis of the poet's overall themes.[27]

Current work on Emily Dickinson continues to be driven by editions of the poetry: Peter Verstegen's *Gedichten 1* (2005) includes "about half of Dickinson's poems from her forty hand-sewn manuscript books from 1858 to 1864 in the order that had been reconstructed by R. W. Franklin (1981)," while Lennart Nyberg's 1993 translation of 90 poems derives its structure from both the Johnson (1955) and Franklin (1981) editions, including a complete Swedish version of fascicle 37.[28] At the same time, translators and commentators can increasingly draw on an expanding archive of work on the poet in their own languages: Swedish publications stretch back to 1931 and include book-length translations in 1950 and 1986, while Giuseppe Ierolli's monumental online edition of *Emily Dickinson: Tutte le Opere* takes its place among a list of some twenty book-length translations of Dickinson in Italian.[29] But many readers who travel to the Emily Dickinson Museum in Amherst and to the Emily Dickinson Room at the Houghton Library at Harvard University do so because of a fascination with the poet's *character*: though the myth of Emily Dickinson's reclusiveness distorts the more gradual and complex nature of the poet's withdrawal from Amherst society, biography has played a substantial role in generating attention to the work.[30] Pete Doherty is not the only musician to refer to the "curious life [of] abstinence": young Norwegian jazz interpreters record a similar fascination with an apparently unusual personal history.[31] Nor is this a recent phenomenon: early reviews in England commented on her isolation, and there has been continuing speculation on the reasons for it since one of the first French studies appeared in 1924 – most recently in an otherwise well-documented biography by South African born Lyndall Gordon that wrongly attributed it to epilepsy.[32] An important revision of the myth was offered by William Luce's *The Belle of Amherst*, a one-woman play first performed in Seattle, Washington, in 1976. It had a worldwide impact: a Portuguese translation of the play toured Brazil in 1984–5, with considerable success, while the Dutch writer Louise van Santen's 1983 adaptation (entitled *Emily*) was performed more than a hundred times in Amsterdam.[33] In Norway, Halldis Moren Vesaas's *Den Kvitkledde fra Amherst* ("the white-dressed one from Amherst") ran from 1977 to 1980, ending up in the Norwegian Theatre in Oslo and broadcast on Norwegian National Radio: Moren Vesaas was one of the leading figures of twentieth-century literary culture, and the Norwegian Theatre was associated with high-quality, often experimental theatre. Whatever its shortcomings, Luce's play was useful because it worked as theatre, and not least as comedy; its best moments challenged the idea of Dickinson as a victim and showed her to be strong, compassionate, funny, and serious about her profession. It also contested the received image of her seclusion in practical ways: the character addresses the audience directly, and is shown engaged in dialogue with others offstage. Though not regarded as a feminist text in the United States or Britain, where its popular appeal was not valued by the academic community, Luce's play was effectively assimilated into other cultures as a political as well as a biographical work (reflecting an ideological potential inherent in the circumstances of the poet's life: for many readers, she is an icon for the politically marginalised or disenfranchised).

Dickinson's international reception is driven by a complex set of factors. She is translated and commented on because she is an important American poet, and since the end of the Second World War American culture has received increasing amounts of attention abroad because of the country's political and military prominence. In the 1940s and 1950s Departments of American Studies were founded throughout Europe in part with important financial contributions from U.S. government offices and foundations, financial institutions, and private benefactors, as America embarked on a diplomatic policy of promoting closer ties with its Cold War allies. This is one of several reasons why Dickinson scholarship is so well established in Germany, Japan, the United Kingdom (and, later, its Commonwealth satellites, not least in India where there has been an American Studies Research Centre in Hyderabad since the early 1960s).

But the recognition of Dickinson's importance by translators and commentators outside of the United States can also be motivated by a desire to "nationalize" foreign works – to give them forms and sometimes a language that are particular to the target culture – or to signal an allegiance or influence from outside the boundaries and paradigm of a national language, literature, and culture, often for the purposes of redefining or expanding them. When Stanislaw Baranczak remarks on a conflict between Polish renderings of Dickinson "as a Victorian poet, mostly following the poetics and style of [the] Polish fin-de-siecle" and lends his support to those that resemble instead "the terse, compressed, and elliptical style of the great poet Cyprian Norwid," he takes part in a discussion that is as much about Polish literature as it is about Dickinson.[34] The act of translation can also be seen as an act of bravura: coping with the linguistic and semantic complexities of this most riddling of poets is a sign that your own vernacular is at least equal to that of the person you are translating, a point Baranczak makes explicit when he writes of the opportunity in translation to "improve" on the original.³⁵ Like the poems themselves, then, Emily Dickinson's international reception can be read in many different ways: as a sign of how successfully American culture has been exported abroad, but also as proof that local cultures adapt that culture and her poems to their own particular needs, idioms, and histories. Dickinson is now read in Argentina, Austria, Australia, Belgium, Brazil, Canada, China, the Czech Republic, Denmark, England, Finland, France, Germany, Greece, Holland, Hungary, Iceland, India, Iraq, Ireland, Israel, Italy, Japan, Korea, Mexico, Norway, Poland, Portugal, Russia, Saudi Arabia, Scotland, South Africa, Spain, Sweden, Switzerland, Taiwan, Thailand, Turkey, Ukraine, the United Kingdom, Uruguay, Venezuela, and Vietnam. The international aspects of that reception might have gladdened rather than taken her aback: she read the literature of Great Britain avidly and that of other countries occasionally (in translation), but also read *about* foreign countries in *The Atlantic Monthly, Harper's Magazine,* and *Scribner's* and wrote about them with fascination in poems and letters. Clearly, the future audience Dickinson imagined for herself in F519/J441 (her "letter to the World") and defined as her "countrymen" is comprised very simply of people who read her anywhere at any time: what might have delighted her is how many of them continue to write back, in their own languages, and on their own terms.

NOTES

1 Walter Grünzweig, "Cries of Distress: Emily Dickinson's Initial German Reception from an Intercultural Perspective," *EDJ* 5.2 (1996), 232.
2 Johan Støren (trans.), *Paradiset hernede og deroppe* (Kristiania: Johannes Bjørnstad, 1914), 141.
3 Gastón Figeuira, *Emily Dickinson in América Latina: Crítica, traducción, influencia, espectáculo* (Montevideo: Biblioteca Artigas–Washington, 1983), 2.
4 Alan Bennett, *The Uncommon Reader* (London: Faber & Faber, 2007), 122. The poem is F1263/J1129.
5 Laura Barton, "Emily Dickinson? She's Hardcore," *The Guardian* (G2) (October 3, 2006), 22.
6 William Dean Howells, "Editor's Study," *Harper's New Monthly Magazine* 82 (January 1891), quoted in *Reception*, 78.
7 Andrew Lang, "The Newest Poet," *Daily News* (January 2, 1891), quoted in *Reception*, 81–3.
8 Quoted in *Reception*, 159, 163.
9 Conrad Aiken, ed., *Selected Poems of Emily Dickinson* (London: Jonathan Cape, 1924). Martha Dickinson Bianchi, ed., *The Complete Poems of Emily Dickinson* (London: Martin Secker, 1924).

10 Aiken, ed., *Selected Poems*, 14.
11 Ibid., 15.
12 Quoted in Caesar Robert Blake and Carlton Frank Wells (eds.), *The Recognition of Emily Dickinson: Selected Criticism since 1890* (Ann Arbor: University of Michigan Press, 1964), 124.
13 Margit Abenius, "Emily Dickinson," *Bonniers Litterära Magasin* 7 (1934), 22–3. Translation mine.
14 Ted Hughes, *A Choice of Emily Dickinson's Verse*, ed. Hughes (London: Faber, 1968); Seamus Heaney, 'Crediting Poetry,' in *Nobel Lectures: From the Literature Laureates, 1986 to 2006* (New York: New Press, 2007), 167.
15 Terry Gifford, *Ted Hughes* (Oxford: Routledge, 2009), 152. See also Aurelia Schober Plath (ed. and introd.), *Sylvia Plath: Letters Home* (London: Faber & Faber, 1976), 110, 5.
16 See Maria Stuart, "Dickinson in England and Ireland," in Domhnall Mitchell and Maria Stuart (eds.), *The International Reception of Emily Dickinson* (London: Continuum, 2009), 204–33.
17 Ted Hughes, "Review of *Emily Dickinson's Poetry* by Charles Anderson," *The Listener* Vol. LXX. No. 1798 (September 1963), 394.
18 Sirkka Heiskanen–Mäkelä, "Dickinsonian Idiom in Finnish, on a Par," *EDJ* 6.2 (1997), 45.
19 Victor Finkel, "Russian Translations of Emily Dickinson's Poetry (1969–1992)," *EDJ 18.1* (2009), 80.
20 Nabil Alawi, "Translating Dickinson's 'There came a Day at Summer's full' into Arabic," *EDJ* 6.2 (1997), 87–8.
21 Ibid., 87.
22 Marvin Zuckerman, "Dickinson in Yiddish," *EDJ* 6.2 (1997), 68–70.
23 Chanthana Chaichit, "Seeking an Artistic Translation of Emily Dickinson: A Thai Perspective," *EDJ* 6.2 (1997), 142.
24 William Dow, "French Responses to Dickinson," *An Emily Dickinson Encyclopedia* ed. Jane Donahue Eberwein (Westport, CT: Greenwood Press, 1998), 118–19.
25 Kikuo Kato (trans.), *The Complete Translation: The Poems of Emily Dickinson* (Tokyo: Kenyu-sha, 1976). Marisa Bulgheroni (trans.), *Emily Dickinson, Tutte le poesie* (Milano: Mondadori, 1997). Kurt Narvesen (trans.), *Samlede dikt: Emily Dickinson, 1* (Oslo: Bokvennen, 2008) and *Samlede dikt: Emily Dickinson, 2* (Oslo: Bokvennen, 2009). Claire Malroux (trans.), *Une âme en incandescence: Cahiers de poèmes, 1861–1863* (Paris: José Corti, 1998). Gunhild Kübler (trans.), *Emily Dickinson: Gedichte* (Munich: Hansler, 2006).
26 See Jennifer Hynes, "Thomas H. Johnson," in *An Emily Dickinson Encyclopedia*, 168; Edina Szalai, "The Critical 'Turn of the Screw' of Emily Dickinson's Reception: The Thomas Johnson Edition (1955)," *The 1950s: Proceedings of the 2003 Biennial Conference of the Hungarian Association of American Studies* (Budapest: ELTE, 2005), 177–81.
27 Roland Hagenbüchle, "Precision and Indeterminacy in the Poetry of Emily Dickinson," *ESQ 20.2* (1974), 137–95; Brita Lindberg-Seyersted, *The Voice of the*

      Poet: Aspects of Style in the Poetry of Emily Dickinson (Cambridge, MA: Harvard University Press, 1968); Mohammad Mansoor Khan, *Emily Dickinson's Poetry: Thematic Design and Texture* (New Delhi: Bahri Publications, 1983).
28 Marianne de Vooght, "Emily Dickinson in the Low Countries," *The International Reception of Emily Dickinson*, 61. Lennart Nyberg (trans.), *Emily Dickinson: Dikter* (Lund: Studentlitteratur, 1993).
29 Giuseppe Ierolli (trans.), *Emily Dickinson: Tutte le opere*. Available at: http://www.emilydickinson.it/.
30 See, e.g., Marisa Bulgheroni, *Nei Sobborghi di un Segreto: Vita di Emily Dickinson* (Milan: Mondadori, 2001); Michiko Iwata, *Emily Dickinson: I Dwell in Possibility* (Tokyo: Kaibunsha-shuppan, 2005).
31 Domhnall Mitchell, "Emily Dickinson in Norway," *The International Reception*, 91–2.
32 Lyndall Gordon, *Lives like Loaded Guns: Emily Dickinson and Her Family's Feud* (London: Virago, 2010).
33 Carlos Daghlian, "Emily Dickinson in Brazil," *The International Reception*, 142–3. de Vooght, "Emily Dickinson in the Low Countries," 59.
34 Stanislaw Baranczak, "Emily Dickinson's 'Because I could not stop for Death' – Remarks of a Polish Translator," *EDJ 6*.2 (1997), 122.
35 Ibid., 124.

Further Reading

1. AMHERST

Carpenter, Edward, and Charles Morehouse. *The History of the Town of Amherst, Massachusetts* (Amherst, MA: Carpenter and Morehouse, 1896).

Carter, Louise. "Gardening with Emily Dickinson," in Judith Farr, *The Gardens of Emily Dickinson* (Cambridge, MA: Harvard University Press, 2004), 214–63.

Eberwein, Jane Donahue. "Outgrowing Genesis? Dickinson, Darwin and the Higher Criticism," *Emily Dickinson and Philosophy*, eds. Jed Deppman, Marianne Noble, and Gary Lee Stonum (Cambridge: Cambridge University Press, 2013).

Habegger, Alfred. *My Wars Are Laid Away in Books: The Life of Emily Dickinson* (New York: Random House, 2001).

Lambert, Robert Graham Jr. *Emily Dickinson's Use of Anglo-American Legal Concepts and Vocabulary in Her Poetry: Muse at the Bar* (Lewiston, NY: Edwin Mellen Press, 1997).

Leyda, Jay. *The Years and Hours of Emily Dickinson* (New Haven, CT: Yale University Press, 1960).

Lombardo, Daniel. *A Hedge Away: The Other Side of Emily Dickinson's Amherst* (Northampton, MA: Daily Hampshire Gazette, 1997).

Longsworth, Polly. *The World of Emily Dickinson* (New York: W. W. Norton, 1990).

The Dickinsons of Amherst (Hanover: The University Press of New England, 2001).

Stuart, Maria. *"Contesting the Word: Emily Dickinson and the Higher Critics,"* Diss. (Cambridge University, 1997).

2. READING IN THE DICKINSON LIBRARIES

Capps, Jack L. *Emily Dickinson's Reading, 1836–1886* (Cambridge, MA: Harvard University Press, 1960).

Gordon, Lyndall. *Lives Like Loaded Guns: Emily Dickinson and Her Family's Feuds* (New York: Viking, 2010).

Horan, Elizabeth. "Mabel Loomis Todd, Martha Dickinson Bianchi, and the Spoils of the Dickinson Legacy," *A Living of Words: American Women in*

Print Culture, ed. Susan Albertine (Knoxville: The University of Tennessee Press, 1995), 65–93.
Lease, Benjamin. *Emily Dickinson's Readings of Men and Books: Sacred Soundings* (New York: St. Martin's Press, 1990).
Morris, Leslie A. "Foreword," *Emily Dickinson's Herbarium: A Facsimile Edition*. (Cambridge MA: The Belknap Press of Harvard University Press, 2006), 7–14. St. Armand, Barton Levi. "Keeper of the Keys: Mary Hampson, the Evergreens, and the Art Within," *The Dickinsons of Amherst*, ed. Jerome Liebling, Christopher Benfey, and Barton Levi St. Armand (Hanover: University Press of New England, 2001), 107–67.

3. EDUCATION

Capps, Jack. *Emily Dickinson's Reading, 1836–1886* (Cambridge: Harvard University Press, 1966).
Crain, Patricia. *The Story of A: The Alphabetization of America from the New England Primer to the Scarlet Letter* (Palo Alto, CA: Stanford University Press, 2000).
Eberwein, Jane Donahue. "Earth's Confiding Time: Childhood Trust and Christian Nurture," *EDJ* 17.1 (2008), 1–24.
Lowenberg, Carleton. *Emily Dickinson's Textbooks* (Lafayette, CA: Carleton Lowenberg, 1986).
Porterfield, Amanda. *Mary Lyon and the Mt. Holyoke Missionaries* (New York: Oxford University Press, 1997).
Scheurer, Erika. "'[S]o of course there was speaking and Composition - ': Dickinson's Early Schooling as a Writer," *EDJ* 18.1 (2009), 1–21.
Sorby, Angela. *Schoolroom Poets: Childhood, Performance, and the Place of American Poetry, 1865–1917* (Durham, NH: University Press of New England, 2005).

4. NEW ENGLAND PURITAN HERITAGE

Eberwein, Jane Donahue. "'Is Immortality True?': Salvaging Faith in an Age of Upheavals. *A Historical Guide to Emily Dickinson*, ed. Vivian R. Pollak (New York: Oxford University Press, 2004), 67–102.
Habegger, Alfred. *My Wars Are Laid Away in Books: The Life of Emily Dickinson* (New York: Random House, 2001).
Jones, Rowena Revis. "The Preparation of a Poet: Puritan Directions in Emily Dickinson's Education," *Studies in the American Renaissance* (Boston: Twayne, 1982), 285–324.
Keller, Karl. *The Only Kangaroo among the Beauty: Emily Dickinson and America* (Baltimore: Johns Hopkins University Press, 1979).
Lundin, Roger. *Emily Dickinson and the Art of Belief* (Grand Rapids, MI: Eerdmans, 1998).

5. NATURE'S INFLUENCE

Abram, David. *Becoming Animal: An Earthly Cosmology* (New York: Pantheon, 2010).

Benfey, Christopher. *A Summer of Hummingbirds: Love, Art, and Scandal in the Intersecting Worlds of Emily Dickinson, Mark Twain, Harriet Beecher Stowe, and Martin Johnson Heade* (New York: Penguin, 2008).

Farr, Judith, with Louise Carter. *The Gardens of Emily Dickinson* (Cambridge, MA: Harvard University Press, 2004).

Fauconnier, Gilles, and Mark Turner. *The Way We Think: Conceptual Blending and the Mind's Hidden Complexities* (New York: Basic Books, 2002).

Johnson, Mark. *The Body in the Mind: The Bodily Basis of Meaning, Imagination, and Reason* (Chicago: The University of Chicago Press, 1987).

Lakoff, George, and Mark Johnson. *Metaphors We Live By* (Chicago: The University of Chicago Press, 1980).

London, Peter. *Drawing Closer to Nature: Making Art in Dialogue with the Natural World* (Boston: Shambala, 2003).

Patterson, Rebecca. *Emily Dickinson's Imagery*, ed. Margaret H. Freeman (Amherst: University of Massachusetts Press, 1979).

6. THE BIBLE

Doriani, Beth Maclay. *Emily Dickinson, Daughter of Prophecy* (Amherst: University of Massachusetts Press, 1996).

Eberwein, Jane Donahue. *Dickinson: Strategies of Limitation* (Amherst: University of Massachusetts Press, 1985).

Freedman, Linda. *Emily Dickinson and the Religious Imagination* (New York: Cambridge University Press, 2011).

Jones, Rowena Revis. "'A Taste for Poison': Dickinson's Departure from Orthodoxy," *EDJ* 2.2 (1993), 47–64.

Lease, Benjamin. *Emily Dickinson's Reading of Men and Books: Sacred Soundings* (New York: St. Martin's, 1990).

Lundin, Roger. *Emily Dickinson and the Art of Belief* (Grand Rapids: Eerdmans, 2004 [1998]).

McIntosh, James. *Nimble Believing: Dickinson and the Unknown* (Ann Arbor: University of Michigan Press, 2004 [2000]).

Oberhaus, Dorothy Huff. *Emily Dickinson's Fascicles: Method and Meaning* (University Park: Pennsylvania State University Press, 1995).

Oliver, Virginia H. *Apocalypse of Green: A Study of Emily Dickinson's Eschatology* (New York: Peter Lang, 1989).

Ostriker, Alicia. "Re-playing the Bible: My Emily Dickinson." *EDJ* 2.2 (1993), 160–71.

7. SHAKESPEARE

Finnerty, Páraic. *Emily Dickinson's Shakespeare* (Amherst, MA: University of Massachusetts Press, 2006).
Gail Marshall. *Shakespeare and Victorian Women* (Cambridge: Cambridge University Press, 2009).
Novy, Marianne, ed. *Women's Re-visions of Shakespeare* (Urbana: University of Illinois Press, 1990).
Rawlings, Peter, ed. *Americans on Shakespeare, 1776–1914* (Aldershot, U.K.: Ashgate, 1999).
Teague, Frances. *Shakespeare and the American Popular Stage* (Cambridge: Cambridge University Press, 2006).
Thompson, Ann, and Sasha Roberts, eds. *Women Reading Shakespeare 1660–1900* (Manchester, U.K.: Manchester University Press, 1997).

8. RENAISSANCE AND EIGHTEENTH-CENTURY LITERATURE

Banzer, Judith (as Judith Farr). "'Compound Manner': Emily Dickinson and the Metaphysical Poets," *American Literature 32.4* (January 1961), 417–33.
Capps, Jack L. *Emily Dickinson's Reading, 1836–1886.* (Cambridge, MA: Harvard University Press, 1966).
Childs, Herbert E. "Emily Dickinson and Sir Thomas Browne," *American Literature 22.4* (1951), 455–65.
Lease, Benjamin. *Emily Dickinson's Readings of Men and Books* (London: Macmillan, 1990).
Pollak, Vivian R. "Emily Dickinson's Literary Allusions," *Essays in Literature 1.1* (Spring l974), 54–68.
Stonum, Gary Lee. "Dickinson's Literary Background," *Handbook*, 44–60.

9. BRITISH ROMANTIC AND VICTORIAN INFLUENCES

Cameron, Sharon. *Lyric Time: Dickinson and the Limits of Genre* (Baltimore: Johns Hopkins University Press, 1979).
Farr, Judith. *The Passion of Emily Dickinson* (Cambridge, MA: Harvard University Press, 1992).
Finnerty, Páraic. "'Dreamed of your meeting Tennyson in Ticknor and Fields - ': A Transatlantic Encounter with Britain's Poet Laureate," *EDJ 20.1* (2011), 56–77.
Jackson, Virginia. *Dickinson's Misery: A Theory of Lyric Reading* (Princeton, NJ: Princeton University Press, 2005).
Loeffelholz, Mary. *Dickinson and the Boundaries of Feminist Theory* (Chicago: University of Illinois Press, 1991).
Willis, Elizabeth. "Dickinson's Species of Narrative," *EDJ 18.1* (2009), 22–31.

10. TRANSATLANTIC WOMEN WRITERS

Chapman, Alison. "'I Think I Was Enchanted': Elizabeth Barrett Browning's Haunting of American Women Poets," *Representations of Death in Nineteenth-Century US Writing and Culture*, ed. Lucy Frank (Aldershot, U.K.: Ashgate, 2007), 109–24.

Doyle, Christine. *Louisa May Alcott and Charlotte Brontë* (Knoxville: University of Tennessee Press, 2000).

Loeffelholz, Mary. *Dickinson and the Boundaries of Feminist Theory* (Urbana and Chicago: University of Illinois Press, 1991).

Mueller, Monika. *George Eliot U.S.: Transatlantic Literary and Cultural Perspectives* (Madison, NJ: Fairleigh Dickinson University Press, 2005).

11. IMMEDIATE U.S. LITERARY PREDECESSORS

Capps, Jack. *Emily Dickinson's Reading, 1846–1886* (Harvard University Press, 1966).

Cohen, Michael. "Whittier, Ballad Reading, and the Culture of Nineteenth-Century Poetry," *Arizona Quarterly* 64.3 (2008), 1–29.

Dickinson, Susan. "Harriet Prescott's Early Work," *Springfield Republican* (January 1903).

Loeffelholz, Mary. *From School to Salon: Reading Nineteenth-Century American Women's Poetry* (Princeton, NJ: Princeton University Press, 2004).

Miller, Cristanne. "Dickinson and the Ballad," *Genre* (forthcoming 2012).

Reading in Time: Dickinson in the Nineteenth Century (University of Massachusetts Press, 2012).

Petrino, Elizabeth A. *Emily Dickinson and Her Contemporaries: Women's Verse in America, 1820–1885* (Hanover, NH: University Press of New England, 1998).

Saint Armand, Barton Levi. *Emily Dickinson and Her Culture: The Soul's Society* (Cambridge: Cambridge University Press, 1984).

Small, Judy Jo. *Positive as Sound: Emily Dickinson's Rhyme* (Athens, GA: University of Georgia Press, 1990).

12. U.S. LITERARY CONTEMPORARIES: DICKINSON'S MODERNS

Bennett, Paula. *Emily Dickinson: Woman Poet* (Iowa City: University of Iowa Press, 1990).

Loeffelholz, Mary. *From School to Salon: Reading Nineteenth-Century American Women's Poetry* (Princeton, NJ: Princeton University Press, 2004).

Petrino, Elizabeth A. *Emily Dickinson and Her Contemporaries: Women's Verse in America, 1820–1885* (Hanover, NH: University Press of New England, 1998).

Walker, Cheryl. *The Nightingale's Burden: Women Poets and American Culture before 1900* (Bloomington: Indiana University Press, 1982).

13. PERIODICAL READING

Kirkby, Joan. "Dickinson Reading," *EDJ* 5.2 (1997), 247–54.

"*The Atlantic Monthly,*" "*The Hampshire and Franklin Express,*" "*Harper's,*" "*Scribners,*" *An Emily Dickinson Encyclopedia,* ed. Jane Donahue Eberwein (Westport, CT and London: Greenwood Press, 1998).

"'[We] thought Darwin Had Thrown the "Redeemer" away': Darwinizing with Emily Dickinson," *EDJ* 19.1 (2010), 1–29.

Lease, Benjamin. *Emily Dickinson's Readings of Men and Books* (Basingstoke and London: Macmillan, 1990).

Lombardo, Daniel. "What the Dickinsons Read," *Tales of Amherst: A Look Back* (Amherst: The Jones Library Inc., 1986), 100–3.

Scholnick Robert J. "'Don't Tell! They'd Advertise': Emily Dickinson in the Round Table," "*The Only Efficient Instrument*": *American Women Writers & the Periodical 1837–1916,* ed. Aleta Feinsod Cane & Susan Alves (Iowa City: University of Iowa Press, 2000), 166–82.

Strickland, Georgiana. "*The Springfield Republican,*" *An Emily Dickinson Encyclopedia,* ed. Jane Donahue Eberwein (Westport, CT: Greenwood Press), 1998.

Thomas Shannon L. "'What News must think when pondering': Emily Dickinson, *The Springfield Daily Republican,* and the Poetics of Mass Communication," *EDJ* 19.1 (2010), 60–80.

14. RELIGION

Buell, Lawrence. *New England Literary Culture: From Revolution through Renaissance* (Cambridge: Cambridge University Press, 1986).

Eberwein, Jane Donahue. *Dickinson: Strategies of Limitation* (Amherst: University of Massachusetts Press, 1985).

"'Is Immortality True?': Salvaging Faith in an Age of Upheavals," *A Historical Guide to Emily Dickinson,* ed. Vivian R. Pollak (New York: Oxford University Press, 2004), 67–102.

Freedman, Linda. *Emily Dickinson and the Religious Imagination* (New York: Cambridge University Press, 2011).

Habegger, Alfred. *My Wars Are Laid Away in Books: The Life of Emily Dickinson* (New York: Random House, 2001).

Jones, Rowena Revis. "The Preparation of a Poet: Puritan Directions in Emily Dickinson's Education," *Studies in the American Renaissance* (1982), 285–324.

Keane, Patrick J. *Emily Dickinson's Approving God: Divine Design and the Problem of Suffering* (Columbus: University of Missouri Press, 2008).

Lundin, Roger. *Emily Dickinson and the Art of Belief.* Second Edition (Grand Rapids, MI: William B. Eerdmans, 2004).

McIntosh, James. *Nimble Believing: Dickinson and the Unknown* (Ann Arbor: University of Michigan Press, 2000).

Oberhaus, Dorothy Huff. "'Tender Pioneer': Emily Dickinson's Poems on the Life of Christ," *American Literature* 59 (1987), 341–58.

St. Armand, Barton Levi. *Emily Dickinson and Her Culture: The Soul's Society* (New York: Cambridge University Press, 1984).
Sewall, Richard B. *The Life of Emily Dickinson* (New York: Farrar, Straus and Giroux, 1974).

15. DEATH AND IMMORTALITY

Cameron, Sharon. *Lyric Time: Dickinson and the Limits of Genre* (Baltimore: John Hopkins University Press, 1979).
Deppman, Jed. "Dickinson, Death, and the Sublime," *EDJ 9*.1 (2000), 1–20.
Ford, Thomas W. *Heaven Beguiles the Tired: Death in the Poetry of Emily Dickinson* (Birmingham: University of Alabama Press, 1966).
Kirkby, Joan. "'A crescent still abides': Emily Dickinson and the Work of Mourning," *Wider than the Sky: Essays and Meditations on the Healing Power of Emily Dickinson*, ed. Cindy MacKenzie and Barbara Dana (Kent, OH: Kent State University, 2007), 129–40.
Petrino, Elizabeth A. "'Alabaster Chambers': Dickinson, Epitaphs, and the Culture of Mourning," *Emily Dickinson and Her Contemporaries* (Hanover, NH: University Press of New England, 1998), 96–129.
Raymond, Claire. *The Posthumous Voice in Women's Writing from Mary Shelley to Sylvia Plath* (London: Ashgate, 2006).
St. Armand, Barton Levi. *Emily Dickinson and Her Culture: The Soul's Society* (Cambridge: Cambridge University Press, 1984).

16. GENDERED POETICS

Dobson, Joanne. *Dickinson and the Strategies of Reticence* (Bloomington: Indiana University Press, 1989).
Elshtein, Jean Bethke. *Private Woman, Public Man* (Princeton, NJ: Princeton University Press, 1981).
Felski, Rita. *Doing Time: Feminist Theory and Postmodern Culture* (New York: New York University Press, 2000).
Gilligan, Carole. *In a Different Voice* (Cambridge, MA: Harvard University Press, 1993).
Miller, Cristanne. *Emily Dickinson: A Poet's Grammar* (Cambridge, MA: Harvard University Press, 1987).
Pateman, Carole. *The Disorder of Women* (Stanford, CA: Stanford University Press, 1989).
Rosaldo, Michelle Zimbalest. "Woman, Culture and Society: A Theoretical Overview," *Women, Culture, Society*, ed. Michelle Zimbalist Rosaldo and Louise Lamphere (Stanford, CA: Stanford University Press, 1975), 17–42.
Ruether, Rosemary Radford, and Rosemary Skinner Keller, eds. *Women and Religion in America*, Vol. 1 (San Francisco: Harper & Row, 1981).
Ryan, Mary. *Women in Public* (Baltimore: The Johns Hopkins Press, 1990).

Smith-Rosenberg, Carroll. *Disorderly Conduct* (New York: Oxford University Press, 1985).
Wolosky, Shira. *Emily Dickinson: A Voice of War* (New Haven, CT: Yale University Press, 1984).
Poetry and Public Discourse (New York: Palgrave Macmillan, 2011).

17. DEMOCRATIC POLITICS

Barrett, Faith. "Public Selves and Private Spheres: Studies of Emily Dickinson and the Civil War, 1984–2007," *EDJ 16*.1 (2007), 92–104.
Crumbley Paul. *Winds of Will: Emily Dickinson and the Sovereignty of Democratic Thought* (Tuscaloosa: University of Alabama Press), 2010.
Erkkila Betsy. "Dickinson and the Art of Politics," *A Historical Guide to Emily Dickinson*, ed. Vivian Pollak (New York: Oxford University Press, 2004), 133–74.
Hutchison Coleman. "'Eastern Exiles': Dickinson, Whiggery, and War," *EDJ 13*.2 (2004), 1–26.
Ruttenburg Nancy. *Democratic Personality: Popular Voice and the Trial of American Authorship* (Stanford, CA: Stanford University Press, 1998).
Sanborn Geoffrey. "Keeping Her Distance: Cisneros, Dickinson, and the Politics of Private Enjoyment," *PMLA 116*.5 (October 2001), 1334–48.
Wolosky Shira. *Poetry and Public Discourse in Nineteenth-Century America* (New York: Palgrave, 2010).

18. ECONOMICS

Burbick, Joan. "Emily Dickinson and the Economics of Desire," *American Literature 58*.3 (1986): 361–78.
Erkkila, Betsy. "Emily Dickinson and Class," *American Literary History 4* (1992), 1–27.
Guthrie, James. "'Some things that I called mine': Dickinson and the Perils of Property Ownership," *EDJ 9*.2 (2000), 16–22.
Horan, Elizabeth. "To Market: The Dickinson Copyright Wars," *EDJ 5*.1 (1996), 88–120.
"Technically Outside the Law: Who Permits, Who Profits, and Why," *EDJ 10*.1 (2001), 34–54.
Merideth, Robert. "Emily Dickinson and the Acquisitive Society," *The New England Quarterly 37*.4 (1964), 435–52.
Mitchell, Domhnall. *Emily Dickinson: Monarch of Perception* (Amherst: University of Massachusetts Press, 2000).
Pollak, Vivian R. "'That Fine Prosperity': Economic Metaphors in Emily Dickinson's Poetry," *Modern Language Quarterly 34*.2 (1973), 161–79.
Stoneley, Peter. "'I - Pay - in Satin Cash - ': Commerce, Gender, and Display in Emily Dickinson's Poetry," *American Literature 72*.3 (2000), 575–94.

19. LAW AND LEGAL DISCOURSE

Dakin, Winthrop. "Lawyers Around Emily Dickinson," *Dickinson Studies 47* (1983), 36–40.

Diehl, Joanne Feit. "'Ransom in a Voice': Language as Defense in Dickinson's Poetry," *Feminist Critics Read Emily Dickinson*, ed. Suzanne Juhasz (Bloomington: Indiana University Press, 1983), 156–75.

Dietrich, Deborah. "Legal Imagery," *An Emily Dickinson Encyclopedia*, ed. Jane Donahue Eberwein (Westport, CT: Greenwood Press, 1998), 172–3.

Erkkila, Betsy. "Emily Dickinson and Class," *American Literary History* 4.1 (1992), 1–27.

  The Wicked Sisters: Women Poets, Literary History, and Discord (Oxford: Oxford University Press, 1992).

Guthrie, James R. "Law, Property, and Provincialism in Dickinson's Letters and Poems to Judge Otis Phillips Lord," *EDJ* 5.1 (1996), 27–44.

  "'Some Things That I Called Mine': Dickinson and the Perils of Property Ownership," *EDJ* 9.2 (2000), 16–22.

  "Darwinian Dickinson: The Scandalous Rise and Noble Fall of the Common Clover." *EDJ* 16.1 (2007), 73–91.

  "Heritable Heaven: Erotic Properties in the Dickinson-Lord Correspondence," *Reading Emily Dickinson's Letters: Critical Essays*, ed. Jane Donahue Eberwein and Cindy MacKenzie (Amherst: University of Massachusetts Press, 2009), 189–212.

Horan, Elizabeth. "Technically Outside the Law: Who Permits, Who Profits, and Why," *EDJ* 10.1 (2001), 34–54.

Howard, William. "Emily Dickinson's Poetic Vocabulary," *PMLA* 72.1 (1957), 225–48.

Lambert, Robert G., *Emily Dickinson's Use of Anglo-American Legal Concepts and Vocabulary in Her Poetry: Muse at the Bar* (Lewiston, NY: Edwin Mellen Press, 1997).

Mitchell, Domhnall. "Emily Dickinson and Class," *The Cambridge Companion to Emily Dickinson*, ed. Wendy Martin (Cambridge: Cambridge University Press, 2002), 191–214.

Sedarat, Roger. *New England Landscape History in American Poetry: A Lacanian View* (Amherst, NY: Cambria Press, 2011).

Smith, B.J. "Vicinity to Laws," *Dickinson Studies 56* (1985), 38–52.

20. SLAVERY AND THE CIVIL WAR

Barrett, Faith. *To Fight Aloud Is Very Brave: American Poetry and the Civil War* (Amherst: University of Massachusetts Press, 2012).

  "Public Selves and Private Spheres: Studies of Emily Dickinson and the Civil War, 1984–2007," *EDJ* 16.1 (2007), 92–104.

Bergland, Renée. "The Eagle's Eye: Dickinson's View of Battle," *A Companion to Emily Dickinson*, ed. Martha Nell Smith and Mary Loeffelholz (Oxford: Blackwell, 2008), 133–56.

Friedlander, Benjamin. "Auctions of the Mind: Emily Dickinson and Abolition," *Arizona Quarterly 54*.1 (1998), 1–25.

"Emily Dickinson and the Battle of Ball's Bluff," *PMLA 124*.5 (2009), 1582–99.

Hutchinson, Coleman. "'Eastern Exiles': Dickinson, Whiggery, and War," *EDJ 13*.2 (2004), 1–26.

Lee, Maurice. "Writing through the War: Melville and Dickinson after the Renaissance," *PMLA 115* (2000), 1124–8.

Miller, Cristanne. *Reading in Time: Dickinson in the Nineteenth Century* (Amherst: University of Massachusetts Press, 2012).

Pollak, Vivian. "Dickinson and the Poetics of Whiteness," *EDJ 9*.2 (2000): 84–95.

Richards, Eliza. "'How News Must Feel When Traveling': Dickinson and Civil War Media," *A Companion to Emily Dickinson*, ed. Martha Nell Smith and Mary Loeffelholz (Oxford: Blackwell, 2008), 157–79.

St. Armand, Barton Levi. *Emily Dickinson and Her Culture: The Soul's Society* (Cambridge: Cambridge University Press, 1984).

Wolosky, Shira. *Emily Dickinson: A Voice of War* (New Haven, CT: Yale University Press, 1984).

21. POPULAR CULTURE

Bean, Annemarie, James V. Hatch, and Brooks McNamara, eds. *Inside the Minstrel Mask: Readings in Nineteenth-Century Blackface Minstrelsy* (Hanover, NH: Wesleyan University Press, 1996).

Cockrell, Dale. *Demons of Disorder: Early Blackface Minstrels and Their World* (Cambridge: Cambridge University Press, 1997).

Dennett, Andrea Stulman. *Weird and Wonderful: The Dime Museum in America.* (New York: New York University Press, 1997).

Finson, Jon W. *The Voices That Are Gone: Themes in Nineteenth-Century American Popular Song* (New York: Oxford University Press, 1994).

Levine, Lawrence W. *Highbrow/Lowbrow: The Emergence of Cultural Hierarchy in America* (Cambridge MA: Harvard University Press, 1988).

Lott, Eric. *Love and Theft: Blackface Minstrelsy and the American Working Class.* (New York: Oxford University Press, 1993).

Mahar, William J. *Behind the Burnt Cork Mask: Early Blackface Minstrelsy and Antebellum American Popular Culture.* (Urbana: University of Illinois Press, 1999).

22. VISUAL ARTS: THE PENTIMENTO

Cikovsky, Nicolai, Jr., and Franklin Kelly. *Winslow Homer* (Washington, DC: National Gallery of Art, 1995).

Danly Susan, ed. *Language as Object: Emily Dickinson and Contemporary Art* (Amherst, MA: Mead Art Museum, 1997).

Farr, Judith. *The Passion of Emily Dickinson* (Cambridge, MA: Harvard University Press, 1992).

Greenhill, Jennifer. "Winslow Homer and the Mechanics of Visual Deadpan," *Art History 32* (April 2009), 351–86.
Nemerov, Alexander. *Acting in the Night: Macbeth and the Places of the Civil War* (Berkeley: University of California Press, 2010).
Richards, Eliza. "'How News Must Feel When Traveling': Dickinson and Civil War Media," *A Companion to Emily Dickinson*, ed. Martha Neil Smith and Mary Loeffelholz (Oxford: Blackwell, 2008), 157–79.
St. Armand, Barton. *Emily Dickinson and Her Culture: The Soul's Society* (Cambridge, MA: Harvard University Press, 1984).
Simpson, Marc, ed. *Winslow Homer Paintings of the Civil War* (San Francisco: The Fine Arts Museums of San Francisco, 1988).

23. NATURAL SCIENCES

Deppman, Jed. *Trying to Think with Emily Dickinson* (Amherst: University of Massachusetts Press, 2008).
Hagenbüchle, Roland. "Precision and Indeterminacy in the Poetry of Emily Dickinson," *Emerson Society Quarterly 20*.1 (1974), 33–56.
Manning, Susan, "How Conscious Could Consciousness Grow? Emily Dickinson and William James," *Soft Canons: American Women Writers and Masculine Tradition*, ed. Karen L. Kilcup (Iowa City: University of Iowa Press, 1999), 306–31.
Otten, Thomas J. "Emily Dickinson's Brain: On Lyric and the History of Anatomy." *Prospects: An Annual of American Cultural Studies*, 29 (2005), 57–83.
Peel, Robin. *Emily Dickinson and the Hill of Science* (Madison: Fairleigh Dickinson University Press, 2010).
Sielke, Sabine. "'The Brain - is wider than the Sky - ' or: Re-Cognizing Emily Dickinson", *EDJ 17*.1 (2008), 68–85.
 "Biology", *The Routledge Companion to Literature and Science*, ed. Bruce Clarke and Manuela Rossini (London: Routledge, 2010), 29–40.
 Fashioning the Female Subject: The Intertextual Networking of Dickinson, Moore and Rich (Ann Arbor: University of Michigan Press, 1997).
Uno, Hiroko. "'Chemical Conviction': Dickinson, Hitchcock and the Poetry of Science," *EDJ 7*.2 (1998), 95–111.
White, Fred D. "'Sweet Skepticism of the Heart': Science in the Poetry of Emily Dickinson." *College Literature 19*.1 (1992), 121–8.

24. NINETEENTH-CENTURY LANGUAGE THEORY AND THE MANUSCRIPT VARIANTS

Berlin, James A. *Writing Instruction in Nineteenth-Century American Colleges* (Carbondale, IL: Southern Illinois University Press, 1984).
Cameron, Sharon. *Choosing Not Choosing: Dickinson's Fascicles* (Chicago: University of Chicago Press, 1992).

Lyric Time: Dickinson and the Limits of Genre (Baltimore: Johns Hopkins University Press, 1979).
Deppman, Jed. *Trying to Think With Emily Dickinson* (Amherst: University of Massachusetts Press, 2008).
Engell, James. "The New Rhetoric and Romantic Poetics," *Rhetorical Traditions and British Romantic Literature*, ed. Don Bialostosky and Lawrence D. Needham (Bloomington: Indiana University Press, 1995).
Scarry, Elaine. *The Body in Pain: The Making and Unmaking of the World* (London: Oxford University Press, 1987).

25. "SAY SOME PHILOSOPHER!"

Deppman, Jed. *Trying to Think with Emily Dickinson* (Amherst: Massachusetts University Press, 2008).
Deppman, Jed, Marianne Noble, and Gary Lee Stonum, eds. *Emily Dickinson and Philosophy* (Cambridge University Press, 2013).
Flower, Elizabeth and Murray G Murphey. *A History of Philosophy in America*, 2 vols. (New York: G. P. Putnam's Sons, 1977).
Gelpi, Albert. *The Mind of the Poet* (Cambridge, MA: Harvard University Press, 1965).
Hedge, Frederic Henry. *Prose Writers of Germany* (Philadelphia: Carey and Hart, 1848).
Juhasz, Suzanne. *The Undiscovered Continent: Emily Dickinson and the Space of the Mind* (Bloomington: Indiana University Press, 1983).
Kuklick, Bruce. *A History of Philosophy in America, 1720–2000* (Oxford: Clarendon Press, 2001).
Porter, David. *The Modern Idiom* (Cambridge, MA: Harvard University Press, 1981).
Stonum, Gary Lee. *The Dickinson Sublime* (Madison: Wisconsin University Press, 1990).
Upham, Thomas Cogwell. *Elements of Mental Philosophy* (New York: Harper and Brothers, 1842).
  Outlines of Imperfect and Disordered Mental Action (New York: Harper and Brothers, 1840).
Watts, Isaac. *On the Improvement of the Mind*, ed. Joseph Emerson (New York: A. S. Barnes, 1849).

26. EDITORIAL HISTORY I: BEGINNINGS TO 1955

Bingham, Millicent Todd. *Ancestors' Brocades: The Literary Debut of Emily Dickinson* (New York: Harper & Brothers, 1945).
Buckingham Willis J. *Emily Dickinson's Reception in the 1890s: A Documentary History* (Pittsburgh: University of Pittsburgh Press, 1989).
Erskine, John. "The Dickinson Feud," *The Memory of Certain Persons* (Philadelphia: J.P. Lippincott, 1947), 128–38.

Franklin, R.W. *The Editing of Emily Dickinson: A Reconsideration* (Madison: University of Wisconsin Press, 1967).
Gordon, Lyndall. *Lives Like Loaded Guns: Emily Dickinson and Her Family's Feuds* (New York: Viking Penguin, 2012).
Lubbers, Klaus. *Emily Dickinson: The Critical Revolution* (Ann Arbor: University of Michigan Press, 1968).
Myerson, Joel. *Emily Dickinson: A Descriptive Bibliography* (Pittsburgh: University of Pittsburgh Press, 1984).
Smith, Martha Nell. *Rowing in Eden: Rereading Emily Dickinson* (Austin: University of Texas Press, 1992).

27. EDITORIAL HISTORY II: 1955 TO THE PRESENT

Bingham, Millicent Todd. *Ancestors' Brocades: The Literary Discovery of Emily Dickinson; The Editing and Publication of her Letters and Poems* (New York: Dover Publications, 1945).
Christensen, Lena. *Editing Emily Dickinson: The Production of an Author* (New York: Routledge, 2008).
Dickie, Margaret. "Dickinson in Context," *American Literary History* 7.2 (1995), 320–33.
Franklin, R. W. *The Editing of Emily Dickinson: A Reconsideration* (Madison: University of Wisconsin Press, 1967).
Jackson, Virginia. *Dickinson's Misery: A Theory of Lyric Reading* (Princeton, NJ: Princeton University Press, 2005).
Loeffelholz, Mary. "What Is a Fascicle? Reading Dickinson's Manuscript Books," *The Harvard Library Bulletin 10* (Spring 1999), 23–42.
Miller, Cristanne. "Controversy in the Study of Emily Dickinson." *Literary Imagination: The Review of the Association of Literary Scholars and Critics 6.*1 (2004), 39–50.
Smith, Martha Nell. *Rowing in Eden: Rereading Emily Dickinson* (Austin: University of Texas Press, 1992).
Werner, Marta L. "'A Woe of Ecstasy': On the Electronic Editing of Emily Dickinson's Late Fragments." *EDJ 16.*2 (2007), 25–52.

28. ON MATERIALITY (AND VIRTUALITY)

Cameron, Sharon. *Choosing Not Choosing: Dickinson's Fascicles* (Chicago: University of Chicago Press, 1992).
Dickinson Electronic Archives. University of Virginia Press. Available at: www.emilydickinson.org/index.html
Franklin, Ralph W., ed. *The Manuscript Books of Emily Dickinson* (Cambridge, MA: Harvard University Press, 1981).
Heginbotham, Eleanor Elson. *Reading the Fascicles of Emily Dickinson: Dwelling in Possibilities* (Columbus: Ohio State University Press, 2003).
Juhasz, Suzanne. "Materiality and the Poet," *Handbook,* 427–39.

Loeffelholz, Mary. "What Is a Fascicle?" *Harvard Library Bulletin* 10.1 (Spring 1999).
Mitchell, Domhnall. *Measures of Possibility: Emily Dickinson's Manuscripts* (Amherst: University of Massachusetts Press, 2005).
Oberhaus, Dorothy. *Emily Dickinson's Fascicles: Method and Meaning* (University Park: Pennsylvania State University Press, 1995).
Smith, Martha Nell, and Ellen Louise Hart, eds. *Open Me Carefully: Emily Dickinson's Intimate Letters to Susan Huntington Dickinson* (Ashfield, MA: Paris Press, 1998).
Socarides, Alexandra. *Dickinson Unbound: Paper, Process, Poetics* (New York: Oxford University Press, 2012).
Werner, Marta, ed. *Emily Dickinson's Open Folios: Scenes of Reading, Surfaces of Writing* (Ann Arbor: University of Michigan Press, 1995).

29. THE LETTERS ARCHIVE

Decker, William Merrill. *Epistolary Practices: Letter Writing in America before Telecommunications* (Chapel Hill: University of North Carolina Press, 1998).
Eberwein, Jane Donahue, and Cindy MacKenzie, eds. *Reading Emily Dickinson's Letters: Critical Essays* (Amherst: University of Massachusetts Press, 2009).
Hewitt, Elizabeth. *Correspondence and American Literature, 1770–1865* (Cambridge: Cambridge University Press, 2004).
Messmer, Marietta. *A Vice for Voices: Reading Emily Dickinson's Correspondences* (Amherst: University of Massachusetts Press, 2001).
Salzka, Agnieszka. "Dickinson's Letters," *Handbook*, 163–80.
Smith, Martha Nell. *Rowing in Eden: Rereading Emily Dickinson* (Austin: University of Texas Press, 1992).

30. CRITICAL HISTORY I: 1890–1955

Blake, Caesar, and Carton Wells, eds. *The Recognition of Emily Dickinson: Selected Criticism since 1890* (Ann Arbor: The University of Michigan Press, 1964);
Buckingham, Willis J. *Emily Dickinson: An Annotated Bibliography; Writings, Scholarship, Criticism and Ana 1850–1968* (Bloomington: Indiana University Press, 1970).
Lubbers, Klaus. *Emily Dickinson: The Critical Revolution* (Ann Arbor: The University of Michigan Press, 1968).
Messmer, Marietta. "Dickinson's Critical Reception," *Handbook*, 299–322.
Sewall, Richard. *Emily Dickinson: A Collection of Critical Essays* (Englewood Cliffs, NJ: Prentice-Hall, 1963).

31. CRITICAL HISTORY II: 1955 TO THE PRESENT

Ackmann, Martha. "Biographical Studies of Dickinson," *Handbook* 11–23.
Barrett, Faith. "Public Selves and Private Spheres: Studies of Emily Dickinson and the Civil War, 1984–2007," *EDJ 16.1* (2007), 92–104.

Dickie, Margaret. "Feminist Conceptions of Dickinson," *Handbook*, 342–55.
Hagenbüchle, Roland. "Dickinson and Literary Theory," *Handbook*, 356–84.
Lubbers, Klaus. *Emily Dickinson: The Critical Revolution* (Ann Arbor: University of Michigan Press, 1968).
Messmer, Marietta. "Dickinson's Critical Reception," *Handbook*, 299–322.
White, Fred. *Approaching Emily Dickinson: Critical Currents and Crosscurrents Since 1960* (Rochester, NY: Camden, 2008).

32. DICKINSON'S INFLUENCE

Benfey, Christopher. "Alcohol and Pearl: Dickinson's Imprint on American Poetry," *Language as Object: Emily Dickinson and Contemporary Art*, ed. Susan Danly (Amherst: University of Massachusetts Press, 1997), 43–50.
Gardner, Thomas. *A Door Ajar: Contemporary Writers and Emily Dickinson* (Oxford: Oxford University Press, 2006).
Gelpi, Albert. "Emily Dickinson's Long Shadow," *EDJ* 17.2 (2008), 100–12.
Hogue, Cynthia. "'The Plucked String': Emily Dickinson, Marianne Moore and the Poetics of Select Defects," *EDJ* 7.1 (1998), 89–109.
Howe, Susan. *The Birth-mark* (Hanover, NH: Wesleyan University Press, 1993).
 My Emily Dickinson (Berkeley: North Atlantic Books, 1985).
Keller, Karl. *The Only Kangaroo among the Beauty: Emily Dickinson and America* (Baltimore: Johns Hopkins University Press, 1979).
Leavell, Linda. "Marianne Moore's Emily Dickinson," *EDJ* 12.2 (2003), 1–20.
Pollak, Vivian R. "American Women Poets Reading Dickinson: The Example of Helen Hunt Jackson," *Handbook*, 322–41.
Sielke, Sabine. *Fashioning the Female Subject: The Intertextual Networking of Dickinson, Moore, and Rich* (Ann Arbor: University of Michigan Press, 1997).
Smith, Martha Nell, ed. "Titanic Operas: A Poet's Corner of Responses to Dickinson's Legacy." *Dickinson Electronic Archives*. Available at: http://www.emilydickinson.org/titanic/.
Weisbuch, Robert. "Prisming Dickinson; or, Gathering Paradise by Letting Go," *Handbook*, 197–223.

33. TRANSLATION AND INTERNATIONAL RECEPTION

Blake, Caesar Robert, and Carlton Frank Wells, eds. *The Recognition of Emily Dickinson: Selected Criticism since 1890* (Ann Arbor: University of Michigan Press, 1964).
Eberwein, Jane Donahue, ed., *An Emily Dickinson Encyclopedia* (Westwood, CT: Greenwood Press, 1998).
Freeman, Margaret H., Gudrun Grabher, and Roland Hagenbüchle, eds. "Translating Dickinson (Special Issue)," *EDJ*, 6.2 (1997), 1–188.
Grabher, Gudrun, Roland Hagenbüchle, and Cristanne Miller, eds. *The Emily Dickinson Handbook* (Amherst, MA: University of Massachusetts Press, 1999).

Lilliedahl, Ann. *Emily Dickinson in Europe: Her Literary Reputation in Selected Countries*, (Washington, DC: University Press of America, 1981).
Lubbers, Klaus, *Emily Dickinson: The Critical Revolution* (Ann Arbor: The University of Michigan, 1968).
Miller, Cristanne, ed. "Special Section: The Global Translation and Reception of Emily Dickinson," *EDJ 18*.1 (2009), 69–104.
Mitchell, Domhnall, and Maria Stuart, eds. *The International Reception of Emily Dickinson* (London: Continuum Press, 2009).

Index

Abbot, John S.C., 151
  The Mother at Home, 151
Abenius, Margit, 346
Abercrombie, John, 165
  Inquiries Concerning the Intellectual Powers, 165
  'Our Knowledge of the Mind', 165
Adams, Allen J., 84
Addison, Joseph, 94, 96
affect, 36, 38, 40, 43
Agricultural College, 140
agriculture, 20, 30, 57, 227
Aiken, Conrad, 311, 345, 346
  Modern American Poets, 345
  Selected Poems of Emily Dickinson, 345
Alawi, Nabil, 347
Alcott, Bronson, 140
Alcott, Louisa May, 81, 117, 141
Aldrich, Thomas Bailey, 311, 312, 317
Allen, George, 96
American Museum, 216
American Whig Review, 110
Amherst Academy, 13, 36, 37, 39, 41, 42, 70, 71, 83, 140, 143, 151, 162, 165, 238, 246, 250, 259, 260, 261
Amherst College, 13, 16, 17, 37, 41, 50, 79, 84, 140, 151, 154, 162, 189, 190, 196, 208, 261, 295
Amherst Female Seminary, 13
Amherst Record, 30, 139
Amherst, Massachusetts, 6, 13–23, 40, 43, 47, 49, 50, 56, 57, 59, 60, 62, 63, 70, 71, 80, 84, 109, 139, 140, 151, 169, 199, 210, 217, 221, 274, 278, 297, 346, 348
Amsterdam, 348
Anderson, Charles, 222, 323
  Emily Dickinson's Poetry: Stairway of Surprise, 323
Andover Divinity School, 48

Anthon, Kate, 306, 316
Arabic, 347
archaeology, 104
Argentina, 350
Arminianism, 49
Asia, 14
astronomy, 4, 28, 29, 236, 238, 258
The Atlantic Monthly, 14, 29, 38, 44, 81, 98, 99, 100, 115, 120, 123, 124, 127, 130, 131, 134, 139, 141, 164, 170, 221, 233, 350
Auden, W.H., 346
Aurora Borealis, 17, 18
Australia, 350
Austria, 350
Azarian School, 134

Bacon, Delia, 81
Bacon, Francis, 91
Baily, George F., 217
Baltimore, Maryland, 200
Baranczak, Stanislaw, 349
Barlow, Francis Channing, 230
Barnum, P.T., 216, 221
Barrett, Faith, 4, 324
Barry, John, 332
Barthes, Roland, 161
Bates, Arlo, 312, 316
Baudelaire, Charles, 141
Baxter Upon the Will, 47
Beadsley, Monroe C., 312
  'The Affective Fallacy', 314
  'The Intentional Fallacy', 314
Beardsley, Monroe C., 314
Beaumont, Francis, 91
Beecher, Henry Ward, 29, 142
  Life of Jesus the Christ, 29
Belchertown, Massachusetts, 16
Belgium, 350
Benfey, Christopher, 100, 308
Bennett, Alan, 344
  The Uncommon Reader, 344

Bennett, Paula, 325, 328
  Emily Dickinson: Woman Poet, 325
Bereaved of all, I went abroad - , 109
Berlin, James A., 246, 247
  Writing Instruction in Nineteenth-Century American Colleges, 246
Bianchi, Martha Dickinson, 31, 32, 276, 277–8, 279, 304, 308, 345
  Emily Dickinson Face to Face: Unpublished Letters with Notes and Reminiscences, 276, 278 304
  Further Poems of Emily Dickinson, 343
  The Life and Letters of Emily Dickinson, 276, 304
  The Single Hound, 276, 343
Bible, 3, 6, 29, 37, 42, 46, 53, 69–77, 83, 89, 91, 94, 95, 140, 143, 151, 153, 162, 218, 283, 328
  Acts, 76
  Corinthians, 163
  Genesis, 104
  Revelations, 76, 105
Bichat, Xavier, 241
Bingham Collection, 32
Bingham, Millicent Todd, 29, 32, 33, 93, 277, 278, 279, 286, 304, 317
  Ancestor's Brocades: The Literary Debut of Emily Dickinson, 278
  Bolts of Melody: New Poems of Emily Dickinson, 93, 278, 343
  Emily Dickinson: A Revelation, 279, 304
  Emily Dickinson's Home: Letters of Edward Dickinson and His Family, 278, 286, 304
biology, 236, 241, 338
Bishop, Elizabeth, 335–6
  'In the Waiting Room', 336
Bishop, Henry, 219
Blackmur, R.P., 311, 312, 314, 316, 318
  'Emily Dickinson: Notes on Prejudice and Fact', 314
Blackstone, William, 199
Blake, Caesar, 311
Boltwood, Mrs. Lucius, 22
Boston, 47, 100, 223, 226, 274
Boston Daily Atlas, 221
Boston Museum, 82, 216
Boston Post, 125, 274
botany, 14, 39, 238, 258
Bowdoin, Elbridge G., 111
Bowles, Gilbert, 22
Bowles, Samuel, 1, 22, 28, 43, 59, 131, 139, 140, 141, 142, 143, 157, 170, 208, 209, 295, 305
Bradstreet, Anne, 48, 52
Brazil, 348, 350

Brock-Broido, Lucie, 339–40
  The Master Letters, 339
Brontë, Anne, 110
  The Tenant of Wildfell Hall, 110
Brontë, Charlotte, 107, 109, 110, 113, 114, 116, 117
  Jane Eyre, 110, 111–12, 113, 116, 130
Brontë, Emily, 107, 109, 110, 116, 117
  Wuthering Heights, 110, 112–13
Brooklyn Daily Union, 274
Brooks, Maria, 274
Brower, Frank, 221
Browles, Samuel, 208
Brown University, 33
Brown, Thomas, 261, 265
Browne, Sir Thomas, 6, 94–5
  Hydriotaphia, 95
  Religio Medici, 94, 95
Browning, Elizabeth Barrett, 31, 32, 94, 105, 109, 114–15, 116, 117, 141
  'A Drama of Exile', 105
  Aurora Leigh, 31, 32, 105, 114, 116, 153
  Essays on Greek Christian Poets, 32
Browning, Robert, 94, 98, 105, 141
  Dramatis Personae, 105
  The Ring and the Book, 105
Bryant, William Cullen, 120, 121, 123, 161
  'A Forest Hymn', 121
  'Death of the Flowers', 120
  'Hymn to Death', 121
  Poems, 120
  'Thanatopsis', 161
Buckingham, J. Willis, 311
Bunyan, John
  Pilgrim's Progress, 47
Burdick, Joan, 191
Burke, Edmund, 141
Burnham Antique Bookstore, 26
Burns, Anthony, 198
Burns, Robert, 51, 90, 96, 107
Burnside, John, 58
Burritt, Elijah H., 29
  Geography of the Heavens and Class Book of Astronomy, 29
Burton, Robert, 95
Bushnell, Horace, 152, 259
  God in Christ, 259
Bust-on-em, E. Plewry, 124
  'Owed to the Charlestown Convenshun', 124
Butler, Samuel, 90
Byron, George Gordon, Lord, 98, 99–100, 141, 144, 203
  'Childe Harold's Pilgrimage', 99
  'The Corsair', 99
  Don Juan, 99
  'The Prisoner of Chillon', 99, 100

Calvin, John, 48
Calvinism, 2, 36–7, 38, 39, 47, 48, 49, 53, 62, 72, 73, 100, 151, 152–3, 155, 157, 158, 159, 201, 321, 327
Cambridge, Massachusetts, 13, 199
Cameron, Sharon, 194, 246, 254, 324, 326
  Choosing Not Choosing: Dickinson's Fascicles, 246, 326
  Lyric Time: Dickinson and the Limits of Genre, 254, 324
Canada, 350
Cape, Jonathan, 345
Capps, Jack, 25, 91, 93, 139, 198, 329
  Emily Dickinson's Reading: 1836–1886, 198, 329
Carlyle, Thomas, 141
Carse, James P., 57, 58
Carter, A.P., 338
Catholicism, 157
Celan, Paul, 346
Century Magazine, 81, 272, 275
Chaichit, Chanthana, 347
Chambers, Robert, 100
  Cyclopedia of English Literature, 100
Charyn, Jerome
  The Secret Life of Emily Dickinson, 2
Chase, Richard, 316
Chaucer, Geoffrey, 91
chemistry, 14, 163, 236, 238, 258, 261
Child, Lydia Maria, 140, 274
China, 350
Chinese, 346
Choate, Rufus, 198
The Christian Intelligencer, 312
Christian Register, 52
Cikovsky, Nicolai Jr., 227, 229, 230
Cincinnati, Ohio, 19
circus, 216–18
  Great Golden Menagerie, 217
  Great North American Circus, 217
  Great Quadruple Combination!, 217
  Raymond and Waring's Menagerie, 217
Civil War, U.S., 3, 23, 98, 99, 127, 139, 153, 157, 169, 170, 179, 185–6, 206–15, 227, 229, 230, 232, 233, 258, 321, 324, 326, 327
  Battle of Antietam, 206
Clarke, James Freeman, 140
class, 29, 169, 205, 214, 215, 220, 224, 321, 323, 327
Cleopatra, 115, 135
Cockrell, Dale, 220
Cody, David, 6, 127, 135
Cody, John, 323
  After Great Pain: The Inner Life of Emily Dickinson, 323

Cold War, 279, 349
Coleman, Eliza, 70
Coleman, Lyman, 16, 70
Coleridge, Samuel Taylor, 99, 123, 251
Colton, Aaron, 151
Conforti, Joseph, 48
Congregational First Church, 15, 16, 49, 51, 151
Congregationalism, 49, 151
Congress, 189, 198
Connecticut River Valley, 60, 64,
  See also Amherst
Cool White, 219
Cornell, Joseph, 226
Cowan, Perez, 166
Cowper, William, 96, 162
  'John Gilpin's Ride', 96
  The Task, 162
Crain, Pat, 38
Crane, Hart, 332–3
  'To Emily Dickinson', 332
Crane, Stephen, 332
  The Black Riders, 332
Crashaw, Richard, 93
Crimean War, 98
critical reception, 4, 127, 179–80, 271, 276, 277, 292–4, 311, 312–13, 329, 330
  international reception, 4, 7, 343–50
criticism, 2–7, 129, 169–70, 185–6, 189, 191–2, 204–5, 207–8, 260, 271, 282, 292–4, 295, 302, 305, 311–18, 321–31, 347–8
  cognitive poetics, 60
  conceptual metaphor theory, 61–3
  deconstructionist criticism, 3
  feminist criticism, 3, 129, 169, 170, 176, 292, 306, 322, 323, 324–5, 328, 329
  formalist criticism, 2, 179, 246, 312–15, 322, 323–4
  historicist criticism, 3, 5, 129, 169, 246, 292, 322, 323, 324, 326–9
  marxist criticism, 322, 327
  New Criticism, 2, 207, 312–15, 316, 318, 323, 324, 346
  Poststructuralist Criticism, 326
  textual criticism, 292
Crosby, L.V.H., 219
Cruden, Alexander, 76
Crumbley, Paul, 4, 6, 325, 327
  Winds of Will: Emily Dickinson and the Sovereignty of Democratic Thought, 4, 327
Cuddy, Lois, 39
Currier, Elizabeth, 84
Cutter, Calvin, 241
  Anatomy and Physiology Designed for Academies and Families, 241
Czech Republic, 350

Daily News, 345
Dana, Barbara, 330
  Wider than the Sky: Essays and Meditations on the Healing Power of Emily Dickinson, 330
Dana, Charles Anderson, 91, 100
  The Household Book of Poetry, 91, 100
Dana, Richard Henry, 78, 80
Dante, 96, 115
Darwin, Charles, 153, 239, 104, 140, 141,
  See also science: evolution
  The Origin of Species, 104, 239
Davis, Rebecca Harding, 99, 120
  Life in the Iron Mills, or, the Korl Woman, 99, 134
Davis, Theo, 2, 6
De Certeau, Michel, 144
de Man, Paul, 102
De Quincey, Thomas, 107
de Tocqueville, Alexis, 140, 174
  Democracy in America, 174
Dean, Gabrielle, 5
death, 23, 42, 47, 54, 56, 59, 60, 62–3, 84, 95, 102, 106, 113, 120, 135–7, 144–6, 153–4, 155, 160–7, 207, 208, 209–12, 214, 227, 251, 254–5, 257, 258, 275, 309, 313, 347, 3, 15, *See also* transience
Decker, William, 308
Declaration of Independence, 112
Defoe, Daniel, 96
Dekker, Thomas, 91
Deleuze, Gilles, 242
democracy, 6, 53, 80, 81, 140, 161, 180, 181–6, 189
Democrats, 20
Denmark, 350
Dennett, Andrea Stulman, 216
  Weird and Wonderful: The Dime Museum in America, 216
Deppman, Jed, 6, 36, 185, 329
  Trying to Think with Emily Dickinson, 329
Derrida, Jacques, 302
  Archive Fever, 302
Descartes, Réné, 57
Dewey, John, 265
The Dial, 262
Diamond, John, 221
Dickens, Charles, 1, 18, 31, 89, 107, 115, 130, 141
  American Notes for General Circulation, 18
Dickinson, Austin, 15, 16, 17, 19, 25, 26, 30, 31, 40, 46, 47, 51, 52, 70, 82, 91, 92, 120, 129, 166, 179, 188, 189, 198, 199, 200, 204, 208, 211, 226, 271, 276, 295, 304, 339
  'Representative Men of the Parish', 51
Dickinson, Ebenezer, 51

Dickinson, Edward, 17, 18, 19, 20, 26, 29, 30, 31, 46, 47, 51, 54, 69, 70, 79, 96, 129, 151, 170, 179, 189, 198–9, 200, 204
Dickinson, Emily, 47
  biographies, 1, 2, 4, 204, 271, 278, 279, 285, 322–3, 348, 349
  education, 6, 13–14, 36–44, 50, 72, 81–2, 83, 104, 119, 143, 190, 238, 247, 258, 259–60, 323
  gardens, 18, 20, 58, 59–60, 63
  herbarium, 18, 30, 58, 238, 293, 298
  humor, 84, 222
  influence on others, 7, 32, 40, 243, 329–30, 332–40, 348–9
  influences, 303, 321, 329
  letters, 6, 7, 13, 14, 16, 17, 18, 19, 20, 21, 22, 23, 26, 28, 31, 33, 36, 37, 38, 39, 41, 43, 44, 46, 47, 51, 52, 53, 54, 56, 57, 58, 70, 71, 74, 75–6, 78, 80, 81, 82, 83–5, 89–93, 94, 95–6, 98, 100, 103, 105, 111, 114, 116, 119–20, 127, 129, 130, 135, 139, 140, 143, 145, 146, 152, 156–7, 159, 161, 162, 166–7, 188, 189–90, 196, 199, 200–1, 202–3, 206, 208, 210, 217, 236, 251, 257, 258, 260, 264, 271, 272–3, 274, 284–6, 287, 293, 296–7, 298, 302–10, 311, 317, 325–6, 329, 330, 335, 340
  marginal writing, 30–1, 32, 39, 69–71, 74, 78, 91, 93, 98, 103, 105, 120, 123, 125, 200, 284
  Master letters, 95, 100, 112, 203, 286, 305–6, 339–40
  physical withdrawal, 1, 19, 44, 56, 100, 169, 171, 176–7, 179, 188, 208, 274, 276, 303, 316, 348–9
  poetic output, 1, 3, 21, 208, 258
  public life, 4, 13, 22–3, 47, 170, 179, 216–25, 321, 337
  reading, 25, 29–30, 31, 33, 51–2, 69, 70, 73, 79, 82, 89, 119–20, 123, 131, 139–46, 151, 153, 179, 198, 260, 329
  religion, 2–3, 15, 38, 42–3, 47–50, 57, 62, 71, 72, 94, 99, 105, 121, 151–9, 162, 166–7, 169, 207, 237, 251, 262, 323, 327–8
  sexuality, 3, 83, 95, 135, 169, 203, 277, 279, 305, 306, 316, 325, 328
Dickinson, Emily Norcross, 15, 17, 19, 20, 31, 151, 159, 166, 198, 204, 306
Dickinson family, 1, 17–21, 49, 50, 51
  family pride, 17, 19, 20, 21
  public life, 16–20, 23, 29, 51, 170, 179, 189
  reading, 14, 26–8, 139–40, 164, 204, 221, 292

Dickinson family library, 14, 31, 33, 38, 50, 70, 72, 91, 92, 93, 98, 110, 124, 190, 219–20, 246, 329, *See also* Dickinson family
Dickinson, Gilbert, 156, 275, 304, 309
Dickinson, Lavinia, 1, 15, 18, 22, 28, 30, 31, 39, 57, 82, 100, 166, 257, 273, 275, 276, 294, 303, 305
Dickinson, Lucretia Gunn, 19
Dickinson, Moses Billings, 84
Dickinson, Nathan, 49
Dickinson, Nathaniel, 49, 51
Dickinson, Samuel Fowler, 17, 19, 39, 51, 198
Dickinson, Susan Huntington Gilbert, 3, 14, 15, 17, 19, 31, 46, 47, 83, 93, 95, 96, 99, 102, 119, 120, 130, 131, 134, 135, 156, 157, 192, 200, 201, 271, 272, 273–7, 278, 287, 294, 296, 299, 304, 306, 309, 322, 325
  Writings by Susan Dickinson, 275
Dickinson, William Cowper, 38
Diehl, Joanne Feit, 101, 325
digital editions, 5, 271, 288–90, 293, 299–300, *See also* the names of individual digital editors
Dobson, Joanne, 3, 325, 328
  Dickinson and the Strategies of Reticence, 325
Doherty, Pete, 344, 348
Donne, John, 31, 91, 93
Doriani, Beth Maclay, 328
  Emily Dickinson: Daughter of Prophecy, 328
Dostoevsky, Fyodor, 157
Drum Beat, 125, 274
Dryden, John, 95, 164
Dwight, Edward, 50

Eberwein, Jane Donahue, 3, 37, 151, 157, 159, 222, 258, 327, 330
  Reading Emily Dickinson's Letters: Critical Essays, 307, 330
economics, 6, 13, 171, 172–4, 175, 176, 177, 180, 188–96, 211–12, 214, 292, 322, 327
Edelman, Gerald M., 243
  Wider than the Sky: The Phenomenal Gift of Consciousness, 243
Eden, 20, 22, 57–8, 113, 114, 154
editorial practices, 271–80, 282–90, 292, 293, 302, 303–10, 317–18, 323, 326, 339
Edwards Church, 46, 48
Edwards, Jonathan, 46, 48, 49, 151, 257
  Faithful Narrative, 48
  History of the Work of Redemption, 49
  The Life of the Late Reverend Mr. David Brainerd, 48

'Sinners in the Hands of an Angry God', 48
Eliot, George, 72, 91, 107, 109, 115–16, 117, 130, 152
  Daniel Deronda, 91, 116, 130, 131, 132
  Middlemarch, 25, 116
Eliot, T.S., 346
Ellis, John Harvard, 52
Elsthain, Jean Bethke, 170
Emancipation Proclamation, 206
Emerson, Ralph Waldo, 26, 37, 43, 72, 78, 80, 94, 102, 119, 123, 126, 140, 141, 152, 154, 184, 185, 201, 239, 240, 251, 253, 259, 262, 265, 297, 324, 329
  'Bacchus', 121
  Collected Poems, 43
  'Education', 37
  'Merlin', 124
  Poems, 120
  Representative Men, 78
  'Self-Reliance', 185
  'Snow-Storm', 120
  The American Scholar, 259
  'The Rommany Girl', 121
  'The Visit', 123
  'Threnody', 124
Emily Dickinson International Society, 321
Emily Dickinson Museum, 348
Emily Dickinson Tutte le Opere, 348
Emmett, Dan, 219
Emsley, Sarah, 93
England, 344, 350
Erkkila, Betsy, 195, 204, 327
  'Emily Dickinson and Class', 327
Escher, M.C., 251
Evans, Rand, 260

Farr, Judith, 58, 59, 93, 307
  The Passion of Emily Dickinson, 307
fascicles, 1, 5, 47, 75, 91, 192, 275, 285, 292–3, 295–8, 299, 300, 326, 347, 348
Faust, Drew Gilpin, 258
Field, Kate, 115
Field, Mrs. Thomas P., 22
financial failure, 19, 20, 192–3, 194, 323
Finkel, Viktor, 346
Finland, 350
Finnerty, Páraic, 4, 6
  Emily Dickinson's Shakespeare, 4, 329
Finnish, 346
Fiske, John, 140, 165
  'The Unseen World', 164
Fletcher, John, 91
Florence, Italy, 115

Flower, Elizabeth, 261, 265
flowers, 14, 22, 28, 30, 46, 56, 58–9, 62, 64, 70, 120, 121, 134, 155, 164, 191, 333, 340
Flynt, Maria, 16
Ford, Emily Fowler, 79
Ford, John, 91
Forest Leaves, 14, 143
Forster, E.M., 344
France, 347, 350
Frank Leslie's Illustrated Weekly, 234
Franklin, R.W., 5, 276, 278, 285–6, 288, 292, 297, 305, 325, 326, 348
  Poems of Emily Dickinson: Variorum edition, 288, 297
  The Manuscript Books of Emily Dickinson, 5, 285–6, 292, 297, 325
  The Master Letters of Emily Dickinson, 286, 305
Fraser, Kathleem, 339
Freedman, Linda, 328
  Emily Dickinson and the Religious Imagination, 328
Freeman, Margaret, 6
French, 347, 348
Frost Library, 25, 29, 31, 32
Frost, Robert, 104, 333–4, 336
  'Acquainted with the Night', 333
  'Desert Places', 333
Fugitive Slave Act, 198
Fulton, Alice, 339
  Sensual Math, 339

Galileo, 115
Gall, Franz Joseph, 241
Gardner, Thomas, 7, 330
  A Door Ajar: Contemporary Writers and Emily Dickinson, 330
Gaskell, Elizabeth, 110, 111, 113, 114
  The Life of Charlotte Brontë, 110
Gautier, Theophile, 141
Gelpi, Albert, 257, 327
  Emily Dickinson: The Mind of the Poet, 327
gender, 3, 29, 39, 40, 42, 79–80, 87, 109–17, 131–7, 146, 169–77, 181, 200, 220, 223, 224, 316, 321, 322, 324–5, 328, 334, 337, 338, 339, 346–7
geography, 14, 258
geology, 4, 14, 39, 41, 56, 104, 258
German, 347
Germany, 347, 349, 350
Gibbons, Thomas, 90
Gilbert, Sandra, 3, 273, 324
  Madwoman in the Attic: The Woman Writer and the Nineteenth-Century Literary Imagination, 3, 324
Giles, Paul, 238

Goldsmith, Oliver, 96
  The Vicar of Wakefield, 96
Goodman, Miriam M., 243
Goodrich, Samuel Griswold, 50
Gordon, Lyndall, 32, 323, 348
  Lives Like Loaded Guns: Emily Dickinson and her Family Feuds, 323
Gorman, Herbert, 257
Gould, George Henry, 16
Graham, Jorie, 332
Graham, Martha, 226
Grahame, James, 90
Gray, John, 164
Great Awakening, 48, 151
Great Migration, 51
Great Britain, 344–6
Greece, 350
Green, Charles, 31
Griswold, Rufus W., 93
  Sacred Poets of England and America, 93
Gubar, Susan, 3, 324
  Madwoman in the Attic: The Woman Writer and the Nineteenth-Century Literary Imagination, 3, 324
Guthrie, James, 6

Habegger, Alfred, 4, 14, 29, 39, 70, 204, 259, 323
  My Wars Are Laid Away in Books: The Life of Emily Dickinson, 4, 323
Hadley, Massachusetts, 49, 57
Hagenbüchle, Roland, 241, 305, 323, 347
Hallam, Arthur, 99
Hamilton, Alexander, 181
  The Federalist, 181
Hampshire and Franklin Express, 26, 29, 71, 139, 140, 144, 145, 146, 217
Hampson Dickinson Collection, 32, 33
Hampson, Alfred Leete, 32, 278, 279
  Poems for Youth by Emily Dickinson, 278
Hampson, Mary, 33, 278
Harde, Roxane, 158, 159
Harper's Magazine, 14, 37, 81, 98, 139, 140–1, 142, 221, 350
Harris, Benjamin, 38
Hart, Ellen Louise, 287, 306, 325
Harte, Bret, 141
Hartford, Connecticut, 49
Harvard University, 32, 33, 36, 40, 42, 49, 69, 70, 98, 196, 198, 199, 279
Hawthorne, Nathaniel, 52, 80, 90, 94, 119, 141, 201
  The Custom House, 90
  The House of Seven Gables, 52
Hay Library, 25

Heaney, Seamus, 346
Hegel, G.W.F., 265
Heginbotham, Eleanor Elson, 6, 326
  Reading the Fascicles of Emily Dickinson, 326
Heidegger, Martin, 264
Heiskanen-Mäkelä, Sirkka, 346
Herbert, George, 93, 94
  Matin Hymn, 93
  Poetical Works, 93
  'The Church-Porch', 93
  The Temple, 93
  'Virtue', 93
Hewitt, Elizabeth, 6
Higginson, Louisa, 92
Higginson, Thomas Wentworth, 1, 28, 36, 37, 40, 43, 47, 73, 75, 76, 83, 90, 92, 94, 100, 114, 119, 120, 127, 130, 131–3, 137, 139, 141, 145, 153, 156, 164, 170, 204, 208, 214, 233, 234, 236, 264, 271, 272, 273, 274, 275, 276, 277, 279, 292, 295, 297, 300, 302, 303, 308, 309, 311, 317, 336
  'Letter to a Young Contributor', 90, 94, 127
  Letters by Emily Dickinson, 271
  'The Life of Birds', 100
  Malbone: An Oldport Romance, 28
  Out-Door Papers, 28
  Poems by Emily Dickinson, 120, 271, 274, 276, 303, 311, 317, 332, 343, 344
  'The Results of Spiritualism', 164
  'Snow', 120, 233
Higher Criticism, 16, 72–3, 153
Hills, Leonard M., 21
Hitchcock, Edward, 14, 30, 41, 42, 79, 104, 151, 154, 162, 167, 238
  Elementary Geology, 42, 104
  The Religion of Geology, 163, 238
Holbein, Hans, 141
Holland, 350
Holland, Elizabeth, 18, 28, 56, 70, 103, 120, 166, 202, 217, 306, 335
Holland, Josiah, 28, 120, 131, 139, 141, 142, 170, 202, 295, 335
Holland, Sophia, 139
Hollander, John, 99, 107
Holmes, Oliver Wendell, 120, 141
  'Bill and Joe', 120
  'The Deacon's Masterpiece Or the Wonderful One-Hoss-Shay', 123
  'The Professor's Story', 120
Holt, Jacob, 70, 71
  'The Bible', 71
Homans, Margaret, 3, 325
  Women Writers and Poetic Identity, 325
Homer, Winslow, 6, 226, 234
  The Brush Harrow, 229–32
  Prisoners from the Front, 229–32
  Veteran in a New Field, 226–8, 229, 234
Homestead, 19, 20, 25, 26, 28, 33, 51, 189, 198, 297, 337
Hooker, Thomas, 49
Hopkins, Gerard Manley, 335
Horan, Elizabeth, 31, 32, 196
Houghton Library, 25, 30, 31, 32, 33, 69, 238, 348
  Emily Dickinson Room, 348
Howe, Julia Ward, 115, 122, 131, 141, 207
  'A New Sculptor', 133–4
  'Battle Hymn of the Republic', 122, 207
  'Rouge Gagne', 132–3, 137
Howe, Susan, 85, 129, 338
  My Emily Dickinson, 338
Howells, William Dean, 179, 180, 186, 332, 344, 345
Hubbard, Melanie, 6
Hudson River School, 226
Hudson, Henry Norman, 78
Hughes, Ted, 161, 346
  A Choice of Emily Dickinson's Verse, 344, 346
Hume, David, 249, 254, 262, 264, 265
Humphrey, Heman, 50, 53, 79, 151
Humphrey, Jane, 41
Hungary, 350
Hutchison Family Singers, 219
Hutchison, Coleman, 179
Hutsvedt, Siri, 243
  The Shaking Woman, or a History of My Self, 243
hymns, 3, 14, 15, 29, 38–9, 53, 89, 96, 121–2, 176, 220, 242, 328

Iceland, 350
Ierolli, Guiseppe, 348
Ik Marvel. *See* Mitchell, Donald Grant
Illinois Staats-Zeitung, 343
Imagism, 129, 311, 345
immortality, 3, 21, 23, 43, 47, 54, 62, 71, 139, 140, 145, 155, 156–7, 161, 254, 265, 276, 302, 310
India, 348, 349, 350
Indicator, 295
industrialization, 21, 57, 189, 297, 298–9
  industry (Amherst's), 21, 58, 258
Iraq, 350
Ireland, 344, 347, 350
Irish, 347
Israel, 350
Italian, 347
Italy, 347, 350

Jackson, Helen Hunt, 81, 131, 136, 272, 273, 328
  'Found Frozen', 136, 137
  Ramona, 81
  'A Woman's Death-Wound', 137
Jackson, Virginia, 4, 180, 226, 228, 229, 233, 234, 311, 326, 330
  Dickinson's Misery: A Theory of Lyric Reading, 4, 226, 326, 328, 330
Jackson, William A., 33
Jakobson, Roman, 170
James, Henry, 31, 100, 115, 134, 141
Japan, 347, 349, 350
Japanese, 346, 347
JB and C Adams, 26
Jenkins, Sarah, 17
Jenks, William, 73
  A Companion to the Bible, 73
Jewett, Sarah Orne, 141
Jiménez, Juan Ramón, 344
John Brown's Body, 122
John Hay Library, 30, 31, 32, 33
Johnson, Mark, 60, 62
Johnson, Robert Underwood, 272
Johnson, Samuel
  Rasselas, 96
Johnson, Thomas H., 5, 20, 33, 43, 52, 89, 278, 279, 282–5, 286, 287, 303, 304, 305, 321, 348
  Emily Dickinson: An Interpretive Biography, 279
  The Complete Poems of Emily Dickinson, 284, 347
  The Editing of Emily Dickinson: A Reconsideration, 285
  The Letters of Emily Dickinson, 284–5, 286, 304, 321
  The Poems of Emily Dickinson, 279, 282, 284, 321, 323, 335, 336
Jones Library, 25, 28, 29, 31
Jones, Rowena Revis, 50
Jonson, Ben, 91
Juhasz, Suzanne, 222, 259, 307, 325

Kant, Immanuel, 265
Kavanagh, Patrick, 23
Keats, John, 94, 98, 100–2, 107, 141, 318, 346
  'Ode on Melancholy', 318
  'On the Grasshopper and the Cricket', 101
  'To Autumn', 101
Keller, Karl, 46, 328
  The Only Kangaroo Among the Beauty: Emily Dickinson and America, 328
Kemble, Fanny, 82
Kent, James
  Commentaries on American Law, 199

Khan, Mansoor, 348
Kidder Trial, 202
Kierkegaard, Søren, 157, 158
Kimball, Benjamin, 203
Kimball, Moses, 216
King Philip's War, 51
Kirkby, Joan, 3, 6
Knight, Charles, 79
Korea, 350
Kyd, Thomas, 91

Ladin, Joy, 129
Lakoff, George, 60
Lambert, Robert, 203, 204
  Emily Dickinson's Use of Anglo-American Legal Concepts and Vocabulary in Her Poetry: Muse at the Bar, 204
Landis, Mary, 32
Lane, William Henry, 221
Lang, Andrew, 344–5
language theory, 246–55, 259
Larcom, Lucy, 274
Laski, Harold, 181
Latin, 39–40, 137
Latin America, 344
Lavoisier, Antoine, 250
law, 6, 17, 176, 198–205, 211, 214
Lease, Benjamin, 31, 93, 94
Leavell, Linda, 334
Lee, Robert E., 206
Legal Tender Act, 211
Leibnitz, Gottfried Wilhelm, 141
Leland, John, 96
Lewes, George Henry, 116
Lewontin, Richard, 239, 241
Leyda, Jay, 70, 71, 286
  The Years and Hours of Emily Dickinson, 286
liberalism, 37
Liebling, Jerome, 28
Lincoln, Abraham, 170, 206, 211, 214
  assassination of Lincoln, 30
Lind, Jenny, 46, 48, 53, 54, 189, 219, 220
Lindberg-Seyersted, Brita, 75
Locke, John, 246, 247, 248, 249, 250, 253, 254, 259, 261
Loeffelholz, Mary, 3, 5, 6, 325, 327, 328
  Companion to Emily Dickinson, 327
  From School to Salon: Reading Nineteenth-Century American Women's Poetry, 328
Lombardo, Daniel, 57
London, 345
London, Peter, 58
Longfellow, Henry Wadsworth, 31, 32, 52, 119, 122, 123, 126, 141

'Catawba Wine', 121, 123
The Courtship of Miles Standish, 52
'The Monk Felix', 124
'Psalm of Life', 120
'The Village Blacksmith', 123, 133
Lord, Otis P., 22, 37, 94, 201, 203, 279, 304, 305
Lothrop, Charles D., 22
Lott, Eric, 220
Lowell, Amy, 129, 311, 345
Lowell, James Russell, 120, 123, 141
  A Fable for Critics, 120, 125
  'First Snow-Flake', 120
  'The Relief of Lucknow', 123
Lowell, Mason
  The Boston Academy's Collection of Church Music, 219
Lowell, Robert, 335, 346
Lowenberg, Carlton, 50
Lubbers, Klaus, 311
Luce, William, 348
  The Belle of Amherst, 348
Lundin, Roger, 154, 157
Lyman, Joseph, 43, 76, 94
Lyon, Mary, 15, 30, 42, 71, 151, 259
Lytton, Bulwer, 141

Mack, David, 19, 51
MacKenzie, Cindy, 6, 307, 330
  A Concordance of the Letters of Emily Dickinson, 307
  Reading Emily Dickinson's Letters: Critical Essays, 307, 330
  Wider than the Sky: Essays and Meditations on the Healing Power of Emily Dickinson, 330
MacNiece, Louis, 346
Mahar, William J., 220
Maher, Margaret, 323, 327
Mangan, James Clarence
  'Karamian's Exile', 122
Manheim, Daniel, 4, 329
Manning, Ann, 91
manuscripts, 5, 54, 137, 206, 273, 275, 276, 277, 278, 283, 285–90, 293, 295, 296–8, 300, 302, 306, 307, 311, 317–18, 322, 323, 325–6, 348
Marlowe, Christopher, 91
Marsden, Joshua, 90
Marshall, William E., 29
Martha Dickinson Bianchi
  The Single Hound, 275
Martin, Wendy, 47
Marvell, Andrew, 93, 94
Mary Magdalene, 115

Mason, Lowell, 219
Massachusetts Agricultural College, 21
Massachusetts Bay Colony, 51
Massachusetts House of Representatives, 96
Massinger, Philip, 91
mathematics, 14, 30, 201, 237, 238, 240
Mather, Cotton, 36
  Corderius Americanus, 36
Matthiessen, F.O., 317–18
McCarthy, William H., 33
McClellan, George B., 206
McDowell, Marta, 58
McGann, Jerome, 23
McIntosh, James, 3, 327
  Nimble Believing: Dickinson and the Unknown, 327
McNeil, Helen, 329
  Emily Dickinson, 329
Melville, Herman, 80, 81, 94, 157, 198, 201
Merideth, Robert, 188
Merrill, Miss, 84
Messmer, Marietta, 306, 307, 311, 322
  A Vice for Voices: Reading Emily Dickinson's Correspondence, 306, 307, 330
metaphysical instability, 16, 36, 99, 327, 329
metaphysical poets, 92–4
Metzinger, Thomas, 243
  Being No One: The Self-Model Theory of Subjectivity, 243
Mexico, 350
Michelangelo, 115
microscopes, 42
Middleton, Thomas, 91
Miles, Susan, 345
Miller, Cristanne, 3, 4, 6, 14, 93, 94, 185, 222, 307, 324, 325, 326, 331
  Emily Dickinson: A Poet's Grammar, 324
  Reading in Time: Emily Dickinson in the Nineteenth Century, 4, 329
  'The Sound of Shifting Paradigms, or Hearing Dickinson in the Twenty-First Century', 326
Miller, James Russell, 343
Miller, Ruth, 91, 93, 326
  The Poetry of Emily Dickinson, 326
Milton, John, 91, 92
  Il Penseroso, 91
  'L'Allegro', 91
  Paradise Lost, 31, 91
  Samson Agonistes, 91
  'To the Lord General Cromwell', 91
minstrelsy, 219–25. *See also* race
Mirabeau, 96

Mitchell, Domhnall, 4, 6, 7, 204, 326, 327, 330
  Emily Dickinson: Monarch of Perception, 4, 327
  Measures of Possibility: Emily Dickinson's manuscripts, 326
  The International Reception of Emily Dickinson, 330
Mitchell, Donald Grant, 89, 119, 130
  Reveries of a Bachelor, 130
modernism, 2, 129, 241, 332–5, 345
Montague, Gilbert Holland, 33
Monteiro, George, 33
Moore, Marianne, 334–5, 346
  'In the Days of Prismatic Color', 334
Moore, Thomas, 90, 219
  Irish Melodies, 219
Morgan, Barbara, 226
Morgan, Victoria, 328
  Emily Dickinson and Hymn Culture, 328
Morris, Leslie, 25, 32
Mossberg, Barbara, 222
Mount Holyoke Female Seminary, 15, 20, 36, 42, 49, 70, 71, 104, 140, 151, 152, 162, 238, 246, 259, 261
Murphey, Murray G., 261, 265
Murray, Aífe, 4, 29, 323, 327
  Maid as Muse: How Servants Changed Emily Dickinson's Life and Language, 4, 323, 327
music, 46, 54, 64, 122–3, 216, 218–25, 240, 284, 324, 338, 345, 348, *See also* hymns

Nathan, Hans, 224
National Academy of Design, 229
National Geographic, 335
nationalism, 80–1, 82, 109, 142, 174, 176, 186, 215, 345, 349–50
nature, 6, 56–65, 95, 98, 100–5, 107, 120, 121, 140, 144, 153, 154, 207, 236, 237–8, 240, 241, 257, 275
Nemerov, Alexander, 6
New York City, 216, 223, 226
New, Elisa, 157, 158, 159
Newman, Samuel P., 246, 247, 250, 253, 254, 255
  Practical System, 246, 247–8
newspapers, 29
Newton, Benjamin Franklin, 26, 43, 152, 156
Newton, Isaac, 41, 261
Nietzche, Friedrich, 265
Nightingale Opera Troupe, 223
Nims, Seth, 20
No Name Series, 272
Noble, Marianne, 4, 328, 329, 330
  The Masochistic Pleasures of Sentimental Literature, 328, 330

Norcross, Frances, 82, 84, 98, 103, 114, 159, 202, 217, 304
Norcross, Joel, 15
Norcross, Louise, 82, 98, 103, 114, 159, 202, 272, 273, 304
North American Review, 110
North Pleasant Street home, 19, 26
Northampton, 46
Northampton Courier, 71
Norway, 348, 350
Norwegian, 343, 347
Nyberg, Lennart, 348

Oberhaus, Dorothy Huff, 326, 327
  Emily Dickinson's fascicles: Method and Meaning, 326
obituaries, 30
orientalism. *See* style (Dickinson's): exoticism
Orpheus, 16
Orsini, Daniel J., 239
Orzeck, Martin, 329
  Dickinson and Audience, 329
Osgood, Frances Sargent, 328
  The Poetry of flowers, and flowers of Poetry, 121
Oslo, 348
Ostriker, Alicia, 185
Otten, Thomas J., 242
Owen, Robert Dale, 141
Oxford English Dictionary, 181

paleontology, 4
Palmo's Burlesque Opera Company, 223
Panic of 1957, 192
Paradise, 114, 116, *See also* Eden
Park, Edwards Amasa, 16, 152, 259
  The Theology of the Intellect and That of the Feelings, 259
Parker, Theodore, 152
Parley's Magazine, 37
Pateman, Carole, 170
Patterson, Rebecca, 60, 63, 279, 316
  The Riddle of Emily Dickinson, 279, 316
Payne, John Howard, 219
Peck, G.W., 110, 112
pedagogy, 39, 41, 43
Peel, Robin, 4, 236, 239, 328
  Emily Dickinson and the Hill of Science, 236, 328
Petrino, Elizabeth A., 3, 6, 90, 328
  'Allusion, Echo, and Literary Influence in Emily Dickinson', 90
  Emily Dickinson and Her Contemporaries: Women's Verse in America, 1820–1885, 328
Phelps, Elizabeth Stuart, 117

Philadelphia, 13, 223
philosophy, 6, 39, 50, 57, 58, 237, 243, 257–65, 329, 331, 338
physics, 236, 237
physiology, 238, 261
Peirce, Charles Sanders, 265
Pike, Marshall, 219
Pilgrims, 51
Plath, Sylvia, 346
Plato, 265
Plymouth, 51
Poe, Edgar Allan, 94, 119, 123
Poland, 349, 350
politics, 13, 141, 179–86, 199, 207, 215, 219, 220, 321, 322, 327, 338
Pollak, Vivian, 188, 222, 326, 330
  Historical Guide to Emily Dickinson, 326
Pollitt, Katha, 181
Pope, Alexander, 94, 96
  'Essay on Man', 96
  The Dunciad, 283
Porter, David, 129, 194, 257, 323, 324, 327
  Art of Emily Dickinson's Early Poetry, 323
  Dickinson: The Modern Idiom, 324
Porter, Ebenezer, 124, 162
  Rhetorical Reader, 124, 162
Porterfield, Amanda, 42
Portugal, 350
Portuguese, 348
postmodernism, 129, 321, 329
Pound, Ezra, 346
Powell, Mary, 91
Powers, Richard, 243
  Galatea 2.2, 243
  The Echo Maker, 243
Pratt, William Fenno, 19
print culture, 6, 14, 20, 28, 81–3, 84, 85, 87, 98, 130, 139–46, 176, 213, 233, 234, 239, 258, 274, 277, 293, 296–9, 324, 335
publication, 1, 5, 20, 22, 26, 31–3, 120, 121, 125–6, 127, 132, 169, 170, 188, 195–6, 210, 213, 233, 236, 271–80, 282–92, 294, 295, 296, 304, 317, 323, 325, 333, 343–4, 347
ownership rights, 32, 196
Puritanism, 2, 37, 38, 46–54, 57, 62, 79, 100, 155, 172, 203, 257

Quarles, Francis, 91
  Emblems, Divine and Moral, 91
Queen Elizabeth I, 90

race, 169, 195, 212–15, 220, 242, 323
railroads, 4, 18, 57, 188, 189, 192
Randall, James, 122
  'My Maryland', 122

Rankka, Kristine M., 158
Rantoul, Robert, 198
rationalism, 37
Read, Mrs. Hanson L., 22
Recollections of Keats, 100
Reed, Sampson, 258
  Observations on the Growth of the Mind, 258
Reid, Thomas, 261
religion, 14, 15–16, 40, 42, 57, 140, 141, 151–9, 161, 171, 174, 175, 176, 177, 181, 207, 209, 214, 215, 218, 220, 238, 257, 258, 259, 261, 264, 303, 326
resurrection, 38, 59, 62, 161, 163, 207
revivalism, 49–50
Rice, T.D., 221
Rich, Adrienne, 22, 324, 336–7
  'I Am in Danger – Sir - ', 336
  'The Spirit of Place', 337
  "'Vesuvius at Home': The Power of Emily Dickinson", 324, 337
Richards, Eliza, 232, 324
romanticism, 6, 36, 37–8, 72, 98, 99–104, 106, 107, 123, 236, 237, 239, 265, 329
  negative capability, 101
Root, Abiah, 39, 162, 258, 260
Rosaldo, Michelle Zimbalest, 170
Rosenbach Company, 33
Ross, Robert, 104
Rossetti, Christina, 107, 294–5
Rossetti, Dante Gabriel, 294
Rossetti, Maria, 294
Rossetti, William Michael, 294
Round Table, 274
Ruether, Rosemary, 158
Runzo, Sandra, 6
Ruskin, John, 3, 94, 226
Russia, 350
Russian, 346
Ryan, Mary, 170

Saito, Naoko, 43
Salska, Agnieszka, 306, 307, 324, 327
  'Dickinson's Letters', 306
Sanborn, Geoffrey, 180
Sand, George, 114
  Histoire de ma Vie, 115
Santayana, George, 265
Sappho, 115
Saudi Arabia, 350
Scandinavia, 347
Scheurer, Erika, 41
Schleiermacher, Friedrich. *See also* Higher Criticism
Scholl, Diane Gabrielsen, 47, 93

science, 4, 6, 14, 36, 41–2, 50, 57, 58, 99, 140, 141, 144, 154, 164–6, 220, 236–43, 258–9, 262, 264, 328, 329, 331, 338
  evolution, 104, 140, *See also* Darwin, Charles
Scotland, 344, 350
Scribner's, 14, 28, 81, 139, 141, 202, 350
Seattle, 348
Second Great Awakening, 2, 15, 48
Sedgwick, Catherine, 274
  Hope Leslie, 26
Seelbinder, Emily, 3, 6
sentimentalism, 36, 37, 43, 121, 133, 234, 328
sermons, 13, 16, 26, 46, 49, 51, 53, 71, 151
servants (Dickinson household), 4
Severn, Joseph, 100
  The Vicissitudes of Keat's Fame, 100
Sewall, Richard, 23, 47, 58, 94, 143, 204, 238, 271, 278, 311, 322, 323, 329
  The Life of Emily Dickinson, 278, 322
Seyersted, Brita Lindberg, 347
Shakespeare, William, 6, 14, 26, 30, 64, 78–87, 89, 91, 94, 116, 220, 283, 313, 329, 337
  A Midsummer Night's Dream, 83
  Antony and Cleopatra, 83
  Hamlet, 30, 86–7, 116
  Henry VI, 82
  Love's Labour's Lost, 64
  Macbeth, 83
  Othello, 82
  Romeo and Juliet, 84
Shaw, Lemuel, 198
Shaw, Robert Gould, 214
Shelley, Percy Bysshe, 98, 102, 103–4
  'Hymn to Intellectual Beauty', 102
  'Ode to the West Wind', 104
  'To a Skylark', 103
Shoptaw, John, 185
  'Dickinson's Civil War Poetics', 185
Sidney, Philip, 91
Sielke, Sabine, 6
Sigourney, Lydia, 123, 328
slavery, 212–13, 214, 221, 169, 188, 198, 207, *See also* race
Small, Judy Jo
  Positive as Sound: Emily Dickinson's Rhyme, 324
Smith, B.J., 203
Smith, Henry Boynton, 16
Smith, Martha Nell, 1, 3, 46, 185, 287, 302, 306, 307, 325, 327
  Companion to Emily Dickinson, 327
  Dickinson Electronic Archives, 288, 299, 300, 307

  Emily Dickinson's Correspondences: A Born-Digital Textual Inquiry, 5, 289–90, 299
  Open Me Carefully: Emily Dickinson's Intimate Letters to Susan Huntington Dickinson, 287, 306
  Rowing in Eden: Rereading Emily Dickinson, 3, 325
Smith, Robert McClure, 329
  The Seductions of Emily Dickinson, 330
Snow, C.P., 236, 240–1
Socarides, Alexandra, 5, 326, 331
  Dickinson Unbound: Paper, Process, Poetics, 326
Socrates, 263
Soelle, Dorothy, 158
Sorby, Angela, 6
South Africa, 350
Spain, 350
Spenser, Edmund, 91
Spiritualism. *See* spirituality
spirituality, 36, 140, 164, 166–7, 172, 218, 252, 261
Spofford, Harriet Prescott, 117, 119, 127, 134, 136, 137
  'Circumstance', 130–1, 135
  'The Amber Gods', 135–6, 137
  'The South Breaker', 135
Springfield Republican, 28, 29, 51, 93, 119, 121, 124, 125, 126, 139, 140, 143, 145, 164, 170, 201, 208, 214, 272, 274, 295, 305
Spurzheim, Johann Gaspar, 241
St. Armand, Barton Levi, 3, 32, 33, 257, 326, 328
  Emily Dickinson and Her Culture: The Soul's Society, 3, 326
Stearns, Frazer, 23, 208–11
Stein, Gertrude, 129
Sterne, Laurence, 95
Stewart, Dugald, 249, 250, 252, 261
  Human Mind, 250–1
Stoddard, Elizabeth, 117
Stoddard, Solomon, 151
Stone, Ruth, 279
Stoneley, Peter, 189, 195
Stonum, Gary Lee, 25, 93, 185, 329
  The Dickinson Sublime, 329
Story, Joseph, 198
Stoughton, William, 51
Stowe, Harriet Beecher, 81, 100
  'The True Story of Lady Byron's Life', 100
  Uncle Tom's Cabin, 31, 129
Stuart, Maria, 330
  The International Reception of Emily Dickinson, 330
style (Dickinson's), 5, 46, 71, 119, 121, 142–6, 171–3, 175–6, 190–5, 202, 203–4, 207, 321, 322, 323, 338, 346–7

Index

alliteration, 40
allusion, 20, 46, 73–7, 83–6, 89–97, 99–107, 117, 120–6, 133, 135, 334
capitalization, 16, 126, 184, 283, 284, 321
dashes, 69, 184, 283, 339
exoticism, 18, 116, 135, 308, *See* travel
form, 296, 297, 331, 345
humor, 41, 46, 47, 72, 84, 96, 125, 145, 193, 200–2, 221, 239, 275, 308, 334
irony, 40, 200, 202, 218, 222, 239, 253, 254, 263
metaphor, 60–5, 71, 106, 126, 137, 190, 206, 207, 212, 222, 235, 239, 6, 56, *See also* flowers
meter, 6, 29, 38, 121, 176, 220, 345
pentimento, 226–35
religious language, 15, 47, 53, 114, 158, 242, 252, 328, 347
rhyme, 15, 50, 133, 324, 345, 346
rythm, 125–7
synaesthesia, 243
syntax, 39, 41, 126, 184, 208, 212, 324, 346
supernaturalism, 21, 153, 236, 308, 338
Sweat, Margaret, 111
Sweden, 350
Swedenborg, Emanuel, 141
Swedish, 346, 347, 348
Sweetser, Luke, 189
Swift, Jonathan, 96
Switzerland, 350

Taggart, Genevieve, 315
  The Life and Mind of Emily Dickinson, 315
Taiwan, 350
Tate, Allen, 139, 257, 311, 312, 313–14, 315, 316, 318
Taylor, Edward, 48, 52
Taylor, Jeremy, 95
Tennyson, Alfred, Lord, 98, 99, 107
  In Memoriam, 99, 105–7
Thackeray, Donald, 318
Thackeray, William, 115, 141
Thailand, 347, 350
The Atlantic Monthly, 14, 29, 37, 43, 81, 98, 99, 100, 115, 120, 123, 124, 127, 130, 131, 134, 139, 141, 164, 170, 221, 233, 350
The Christian Intelligencer, 312
The Dial, 262
The Emily Dickinson Journal, 4, 321, 329
The Enlightenment, 261
The Evergreens, 19, 20, 22, 25, 28, 33, 226, 273
The Evergreens' Library, 28
The Guardian, 344
The Harmoneon Family, 219
The Hutchison Family, 220, 223

The Kalevala, 122
The London Mercury, 345
The Mayflower, 51
The New England Primer, 38–9, 46, 47, 50, 52, 54, 151
theology, 4, 16, 29, 48, 49, 62, 136, 140, 144, 164, 242
  feminist Christan theology, 158
  theology of the feelings, 16, 152, 259
Thoreau, Henry David, 94, 119, 141, 152, 201
Todd Collection, 32, 33
Todd, David, 304
Todd, Mabel Loomis, 32, 52, 56, 57, 127, 236, 271, 272, 273, 275–7, 278, 279, 292, 294, 297, 300, 303, 304, 305, 306, 317, 334
  The Letters of Emily Dickinson, 303
  affair with Austin Dickinson, 304, 323, *See also* Dickinson, Austin
  Poems by Emily Dickinson, 120, 271, 274, 276, 303, 311, 317, 332, 343, 344
Tourneur, Cyril, 91
transcendence, 38, 103, 106, 109, 117, 218, 259
transcendentalism, 2, 72, 121, 157, 201, 238, 239, 246, 259, 262, 265, 321
transience, 20, 21, 101
translation, 343–4, 346–50
travel, 7, 13, 14, 18, 25, 56, 60–3, 99, 109–10, 111, 113, 114, 117, 238
Trelawney, Edward John, 100
  Recollections of the Last Days of Byron and Shelley, 100
Trench, Richard, 246, 247, 252, 253, 255
  On the Study of Words, 246, 251–2
Tuckerman, Edward, 22
Turkey, 350
Turner, James, 157
Twain, Mark, 140

Ukraine, 350
Unitarianism, 49, 52, 152–3, 154, 157
United Kingdom, 347, 349, 350
Upham, Thomas C., 260, 261, 264
  Elements of Mental Philosophy, 260, 263
  Outlines of Imperfect and Disordered Mental Action, 260–1
Uruguay, 350

van Santen, Louise, 348
  Emily, 348
Vaughan, Henry, 92, 93, 94
  Silex Scintillans, 92
Vendler, Helen, 233, 234, 324
  Dickinson: Selected Poems and Commentaries, 324

Venezuela, 350
Verstegen, Peter, 348
  Gedichten 1, 348
Vesaas, Halden Moren, 348
  Den Kvitkledde fra Amherst, 348
Vetter, Lara
  Emily Dickinson's Correspondences: A Born-Digital Textual Inquiry, 5, 289–90, 299
Vietnam, 350
Virgil, 30, 39, 40, 115
  The Aeneid, 39, 40
Virgin, Mary, 115
Virginia Minstrels, 219, 221
visual arts, 226–35, 275

Wadsworth, Charles, 43, 305, 308
Wald, Jane, 26
Wales, 344
Walker, Amasa, 190
  The Science of Wealth, 190
Walker, Cheryl, 3, 132, 325, 328
  Nightingale's Burden: Women Poets and American Culture Before 1900, 325
Waller, Edmund, 93
Ward, Mrs. Humphrey, 141
Ward, Theodora, 284, 286, 304
  Emily Dickinson's Letters to Dr. and Mrs. Josiah Gilbert Holland, 304
Wardrop, Daneen, 327
  Emily Dickinson and the Labor of Clothing, 327
  Emily Dickinson's Gothic: Goblin with a Guage, 328
Washington D.C., 13
  Morrison's Stranger's Guide to the City of Washington, 30
Watts, Isaac, 14, 29, 38–9, 40, 41, 96, 121, 261
  On the Improvement of the Mind, 261
  The Psalms, Hymns, and Spiritual Songs of the Rev. Isaac Watts, 219
Weber, Max, 172
Webster, Daniel, 200
Webster, John, 91
Webster, Noah, 13, 38, 50, 53
  American Dictionary of the English Language, 53, 181
  Speller, 50
Weisbuch, Robert, 185, 323, 324, 329
  Dickinson and Audience, 329
Wells, Carlton, 311
Werner, Marta L., 5, 286, 287, 289, 305, 325
  Emily Dickinson's Open Folios: Scenes of Reading, Surfaces of Writing, 287, 305
  Radical Scatters, 5, 289–90, 299, 300
Westminster Assembly Shorter Catechism, 50

Whateley, Richard, 246, 247, 251, 252, 253, 254, 255
  Elements of Rhetoric, 246, 249–50
Whicher, George Frisbie, 91, 93, 143, 260, 278, 311, 315, 316
  This Was a Poet, 93, 315–16
Whigs, 20, 200, 327
Whipple, E.P., 110, 111
White, Fred, 153, 322
  Approaching Emily Dickinson, 322
White, Melissa, 306
  'Letter to the Light Discoveries in Dickinson's Correspondence', 306
White, Richard Grant, 80
Whiting, Lilian, 312
Whitlock, William, 219, 221
Whitman, Walt, 16, 80, 102, 184, 185, 194, 239, 273, 294, 295
  'As I ebb'd with the ocean of life', 124
  'Democratic Vistas', 184
  Leaves of Grass, 283, 294
Whittier, John Greenleaf, 123
  'Skipper Ireson's Ride', 123
Wimsatt, W.K., 312, 314
  'The Affective Fallacy', 314
  'The Intentional Fallacy', 314
Wineapple, Brenda, 323
  White Heat: The Friendship of Emily Dickinson and Thomas Wentworth Higginson, 323
Winslow, Hubbard, 165
  Elements of Intellectual philosophy, 165
Winters, Yvor, 311, 312–14, 316, 318
  'Emily Dickinson and the Limits of Judgement', 312
Winthrop, John, 51
Wittke, Carl, 217
Wodehouse, Richard, 100
Wolff, Cynthia Griffin, 204, 259, 323, 327
  Emily Dickinson, 323
Wolosky, Shira, 3, 185, 186, 326, 327
  Emily Dickinson: A Voice of War, 185, 326
  Poetry and Public Discourse in Ninteenth-Century America, 186
Woman's Journal, 273
Woolson, Constance Fenimore, 117
Wordsworth, William, 31, 98, 99, 102–3, 123
  'Elegiac Stanzas, suggested by a Picture of Peele Castle', 102, 103
  'Lines Written Among the Eugenean Hills', 102
  'Mont Blanc', 102
  The Prelude, 102
  'The Sunset', 102
World War II, 349

Wright, Charles, 332, 338–9
  Zone Journals, 338
Wylder, Edith, 325
  The Last Face: Emily Dickinson's Manuscripts, 325

Yale Divinity School, 48
Yale Law School, 199
Yellowstone Park, 141

Yiddish, 347
Young, Edward, 90, 96, 162, 167
  Night Thoughts on Life, Death, and Immortality, 96, 162
  Religious Lectures on the Phenomena of the Four Seasons, 162–4

Zapedowska, Magdalena, 4
Zuckerman, Marvin, 347

Index of Emily Dickinson's Poems

A Bird came down the Walk, 122
A Counterfeit - A Plated Person - , 22
A Deed knocks first at Thought, 181
A narrow Fellow in the Grass, 272
A precious - mouldering pleasure - 'tis - , 25, 95
A Prison gets to be a friend - , 183
A prompt - executive Bird is the Jay - , 204
A Route of Evanescence, 308
A Sloop of Amber slips away, 61
A soft Sea washed around the House, 61
A solemn thing - it was - I said - , 277
A South Wind - has a pathos, 60
A transport one cannot contain, 218
A Word dropped careless on a Page, 95, 251
A word made Flesh is seldom, 72, 156, 252
After great pain, a formal feeling comes - , 106, 126, 160, 243
All overgrown by cunning moss, 113
An altered look about the hills - , 154
'Arcturus' is his other name - , 238
As by the dead we love to sit - , 145, 160
As if I asked a common Alms, 192
As imperceptibly as Grief, 60

Because I could not stop for Death - , 23, 136, 144, 156, 160, 346
Before I got my eye put out - , 143
Besides the Autumn poets sing, 120
Blazing in Gold - and, 18, 217
By a flower - By a letter, 59

Color - Caste - Denomination, 213
Come slowly - Eden!, 113
Dare you see a Soul at the 'White Heat'?, 133
Death is the supple Suitor, 160
Departed - to the Judgement, 137
Did life's penurious length, 264
Do people moulder equally, 163
Doom is the House without the Door - , 63
Doubt me! My Dim Companion!, 146

Drama's Vitallest Expression is the Common Day, 85

Eden is that old fashioned House, 58
Escaping backward to perceive, 158
Expectation - is Contentment - , 191

'Faith' is a fine invention, 42, 238
Fame is a bee, 343
Fame is a fickle food, 100
Flowers - Well - if anybody, 63, 125

God is a distant - stately Lover - , 52
Going to Heaven!, 158

He ate and drank the precious Words - , 71, 109
He fumbles at your Soul, 16
He put the Belt around my life - , 145
Heaven is so far of the Mind, 264
Her - last Poems - , 114
Her Losses made our Gains ashamed - , 116
'Hope' is the thing with feathers - , 104

I am afraid to own a Body - , 195
I came to buy a smile - today - , 195
I cannot dance upon my Toes - , 222
I cannot live with You - , 156
I dwell in Possibility - , 20, 333
I felt a Cleaving in My Mind - , 243
I felt a Funeral, in my Brain, 120, 136, 154
I found the words to every thought, 248
I gave Myself to Him - , 193
I had a guinea golden - , 192
I had been hungry, all the Years - , 62, 194
I heard a Fly buzz - when I died - , 136, 144, 160
I like to see it lap the Miles - , 18, 19
I live with Him - I see His face, 137
I lost a World - the other day!, 188–90
I measure every Grief I meet, 160
I never felt at Home - Below - , 113
I never lost as much but twice - , 192

I never saw a Moor, 60
I play at Riches - to appease, 172, 183, 191, 194
I reason, Earth is short - , 265
I reckon - When I count at all - , 122
I rose - because He sank - , 112
I saw no Way - The Heavens were stitched - , 165, 335, 336
I send Two Sunsets - , 343
I should have been too glad, I see - , 63
I taste a liquor never brewed - , 121
I tend my flowers for thee - , 18
I think I was enchanted, 114
I think the Hemlock likes to stand, 54
I tie my Hat - I crease my shawl - , 21
I took one Draught of Life - , 190, 344
I went to thank Her - , 114
If I may have it, when it's dead, 144, 160
If I should die - , 192
If *she* had been the Mistletoe, 59
I'll tell you how the Sun rose - , 60, 160
I'm ceded - I've stopped being Their's - , 53
I'm Nobody! Who are you?, 23, 144, 243
I'm 'wife' - I've finished that - , 112
In Ebon Box, when years have flown, 95
Is Bliss then, such Abyss - , 202
Is it true, dear Sue?, 72
It always felt to me - a wrong, 72
It bloomed and dropt - a Single Noon - , 239
It don't sound so terrible - quite - as it did - , 208
It feels a shame to be Alive - , 211
It sifts from Leaden Sieves - , 120, 232, 333
It was a quiet way - , 165
It was not Death, for I stood up, 143, 154, 163
It would have starved a Gnat - , 194
It's all I have to bring today - , 192
I've known a Heaven, like a Tent - , 61, 217

Just lost, when I was saved!, 333

Knows how to forget!, 263, 264

Let Us play Yesterday - , 25
Life - is what we make it - , 155
Low at my problem bending, 194

Midsummer, was it, when They died - , 101
Mine - by the Right of the White Election!, 53
My Cocoon tightens - Colors teaze - , 63
My Life had stood - a Loaded Gun - , 254, 337
My Reward for Being - was this - , 53
Myself was formed - a Carpenter - , 21, 250

Nature and God - I neither knew, 240
Nature - the Gentlest Mother is, 57
No Crowd that has occurred, 95

No Prisoner be - , 183
No Rack can torture me - , 183
Nobody knows this little rose, 125
Now I lay thee down to Sleep - , 38

Of Bronze - and Blaze - , 18, 126
Of Death I try to think like this, 264
Of God we ask one favor, 15
Of nearness to her Sundered Things, 166
Of Tribulation - these are They - , 73, 74–6
On the World you colored, 226
One life of so much consequence!, 190
One Sister have I in our house, 277
Our little Kinsmen - after Rain, 239
Over and over, like a Tune - , 210

Paradise is that old mansion, 20
Perception of an Object costs, 240, 242, 264
Publication - is the Auction - , 20, 32, 188, 212, 272

'Red Sea,' indeed! Talk not to me, 60
Removed from Accident of Loss, 192
Renunciation - is a piercing Virtue - , 242
Revolution is the Pod, 182

Safe in their Alabaster Chambers - , 63, 122, 125, 164, 274
September's Baccalaureate, 101
Shall I take thee, the Poet said, 249
She rose to His Requirement - dropt, 137, 146
Sic transit gloria mundi, 40, 50
So gay a Flower, 262
Some - Work for immortality - , 274
Soul, Wilt thou toss again?, 132
Split the Lark - and you'll find the Music - , 240
Success is counted sweetest, 272

That it will never come again, 160
The Admirations - and Contempts - of time - , 242
The Bible is an antique Volume - , 16, 72
The Brain - is wider than the Sky - , 241, 242
The Bumble Bee's religion - , 46
The Bustle in a House, 160
The Chemical conviction, 163, 238
The Frost of Death was on the Pane - , 154
The gleam of an heroic act, 344
The last Night that she Lived, 160
The Malay - took the Pearl - , 195
The Martyr Poets - did not tell - , 154
The most important population, 239
The name - of it - is 'Autumn' - , 63, 206
The nearest Dream recedes - unrealized - , 265
The only news I know, 1, 29, 204

The Past is such a curious Creature, 72
The Poets light but Lamps - , 25
The Props assist the House, 63
The Robin's my Criterion for Tune - , 54, 63
The Show is not the Show, 217
The Soul has Bandaged moments - , 60
The Soul selects her own Society - , 89
The Soul that hath a Guest, 343
The Soul's distinct connection, 143
The Spider holds a Silver Ball, 2
The Spirit lasts - but in what mode - , 156, 163
The World - stands - solemner - to
    me - , 146, 175
There came a Day - at Summer's full - , 73, 156
There is no Frigate like a Book, 25, 71, 109
There's a certain Slant of light, 338, 347
There's been a Death, in the Opposite
    House, 160
They dropped like Flakes - , 126, 207
They say that 'Time assuages' - , 41
They shut me up in Prose - , 109, 183
This Consciousness that is aware, 145
This is a Blossom of the Brain - , 155
This is my letter to the World, 1, 64, 350
This World is not conclusion, 106, 158, 160, 243
Tho' my destiny be Fustian - , 121
Those - dying then, 265
Though the great waters sleep, 22
Through lane it lay - thro' bramble - , 62
'Tis so appalling - it exhilarates - , 163

'Tis so much joy! 'Tis so much joy!, 132
Title Divine - is mine!, 116, 137
To hear an Oriole sing, 264
To lose - if One can find again - , 192
To put this World down, like a Bundle - , 62
'Twas just this time, last year, I died, 136
'Twas like a Maelstrom, with a notch, 135
'Twas the old - road - through pain - , 62
'Twas warm - at first - like Us - , 163

Unto like Story - Trouble has enticed
    me - , 183
Unto my Books - so good to turn - , 25

We grow accustomed to the Dark - , 334
We learned the Whole of Love - , 44
We lose - because we win - , 192
What if I say I shall not wait!, 86, 160
What mystery pervades a well!, 240
What would I give to see his face his face?,
    191, 195
When the Astronomer stops seeking, 146
Who were 'the Father and the Son', 152
Whole Gulfs - of Red, and Fleets - of Red - , 60
Whose cheek is this?, 47
Why - do they shut me out of Heaven?, 113
Wild nights - Wild nights!, 113
Within my garden, rides a Bird, 63

Your Riches - taught me - Poverty, 192

Lightning Source UK Ltd.
Milton Keynes UK
UKHW012130041019
351052UK00004B/19/P